*Culture of Qiang / Culture de Qiang*

# 羌 族 文 化

主　编　陈蜀玉

副主编　徐友香　王维民　严学玉

编　委　孙念红　代智勇　蒋　婧

　　　　陈思本　沈一新

西南交通大学出版社

·成　都·

图书在版编目（ＣＩＰ）数据

羌族文化 / 陈蜀玉主编. —成都：西南交通大学
出版社，2015.8
ISBN 978-7-5643-4171-8

Ⅰ.①羌… Ⅱ.①陈… Ⅲ.①羌族－民族文化－中国
Ⅳ.①K287.4

中国版本图书馆 CIP 数据核字（2015）第 189006 号

## 羌 族 文 化

### 主编　陈蜀玉

| | |
|---|---|
| 责 任 编 辑 | 王小碧 |
| 特 邀 编 辑 | 王小龙 |
| 封 面 设 计 | 原谋书装 |
| 出 版 发 行 | 西南交通大学出版社<br>（四川省成都市金牛区交大路 146 号） |
| 发 行 部 电 话 | 028-87600564　028-87600533 |
| 邮 政 编 码 | 610031 |
| 网　　　址 | http://www.xnjdcbs.com |
| 印　　　刷 | 成都蜀通印务有限责任公司 |
| 成 品 尺 寸 | 167 mm × 236 mm |
| 印　　　张 | 24.75 |
| 字　　　数 | 575 千 |
| 版　　　次 | 2015 年 8 月第 1 版 |
| 印　　　次 | 2015 年 8 月第 1 次 |
| 书　　　号 | ISBN 978-7-5643-4171-8 |
| 定　　　价 | 78.00 元 |

# 前　言

　　一个偶然的机会，在上个世纪末，我陪同外宾参观了羌寨：羌碉、羌笛、羌族服饰和歌舞，等等。羌族文化第一次如此生动地展现在我眼前，印象非常深刻。从此，工作之余、闲暇之时我便开始阅读一些关于羌族的书籍。尽管我不是学民族学出身，且对羌族文化的了解仅限于一鳞半爪，但是羌族文化的魅力——悠久的历史、多样化的文学、口耳相传的语言以及羌族文化的现况，均构成我心中挥之不去的情结。结情之后，不禁心痒，跃跃欲试，虽力不能逮，但仍想走近羌族文化，为羌族文化的发展尽绵薄之力。毕竟个人的能力十分有限，但是教师的点滴影响，可以使青年一代开始了解羌族，通过网络、书籍和对外文字宣传，羌族文化必日久弥新；虽然发展民族文化不可能一蹴而就，但是我们可以用有限的知识去追溯羌族文化的发展脉络，去开拓羌族文化的发展空间。

　　又是一个偶然的机会，我结识了福特基金会。这些想法得到福特基金会文化和教育项目官员何进博士的认同。在他的鼎力支持下，我们组织了课题组，师生们做了大量的实地考察、案头写作、资料查阅、网络建设、系列讲座、问卷调查，以及中、英、法三种文字的写作和翻译。这一过程不仅提高了师生们的个人能力，而且使大家认识到，民族文化的生存取决于自身的发展，而发展的途径必须不断创新。

　　在此基础上，课题得到了四川省人大、四川省民族委员会、阿坝州党委、阿坝师范专科学校、西南交通大学 211 办公室等部门和单位的通力合作。四川省人大纽晓明副主任在百忙之中多次关心课题进展情况。《羌族文化》一书已经过四川省民族事务委员会专家审阅，省民族事务委员会周发成处长和省民族宗教委员会周礼成主任亲自执笔修改。阿坝藏族羌族自治州党委王建民副书记和杜林先生也曾细致入微地关心课题进展的每一个细节。阿坝师范专科学校副校长陈兴龙教授对《羌族文化》一书提出了宝贵的修改意见。在成书之际，西南交通大学 211 办公室的郑凯锋教授对《羌族文化》的出版给予了大力支持。没有以上各位领导和师长的帮助，就没有《羌族文化》这一成果。不仅如此，西南民族大学科研处王康教授、文学院副院长徐希平教授都在课题出现困难时伸出了援助之手。还有四川大学法学院研究生黄亚菲同学和邹俊彬同学，他们对所承担的工作竭尽全力。特别是贺运和刘安两位同学，他们吃苦耐劳、任劳任怨，出色地完成了课题组中最艰苦的工作。在英语翻译过程中，西南交通大学外国语学院的代智勇和蒋婧老师做了大量的前期工作。随后由美国康奈尔大学余同乐同学和余丹娜同学、西南交通大学外国语学院的孙念红和 Denise O'Toole 老师对原稿做了修改，最后由 Rachel Meakin（白洁）女士校订完成。

还是很偶然，我原本只打算出版一本中英文对照的《羌族文化》，2004 年恰逢西南交通大学法语系诞生，师生们对羌族文化产生了浓厚的兴趣，部分师生参加了项目工作，他们的热情鼓励了我。在我们的共同努力下，完成了法语译本。在修改法语译本的过程中，王婷婷老师付出了大量的时间和精力，同时 Guillaume Larsen，Babaud Alain 和 Ye Ma 也参加了校订工作。其实还有很多人与我们有同样的情结：他们访问过我们的网站，参加过我们的活动，试译过我们的文本，与我们共同努力。由于人数很多，唯恐挂一漏万，恕不一一列出，在此一并感谢。

应该承认，具有独特性的民族文化在科学化、商业化、全球一体化的竞争中处于劣势，现代性强烈地冲击着民族性。在民族文化求生存、谋发展的过程中，应该对本土文化进行保护，这种保护意味着对民族文化的扶持和挽救：扶持被流行趋势冲击的民族文化原形，挽救被强势文化忽视的原生态。这些文化原形和文化原生态是民族文化的根基，也是全人类的共同财富。因此，民族文化唯有先生存才能发展，唯有发展才能体现其价值。

我们课题组提出了促进羌族文化发展的三种保护手段：文化手段、网络手段、法律手段。保护是手段，发展是目的。尽管用有限的手段去保护无限的文化显得杯水车薪，用固定的方式展示发展的内容，更是捉襟见肘，对每一种民族文化形态都立法保护，尤为力不能逮，但是这些手段奠定了发展的基础。《羌族文化》一书就是保护和发展链条中的一个有机环节：用中、英、法三种文字向外界介绍羌族文化，让羌族走出羌寨；通过文字反映羌族历史、建筑、语言、文学、音乐舞蹈、衣食住行和风土人情，让世界了解羌族。用三种语言的互动促进民族文化的发展，是我们课题的创新之处。我们期待这一尝试能得到法语国家、英语国家和我们本民族的共同认可。

如果我们的共同努力能使羌族文化走进世界民族文化之林，如果通过我们中、英、法三种文字所开启的小小窗口能管窥博大精深的羌族文化，我们对羌族文化的爱慕之情便得以表达。若夫文果载心，故余心有寄。

陈蜀玉

# 目　录

Culture of Qiang

# 羌族文化

Culture de Qiang

# 第一章　羌族历史

羌族是中国最古老的民族之一，起源于上古史前时期。在中国古老的历史传说资料中有许多关于羌人的记载。许慎在《说文解字》中说："羌，西戎牧羊人也。从人，从羊。"古代文献都把"羌"作为从事畜牧业且以养羊为特色的一个民族。范晔在《后汉书·西羌传》中说：羌人"以产牧为业"。牧就是牧羊，产就是粗耕。这说明他们以牧羊为主要生产，而以粗耕为辅。根据考古发现，距今四五千年前的新石器时期，在今甘肃、青海河湟东至陕西泾渭流域的广大地区，即有我国先民的活动遗址，这些先民正是古代的羌人。《后汉书·西羌传》又载："西羌之本，出自三苗，姜姓之别也。"根据历史传说，三苗是帝舜时期的一个部族，是黄帝的夏官缙云氏之后。缙云氏姓姜，炎帝之苗裔。这里追溯到西羌的本源，即是上古姜姓部族炎帝之后。

上古畜牧起源于狩猎，是男子从事的产业。农业种植起源于采集，是女子操作的劳动。传说中的姜姓部落多与农业有关,早于神农的共工氏就是姜姓部落的一支。传说共工氏之王，水处什之七，陆处什之三，

# CHAPTER ONE    HISTORY OF THE QIANG

The Qiang, whose origin can be dated back to prehistoric times, are one of the most ancient ethnic groups in China. Many records of the Qiang people can be found in historical documents about Chinese antiquity. Xu Shen's most important work, the *Shuowen Jiezi (Origin of Chinese Characters)*, gives us a clear definition of the Qiang: "shepherds who share common ancestry with the Western Rong nationality; the character itself can be divided into two root words: 'people' and 'sheep'." Historical documents all characterize the "Qiang" as an ethnic group dependent on animal husbandry, especially sheep, for their livelihood. In the *History of the Later Han Dynasty: the History of the Western Qiang*, the author Fan Ye says "the Qiang depend on sheep herding and farming," which indicates that the main industry of the Qiang at that time was raising sheep, supplemented by some primitive form of farming. In a wide area spanning from the Huangshui river in Gansu and Qinghai provinces eastwards to the valleys of the Jing and Wei rivers in Shaanxi Province, archaeologists have discovered relics of ancient Chinese people living in the Neolithic Age four or five thousand years ago. These people were the ancient Qiang. Fan Ye also states that "the Western Qiang originated from the San Miao," a branch of the Jiang family. According to historical legends, the San Miao was a tribe which existed during the period when the legendary monarch Shun was in power. The ancestor of the San Miao was Jin Yun, whose husband was a government official serving Huang Di, the legendary Huang Emperor, around 3000 BC. Jin Yun was named Jiang. Thus, the San Miao tribe, who were also descendants of Yan Di (the Yan Emperor), belonged to the Jiang Family. The origins of the Western Qiang can be traced to the Jiang tribe, whose forefather was Yan Di.

In ancient times, the men usually took care of the livestock while the women farmed the land. According to legend, most of the Jiang tribes were involved in agriculture. The Gonggong tribe was one of the earliest Jiang tribes, even earlier than Shen Nong (the Chinese God of agriculture). Legend has it that seventy percent of the area ruled by the Gonggong tribe was covered by water.

乃是洪水泛滥的时代。共工氏及其后代都致力于防治洪水。"共工氏之霸九州也,其子曰后土,能平九州,故祀以为社(神)。"(《礼记·祭法》)共工氏子孙在黄帝时任"土官",少皞时任"水官",禹之时四岳继续协助禹治水。水是早期文明的先决条件,也是原始农业发展的基础。传说姜姓共工氏不仅是古羌人中也是中国古代先民中最早进行农业生产的部落之一。从这个意义上讲,古代羌人姜姓部落开启了中国的农耕文明。

同时,古羌人是汉族前身华夏族的重要组成部分。《国语·晋语》有云:"昔少典娶于有蟜氏,生黄帝、炎帝。黄帝以姬水成,炎帝以姜水成。成而异德,故黄帝为姬,炎帝为姜。"姜姓部落联盟不断扩张壮大,大举东进。"阪泉氏蚩尤,姜姓炎帝之裔也。"(《路史》)相传,蚩尤作五兵(器),即戈、矛、戟、酋矛、夷矛。这些金属兵器的制作表现出他们卓越的制造才能,所以后世把蚩尤奉为主兵之神。至于夏禹,也有史料传说他是羌人的后裔。自汉司马迁《史记·六国年表》至晋500年间的许多文献,都说禹生于西羌石纽,是西羌(夷)人。所以,有学者据此认为"夏王朝的主要部族是羌(人)"。

Flooding was a continual problem and successive generations of Gonggong devoted their lives to flood prevention. "The Gonggong tribe dominated all of China. A son of the Gonggong, named Hou Tu, took care of the country and the people all worshipped him as the God of the Land." (*Book of Rites: Sacrificial Offering*) Under the Huang Emperor, the descendants of the Gonggong tribe were in charge of land management, whereas under Shao Hao, the son of the Huang Emperor, they managed the water resources. Under Emperor Yu, they held the post of "Si yue", their main duty being to assist Yu in regulating the rivers and watercourses, a prerequisite in the early stages of civilization with water being foundational to the development of primitive agriculture. Thus, the Gonggong people of the Jiang were among the earliest of the ancient Qiang and were also possibly the earliest ancestors of the Chinese to take up agriculture as a way of life. In this sense, it is the Jiang tribe of the ancient Qiang who initiated the agricultural civilization of China.

In addition, the ancient Qiang are one of the ethnic groups that composed the Hua Xia nationality, out of which grew the Han nationality. According to the *Guo Yu*, a collection of historical anecdotes making up pre-Imperial China's most important body of historical narratives, "Shao Dian married You Jiao and gave birth to two sons, Huang Di and Yan Di. Huang Di grew up by the Ji River whereas Yan Di grew up by the Jiang River. As a result of these differences in background, Huang Di bore Ji as his family name whereas Yan Di bore Jiang as his family name." With the alliance of these Qiang tribes, the Jiang family name grew stronger and stronger and they moved eastward in large numbers. The book of *Lu Shi* relates that the Chiyou people of the Banquan tribe, who were descended from Yan Di of the Jiang, were good at making five kinds of weapons, namely, daggers, spears, halberds, the Qiu spear and the Yi spear. This highlights the great skill of the Chiyou people in weapon manufacturing, a skill which caused them to be worshipped later as the God of Weaponry. As for Yu, the reputed founder of the Xia Dynasty, some legends regard him as a descendant of the Qiang. According to many documents written during the five hundred year period from Sima Qian's Han Dynasty *Historical Records: the Chronological Table of the Six States* until the Jin Dynasty, Yu was born in Shiniu, in the Western Qiang area, and was a descendant of the Qiang. Therefore, some scholars even conclude that the Qiang was the dominant tribe in the Xia Dynasty.

在史前时期，居住在西北的古羌人中一支姓姜的部落，以及共工氏、炎帝、蚩尤等部落最先进入中原，相继并入以黄帝为代表的部落。经过长期的迁徙和交往，逐步融合为一体。可见古羌人是汉族前身华夏民族的重要组成部分。至于未进入中原的古羌人部落，散布于甘肃、青海河湟及陕西的部分地区，继续从事游牧生活，发展缓慢，其后裔便成为毗邻于殷商的羌方、羌人。甲骨文中大量记载了他们的活动以及他们与殷商长期交战的史实。自此以后，羌人的历史进入了文字记载时期。

到了商代，羌与商时常交战，并以被商征伐为多。商朝对羌方用兵，主要目的是掳掠奴隶，同时也用掳掠的羌人奴隶作人牲供祭祀。据卜辞记载，商朝将羌人与牛牲一起用于祭祀，而且以五羌配三牛，三羌配二牛，等等，羌人的身价还不如牛。据现有资料的初步统计，被用作祭品的羌俘多达 7 750 人。羌俘除了被用于祭祀外，还是殉葬品。据现有资料统计，被用作殉葬品的羌人达 5 178 人以上。

周代羌人有了很大的发展，种姓繁衍，遍布西北，其中一部分进入中原。西周建国之初，面临国内外诸多困难，周王室为了巩固周的统治，继续加强与姜姓的联盟，封姜姓之国申、吕和许等于江汉及淮河流域。并建立东方的大国齐国，以镇压反叛的淮夷。周建立的姜姓之国还有纪（今山东寿光）、向（今安徽怀远）、州（今山东安丘）、郭（今山东东平）、

In the prehistoric period, an ancient Qiang tribe called the Jiang lived in northwestern China, and together with the Gonggo and integration they merged into one tribe represented by Huang Di. Thus, it is clear that the ancient Qiang were one of the people groups that formed the Hua Xia nationality, out of which grew the Han nationality. The ancient Qiang tribes that did not enter central China were spread over the Huangshui River valley in Gansu Province, Qinghai Province and some parts of Shaanxi Province, continuing their nomadic existence. Their descendants lived in the border area of the Shang Dynasty territory. Many records have been found in the form of inscriptions on tortoise shells, relating the lives of these Qiang people and their long-time wars with the Shang Dynasty. Thenceforth, the history of the Qiang entered into a new era with written records. Yan Di, Chiyou and other tribes, they were the first to gradually enter central China after many years of association.

In the Shang Dynasty, the Qiang and the Shang were often at war with each other, with the Shang more frequently the victors. The Shang would go on expeditions with the express purpose of capturing Qiang people to be used either as slaves or in sacrificial rituals. Shang Dynasty oracle inscriptions on tortoise shells or animal bones indicate that in such a sacrificial ritual either five Qiang slaves with three cattle or three Qiang slaves with two cattle were used. The price of Qiang slaves at that time was even lower than that of cattle. Moreover, the Qiang slaves were sometimes buried alive with the dead. Statistical data show that a total of 7,750 Qiang slaves were sacrificed and more than 5,178 slaves were used as grave goods.

In the Zhou Dynasty, the Qiang developed rapidly in terms of both population and number of family names. They spread all over northwestern China, and some of them settled down in central China. After the foundation of the Western Zhou Dynasty, the Zhou royal family encountered great difficulties both at home and abroad. To consolidate their ruling power, they strengthened their alliance with the Qiang. Some Qiang nobles were offered official posts, becoming heads of the states of Shen, Lü and Xu in the Jiang Han valley and Huai River valley. The powerful state of Qi was set up in the east to suppress the rebellious Yi in the Huai River valley. Other states established by the Zhou and administered by Qiang nobles included the states of Ji (now Shouguang in Shandong Province), Xiang (now Huaiyuan in Anhui Province), Zhou (now Anqiu in Shandong Province), Zhang (now Dongping in Shandong Province),

厉（今湖北随州）等。他们和齐、吕、许等大国一样处于周王朝的周边要塞地区，共同起着屏藩周王室的重要作用。西周末年，周幽王宠褒姒（褒姒娘家为姒姓之国）废申后。申后之父申侯（姜姓）联合缯及犬戎攻杀幽王于骊山。在申侯的主持下，太子宜臼被立为平王。西周故地为犬戎所侵，西周告亡。西周灭亡后，平王被迫东迁洛邑。由于周姜联盟破裂，周王室一蹶不振。

姜氏戎（四岳之后）与齐、吕、申、许同为姜姓。这些国家都是最先进入中原的。齐、吕、申、许做了诸侯、贵族，均自称是华夏（族）。到了周代，已形成一个比较普遍的概念，即重视遵守周礼，接受华夏文明，所谓"诸夏用夷狄礼则夷狄之，夷狄用诸夏礼则诸夏之"①。除羌人中的姜姓部落在西周时已开始融入华夏外，还有部分羌人在春秋战国时期建立了"义渠国"，都城在今甘肃宁县。他们已能建筑城堡，实行定居，农业生产水平较高，对死者实行火葬，这些都是羌人的习俗。随后秦灭义渠，以羌人为主要成分的西方诸戎（一般统称为西戎）大都融合于秦。所以，《后汉书·西羌传》评价说："自是中国无戎寇。"

---

① 范文澜：《中国通史简编》（第一册），中国人民出版社1953年版，第107~108页。

and Li (now Suizhou in Hubei Province). These states were situated as important garrisons in the border areas of the Zhou Dynasty territory, forming a kind of natural defense against foreign invasion. In the final years of the Western Zhou Dynasty, the last Zhou emperor, You Wang, bestowed his favour on Bao Si, one of his imperial concubines, who was from a state governed by the Si family, and dethroned his queen, Shen Hou. Shen Hou's father, a Qiang noble and head of the state of Shen, conspired with Quan Rong to kill You Wang at the foot of Li Mountain. A ceremony was then held, presided over by the father of Shen Hou, in which Yi Jiu, the crown prince, was enthroned as Emperor Ping Wang. However, Quan Rong then invaded the Zhou territory and Emperor Ping Wang was forced to move eastward to Lou Yi. Owing to the break-up of the alliance between the Zhou and the Qiang, the Zhou royal family fell into disarray and the dynasty finally came to an end.

The head of the state of Rong and the heads of the states of Qi, Lü, Shen and Xu were all Jiang. These Jiang people were the first to enter central China where they became nobles, dukes or feudal princes and claimed membership of the Hua Xia. By the time of the Zhou Dynasty, it was widely accepted that all people should conform to the ceremonial rites and regulations of the Zhou and adopt Hua Xia traditions. The general belief at that time was that "if China adopted barbarian etiquette, all the Hua Xia people would become barbarians, whereas if barbarians adopted Chinese etiquette, then they would become part of Hua Xia" (Fan Wen Lan. *General History of China. Vol. 1.* pp. 107-108. Beijing: People's Publishing Company, 1953). Although the Qiang tribe of Jiang merged into Hua Xia society during the Western Zhou Dynasty, there were other Qiang tribes who founded a state called "Yiqu" during the Spring and Autumn period and the Warring States period. In Yiqu, these tribes settled down and built fortresses, engaging in relatively advanced agriculture and practising cremation, a tradition of the Qiang. Their capital was located in Ning County, Gansu Province. This state of Yiqu was later destroyed by the Qin, who unified the whole country and established the first centralized imperial government in China. Thus the tribes from western China (generally called the Xi Rong or Western Rong), most of which were Qiang, gradually merged with the people of Qin. The *History of the Later Han Dynasty: the History of the Western Qiang* states that "there were no invaders from the west after the unification of the country".

到了汉代，原来进入中原的羌人，已与汉族融合。而未进入中原的则形成众多部落，各有酋长，散布于长城以南的陇西和青海河湟地区。这些部落名号不同，不相统属，常互相攻战掳掠，"强则分种为酋豪，弱则为人附落"（《后汉书·西羌传》）。他们大多处于原始社会氏族部落末期至阶级社会初期，与西周初年建立的齐、吕、申、许等羌人大不相同。众多部落中最强的有先零羌和烧当羌。其次则有钟羌、勒姐羌、卑湳羌、当煎羌、开羌、罕羌、且冻羌、沈氐羌、虔人羌、牢姐羌、封养羌、彡姐羌、烧何羌、巩唐羌，以及效功、傅难、当阗、乌吾、零悟、滇那、黄羝等羌族部落。他们分布在今甘肃、青海和陕西西南部，与汉王朝都曾发生过大小不同的冲突，对汉叛服无常，但最后大部分羌人部落都失败降服，被分散内迁至边塞诸郡安置。没有降附的仍居塞外，被称为外羌。

武帝期间，加强中央集权，发展社会经济，维护西北地区的正常活动，实现了与西域各国的友好交流。但匈奴贵族联合羌人豪酋反叛，图谋破坏汉王朝的努力，汉王朝多次出兵征讨。到宣帝时，先零等羌族部落联合起兵，攻城邑，杀长史，进攻金城，大败汉军。宣帝派赵充国率兵前往救援，并颁布命令"大兵诛有罪者……"（《汉书·赵充国传》）羌人若协助汉军诛"有罪者"，给予重赏。

During the Han Dynasty, those Qiang people who had already entered central China integrated with the Han. Those who had remained outside central China lived in the area of Longxi and the Huangshui River to the south of the Great Wall and were divided into many tribes each with their own leader. This tribal autonomy led to bitter rivalries and conflicts between them. "The more powerful tribes usually became overlords and the weak were annexed to the strong." (*History of the Later Han Dynasty: the History of the Western Qiang*) These tribes were in the transitional period from the last tribal clan stage of primitive society to the beginning of a hierarchical society, and were different from the Qiang who had been living in the states of Qi, Lü, Shen and Xu since the early Western Zhou period. Among these autonomous tribes, the most powerful ones were the Xianling and Shaodang, followed by the Zhong, Lejie, Beinan, Dangjian, Jian, Han, Qiedong, Shendi, Qianren, Laojie, Fengyang, Shanjie, Shaohe, Gongtang, Xiaogong, Funan, Dangtian, Wuwu, Lingwu, Dianna and Huangdi. These were distributed over present-day Gansu, Qinghai and southwest Shaanxi provinces. During this period, these Qiang tribes came into varying degrees of conflict with the Han and were unsure whether to rebel against or capitulate to this dominant power. Eventually, most of the Qiang tribes were defeated and pledged allegiance to the ruling Han. They were scattered and moved inwards to the frontier villages of different counties. Those who didn't surrender still lived beyond the Great Wall and were called the "Outside Qiang".

When Wu Di ascended the Han throne, he strengthened the centralization of state power, developed the economy, safeguarded normal daily life in the northwest, and established friendly communications with countries in the western regions. In an effort to reverse these measures, the Xiongnu leaders joined forces with some of the Qiang leaders, plundering and pillaging neighboring states that were under the rule of the Han court. In response to this, the Han Dynasty regularly dispatched troops on punitive expeditions against the rebels. After Xuan Di came to power, some Qiang tribes, such as the Xianling, rose in revolt, attacking cities (in particular the city of Jincheng), killing officials, and utterly defeating the Han armies. In response, Xuan Di mobilized the whole country and sent Zhao Chongguo, a distinguished general, to strengthen the Han army. Xuan Di even issued the decree to "kill the guilty with many troops" (*History of the Later Han Dynasty: Biography of Zhao Chongguo*) and granted handsome rewards to any Qiang who assisted the Han troops.

赵充国部用了5个月的时间结束了这场战争。为了巩固战争的胜利，赵充国向汉王朝提出"屯田"戍边的主张。这一主张的实行，保证了西北边塞的安宁。

汉代在西羌地区设置了行政管理机构。先设军事机构——西平亭（今青海西宁市），然后设置郡县，其行政长官为郡守县令。同时还针对羌区的特殊情况增设"属国都尉"，其任务是"主蛮夷降者"（《后汉书·百官志》）。管辖西羌的最重要的官吏是护羌校尉，其主要任务是直接奉汉王朝使命，专管西羌事务，调解部落矛盾，处理羌汉纠纷，按时巡视访察边民疾苦，不时派通晓羌语的人了解羌人动向以便警戒设防。东汉时期，羌人三次大规模起义，先后延续了60余年，终被东汉王朝镇压。但羌人的反抗也给东汉王朝以沉重的打击，促使其走向衰亡。所以《后汉书·西羌传》评价说："寇敌略定矣，汉祚亦衰焉。"

汉代，羌族部落在今新疆、西藏和内蒙古等地区分布较广，同时，在西南也有牦牛羌、白马羌、参狼羌、青衣羌等羌族部落。其中，冉駹地区的羌人居住在广大的川西地区和岷江上游今阿坝藏族羌族自治州（以下简称"阿坝州"）汶川、理县、茂县等地。"冉駹夷者，武帝所开，元鼎六年以为汶山郡……其山有六夷、七羌、九氏，

Fortunately, the war ended after five months. To consolidate their victory and maintain the peace of frontier villages in the northwest, the Han court then stationed garrison troops who opened up wasteland and grew crops on the frontier.

The government of the Han Dynasty established some administrative and management institutions in the Western Qiang region. Initially, a military institution called Xi Pingting (now the city of Xining in Qinghai Province) was established. This was then followed by the establishment of counties with magistrates as administrators. Furthermore, to cope with the special situation in the Qiang area, a military officer, the "Shuguo Duwei", was assigned to take charge of "compliant indigenous tribes or minority nationalities" (*History of the Later Han Dynasty: Annals of Officials of All Ranks and Descriptions*). The most important government post of the Western Qiang was the Official Protector of the Qiang, who was directly in charge of Qiang affairs, on imperial orders from the Han Dynasty. This official was also responsible for reconciling conflicts among the Qiang tribes, mediating disputes between the Qiang and Han, patrolling the frontiers, and regularly visiting the Qiang people. To ensure that the Han were properly prepared for any potential rebellion, his duty also included constantly sending people who understood the Qiang language to learn whether there was any possible intention to revolt. In the period of the Eastern Han Dynasty, the Qiang raised three large-scale revolts against the government, which together lasted more than sixty years. Although the revolts were cruelly suppressed, they tarnished the reign of the Han court, thereby contributing to the decline and fall of the Eastern Han Dynasty. *History of the Later Han Dynasty: the History of the Western Qiang* states: "the enemy had almost been vanquished but the throne of the Han waned."

During the Han Dynasty many Qiang tribes were living in present-day Xinjiang, Tibet and Inner Mongolia, scattered over a wide area. At the same time, in the southwest, there were also the Qiang tribes of the Mao Niu, Baima, Canlang, and Qingyi. Among the latter, the Qiang people of the Ranmang area lived in the extensive area of western Sichuan and in the counties of Wenchuan, Li and Mao around the upper reaches of the Min River in Sichuan Province. "It is Wu Di, an emperor of the Han Dynasty, who, in the sixth year of his reign, set up Wen Shan County for the minority nationalities, in the area of Ranmang. In this county there are six Yi tribes, seven Qiang tribes and nine Di tribes.

各有部落。……故夷人冬则避寒，入蜀为佣；夏则违暑，反其邑。"（《后汉书·南蛮西南夷传》）他们与汉区交往频繁，受影响较深。尽管土地贫瘠，农业较差，但畜牧业较发达。例如，饲养牦牛，编织牛毛毡毯。他们还积累了独特的治疗病毒的医药经验。在建筑方面更有独特性，"垒石为室，高者至十余丈为邛笼"。这些具有羌族特色的建筑，在羌民族中至今尚在使用。总之，在汉代长达400多年的统治中，羌汉人民往来加深，兼之汉王朝一些政策的实施，也从客观上促进了羌族社会经济的发展和羌汉人民之间的融合。

公元 3 世纪初叶，东汉王朝崩溃，形成魏、蜀、吴鼎立的局面，长期战争，生产破坏，人口锐减。为了增加兵源和劳动力，三国的统治者都把目光和注意力投向周边的少数民族，羌人首先成为争夺的对象。北方魏、晋的统治者招引匈奴、鲜卑、羯、氐、羌等族内迁，与汉人杂居。曹操的军队中有匈奴、乌桓、氐、羌等人。魏、蜀战争中双方都尽力争夺羌人。在云贵地区，吴蜀也展开对少数民族的争夺，结果使少数民族不断向内地迁徙，与汉人杂处。到了西晋时期（公元 265—317 年），羌人几乎遍布关中一带。由于持"胡人猥多"观点的人具有相当的势力，便提出"宜先为其防"（《晋书·北狄匈奴传》）的观点。此时，各种民族矛盾日益尖锐。

These people come to the state of Shu and work as servants in winter to avoid the cold weather. In summer, they return to the mountains to escape the heat." (*History of the Later Han Dynasty: Biography of the Southern and Southwestern Minorities*) Through these intensive contacts the Qiang were greatly influenced by the Han. Although the Qiang area was barren and infertile, resulting in under-developed agriculture, their animal husbandry flourished, especially the raising of yak and the weaving of felt carpet with ox hair. They discovered unique medical methods for curing diseases and also developed a unique architectural style. Their houses were usually built with stones, sometimes towering to a height of more than 10 "zhangs". (A "zhang" was a unit of length in ancient China, approximately equal to 3.3 meters). This distinctive architectural style is still used by the Qiang people today. From the above it can be seen that during the four-hundred-year rule of the Han dynasty, interaction between the Qiang and the Han increased and the Qiang also experienced considerable social and economic development as a result of the policies and measures implemented by the Han.

In the early years of the third century, the Eastern Han Dynasty collapsed and was succeeded by the tripartite confrontation of the Three Kingdoms, namely, Wei, Shu, and Wu. The war destroyed social productivity and took many lives. To augment their military and labour forces, the rulers of the Three Kingdoms turned their attention to the surrounding minorities. The Qiang became the first target. The rulers of the Wei and the Jin in northern China encouraged the Xiongnu, Jie, Di, Qiang and Xianbei minorities to move further into Han territory and live among the Han. In Cao Cao's army there were soldiers from the Xiongnu, Wuhuan, Di, Qiang and other nationalities. During the war between the kingdoms of Wei and Shu, both sides competed to recruit the Qiang. The same thing happened during the war between the kingdoms of Wu and Shu in Yunnan and Guizhou. This increased army recruitment resulted in minority groups continuously moving further into Han territory. By the time of the Western Jin Dynasty (265 A.D. to 317 A.D.), Qiang people were to be found everywhere in the central Shaanxi Plain. This situation quickly drew the attention of the powerful and influential who felt "there were too many minorities in central China". They put forward the suggestion of "being cautious of the minorities" (*History of Jin Dynasty:Biography of the Northern Xiongnu*) and, consequently, tensions increased between the minorities and the Han.

晋惠帝元康初年（公元 291 年），关中氐羌举兵，氐人齐万年称帝。元康四年（公元 294 年），匈奴人郝散起兵，随后其弟郝度元起义。西晋统治者中有人已预见到危机，提出《徙戎论》，主张借助平定齐万年的军威，及早将氐、羌迁出境外，返其故土。随之而来的是民族矛盾进一步激化，以汉族和氐、羌为主体的流民大起义终于爆发。

西晋末年，原先在汉末进入中原的匈奴、鲜卑、羯、氐、羌五族先后起兵反晋，各族统治者先后在北方和巴蜀建立割据政权，计有 16 个国家，史称"十六国"。其中羌人豪酋姚苌建立了后秦。姚氏先人属汉代烧当羌，世为羌人首领。姚苌之父曾告诫诸子说："自古以来未有戎狄作天子者。我死，汝便归晋，当竭尽臣节，无为不义之事。"（《晋书·载记十六》）姚氏建立后秦国后，视儒家思想为正统。这不仅体现了后秦国的治国理念，也表明汉文化对姚氏的影响。建初九年（公元 393 年），姚苌死，子姚兴继位。姚兴时期是后秦国颇有作为的时期：招抚流民，抑制羌、汉豪强；境内平民凡因饥荒沦为奴隶的，一律赦免为良人；俭省法令；谨慎断狱；设律学于长安；奖励清廉官吏，严惩贪污；设置学官，

In the first year of Hui Di's reign in the Jin Dynasty, the Di and Qiang ethnic groups raised a revolt in the central Shaanxi Plain. Then, in the fourth year of Hui Di's reign, Hao San of the Xiongnu rebelled. Later, Hao San's brother, Hao Duyuan led a further revolt. Some government officials realized the danger of the crisis and proposed the idea of "banishing the minorities", which was aimed at driving the people of Qiang and Di out of central China, forcing them to return to their native territory. This tension between the minority nationalities and the Han provoked large-scale resistance by Di and Qiang refugees.

In the last years of the Western Jin Dynasty, five nationalities, the Xiongnu, Jie, Di, Qiang and Xianbei, who had entered central China during the Han Dynasty, raised successive revolts against the Jin Dynasty. They set up sixteen independent regimes called the "Sixteen States". One of these, the state of Hou Qin, was established by a Qiang noble, Yao Chang, whilst a Di noble named Fu had established the state of Qian Qin. The Sixteen States ruled their separate regions by force in northern China, attacking cities and plundering towns. The military chaos continued, forcing the royal family of the Western Jin Dynasty to move southwards where they only retained sovereignty over areas south of the Yangtze River. Yao Chang's forefathers, who had been leaders of the Qiang, belonged to the Shaodang tribe during the Han Dynasty. Yao Chang's father had once exhorted his sons saying that "from ancient times no one from the minority nationalities should become Emperor. When I die, you should yield to the Jin and serve your rulers loyally and wholeheartedly" (*History of the Jin Dynasty: Chapter Sixteen*). This shows quite clearly how the rulers of the state of Hou Qin managed state affairs and also demonstrates the influence of Han culture on the Yao family.

The year 394 A.D. witnessed the death of Yao Chang and the succession of his son, Yao Xing, to the throne. In this period, great accomplishments were achieved by the state of Hou Qin: it offered amnesty and enlistment to refugees to help resist those oppressing both the Qiang and Han; it liberated all civilians in the state who had become slaves as a result of famine; it abolished excessive implementation of laws and regulations and exercised more caution in hearing and passing judgment on cases; it established law studies in Chang'an; it promoted honest and upright officials while punishing corruption with utmost severity; it also set up a system to supervise government officials and offered

考试优劣，随才擢拔；信奉佛教，在长安重新考校翻译佛教经典 300 余卷。姚兴晚年，诸子争位，内部矛盾尖锐。姚兴死后，姚泓继位。此时相继发生羌民和匈奴的叛乱以及统治集团的内讧。随后晋军攻破长安，姚泓被杀，后秦灭亡。后秦传国 31 年。

"十六国"时期，西北甘、青地区先后有前凉、后凉、西秦、南凉、北凉等政权，战争频繁，兵连祸结，使该地区的羌族和其他各族人民都过着动乱不安的痛苦生活。随后鲜卑族拓跋氏结束了"十六国"的纷争局面，建立了北魏，统一了北方。民生得到暂时的休养，经济得以发展。但是北魏统治者实施了一系列残酷的法律以镇压人民："谋反大逆者，亲族男女无论少长皆斩。"不仅如此，刑法条文不断增加，大辟（砍头）140条，后增至 235 条。而且赋税征收数额不断增加，致使民众怨声载道。北魏时期，各民族的反抗斗争此起彼伏，其中影响力较大的是盖吴领导的十万人起义和莫折氏父子领导的羌汉人民大起义。这场持续了五年多的起义从根本上动摇了北魏王朝的统治，羌、氐、匈奴、汉在共同的斗争中消除了民族隔阂，促进了各民族的融合。

魏晋南北朝是中国历史上很有特色的时期：政治混乱而思想活跃；国家动荡却文化繁荣。从羌族历史的角度看，这一时期战争频仍，中原大地成为各族统治者逐鹿的战场，然而共同的灾难和痛苦

promotion according to their ability and performance. Yao Xing, a Buddhist, had more than three hundred volumes of Buddhist classics collated and translated in Chang'an. In Yao Xing's later years, all his sons contended for the throne, provoking internal conflict. After Yao Xing's death, Yao Hong succeeded to the throne. Under his reign, revolts were incited by the Qiang and the Xiongnu, whilst conflicts also occurred within the royal family. Eventually, the city of Chang'an was captured by the troops of Jin, resulting in Yao Hong's death. The state of Hou Qin finally came to an end after existing for thirty-one years.

In the period of the Sixteen States, there were several states in the northwest area of Gansu and Qinghai such as the Former Liang, Later Liang, Western Qin, Southern Liang and Northern Liang. This was a highly turbulent and unstable time for the Qiang and other nationalities in northwest China, who were subjected to endless wars and disasters. The Tuoba tribe of the Xianbei nationality finally ended the "Sixteen States' War", unifying north China and establishing the state of Northern Wei. This brought an improvement in living standards and economic conditions, but parallel with this the rulers of the Northern Wei implemented a series of brutally repressive laws. Anyone who conspired against the state would be decapitated together with all their relatives, regardless of gender and age and despite their innocence. Even worse, the number of these laws continued to expand: the crimes that were to be punished with decapitation increased from one hundred and forty to two hundred and thirty-five. Complaints about the increasing number of taxes levied were heard everywhere and revolts broke out against the government. The most influential ones were the "Hundred Thousand Men Insurgence" led by Gai Wu and the uprising of the Qiang and Han people led by Mo Zhe and his son. These revolts lasted for five years and radically weakened the power of the Northern Wei Dynasty. Through their collective efforts against a common enemy, inter-tribal relations improved among the Qiang, Di, Xiongnu and Han, increasing the degree of ethnic integration among them.

The Northern and Southern Dynasties period was an interesting era in Chinese history. It was politically unstable and ideologically active, socially turbulent but culturally prosperous. From the perspective of Qiang history, the frequent wars had made central China a battlefield where rulers of different nationalities fought for the throne. However, these same disasters and sufferings

却增进了羌民族与各民族之间的理解和交往。这一时期为羌族和其他民族的融合提供了条件，使民族大融合成为可能。首先，自东汉以来，羌族和其他少数民族陆续迁入内地，一部分羌族草原牧人变为从事农耕的农民，生活方式发生改变，逐渐接受了中原的文化。其次，频繁的割据战争和共同的反抗压迫把羌族和其他民族紧密联系起来，使他们有共同的利益所在，从而增进了各民族之间的了解。再者，封建王朝政权在羌区不断增设郡县并任命羌人酋豪做官，不同程度地打破了部落组织的封闭分割状态，促使羌族上层主动吸收其他民族的优点。不仅如此，战乱流亡和民族迁徙造成羌族和其他民族特别是汉族的杂居局面，使各族人民逐渐过着共同的经济、政治和文化生活。当然，后秦和北魏推行"汉化"、提倡儒学也为民族融合起了一定的推动作用。可以说，动乱的南北朝也是羌、汉等各民族融合、发展的南北朝。

公元 589 年，隋朝统一中国，结束了数百年分裂的局面。对于羌族等少数民族，隋文帝本着"志存安养"、"群方无事"(《隋书·高祖记》)的原则，反对动辄诉诸武力，发兵征讨，希望用怀柔政策团结各民族上层贵族，推行教化，以解决民族问题。在岷江上游及今甘肃、四川交界一带设置郡县。在北周设置郡县的基础上，隋初经过调整，到隋炀帝时设置汶山郡，郡治在今茂县凤仪镇，管辖 11 个县。汶山郡是四川地区管辖最广的大郡之一。通过设置郡县，隋朝加强了对羌区的统治管理。

promoted understanding and interaction between the Qiang and other Chinese nationalities, facilitating the amalgamation of different ethnic groups. This came about firstly when, under the Eastern Han Dynasty, the Qiang and other minorities started moving further into central China, from which time some of the Qiang switched from their nomadic lifestyle to land cultivation and gradually adopted the culture of central China. Secondly, the frequent separatist wars and common revolts resulted in closer ties between the Qiang and other nationalities. Their common interests promoted mutual understanding among the various ethnic groups. Thirdly, as the number of administrative counties increased under feudal dynastic rule and since Qiang nobles were increasingly being appointed as officials, the autonomy and segregation of the different Qiang tribes changed to varying degrees and the upper echelons among the Qiang were forced to assimilate with other nationalities. Furthermore, the chaos and exile caused by war and the movement of different ethnic groups meant that the Qiang had to coexist with other Chinese nationalities, especially the Han, with the different groups increasingly sharing similar political, economic and cultural spheres. Also, the promotion of Han culture and the advocacy of Confucianism by rulers of the Northern Wei and Hou Qin contributed to the eventual union of various ethnic groups in China. Thus, the turbulent Northern and Southern Dynasties period was a time of development and amalgamation of different nationalities.

In 589, Emperor Wen of the Sui Dynasty reunified the whole country, bringing to an end the disunity and chaos that had lasted for several hundred years. In the early years of the Sui, Emperor Wen adopted many policies to strengthen his regime. Based on the principle of "peaceful coexistence", he hoped that by using conciliatory policies instead of military force, he could unite the Qiang nobles to resolve ethnic minority issues by means of cultural education. He also established administrative counties around the upper reaches of the Min River and in the border region between present-day Gansu and Sichuan provinces. The second emperor of the Sui Dynasty, Emperor Yang, benefited from the reforms introduced by his predecessor and set up Wen Shan administrative county in the present-day town of Fengyi in Mao County, which administered eleven shires. Wen Shan was the largest county in Sichuan at that time. By establishing administrative counties, the central government strengthened its governance and administration over the Qiang area. The

总之，隋朝的怀柔政策产生了良好的政治效应，并带来了社会安定的结果。

隋亡唐兴，唐太宗不再坚持"贵中华，贱夷狄"的传统偏见，主张用平等的态度对待包括羌族在内的各个少数民族。具体表现有：首先，军事进攻着重于打击那些严重威胁国家安全的民族部落，把主要力量放在加强边区的军事设置和增强边防实力方面。其次，充分利用少数民族首领豪酋，并委以刺使或都督，子孙世袭。再者，民族地区的羁縻州在本州内有自主权，朝廷只要求其在政治上接受管辖，不要求在经济上交纳贡赋。最后，羁縻州可因时势不同而变更建制，条件成熟时可升为正州，成为唐王朝的直属州；正州若时局不稳可降为羁縻州。

7 世纪，在藏北高原羌塘一带有一苏毗国，她是以羌族女性为王的国家。《隋书·女国传》有云：苏毗在"葱岭之南，其国代以女为王，王姓苏毗，字末羯，在位二十年，女王之夫号曰'金聚'，不知（管理）政事。国内丈夫唯以征伐为务。……其俗妇人轻丈夫而不嫉妒，男女皆以彩色涂面，一日之中或数度变改之"。《通典》（卷 193）记载："在葱岭之南，男子皆披发，妇女辫发而縈之。……女子贵者，则多有侍男，男子不得有侍女。虽贱庶之女，尽为家长，有数夫焉，生子皆从母姓。"玄奘《大唐西域记》也说到

placatory policies implemented by the Sui Dynasty thus produced favorable political effects and brought about social stability.

With the decline of the Sui Dynasty, the Tang Dynasty rose to power. Emperor Tai Zong, the second emperor of the Tang Dynasty, no longer held to the traditional prejudice of "attaching importance to the Han nationality while looking down upon the minorities". He advocated an objective attitude towards minorities, including the Qiang people. This was demonstrated in the following ways: firstly, strong measures, especially military attacks, were taken only against powerful minority tribes that could threaten the country's safety, whilst emphasis was placed on reinforcing military defenses in the border areas. Secondly, leaders and nobles of minority tribes were appointed on a hereditary basis as military governors. Thirdly, the system of "Jimi" was introduced for the minorities at a local level. This meant that within a "Jimi" prefecture, Qiang people had full autonomy and did not have to pay tribute to the central government, although politically the "Jimi" prefectures were under the administration of the imperial court. Last, in certain situations a "Jimi" prefecture was allowed to change its administrative status. In other words, it could be promoted to a regular prefecture directly under the jurisdiction of the imperial court, or demoted from a regular prefecture to a "Jimi" prefecture in the case of political instability.

In the seventh century, there was a kingdom called Supi in the north of the Tibetan Plateau. The Kingdom of Supi was mainly composed of Qiang women. As the book *History of the Sui Dynasty: the History of the Kingdom of Women* says, "A kingdom located to the south of the Green Mountain had a queen called Su Pi. Su Pi was on the throne for twenty years and she, rather than her husband, Jin Ju, was in charge of state affairs. The only employment for men in the kingdom was soldiering. It was customary for women to despise men. Men and women in the kingdom all painted their faces with different colors and would change the colors several times a day." The book of *Tongdian* also says, "In the kingdom situated to the south of Green Mountain, the men had disheveled hair and the women wore their hair in braids. Most of the noble women had private male servants but men were not allowed to have maidservants. Even an ordinary woman was the master in her family and had several husbands. Children in the family all took the surname of their mother." The monk, Xuan Zang, mentioned in his book *A Journey to the West in the Tang Dynasty* that the geographical

东女国"东西长,南北狭","东接吐蕃国,北接于阗国,西接三波阿国(在印度恒河上游)"。《新唐书·苏毗传》载:"苏毗本西羌族,为吐蕃所并,号孙波,在诸部最大。"冉光荣《羌族史》认为,还有另一个羌人建立的以女性为王的国家,在史书上也称"东女"。《旧唐书·东女国传》载:"东女国,西羌之别种,以西海中复有女国(因已有西女国存在),故称东女焉。俗以女为王。东与茂州党项羌,东南与雅州接,界隔罗女蛮及白狼夷。"这些历史资料说明在羌族历史上有明显的母系社会的印迹。这对研究少数民族女性发展状况提供了依据,也是中国女性研究的重要内容。其实,在阿坝州的汶、理、茂等地区至今还沿袭着女婿倒插门的习俗,且子女从母姓。这与历史上的东女国应该存在某种渊源关系。

民族之间迁徙、融合的痕迹总是在语言发展和演变中沉淀下来。语言是一个民族共同体的主要特征之一,具有相对的稳定性。换言之,共同语系中的语族之间在历史上的联系必然是紧密的。

藏语和羌语同属藏缅语族的两个支系。古代羌人的一支与西藏高原的原住居民融合,成为唐代的吐蕃,而吐蕃又逐步融合了许多支羌人部落,从而形成了今天的藏族。景颇语也是藏缅语族中的一个支系。景颇族的先民自西藏高原沿横断山脉南下,唐代居住在今德宏州以北,怒江以西。

shape of the Eastern Kingdom of Women was "wide from west to east and narrow from north to south." "It was located to the west of the Kingdom of Tubo, to the south of the Kingdom of Yutian, and to the east of the Kingdom of Sanboa (near the upper reaches of the Ganges River in India)." The *New History of the Tang Dynasty: Biography of Supi* says, "Supi actually belonged to the Qiang. Later the kingdom was annexed by the Kingdom of Tubo and renamed as Sunbo." Ran Guangrong writes in his book *The History of the Qiang* that in addition to Supi, there was another kingdom dominated by Qiang women, which was also called the Eastern Kingdom of Women. The *Old History of the Tang Dynasty: Biography of the Eastern Kingdom of Women* says, "The Qiang founded the Eastern Kingdom of Women. As there had already been a Western Kingdom of Women, the Qiang named it the Eastern Kingdom of Women. Traditionally, women were in charge of state affairs in such a society. To the east of the kingdom was the Dangxiang Qiang tribe in Mao Prefecture, and to the southeast was Ya Prefecture." All of these historical references prove that there were clear features of matriarchal society in the history of the Qiang, something which provides valuable material for the study of minority women in China. In fact, the tradition of the husband living with his wife's family and the habit of naming children after their mother are still carried out today in the areas of Li, Wen and Mao counties in Aba Autonomous Prefecture. The Eastern Kingdom of Women might be the source of the phenomenon.

Traces of the migration and assimilation of ethnic groups are always found in the development and evolution of their languages. Language, as a relatively stable marker, is one of the principal features symbolizing an ethnic community. In other words, between language groups within the same language family, historically close connections are inevitable.

Both the Tibetan and Qiang languages are branches of the Tibeto-Burman language family. A tribe of ancient Qiang people once lived together with the indigenous people on the Tibetan Plateau and, during the Tang Dynasty, these two groups formed the Tubo nationality. The Tubo gradually mixed with many other Qiang tribes, eventually becoming the present-day Tibetans. The Jingpo language is also a branch of the Tibeto-Burman language family. Ancestors of the Jingpo travelled from the Tibetan Plateau along the mountain ranges leading southwards and during the Tang Dynasty they lived in the area to the north of Dehong prefecture and to the west of the Nu River. According to Jingpo custom,

据考，景颇父老死后送魂路线直至昆仑山。以此可知景颇族的祖先也曾居住于青藏高原澜沧江和怒江的发源地，而那里正是古羌人居住的地方。彝语与古代羌人的关系也十分密切。彝族传说和彝文文献记载都说彝族先民是从西北高原大雪山下逐步迁徙到今四川、云南的。汉文献也对此有印证。彝族的很多民俗，如着披毡、父子联名制、行火葬等都与羌族习惯相似。白族也是从古羌人中分化出来的。白族在汉代以前称僰。"僰，羌人之别种也。"（《史记·司马相如传·集解》）汉代往往羌僰并称，或氐僰并称。不仅如此，哈尼族、纳西族、傈僳族、土家族等民族，他们先民的构成都有古羌人。可见，古代羌人的不同支系，在不同的历史时期和不同的社会条件下融入不同的种族而形成许多新的民族。这一点是古代羌人从一个很大的族群演变成为今天一个人口较少的民族的重要原因之一。

宋朝建立以后，宋王朝对羌区的政策是"恃文教而略武备"。宋朝统治者认为："欲竭上腴之征，以取不毛之地，疲易使之众，而得梗化之氓，诚何益哉！"（《宋史·蛮夷一》）宋仁宗景祐五年（公元 1038 年），党项羌后裔元昊称帝，国号大夏，史称西夏。西夏国恢复了党项羌的发式，废除了唐、宋王朝给拓跋家族的赐姓李和赵，改用党项姓"嵬名"，

the living should see off the soul of the dead. Research indicates that the route along which people accompanied the soul of the dead reached as far as the Kunlun Mountains. The ancestors of the Jingpo people once lived in the cradle of the Lancang and Nu Rivers near the Qinghai-Tibet Plateau where the ancient Qiang also lived.

The language of the Yi people in China is also closely related to the ancient Qiang. Yi legends, literature, and documents all record the migration of ancestors of the Yi from the snow-covered mountains on China's northwestern plateau to present-day Sichuan and Yunnan provinces. Han literature also confirms this. Many folk customs of the Yi, such as wearing felt capes, taking one or two characters of the father's name for the son's name, and the practice of cremation, are very similar to Qiang customs.

The Bai are also an ethnic group which evolved from the ancient Qiang. Prior to the Han Dynasty the Bai people were called Bo: "Bo is a subdivision of the Qiang." (*Historical Records: Annotations of the Biography of Sima Xiangru*) During the Han Dynasty, the Bo and Qiang nationalities were often considered as one by the Han people, as were the Bo and Di nationalities. Furthermore, the ancestors of many minority nationalities, such as Hani, Naxi, Lisu and Tujia, were composed partly of ancient Qiang people. One can see that different branches of the ancient Qiang people merged with other nationalities in different historical periods and under different social conditions. Thus many new nationalities were formed, which also explains how the ancient Qiang evolved from a large group of tribes to its presently small population.

After the Song Dynasty was founded, its rulers focused on the development of culture and education rather than strengthening military forces in the Qiang region. They held that " if they dispatch troops to the remote hill areas of the minorities to conquer their wastelands, all the land taxes paid by the Han people will be consumed and the common people in central China will be worn down; their only gain will be those stubborn minority people. It's obviously not worth doing that!" (*History of the Song Dynasty: One of the Minorities*)

In 1038 (the fifth year of the reign of Emperor Ren Zong), a Dangxiang Qiang descendant named Yuan Hao founded the Kingdom of Western Xia. Under his rule the traditional hairstyle of the Dangxiang Qiang was resumed, the surnames of Li and Zhao that had been bestowed by the Tang and Song were abandoned, and the traditional Dangxing surname, Weiming, was adopted. A

并采取一系列措施，如立官制、定兵制、造文字、定仪服、制礼乐等，建立了完备的西夏国。这是羌族史上的一件重大事件。公元 1126 年，成吉思汗亲领大军侵入西夏国。西夏国军民抵抗一年，西夏于 1127 年灭亡，立国 190 年。

　　元朝是以蒙古族为主体建立的封建王朝。元朝废除了唐以来在羌人地区设置的羁縻州，在军事上派大军驻守、巡视，以加强军威和震慑力。元朝统治者还大力提倡喇嘛教，羌区也广修寺院。羌人在宗教信仰方面深受影响，一部分人开始放弃本民族信仰，而改信喇嘛教。元代在四川建立行省，其下设"诸蛮夷部宣慰使司"，管理全行省的少数民族。

　　在 14 世纪中叶的明王朝时期，羌族社会经济有了进一步的发展，各族人民之间的交往也更加频繁，为羌族地区与中央政权之间建立更紧密的政治关系创造了条件。由元朝首创的土司制度（由民族地区各族首领对本部落或地区实行的世袭管理制度，史称"土司"制度），在明朝得以完善。明初四川统一，原有的羌族首领纷纷归顺京朝，土司制度得以施行，例如，今阿坝州一带当时也由土司管理境内的羌民，同时，修筑关、堡、墩台、护城河等，保证羌区的安宁，推动羌民发展生产。

series of measures were also implemented which included the establishment of recruitment systems for officials and the army and the creation of their own script, uniforms and formal etiquette. Thus a complete kingdom was established, which was a significant event in the history of the Qiang. In 1127, Genghis Khan, the Mongol conqueror, annexed the Kingdom of Western Xia. As the most thriving period in the history of the Qiang, this Western Xia Kingdom had lasted for 190 years.

The Yuan Dynasty was established according to Mongol tradition, and under its rule the "Jimi" prefectures in the Qiang area, which had existed since the Tang Dynasty, were abolished. Instead, numerous troops were stationed there and military patrols were carried out both to promote military prestige and to intimidate. In addition, rulers of the Yuan Dynasty were vigorous advocates of Lamaism. Many temples were built in the Qiang area, subjecting the Qiang to strong Lamaistic influence. Some people even gave up their own beliefs and converted to Lamaism. The Yuan Dynasty also established an administrative province in Sichuan under which a department was set up to take charge of all minority affairs.

During the Ming Dynasty, the social economy of the Qiang developed further and there was increased interaction between different ethnic groups, which gave rise to the establishment of a closer political relationship between the Qiang and the central government. A system of "Tusi", originally initiated in the Yuan Dynasty, was continued during the Ming period. Under this system, leaders of different tribes were given the title of "Tusi" by the central government and authorized to take charge of tribal affairs. The position of "Tusi" was hereditary. The "Tusi" system was employed by the imperial court to manage and govern minority nationalities. In the early years of the Ming Dynasty, Sichuan was unified and all the leaders of Qiang tribes gradually surrendered. Once they had pledged allegiance to the imperial court, the "Tusi" system could be implemented. For example, in the area of today's Aba Prefecture, the Qiang people were supervised by their "Tusi". At the same time, they built passes, forts, protective mounds and moats to ensure the peace of the Qiang region and the development of local productivity.

清朝废除了世袭土司制度，改行"流官"统治。由朝廷任命流官，在土司区丈量土地，编订户籍，由朝廷的地方官统一征税，实行与汉区相同的政治制度。此项改革首先在云南实行，后在贵州、广西、四川等地推广并获得成功。四川羌族地区的"改土归流"虽然在明朝后期已经开始，但大规模实行还是在清高宗十七年（1752年）以后。羌区"改土归流"加强了清王朝对边远地区的统治，使统一的多民族国家更为巩固，也促进了少数民族地区经济文化的发展。但当时的改革并不彻底，在边远偏僻的少数羌寨仍然有土司的残余统治，这种情况一直延续到新中国成立前夕。

1949年10月中华人民共和国诞生，同年12月成都解放。1950年1月，解放军挺进羌区，汶川、茂县、理县等羌区城乡相继解放。1958年7月，羌族人民聚居的茂县、汶川和理县合并建茂汶羌族自治县。1963年3月，恢复汶川、理县建制，茂汶羌族自治县辖原茂县。1987年，阿坝藏族自治州更名为阿坝藏族羌族自治州，同时撤销茂汶羌族自治县，恢复茂县建制。2003年，国务院批准建立北川羌族自治县，辖原北川县。今天，二十一世纪的羌族人民正在用自己的智慧和勤劳开创民族繁荣和经济文化的发展。

（陈蜀玉　陈华新）

In the Qing Dynasty, the "Tusi" system was abolished throughout China and the position of responsibility for minority affairs ceased to be hereditary. In places where the "Tusi" formerly governed, a "Liuguan" or local governor was appointed by the imperial court who levied taxes on every household and on land registered and measured by the government. Such reforms were carried out first in Yunnan, then in Guizhou, Guangxi and Sichuan. However, although the reform in the Qiang area of Sichuan had already been initiated in the late years of Ming Dynasty, it did not reach full momentum until the seventeenth year of Qianlong's reign (1752 A.D.). The reforms carried out in the Qiang area not only strengthened the controlling power of the Qing Dynasty over remote areas, helping to stabilize such a multi-ethnic country, but also enhanced the economic and cultural development of the minority groups. However, the reforms of this period failed to reach some areas and the Qiang people in some remote villages continued to be ruled by "Tusi" until 1949.

On October 1$^{st}$, 1949, the People's Republic of China was founded. In December of the same year, Chengdu was liberated. In January of the following year, the Chinese People's Liberation Army moved into the Qiang region. Urban and rural areas in Wenchuan, Mao and Li counties were subsequently liberated. In July 1958, these counties were merged to form the Maowen Qiang Autonomous County. In March 1963, the former administrative systems of Wenchuan and Li County were reinstated while what had been Mao County continued to be administered as Maowen Qiang Autonomous County. In 1987, Aba Tibetan Autonomous Prefecture was renamed Aba Tibetan and Qiang Autonomous Prefecture and at the same time Maowen Qiang Autonomous County once again became Mao County. In 2003, the State Council of China approved the establishment of Beichuan Qiang Autonomous County to administer what was formerly Beichuan County. Today, the Qiang people of the twenty-first century are using their own wisdom and hard work to initiate and develop economic and cultural prosperity.

（Translated by Dai Zhiyong, Chen Shuyu）

# 第二章　羌族碉楼

羌族建筑在中国少数民族建筑中有其自身的独特性。羌族建筑包括碉楼、石砌住宅、板屋土屋、官寨、聚落、桥梁和栈道等。《后汉书·西南夷传》中就描述过早在 2 000 年前的冉駹人的住房，"依山居止，垒石为室，高者至十余丈"，称为"邛笼"。邛笼是羌语碉楼的音译。碉楼见证了羌族的历史，最能代表羌族建筑，展现羌族建筑的风格。

根据四川阿坝藏族羌族自治州内的文物普查，全州 13 县中，除红原、若尔盖、九寨沟 3 县外，其他 10 县均有碉楼，尤以马尔康、汶、理、茂 4 县居多。4 县中就有 3 县为羌族聚居地区。因此，单从数量而言，羌族碉楼无疑集中在阿坝州境内。

碉楼的产生和发展有着不同的说法。

一种观点认为，西北羌人自汉代沿岷江河谷南下，而汉文化又溯岷江北上，在岷江这条各民族频繁交汇、活动的大走廊里，战争不可避免，导致了碉楼的产生。

另一种观点则认为，碉楼的建造跟羌族宗教有直接关系，并涉及释比（羌族不同的方言又称"许"，汉语叫"端公"）所起的重要作用。释比为羌族的精神领袖，自然对建筑规划、设计、营造有绝对的解释权。他认为万物有灵，碉楼（或谓邛笼）是"天宫"，而白石神最灵，那么垒砌碉楼和建房则又是祭放白石的工序和仪式。

## CHAPTER TWO    QIANG WATCHTOWERS

The architecture of the Qiang is distinct from that of other minority groups in China. It includes watchtowers, stone houses, houses made of wood and of earth, magistrate stockades (government offices of local rulers in earlier times), bridges, and plank roads along cliffs. Descriptions of the housing of the Ranmang people, who lived in this area as early as two thousand years ago, can be found in *The History of the Later Han Dynasty: Minorities in the Southwest*: "They lived in the mountains and built stone houses which could be as tall as ten 'zhangs'" (over 30 meters). Called "Qionglong", which is a transliteration of "watchtower" in the Qiang language, these watchtowers have witnessed the history of the Qiang and best typify Qiang-style architecture.

Research into cultural relics conducted within Aba Tibetan and Qiang Autonomous Prefecture show that of the thirteen counties in the prefecture, all have watchtowers except for Hongyuan, Ruoergai and Jiuzhaigou. The four counties of Maerkang, Wenchuan, Li and Mao have the largest number of watchtowers, with Qiang living predominantly in the latter three counties.

Several explanations can account for the emergence and development of the watchtower. One is that the Qiang people living in the northwest during the Han Dynasty moved southward along the Min River valley, while Han culture was simultaneously spreading northward. In the Min River corridor, the conflict between the two cultures resulted in frequent fierce battles, which necessitated the building of the watchtowers for defense.

Others hold that watchtower construction has close connections with the religion of the Qiang and the important role played by the "Shibi" (also called "Xu", or "Duangong" in Chinese). The Shibi is the spiritual leader of the Qiang and he has supreme authority over the planning, design and construction of any building. He believes that everything has a spirit, that the watchtower (or Qionglong) is the "palace of heaven", and that the God of the white stone is of greatest significance in their religion. For this reason, the building of watchtowers and houses is not just a normal building procedure but is also a ritual including sacrifice and the placing of white stones. Customarily, five

白石又常以五块分别代表天、地、山、树（森林）、寨（人间）等五个保护神。而碉楼之高可以把诸神抬举到距天最近的地方，犹如通天云梯、通天之道。释比可以通过它来寄托宗教情感和想象。并以下宽上窄收分的锥状体，投射到天宇之中，那里正是天神、火神和太阳神所在的境界。

再有现代羌人解释为是汉人"风水"塔在羌寨的翻版一说。

无论什么观点，在今羌族聚居区内遗存的大量碉楼，作为一种极特殊的空间形态，在中国乃至世界范围的建筑中，以不可替代的历史、科技、艺术价值昭示人类，展示着独特的空间创造和极不寻常的文化发展。其密度、广度、空间、营造、宗教性等都是世界罕见的。

尽管藏族也有碉楼，且主要分布在古冉駹羌人居住之地，但藏族碉楼多与官寨共生，形体高大，建造严谨，最高者马尔康白赊碉通高 43.2 米，一般的都在 30 米以上，有浓厚的以强大的经济实力为后盾的官府色彩和宗教气氛。而羌族碉楼多为民间建造，现存的羌碉，通高多在 30 米左右，且形多类杂、丰富多彩。构筑相对粗糙，但生动别致，富于变化，充满民间创造风格。羌族碉楼的设计特点有别于前者，造型特色亦非常突出，可惜由于地震、战争和其他原因，50 米上下高度的碉楼应已被毁掉或拆除，实为憾事。藏族碉楼和羌族碉楼应为完全不同的文化背景所产生，是截然不同的两种建筑体系的空间表现。

羌族碉楼空间内外形态跟其分布地区直接相关，大致分为茂县、杂谷脑河下游、羌峰地区三类。茂县地区以黑虎、三龙、曲谷、白溪、洼底、维城等乡为羌族碉楼最具原始特点地区。平面有四、六、八角多形，还有多至十三角的。内或圆或方或六边、八边，内外均有收分。顶部为平顶，通体成锥体，边长 3 至

white stones together symbolize the five tutelary gods of heaven, earth, mountains, trees (forests) and villages (man's world). The lofty watchtower elevates these tutelary gods to the nearest point to heaven like a scaling ladder or road leading upwards. Thus the religious aspirations and sentiments of the Shibi are all closely linked to the watchtower. Furthermore, by means of this tall, tapering structure, these religious thoughts and aspirations are projected into the place where the gods of heaven, fire, and the sun are located.

Some Qiang people nowadays believe that the function of their watchtower is similar to the "fengshui" tower in Han culture which serves as a protective symbol. Whatever the explanation, the remaining watchtowers exhibit to the world their irreplaceably historical, technological and artistic value. As a unique example of local architecture both in China and beyond, the watchtowers of the Qiang reveal a unique creation of space and an extraordinary cultural development. They are extremely unusual in terms of their density, height, space, mode of construction and spiritual significance.

Although Tibetans also have watchtowers distributed over the areas where the ancient Ranmang people of the Qiang used to live, most of the Tibetan watchtowers are tall and compact and constructed as part of a magistrate stockade. The tallest Tibetan watchtower, the Baishe Tower located in Maerkang City, measures 43.2 meters in height. Generally, Tibetan watchtowers are over thirty meters high, are expensively built in an official style, and have a religious quality. Qiang watchtowers, on the contrary, have a less official style. The Qiang watchtowers still in existence are mostly about thirty meters high and have various shapes. These constructions are relatively simple but nonetheless full of character. Unfortunately, due to earthquakes, wars and other factors, the taller Qiang watchtowers, some around fifty meters high, have been destroyed or removed. Belonging to different cultural backgrounds, the Tibetan and Qiang watchtowers are spatial realizations of two completely different architectural systems.

The inner and outer spatiality of the Qiang watchtowers relates directly to where they are located, and they can roughly be divided into the following three areas: a) Mao County; b) along the lower reaches of the Zagunao River; c) in the area of Qiangfeng. In Mao County, the villages of Heihu, Sanlong, Qugu, Baixi, Wadi and Weicheng contain the most of those watchtowers which have retained their original form. The towers have flat sides, which range from three

6 米不等。全为石砌，通高在 20 米上下，底墙厚 0.7～1 米。分公共、隘口、私家碉楼多类。内部全为墙体承重木构分层空间，多者 13 层，少者 3～4 层，有圆木锯状楼梯上下。外观雄浑古朴，坚固沉稳。外墙面多以凹面内收弧线形成锥状"乾棱子"造型，是适应地震多发区的独特构造。现存的羌碉经受了 1933 年叠溪 7.5 级大地震的检验。

杂谷脑河下游地区碉楼花样翻新。突出的特点有：① 以方形平面呈整体方锥形居多。② 以土泥夯筑墙体，有高达 20 多米的布瓦寨群碉。③ 顶端普遍呈椅子形造型。④ 最高的碉楼一层和二层有木桃枋从墙体中挑出，以搁置木板构成了望台。布瓦泥碉顶部还用斗拱挑承檐口。它直接受民居屋顶设计影响，并在防御中讲究审美需要，是羌族地区碉楼空间形态的一大发展。

羌峰一带包括草坡藏羌混居地区，因其接近汉区，除目前所见羌峰寨碉楼为正宗羌族碉楼外，草坡一带的碉楼如码头碉，不仅体宽形大，顶部亦采用汉族两坡水悬山屋面，风格气韵走形较大，是汉羌两族文化碰撞的一星火花。

to six meters wide, and they can be four-, six-, eight-, or even thirteen-sided. The interior can be round, square, six-, or eight-sided. The interior and exterior walls converge gradually from bottom to top, creating a tapering structure topped with a flat roof. The whole tower is constructed with layers of stones to a height of around 20 meters with the base walls being around 70 cm to 1 meter thick.

There are various kinds of towers, including those for communal use, those built on mountain passes, and private family watchtowers. On the inside these towers are divided into stories and have timber structures which support the walls. They may have as many as thirteen stories or just three or four. The stories are connected by ladders made from circular wooden beams with steps cut into them. In spite of their simple appearance, the watchtowers were carefully constructed for both strength and stability and those still in existence today managed to withstand the 1933 Diexi earthquake, which measured 7.5 on the Richter Scale.

The watchtowers around the lower reaches of the Zagunao River have been modified and display the following features: ① most of the watchtowers are square and tapering; ② the walls of the watchtowers are made of rammed soil, as exemplified by the twenty to thirty meter tall group of watchtowers in Buwa village; ③ the tops of the watchtowers are chair-shaped with one wall higher than the rest; ④ the top two stories of the towers have lookout platforms made of wooden rods extending out from the walls, overlaid with wooden planks. These Buwa watchtowers use a system of brackets, which in traditional Chinese buildings is called "Dougong", to support the cornices at the top of the towers. Such structures show the influence of residential-style buildings and indicate a development in watchtower design in which aesthetic considerations complement the basic function of defense.

With the exception of the watchtowers in the village of Qiangfeng itself, the towers in the Qiangfeng area cannot be regarded as typically Qiang, particularly the towers around Caopo, which is an area where both Qiang and Tibetan people live. Due to Caopo's proximity to the area where Han people reside, the watchtowers there are huge in both form and structure, like those typically found at a dockside. Their roofs show a strong resemblance to Han residential-style buildings and the overall architectural style reflects a combination of Han and Qiang cultures.

从碉楼和村寨的角度看，由于羌族碉楼存在着单独的碉楼和与民居结合在一起的碉楼两种空间形态，因此，必然涉及各自的功能以及其在村寨规划上的不同作用。

单独的碉楼往往属于公共性质的，可以分为两类。一类是分设在一寨或几寨的隘口、险关或咽喉之地的碉楼。它像寨子的眼睛，起了望和向各寨通风报信的作用，同时又具有前哨防御功能，姑且称之为哨碉。这种碉楼数量不等，视具体情况和环境而定。比如黑虎等寨均要通过一河谷咽喉狭窄险要之地，然后进入开阔的黑虎地区，那么碉楼选址则必须是山内各寨放哨者视线均能所及的位置，如发现来敌，以烟火或声响等方式报警，做好迎击犯敌的准备。所以，原有哨碉立于河谷咽喉之地。今杨氏将军寨就是由哨碉逐渐组群发展而来的。曲谷河西群碉地处半山腰台地，三面环山，前有陡坡高临河谷。河谷是犯敌必经之地，于是在陡坡边沿最易于观察河谷的位置单独设立巨型哨碉，而此处恰又是山上各寨均可俯视的选址。类似之碉还有布瓦山顶龙山寨石碉等。这类碉楼在选址上和汉"风水"塔有相似之处，但功能迥然不同，前者是为了观察敌情。这类碉楼虽然在空间上和村寨空间不发生直接关系，但其表现形式和村寨空间有着紧密的联系，这一点和汉"风水"塔有一定相似之处，只不过一个是"武"，一个是"文"而已。或者说一个是为生存，另一个是为发展。这种空间现象直接影响村寨选址和寨内居民布局。最基本点则表现在任何居住建筑的出现，均不允许有障碍物阻挡其与公共碉楼在视觉上的可见性。因此，黑虎鹰嘴寨民居为什么不错落设置而是一字沿山脊展开布局，其最根本原因即是相互之间不能阻碍视线。通观羌寨凡设立哨碉者，可谓无一例外。这就为村寨及民居选址和等高线的关系注入了新的内涵。

Freestanding watchtowers and watchtowers that are combined with dwellings have different functions and usually the layout of the villages in which they are located is also different. Freestanding watchtowers are often positioned on strategic passes near one or several villages in an area. They are for communal use and serve as the eyes of the village, providing a wide-ranging view of the area, and therefore play an important defensive role against surprise attacks, hence the name "lookout towers". The number of towers needed for an area depends on the nature of the location and the surrounding geography. In Heihu, for example, one has to negotiate a narrow gorge section of the river valley before the terrain opens out to the broad area where the Heihu villages are located. A watchtower is built above this strategic point at a site where it is visible from all the villages in the area. In the case of an attack, the watchman on the tower sets off fireworks or makes a loud noise, giving the villagers advance warning to prepare themselves against the enemy.

The watchtowers in Jiang Jun village, which is named after an army general of the Yang clan, are good examples of the value of lookout towers. This group of towers to the west of the Qugu River is located on a flat area of land halfway up the mountainside. This plateau area is framed on three sides by the mountain while its front side drops away in a steep slope to the river valley at the foot of the mountain. Since the valley is the only way to the villages, the giant watchtowers are built at the edge of the slope where they have the best view of the valley and are also visible to any villager on the mountain. Watchtowers with a similar function include the stone towers of Longshan village at the top of Buwa Mountain.

Generally, the Qiang lookout tower and the "fengshui" tower of Han culture share some similarities, particularly regarding site selection. However, they differ in their purposes. The primary function of the Qiang watchtowers is for defense while the Han "fengshui" tower serves a civil kind of purpose. These location-related functions have direct influence on the position and layout of the villages. The most important principle is that the watchtowers must be visible from every dwelling with nothing in between to block the line of sight. It comes as no surprise that archeological findings show dwellings in the village of Yingzui, in the area of Heihu, situated in a line along the hill ridge rather than being strewn at random. We presume the underlying reason for this is to prevent anything obstructing a view of the watchtower. Clearly, there is a correlation between contour lines and the location of village structures.

　　另一类单独的碉楼是立于寨中或四周恰当位置者，和前者不同的是，此类碉楼不仅作了望观察之用，同时又是犯敌入寨后寨中居民共同躲避和防御之所。村寨居民数量、财力、环境等决定碉楼的多少。布瓦寨曾经多达48个碉楼，而羌峰寨仅一个碉楼。山岭叠嶂之地，碉楼高一尺，视野即宽数里，故碉高无一雷同者，全视具体地形、环境而定，这是羌寨众多单独碉楼为什么高度不一致的根本原因。此类立于寨中或寨子四周的碉楼，在空间形态上和民居距离较近，在村寨整体空间上产生一种壁垒森严的威武雄壮气氛。又由于起伏错落的高差，墙体各立面大小不同的组合，石、泥材料及工艺的粗犷，它们呈现出一种悲壮的原始沧桑和豪迈之美。而哨碉因与村寨有较远的距离，在空间上与村寨较疏远，缺少亲和感。从空间分布层次讲，它与村寨是空间形态的次序组合。

　　从碉楼和民居的空间关系角度看，如果把上述两类单独的碉楼比喻成空间形态中的第一道防御层次的话，那么，作为碉楼发展的更深层次则是碉楼与民居直接在空间上亲和，出现另一类空间形态，即碉楼民居，亦可谓村寨防御体系中的第二道防御层次。在一些地区的村寨中出现家家有碉楼，各个地区或各个村寨碉楼与民居皆不同的碉楼民居大观。尤其是茂县地区，有的村寨不仅有公共哨碉，进入村寨又家家有私碉，且各寨碉楼与民居皆有不同做法及形态的建筑特色。

　　碉楼民居发达地区集中在茂县曲谷、三龙、黑虎、白溪、洼底、赤不苏、维城等黑水河流域各乡各寨，即羌族传统文化保留较完整的核心区域，散见于杂谷脑河下游流域各寨，反而罕见于松、茂、汶、灌

There is another type of freestanding watchtower which is usually located in the center of the village or at another appropriate position within the village. Unlike the towers previously mentioned, this type of tower serves not only as a lookout tower but also as a shelter and a defensive position for the villagers when enemies invade the village.

Population size, financial resources, and village environment are all factors that determine how many towers are to be built. There were once as many as 48 towers in the village of Buwa. In the village of Qiangfeng, however, there was only one tower. As for the towers built on mountain ridges, if the height of a tower is increased even by a third of a meter, the field of vision from the tower can be extended by a few kilometers. Consequently, the height of the tower depends on the local topography and environment, which explains why so many watchtowers of the Qiang villages differ in height. No matter whether the towers are positioned in the village center or all around the village, or are freestanding or attached to people's dwellings, they give the village a sense of power and strong fortification. The differing widths and heights of the towers, and the rough nature of the stone, mud and building technology, combine to present a kind of heroic beauty and a solemn sense of times past.

Moreover, although the towers which stand in open space can be close to or relatively far from the village, they are still positioned in an ordered kind of sequence. Looking at the relationship between the watchtower and the other dwellings, if one sees the free-standing watchtower erected in open space as the first line of defense, then those towers built as part of people's homes constitute the second line or point of defense.

In some places, each home in the village has a watchtower and where these differ from one another it can be an impressive sight. In Mao County in particular, some villages not only have a communal lookout tower but each home also has its own private tower and each of these homes and towers have their own distinctive architectural features. A large number of these combined watchtowers and dwellings can be found in the villages of Qugu, Sanlong, Heihu, Baixi, Wadi, Chibusu, and Weicheng in Mao County, and in the townships and villages around the valley of the Heishui River where the core of traditional Qiang culture has been well preserved. A few watchtowers with dwellings are scattered in the villages around the lower reaches of the Zagunao River but in Songpan, Mao, Wenchuan and Guan counties they are rare in the

岷江河谷官道附近的村寨。是官道历来驻有汉兵弹压，羌民慑服，防御建筑已失去意义？还是汉化程度较高，逐渐消失了固有的建筑文化特色？这是很值得思考的问题。总之，我们认为任何空间现象绝不是偶然的，在其背后定然存在历史、社会等方面的影响因素。

碉楼与民居在空间上的亲和，是羌族向封建农业经济社会发展在建筑上的注脚。如果还留有公共防御碉楼同时存在于村寨的话，则是由于封建农奴制度并存的社会背景。因此，碉楼民居现象在某种程度上反映出小农经济在维护农奴制度一统天下的同时又必须自保的空间发展，显然这是封建农业经济制度的萌芽状态，不可能像成熟的汉族封建制度一样，对建筑作出严格的形制规范。恰如此，给羌族碉楼民居在空间创造上带来了毫无制约的平面创造。因此，羌族民居与碉楼在亲和方面出现了非常不平凡的、每幢住宅均不同的平面。这种平面意识虽然主要是在维护主宅与碉楼平面的前提下，其他诸如卧室、畜养、杂物间显得比较随意，然而，正是这种层次明晰的主次平面构成，给空间组合造成了大小、疏密、紧松、开合、明暗等美妙的空间气氛。这也是很值得思考的空间现象。

就碉楼本身的结构而言，碉楼基本上是墙承重结构体系，无论是石砌或者土夯墙碉楼，由于内空间跨度极少超过 5 米，一般都在 4 米左右，因此，各层楼和楼顶的梁两端都穿搁在墙上，使楼内荷载都由内外墙负担。由于墙身极高，自重、载重都大，自然加厚墙基，形成收分，以致有的碉楼顶只有簸箕大面积。羌族地区为地震多发区，墙身的防震处理至关重要。为了稳固，必须加厚基脚，基墙一体，

villages near the main road along the Min River. This could be because the Qiang people were afraid of the military force of Han troops stationed along the roads, or because these villages were so influenced by Han culture that they gradually lost their distinctive architectural culture. Whatever the reason, one can see that the spatial location of the towers was highly intentional, with significant historical and social factors influencing their construction and this is something which merits further research.

Where the watchtowers and dwellings are in close proximity, this could be seen as an architectural footnote from the time when the Qiang were moving towards a feudal agricultural economy. However, where communal defense towers still remain in a village, they could be understood as a remnant of the co-existence of feudal and serf systems. The architectural form of combined watchtower and dwelling, although possibly reflecting the small-scale peasant economy of the serf system, was also a form of self-protection, all of which indicates an early stage in social development. Unlike the well-established feudal system of the Han, the serf system of the Qiang did not have strict regulations for architectural forms, and this liberty to design and locate towers as they saw fit resulted in a great variety of styles and spatial location. However, they all share the prerequisite that priority in spatial layout be given to the main rooms and the watchtowers, while other rooms, such as for sleeping, storage and livestock, could be arranged as desired. It is this kind of clear ordering of primary and secondary level spaces which creates a wonderful sense of large and small, restricted and spacious, open and enclosed, light and dark.

The watchtower itself, whether it is layered stone or rammed earth, is essentially a structure with load-bearing walls. Because the width of the watchtower rarely exceeds 5 meters and is more often 4 meters, both ends of the crossbeams for each story and for the roof are set into the walls, which means that the inner and outer walls bear the load of the interior structure. In order to support the great height and weight of the tower, the walls are extremely thick at the base and taper from the base to the top. As a result, the tops of some watchtowers are only the size of a winnowing fan.

Because the Qiang region is an area of seismic activity, it is important that the walls should be quake-resistant. To ensure the stability of the towers, the thick foundation and the base walls must be built as one structure and the

逐层收分，增加转角。墙角下入地下的深度，以见硬度（即坚硬的石头及硬泥）为准。但羌民居住地多陡坡，也有一些碉楼在背后一面墙身的处理上不下基脚，比如羌峰寨碉楼就是把后墙身直接砌在石底盘上的，而其他三面仍需下基脚。在收分上，往往碉楼下半部分收分多一些，上半部分收分少一些。这种分段收分做法可降低重心，增加稳定性。所以从外观上看碉楼，感到轮廓线不是直线即因此理。为了达到更加稳定的目的，在茂县一带的碉楼，平面外轮廓还形成凹面，似内收弧线，这就在各墙面产生变更方向的转角，也就是各墙面相交处角变得尖锐，羌人谓之"乾棱子"，无论四角、六角还是八角碉楼，都有此状。这种平面极类似帐幕边缘之形，是否是古羌游牧时代遗下的情结，尚可作些推测联想。

碉楼一般采取分层构筑法，石砌与土夯都如此。当砌筑一层后，便搁梁置桴放楼板，然后进行第二层，再层层加高。每加一层要间隙一段时间，待其整体全干之后方可进行上一层的砌筑。原因在于下层若是湿土润泥，或石泥尚未黏合牢固，那么无法承受压力，上下层必然坍塌。所以有的碉楼要砌筑多年方可竣工。碉楼顶的构造各地略有差别，但和当地住宅屋顶的做法相同，目的是遮漏防雨。程序是大梁上加小梁或劈柴，再加树枝或竹枝，上铺高山耐寒硬草（龙胆草之类），再铺含沙土层并拍打磨光，形成一面倾斜散水坡，凿墙穿眼接简槽挑出以排水。

corners are added as the walls narrow from one floor to the next. The depth of a tower's foundation depends on the hardness of the rock and the earth. Because of the steep nature of many Qiang areas, some watchtowers have no foundation on the side that is further up the hillside. For example, the watchtower in the village of Qiangfeng has a rear wall which has been built directly on to the rock face, while the other walls have proper foundations.

The outline of many watchtowers is distinctive in that the lower part often has a sharper incline than the upper part, which is presumably in order to lower the tower's center of gravity, thereby increasing its stability. For this reason the outline of the watchtower does not always appear to be a straight line. Examples of this can be seen in the area around Mao County, where the exterior walls of the towers curve inwards in a kind of arc, also increasing their stability. This results in pointed angles as the walls curve outwards at the wall intersections. The Qiang people call this design "Qianlengzi" (celestial angles). Whether the towers are square, hexagonal or octagonal, they all follow this style. One could conjecture that as this kind of structure is very similar to the curved walls and pointed intersections of a tent, it bears a trace of the nomadic lifestyle of the ancient Qiang.

Whether they are stone or rammed earth, the watchtowers are generally built floor by floor. Once the first level is constructed, main beams are put in place to support the secondary beams placed on top of them and then the next floor is constructed. Once a floor of the tower is completed, time is allowed for it to dry out completely before the construction of the next floor begins. If the mud of the lower floor is still moist, or if the mud and stone have not set firmly, the structure will not support the pressure of any weight and both floors will collapse. For these reasons, the construction of a single watchtower can take many years.

There are slight regional differences in how the tops of the towers are constructed, but they tend to be similar in structure to the roof style of houses in their locality, which are designed to keep out the rain. In the construction process, main beams are overlaid with smaller beams, followed by tree branches or bamboo branches. The next layer is of hardy, high mountain plants such as gentian, on top of which is applied a layer of mud mixed with sand which is spread out to form a slightly sloping surface to facilitate drainage. Lastly, a bamboo drainage trough is connected to a hole in the roof parapet to drain off the water.

碉楼顶层一般还开楼梯孔道上顶，亦有加木盖或薄石片的。因为西北少雨，亦常全开着。各层上下多用圆木锯齿状楼梯。极个别的底层不开门，从二层开门加梯上下。待人上去以后，抽梯上楼，以防不测。

总之，羌碉以其自身的独特结构和与村寨、民居的结合构成了一个和谐的空间组合。以羌碉为代表的羌建筑是羌族人民勤劳智慧的结晶，通过威严、沧桑的羌碉，我们可以管窥羌族文化发展、社会变迁的历程。今天，理县桃坪羌寨等一批羌族建筑正在向联合国教科文组织申请世界文化遗产。我们相信，不久的将来，羌碉将在人类建筑史上受到全人类的关注。

（贺运　季富政）

From the top floor of the watchtower a stairway leads to the roof. Sometimes the opening at the top of this stairway is covered by a wooden board or a thin stone slab but with the semi-aridity of this northwestern area of Sichuan it is often left open. The floors are connected by round beams with steps cut into them. In exceptional cases where the watchtower does not have a ground-level door, the tower has to be accessed by a door on the second floor, with the aid of a ladder. Then, if necessary, the ladder can then be pulled up to enhance security.

The distinctive structure of the Qiang watchtowers and their relationship with the village and its dwellings all combine to create a harmonious, spatial landscape. The watchtowers can be seen as a jewel in the crown of Qiang architecture and are a symbol of the wisdom and industriousness of the Qiang people. For this reason, these stately structures, which have survived the tests of time, can serve as a textbook for us, widening our knowledge of Qiang cultural development and social change. Recently, applications have been made to the United Nations Educational, Scientific and Cultural Organization (UNESCO) for the inclusion of some Qiang buildings in Li County's Taoping village on the UN list of World Cultural Heritage Sites. We hope and believe that these Qiang towers will increasingly be seen as a point of interest in the history of world architecture.

( Translated by Dai Zhiyong, Chen Shuyu )

# 第三章  羌族语言

羌族有自己的民族语言而没有民族文字，只有新中国成立后的新创拼音文字。羌语属于汉藏语系藏缅语族的羌语支。说羌语的羌族居民，有自称"尔玛"的传统。羌族在历史上不间断的迁徙生活，使众多部落中丰富的语汇难以得到统一和完善，于是出现了如下特殊的语言现象：同在岷江河谷但大区域内语音大差异，小区域内语音小差异，即使同住一座山，高处半山腰的羌族居民与河坝上的羌族居民的语言在语音上也不尽相同。这种差异性和多样性，既反映出羌语在本民族语言交流中的某些语言障碍，也反映出历史给这个民族带来的丰富的语言地区特色。

## 一、羌语方言

根据几十年来民族语言工作者调查分析的一致结论，羌语分为南部和北部两种方言。阿坝藏族羌族自治州汶川、理县的大部分地区和茂县凤仪等地区羌语属于南部方言；黑水县大部分地区、茂县绝大部分地区、松潘县羌区、北川羌族自治县、平武县等地区羌语属于北部方言。

南北方言差别较大，主要表现在以下几个方面：

（1）语音方面。北部方言复辅音丰富，元音分长短和卷舌、不卷舌，辅音韵尾丰富，并有复辅音韵尾，有轻声，无声调。在构词和构形中语音变化现象很丰富，常见的有辅音的弱化、浊化、换位、交替，元音的和谐、清化、

# CHAPTER THREE   THE LANGUAGE OF THE QIANG

The Qiang language belongs to the Tibeto-Burman branch of the Sino-Tibetan family. Although the Qiang have their own spoken language they have no Qiang script. Only after 1949 was an alphabetic writing system began to create. Native Qiang people have the tradition of calling themselves "Erma". Because of the constant migration in the history of the Qiang it has been difficult to combine the extensive vocabulary of the various tribes into one unified language and this has resulted in a very distinctive linguistic situation. In the valley of the Min River, differences in pronunciation can be found not only within large areas but also between each pocket of speakers. Even on the same mountain, those living at the foot of the mountain and those living higher up may have variations in the way they speak. Such diversity reflects the issue of language barriers among the Qiang themselves but also reflects the richness that history has bequeathed to their regional linguistic features.

## I. Dialects of the Qiang

After decades of study and investigation, minority language researchers have concluded that the language of the Qiang can be generally divided into two branches: the southern dialect and the northern dialect. The southern dialect exists in Wenchuan County, most parts of Li County and the Fengyi area of Mao County. The northern dialect is found in most parts of Heishui County and Mao County, and among the Qiang of Songpan County, Pingwu County, and the Qiang Autonomous County of Beichuan.

Great differences exist between the southern and northern dialect, mainly in phonetics, lexis and grammar.

Phonetics: In the northern dialect, vowels are divided into long and short, retroflex and non-retroflex. There are many consonant clusters and many final consonants, including final consonant clusters. Except for light tones there are no tones in the northern dialect. Considerable changes are occurring in the formation of words, the more common being consonants becoming weaker, voiced, metathesized or replaced and vowels being harmonized, elided,

脱落、增加等。南部方言复辅音比较少，无卷舌元音，只有少数地区的元音有长短之分，一般只有两个鼻音韵尾，有声调，语音变化现象略有残迹。南部方言声调区别词义的作用很小，形态的区别作用较大。

（2）词汇方面。南北两个方言区的基本词汇是相同的，异源词占总词汇的 10% 左右。南部方言在语音、词汇、语法等方面受汉语影响较深，北部方言则受汉语影响较小。此外，还受藏语的影响。虽然南北两种方言有些词在读音上有差别，但有严格的语音对应规律。

（3）语法方面。北部方言的语法表现形式比较复杂，靠内部变化和添加附加成分等形态手段来表达语法规律的情况比南部方言多；北部方言内部差别较小，而南部方言内部差别较大。在语法范畴上也有差别，如南部方言的人称代词有主、宾等格，北部方言则没有。同一语法范畴的表现形式也有若干差别，如北部方言动词命令式的前加成分同趋向范畴基本相同，有八个不同的前加成分，南部方言的前加成分只有一种。

就各方言区内语音和语法之间的差异来看，可在一个方言区内划分若干种土语。[①] 现分列如下：

南部方言有以下 6 种土语[②]：

① 雁门土语。分布在汶川县的雁门乡和茂县的耙川村、利谷村等地。

② 龙溪土语。分布在汶川县龙溪乡、克枯乡和威州镇的岷江河以西地区。

---

① 方言土语的划分主要引用了徐平、徐丹著的《东方大族之谜》一书，知识出版社 2001 年版，第 92～93 页。

② 有的研究者将蒲溪土语和木卡土语合称为大岐山语，所包括地区为理县的蒲溪乡、薛城镇、甘堡乡、农家乐乡和杂谷脑镇等地的部分村寨，木卡乡的三寨、木卡村、九子村、列列村，通化乡的水塘村、沙金村和汶山村等地，以及上孟乡和下孟乡的少数村寨。

epenthesized or devoiced. In the southern dialect there are relatively few consonant clusters and no retroflexed vowels. Only a few areas have the division of long and short vowel sounds, and, generally speaking, there are only two nasal terminal vowels. The southern dialect has tones and these tones serve mainly to differentiate morphology (word formation) rather than word meaning.

Lexis: The southern and northern dialects share almost the same lexis, of which heterogenous words only constitute approximately 10%. The southern dialect is greatly influenced by Chinese in phonetics, lexis and grammar while the northern one has little relation to Chinese but has been to some extent influenced by Tibetan. Although some words are pronounced differently in the southern and northern dialects, strict rules of pronunciation still exist.

Grammar: The grammatical differences between the southern and northern dialects mainly lie in the more complicated grammatical expressions of the northern dialect, which relies on internal inflection and affixation. Grammatical differences between sub-branches of the northern dialect are less noticeable than those of the southern dialect. In terms of grammatical categories, personal pronouns in the southern dialect have nominative and accusative cases whereas these do not exist in the northern dialect. Even within the same grammatical categories, ways of expression in the two dialects are somewhat different. Take the verbal imperative as an example: the northern dialect has eight prefixes and they are always consistent with the direction manifested by the verb, whereas the southern dialect has only one.

As far as the phonetic and grammatical differences within one dialectal area are concerned, several kinds of vernacular are further divided[1]:

Six Vernaculars in the Southern Dialect[2] and Their Distribution:

(1) Yanmen vernacular: Yanmen Village of Wenchuan County; Bachuan and Ligu of Mao County.

(2) Longxi vernacular: Longxi Village and Keku Village of Wenchuan County; the area west of the Min River in Weizhou.

---

① The division of vernaculars is based on The Mystery of the Great Eastern Nation by Xu Ping and Xu Dan, p92-93.
② Some scholars put Puxi vernacular and Muka vernacular together and name it Daqishan vernacular. It is used in Puxi Village, Xuecheng, Ganbao Village, Nongjiale Village, Zagunao Village, Sanzhai, Muka, Jiuzi and Lielie of Muka Village, Shuitang, Shajin and Wenshan of Tonghua Village, few parts of Shangmeng Village and Xiameng Village in Li County.

③ 绵池土语。分布在汶川县的绵池镇和草坡乡、三江、玉龙等地。

④ 蒲溪土语。分布在理县的蒲溪乡、薛城镇，以及甘堡乡、农家乐乡和杂谷脑镇等地的部分村寨，还有木卡乡的三寨和通化乡的汶山村等地。

⑤ 木卡土语。分布在理县木卡乡的木卡村、九子村、列列村，通化乡的水塘村、沙金村，以及上孟乡和下孟乡的少数村寨。另外，分布在甘孜藏族自治州丹巴县的羌族大多数居民也说木卡话。

⑥ 桃坪土语。分布在理县的桃坪、通化两乡。

北部方言有以下 9 种土语①：

① 镇平土语。分布在松潘县的小姓乡、镇坪乡、白羊乡，茂县的太平乡、松坪沟乡、校场乡和石大关乡等地区。

② 曲谷土语。分布在茂县的曲谷乡、雅都乡、维城乡、洼底乡、白溪乡等地。

③ 回龙土语。分布在茂县的回龙乡、三龙乡、石大关乡和校场乡的南部地区。

④ 黑虎土语。分布在茂县的黑虎乡和飞虹乡的水草坪村、苏家坪村等地。

⑤ 渭门土语。分布在茂县的沟口乡、渭门乡和永和乡。

⑥ 维古土语。分布在黑水县的维古乡、木苏乡、洛多乡、龙坝乡、石碉楼乡、色尔古乡、瓦钵梁子乡等地。

⑦ 知木林土语。分布在黑水县知木林乡、乌木树乡、慈坝乡以及晴朗乡、麦扎乡的部分地区。

⑧ 麻窝土语。分布在黑水县的麻窝乡、红岩乡、西尔乡、双溜索乡、扎窝乡等地。

⑨ 芦花土语。分布在黑水县沙石多乡的洋茸村、昌德村、泽盖村、二古鲁村、热拉村，芦花镇的米尔垮村、四美村、沙板沟村、罗坝街村、竹格都村等地。

---

① 有些学者认为，北部方言只有6种，即上面提到的镇平土语、曲谷土语、黑虎土语、知木林土语、麻窝土语和芦花土语。将渭门土语归为黑虎土语，将回龙土语和维古土语归为曲谷土语。

(3) Mianchi vernacular: Mianchi, Caopo Village, Sanjiang and Yulong of Wenchuan County.

(4) Puxi vernacular: Puxi Village and Xuecheng of Li County; some parts of Ganbao Village, Nongjiale Village and Zagunao; Sanzhai of Muka Village and Wenshan of Tonghua Village.

(5) Muka vernacular: Muka, Jiuzi and Leilei in Mula Village of Li County; Shuitang and Shajin of Tonghua Village; and a few parts of Shangmeng Village and Xiameng Village. In addition, most Qiang inhabitants in Danba County of Ganzi Tibetan Autonomous Prefecture also speak the Muka vernacular.

(6) Taoping vernacular: Taoping Village and Tonghua Village of Li County.
Nine Vernaculars in the Northern Dialect[①] and Their Distribution:

(1) Zhenping vernacular: Xiaoxing Village, Zhenping Village and Baiyang Village of Songpan County; Taiping Village, Songpinggou Village, Jiaochang Village and Shidaguan Village of Mao County.

(2) Qugu vernacular: Qugu Village, Yadu Village, Weicheng Village, Wadi Village and Baixi Village of Mao County.

(3) Huilong vernacular: Huilong Village, Sanlong Village, Shidaguan Village and the southern part of Jiaochang Village of Mao County.

(4) Heihu vernacular: Heihu Village, Shuicaoping and Sujiaping in Feihong Village of Mao County.

(5) Weimen vernacular: Goukou Village, Weimen Village and Yonghe Village of Mao County.

(6) Weigu vernacular: Weigu Village, Musu Village, Luoduo Village, Longba Village, Shidiaolou Village, Seergu Village and Waboliangzi Village of Heishui County.

(7) Zhi Mulin vernacular: Zhimulin Village, Wumushu Village, Ciba Village, some parts of Qinglang Village and Maizha Village of Heishui County.

(8) Mawo vernacular: Mawo Village, Hongyan Village, Xier Village, Shuangliusuo Village and Zhawo Village of Heishui County.

(9) Luhua vernacular: Yangrong and Changde in Shashiduo Village of Heishui County, and other places like Zegai, Ergulu, Rela, Mierkua, Simei, Shabangou, Luobajie and Zhugedu of Heishui County.

---

① Some scholars hold that there are only six kinds of vernacular in the northern dialect, i.e. the above-mentioned Zhenping vernacular, Qugu vernacular, Heihu vernacular, Zhimulin vernacular, Woma vernacular, Luhua vernacular. They classify Weimen vernacular into Heihu vernacular, put Huilong vernacular and Weigu vernacular into Qugu vernacular.

## 二、羌语的基本特点

### （一）语音特点

#### 1. 声母

各方言一般都有 40 个单辅音声母，塞音、塞擦音一般都分清音、清送气音、浊音三套，塞擦音一般都有舌尖前、卷舌、舌叶、舌面四套，有小舌部位的塞音和擦音。北部方言复辅音较丰富，一般都在 45 个以上；南部方言的复辅音少于北部方言，个别地区的复辅音已基本消失。复辅音大都是二合的，由基本辅音加前置或后置辅音构成，三合辅音较少。如北部方言曲谷话有单辅音声母 42 个，复辅音声母 49 个，它们的结构是二合的；南部方言雁门话有单辅音声母 41 个，复辅音声母 18 个，其结构也是二合的。

（1）单辅音声母，见表 1。

表 1　单辅音声母表

| 发音方法 | | 发音部位 | 双唇 | 舌尖前 | 舌尖中 | 舌尖后 | 舌叶 | 舌面前 | 舌根 | 小舌 | 声门 |
|---|---|---|---|---|---|---|---|---|---|---|---|
| 塞音 | 清 | 不送气 | p | | t | | | | k | q | (ʔ) |
| | | 送气 | ph | | th | | | | kh | qh | |
| | 浊 | 不送气 | b | | d | | | | g | | |
| 塞擦音 | 清 | 不送气 | | ts | | tʂ | tʃ | tɕ | | | |
| | | 送气 | | tsh | | tʂh | tʃh | tɕh | | | |
| | 浊 | 不送气 | | dz | | dʐ | dʒ① | dʑ | | | |
| 擦音 | 清 | | f | s | ɬ | ʂ | | ɕ | x | χ | h |
| | 浊 | | | z | | ʐ | | ʑ | ɣ | ʁ | ɦ |
| 鼻音 | | | m | | n | | | ɲ | ŋ | | |
| 边音 | | | | | l | | | | | | |
| 颤音 | | | | | r | | | | | | |
| 半元音 | | | w | | | ɻ② | | j | | | |

---

① 有的研究者认为羌语里没有舌尖后塞擦音。

② 有的研究者认为羌语里没有舌尖后半元音。

## II. Basic Features of the Qiang Language

### 1. Phonetic Features

#### 1) Shengmu

In languages of monosyllabic morphemes such as Sinitic languages and many Tibeto-Burmese languages, the "shengmu" is the initial consonant of the syllable, usually followed by a vowel (yunmu).

There are about 40 of these simple initial consonants in each dialect. Stops and affricates are generally divided into voiceless, aspirated voiceless and voiced according to manners of articulation. Moreover, four different places of articulation result in different types of affricates: apical, retroflexed, blade and tongue center. Also, there are some stops and fricatives produced by the uvula. The northern dialect has more than 45 consonant clusters, much more than those in the southern dialect. In one or two southern dialectal areas, consonant clusters have even disappeared. Most consonant clusters are composed of two parts, i.e., one cardinal consonant plus one pre-consonant or post-consonant. A few are made up of three parts. For example, the Qugu vernacular, a sub-branch of the northern dialect, has 42 simple initial consonants and 49 initial consonant clusters, and all of which include two parts. A further example is Yanmen vernacular in the southern dialect which has 41 simple initial consonants and 18 initial consonant clusters, also with two-part structures.

(1) Simple initial consonants (see Table1).

Table1　Simple initial consonants

| manners of articulation \ places of articulation | | | bilabial | front apex | central apex | back apex | blade | front blade | radix | uvula | glottis |
|---|---|---|---|---|---|---|---|---|---|---|---|
| stop | voiceless | unaspirated | p | | t | | | | k | q | (ʔ) |
| | | aspirated | ph | | th | | | | kh | qh | |
| | voiced | unaspirated | b | | d | | | | g | | |
| affricate | voiceless | unaspirated | | ts | | tʂ | tʃ | tɕ | | | |
| | | aspirated | | tsh | | tʂh | tʃh | tɕh | | | |
| | voiced | unaspirated | | dz | | dʐ | dʒ① | dʑ | | | |
| fricative | voiceless | | f | S | ɬ | ʂ | ɕ | x | χ | h | |
| | voiced | | | z | | ʐ | ʑ | ɣ | ʁ | ɦ | |
| nasal | | | m | | n | | ȵ | ŋ | | | |
| lateral | | | | | l | | | | | | |
| trill | | | | | r | | | | | | |
| semi-vowel | | | w | | ɻ② | | j | | | | |

---

① Some scholars think there is no back apex affricate in the Qiang language.
② Some scholars think there is no back apex semi-vowel in the Qiang language.

说明：

① 舌尖塞音、塞擦音在介音 u 前有唇化现象，气流强时，还发生轻微的颤唇，如 tuə（扛）。

② l 有前置辅音 x 时常念成 ɬ，如 xli（骨髓）。

③ j，w 在音节首和音节尾都出现，实际发音分别相当于元音 i，u，如 juju（分），tʂhij（花椒），we（有），aw（姑母）。j 在 u 后受其圆唇影响读作 y，如 tuj（连枷）。

④ x 在高位元音前常读作 ɕ，如 xie/ɕie（骂）。

⑤ ŋ 存在明显的唇化现象，如 ŋeu（奶牛），qəŋ（头发）。汉语借词中的 ŋ 多数不唇化，也有少数唇化，如 ten leŋ（灯笼）。

⑥ r 不作词首音节的声母，ʁ 只作复辅音的前置辅音，x 在大多数情况下也是作前置辅音，h 只在词首音节的开头出现。

⑦ 凡元音起头的音节，元音前都带喉塞音ʔ，如 ʔas（一天）。因ʔ在语流中常消失，不作音位。

例如：

| p | pə | 买 | ph | phə | 皱纹 |
| b | bə | 蜜蜂 | m | mə | 火 |
| Φ | Φa | 衣服 | tsh | tshə | 盐 |
| dz | dzə | 吃 | ʁ | ʁu | 愿意，能 |
| h | har | 朝后看 | x | xu | 香 |

（2）复辅音声母。复辅音全是二合的，大部分是清音与清音相配，浊音与浊音相配。分擦音在前或在后两种类型：擦音在前的有 sts，st，sq，zd，ʂp，ʂk，ʂq 等；擦音在后的有 phʂ，khs，gz，qhs 等。例如：

| st | stə | 老鹰 | sq | pie sqam | 小雪花 |
| zd | zdə | 独木梯 | zb | zbə | 牦牛 |

56

Notes:

① Apical stops and affricates are labialised before the initial "yunmu" "u". Besides, a slight trill will occur if the air-stream is very strong, as in "tuə" (carry).

② "l" is pronounced as "ɫ" when the pre-consonant "x" appears, as in "xli" (marrow).

③ "j" and "w" may appear at both the end and the beginning of a syllable, and their actual pronunciations are more like the vowels "i" and "u" respectively, as in "juju" (distribute), "tʂhij" (pepper), "we" (have), "aw" (aunt). "j" is read as "y" after the rounded vowel "u", as in "tuj" (flail).

④ When "x" is put in front of high vowels, it changes phonetically into "ɕ", as in "xie"/ "ɕie" (scold).

⑤ "ŋ" is obviously labialised, as in "ŋuə" (milch cow), "qəŋ" (hair). But the "ŋ" in loanwords from Chinese is generally not labialised and there are just a few exceptions as in "ten leŋ" (lantern).

⑥ "r" does not appear as the initial consonant of an initial syllable; "ɣ" can only be put in the front of a consonant cluster; "x", under most conditions, is taken as a pre-consonant; "h" is only found at the beginning of an initial syllable.

⑦ Syllables beginning with a vowel always have the glottal stop "ʔ" before the vowel, as in "ʔas" (one day). Because "ʔ" is often lost in a flow of words, it cannot be used as a phoneme.

Examples:

| p | pə | buy | ph | phə | wrinkle |
|---|---|---|---|---|---|
| b | bə | bee | m | mə | fire |
| Φ | Φa | clothes | tsh | tshə | salt |
| dz | dzə | eat | ʁ | ʁu | can |
| h | har | look back | x | xu | fragrant |

(2) Initial consonant clusters. Consonant clusters are all made up of two parts, mostly a voiceless with a voiceless, or a voiced with a voiced. They are divided into two types: one with fricatives in front like sts, st, sq, zd, ʂp, ʂk, ʂq, and etc; the other with fricatives at the end like phʂ, khs, gz, qhs, and etc.

Examples:

| st | stə | eagle | sq | pie sqam | flurry |
|---|---|---|---|---|---|
| zd | zdə | one-plank bridge | zb | zbə | yak |

| ɣʐ | ɣʐə | 足够 | gz | gzə | 辣 |
| qhʂ | qhʂe | 野羊 | χʨ | χʨue | 闭（眼） |

## 2. 韵母

（1）单元音韵母（见表 2）。单元音韵母较丰富，北部方言有长与短、卷舌与不卷舌、鼻化与非鼻化的对立，南部方言也有卷舌和鼻化的现象。如：曲谷话有 8 个舌面元音韵母，8 个长元音韵母，5 个卷舌元音韵母，3 个卷舌长元音韵母，2 个鼻化元音韵母，3 个卷舌鼻化元音韵母，1 个长卷舌鼻化元音韵母；雁门话有 8 个单元音韵母，2 个卷舌元音韵母。

**表 2　单元音韵母表**

| 舌位 | 长短唇形平卷 | | 不卷舌 | | 卷舌 | |
| --- | --- | --- | --- | --- | --- | --- |
| | | | 短 | 长 | 短 | 长 |
| 高 | 前 | 展 | i | i: | iʅ | i:ʅ |
| | | 圆 | y | | | |
| | 后 | 圆 | u | u: | uʅ | u:ʅ |
| 次高 | 前 | 展 | e | e: | eʅ | e:ʅ |
| | 后 | 圆 | o | o: | | |
| 低 | 前 | 展 | a | a: | aʅ | a:ʅ |
| | 后 | 圆 | ɑ | ɑ: | ɑʅ | ɑ:ʅ |
| 央 | | | ə | | əʅ | ə:ʅ |

说明：

① 长元音 i:，u:舌位较高，分别相当于标准元音 [i] 和 [u]。短元音 i，u 舌位较低，分别相当于 [i] 和 [v]；作介音时，舌位也分别与 [i] 和 [u] 相同。u 在小舌音和舌尖中音后，唇的开合接近

| ɣr | ɣrə | enough | gz | gzə | peppery |
| qhs | qhse | wild sheep | χʧ | χʧue | close (eyes) |

**2) Yunmu**

(1) Monophthongal "Yunmu" (Table 2). Monophthong yunmu are abundant in the Qiang language. In the southern dialect, they can be retroflexed and nasalized. In the northern dialect, they are divided into long and short, retroflexed and non-retroflexed, nasalized and non-nasalized. For instance, the Qugu vernacular has 8 blade-voweled yunmu, 8 long-voweled yunmu, 5 retroflexed-voweled yunmu, 3 long-retroflexed-voweled yunmu, 2 nasalized-voweled yunmu, 3 nasalized-retroflexed-voweled yunmu, and 1 long-nasalized-retroflexed-voweled yunmu; the Yanmen vernacular has 8 monophthongal yunmu and 2 retroflexed-voweled yunmu.

Table 2　Monophthongal Yunmu

| the Position of the Tongue / Length / the Degree of Lip Rrounding / Retroflection | | | non-retroflexed | | retroflexed | |
|---|---|---|---|---|---|---|
| | | | short | long | short | long |
| high | front | unrounded | i | i: | iɻ | i:ɻ |
| | | rounded | y | | | |
| | back | rounded | u | u: | uɻ | u:ɻ |
| mid | front | unrouned | e | e: | eɻ | e:ɻ |
| | back | rounded | o | o: | | |
| low | front | unrounded | a | a: | aɻ | a:ɻ |
| | back | rounded | a | a: | aɻ | a:ɻ |
| central | | | ə | | əɻ | ə:ɻ |

Notes:

① In the long vowels "i:" and "u:" the tongue is raised quite high, as in the utterance of the standard vowels [i] and [u]. In the short vowels "i" and "u" the tongue is lower, equivalent to the position in [I] and [v] respectively. But when they are used as initial yunmu, the tongue position is the same as that in [i] and [u]. When "u" is post-uvular and central apex, the lip aperture is approximately

于 [o]，在舌面前音后读作 [y]，在声母 h 后鼻化，读作 [ŭ]。

②a 相当于 [æ]，比 [ʌ] 略后。

③ə 比央元音 [ə] 略低略后。

④ 卷舌元音因受卷舌影响，其舌位都略向舌中靠近。iɹ 只在复元音 uiɹ 中出现；i:ɹ，aɹ，a:ɹ 只在构形中出现。

例如：

| a: | ba: | 布 | ə | pə | 买 |
| o | oqu | 一家 | e | tshe | 山羊 |
| a:ɹ | χa:ɹ | 肋骨 | aɹ | qhaɹ | 稀疏 |

（2）复元音韵母。复元音韵母以后响的为主，也较丰富。南部方言少数地区还出现前响的复元音。复元音分二合元音和三合元音。二合元音都是后响的，前面的介音为 i 或 u。三合元音 iau，uai 只出现在汉语借词中。例如：

| ie | pie | 猪 | ia | siaqa | 选 |
| ui | tuitue | 和睦 | iau | phiau | 票（汉） |

（3）带辅音尾韵母。共 189 个，除 27 个单辅音韵尾外，还有 17 个复辅音韵尾，因限于篇幅，只举几例如下：

| p | kep | 孤儿 | n | tsun | 跳蚤 |
| t | pet | 青铜 | d | sed | 镰刀 |

南北两种方言间的辅音韵尾差别很大，南部方言的辅音韵尾大多已消失，而北部方言有丰富的单辅音韵尾和复辅音韵尾。北部方言在音节里一般有 30 个以上的辅音可作辅音韵尾，构成的韵母达 250 个以上；南部方言则很少，一般只有 20 个左右。

like that in [o]; if it is put behind the front blade, it is pronounced as [y]; if it follows a shengmu "h", it will be nasalized as [Ǔ].

② The tongue position for "a" is like that of [æ] and is a little farther back than that of [ʌ].

③ The tongue position for "ə" is a little lower and further back than that of the central vowel [ə].

④ Under the influence of retroflexion, retroflexed vowels are produced close to the center of the tongue. "iɹ" only appears in the compound vowel "uiɹ", while " I:ɹ ,aɹ, and   a:ɹ" only occur when a word changes form.

Examples:

| a: | ba: | cloth | | ə | pə | buy |
|---|---|---|---|---|---|---|
| o | oqu | family | | e | tʂhe | goat |
| a:ɹ | χa:ɹ | rib | | aɹ | qhaɹ | sparseness |

(2) Compound-vowel Yunmu. A compound-vowel yunmu mainly takes a post-sonorant form except that in a few southern dialectal areas some compound vowels turn up in a pre-sonorant form. Compound vowels are divided into diphthongs and triphthongs. Diphthongs are all post-sonorant with the initial yunmu "i" or "u" in front. Triphthongs of "iau" and "uai" only appear in loanwords from Chinese.

Examples:

| ie | pie | pig | | ia | siaqa | choose |
|---|---|---|---|---|---|---|
| ui | tuitue | harmonious | | iau | phiau | ticket (Chinese) |

(3) Yunmu with Consonantal Coda (or "final consonant"). 27 simple-consonantal codas and 17 compound-consonantal codas make a total of 189 combinations with the various yunmu. Here are a few examples:

| p | kep | orphan | | n | tsun | flea |
|---|---|---|---|---|---|---|
| t | pet | bronze | | d | sed | sickle |

There are great differences in consonantal codas between the southern and northern dialect. Most consonantal codas in the southern dialect have disappeared, while in the northern dialect a great number of simple and compound consonantal codas still exist. More than 30 consonants in the northern dialect still serve as final consonants, which produces over 250 combinations with the various yunmu. Generally the southern dialect only has about 20 such consonants much fewer than the northern one.

### 3. 轻声

北部方言没有区别意义的声调，但大部分本语词有固定的音高，单音节词多读高平调，双音节词多半是前音节读中平调，后音节读高平调。汉语借词音高极不稳定，有的按本语词习惯调整读，有的按当地汉语声调读。

有部分词的非词首音节念轻声，轻声音节不仅音高低，音势弱，而且元音清化。由带有清化符号"。"的元音构成的音节即为轻声音节。

北部方言有丰富的语音变化现象，构形或者连读中常常发生辅音弱化、清化、换位，元音和谐、脱落、清化，音节脱落、合并等。

北部方言无声调，少数词用轻重音区别词义；南部方言则有声调，少的 2 个，多的 6 个，但是区别词义和语法意义的作用都不大。如曲谷话无声调，而雁门话有 3 个声调，它们的调值分别为 55，31，35。

### （二）语法特点

羌语多以虚词和词序为主要语法手段。由于方言土语众多，不能一一列举，这里试以较有代表性的北部方言土语为例，阐述羌语的基本语法特征。

### 1. 词的构成

（1）单纯词。以单音节的居多，如 mə（火），na（好）。两个音节的多半是动词，其中有相当一部分是叠音词和双声词，如 tuətuə（皱），məma（涂抹），tʂhutʂhuə（[鸡]斗），khu(e)khue（生气）。两个音节以上的单纯词很少。

（2）合成词。有以下两种构词方式：

### 3) Light Tones

The northern dialect does not have tones to distinguish word meanings. Nonetheless, almost every native word has a fixed pitch. Monosyllables are mostly high-toned. In a disyllable, the front syllable is usually mid-toned while the second is high-toned. The pitches of loanwords from Chinese are quite flexible. Some become adjusted to the pronunciation habits of the Qiang language while some follow local Chinese tones.

There are some words whose non-initial syllables are pronounced lightly. These syllables are marked by low pitch, weak intensity and devoiced vowels. Syllables including vowels with the devoiced mark " ₒ " are light syllables.

The northern dialect has a variety of phonetic changes. In word formation and liaison the following phenomena often appear: consonantal reduction, devoicing, metathesis, vowel harmony, elision, and syllabic elision and mergence.

The northern dialect has no tones although some words use light or stressed syllables to distinguish meanings. On the contrary, the southern dialect has at least two and at most six different tones but their function is rarely to differentiate lexical and grammatical meanings. For instance, the northern Qugu vernacular has no tones whereas the southern Yanmen vernacular has three, with tone pitches of 55, 31 and 35 respectively.

## 2. Grammatical Features

The main grammatical devices of the Qiang language are word function and word order. Since it is impossible to list every Qiang vernacular, the relatively representative northern dialect is taken as an example to show the basic grammatical characteristics of the Qiang language.

### 1) Word Formation

(1) Single-morpheme words (Monosemy). Most of these are monosyllabic, such as "mə" (fire) and "na" (good). Those which are disyllabic are usually verbs, of which a fair number are repeated sounds or two sounds with the same initial consonant such as "tuətuə" (to wrinkle), "məma" (to paint), "tʂhutʂhuə" (to fight (of chickens)) and "khu(e)khue" (to get angry). Single-morpheme words of more than two syllables are rare.

(2) Compound Words.

① 复合式。词根加词根的复合式以偏正式的居多。一种是前偏后正的，如 dzuaʁl（磨子）tɕi（房子）→dzuaʁl tɕi（磨房）。一种是前正后偏的，如 tɕui（鸡）pi（公）→tɕui pi（公鸡）。

② 附加式。附加成分有前缀、后缀两种。前缀有 a-（表亲属称谓名称的前缀），ha-（表"十一"至"十九"的数词的前缀）等。例如：

| | | | |
|---|---|---|---|
| apa | 祖父，外祖父 | akua | 舅父 |
| opu | 叔父 | ow | 祖母，外祖母 |
| hekheɹ | 十八 | hoŋ | 十五 |

前缀 a-、ha- 因元音与词根元音和谐，分别有 e-、o-、he-、ho- 等不同形式。

后缀有 -m（加在动词性词素后，表示动作的实施者），-s（加在动词性词素后，构成表示物件的名词）等。

| | | | | |
|---|---|---|---|---|
| -m | qhuɹ | 打猎 | qhuɹm | 猎人 |
| | təs pu | 做生意 | təs pum | 商人 |
| -s | dzə | 吃 | dzəs | 吃的 |

（3）借词。汉语借词很多，在记录的近 4 000 个词中，汉语借词约占 19%，如：χu（虎），gantsə（鞍子），sen tshan tui（生产队）。汉语单音节动词和形容词借入后要加后缀 -tha，如 khau tha（考），pentha（笨）；复合动词借入后要加词素 pu，如 ʁuakhu pu（挖苦）。

还有少量藏语借词，多半是宗教方面的，如 piuru（珊瑚）等。

**2. 词类**

（1）名词。名词后加 xsa 表示复数，加 tsi 表示小。方位词能被副词"最"修饰，且较丰富，如表示垂直空间上下与地势、河流上下等方位的方位词还分泛指、近指、中指、远指：

① Combination patterns. The compounding of two root words can be divided into two types, one being where the main meaning comes second, as in dzuaʁl (milling) təI (house) →dzuaʁl təI (milling house), and the other where the main meaning comes first as in tɕui (chicken) pi (male) →tɕui pi (rooster).

② Affixation. There are two kinds of affixes: the prefix and the suffix. For instance, "a-" (used to indicate the titles of relatives) and "ha-" (used to indicate the numerals from eleven to nineteen) are both prefixes.

| apa | grandfather | akua | uncle (mother's brother) |
| opu | uncle (father's brother) | ow | grandmother |
| hekheɹ | eighteen | hoŋ | fifteen |

To maintain vowel harmony between the prefixes "a-" and "ha-" and the root word vowels, these prefixes can also take on other forms, such as "e-", "o-", "he-" and "ho-".

The suffix "-m" is added after a verb morpheme to form a noun indicating the person performing the action and another suffix "-s" is put after a verb morpheme to form a noun referring to the correlative object.

| -m | qhuɹ | hunt | qhuɹm | hunter |
| | təs pu | doing business | təs pum | businessman |
| -s | dzə | eat | dzəs | food |

(3) Loanwords. There are many loanwords from Chinese, which account for approximately 19% of the nearly 4,000 recorded Qiang words. Typical examples are "χu" (tiger), "gantsə" (saddle), and "sen tshan tui" (production team). When monosyllabic verbs and adjectives are borrowed from Chinese, the suffix "-tha" is added, as in "khau tha" (test) and "pentha" (foolish), while for compound verbs from Chinese, the morpheme "pu" is added, as in "ʁuakhu pu" (satirize).

There are a few loanwords from Tibetan. Most of them are related to religion, such as "piuru" (coral).

**2) Parts of Speech**

(1) Noun form: "xsa" added after a noun makes the plural form; "tsi" added after a noun indicates "smallness". Nouns of locality can be modified by the adverb "zui" (most). The most frequent nouns of locality such as words indicating up and down, upriver and downriver can be classified into four categories: (A) generic, (B) short-distance, (C), middle-distance and (D) far-distance.

|  | 泛指 | 近指 | 中指 | 远指 |
|---|---|---|---|---|
| 上方 | məq | tsuməq | məχta | mə:χta |
| 下方 | qəl | tsuqəl | qəlla | qə:lla |
| 上游方 | niz | tsuniz | nizta | ni:zta |
| 下游方 | khsiz | tsukhisiz | khsizta | khsi:zta |

（2）人称代词。人称代词有第一、第二和第三人称，每个人称又分单数、双数和多数。第三人称代词来源于指示代词。除第一人称单数外，加强语气代词均用代词本身的重叠形式表示。

第一、第二人称单数和第三人称单双数还有反身代词，如 gui（我自己），kui（你自己），nili（他们自己）。

（3）数词。1 至 9 的基数词通常要与量词 wu（个）连用。表示 10 的数词有两个。

（4）量词。量词比较丰富，分名量词和动量词两类，一般需和数词或指示代词结合使用，词序是量词在数词后面。许多量词借名词或动词词根，如 quat（斗），tsua（抓）。量词与数词或指示代词结合较紧，与数词结合时，数词元音与量词元音和谐，如 o qhsu（一跳），ra（四根）。

（5）动词。动词有人称（第一、二、三人称）、数（复、单）、时（现在、未来、过去）、式（陈述、命令、祈求、禁止、否定）、体（将行、已行、曾行）、语气（一般、确定、不确定）、态（自动、使用）、趋向（空间上下、河流上下、向里向外、向此向彼）、及物与不及物等范畴，形容词作谓语时也有上述大部分范畴。

这些范畴用内部屈折与增加附加成分表示，以动词 azə（吃）为例。

命令式一般与第二人称过去时相同，有的变换前加成分，单数一般不加

|        | A      | B         | C        | D          |
|--------|--------|-----------|----------|------------|
| up     | məq    | tsuməp    | məχta    | mə:χta     |
| down   | qəl    | tsuqəl    | qəlla    | qə:lla     |
| upriver| niz    | tsuniz    | nizta    | ni:zta     |
| downriver | khsiz | tsukhisiz | khsizta | khisi:zta |

(2) Personal pronouns include first, second and third person pronouns, each of which is subdivided into singular, dual and plural. Third person pronouns originate from demonstrative pronouns. Reduplicated forms of such pronouns are employed to intensify mood for the second and third person singular and for the dual and plural form of the first, second, and third person.

The singular form of the first and second person, and the singular and dual form of the third person all have corresponding reflexive pronouns, such as "gui" (myself), "kui" (yourself) and "nili" (themselves).

(3) The cardinal numbers from one to nine are usually used together with the quantifier "wu" (equal to "ge" in Chinese); there are two other numerals that can express the concept of ten.

(4) There are many measure words. These are categorized into verbal quantifiers and nominal quantifiers, both of which must generally be used in combination with numerals and demonstrative pronouns. Quantifiers must be placed after numerals. Many quantifiers make use of nominal and verbal roots, such as "quat" (a kind of measuring implement) and "tsua" (a handful of). When quantifiers are used together with numerals, their vowels are harmonized, as in "o qhsu" (a jump) and "ra" (four pieces).

(5) Verbs have many different categories, such as person (first, second, third), number (singular, plural), tense (past, present, future), mode (declarative, imperative, invocative, prohibitive, negative), aspect (past perfective, present perfective, future perfective), mood (general, definite, indefinite), voice (active, passive), direction (up and down, upriver and downriver, inwards and outwards, here and there), transitive and intransitive etc. When adjectives function as the predicate, they also have most of the categories above mentioned.

All these categories are expressed by means of internal inflection and affixes. The verb "dzə" (to eat) is given below as an example:

Generally, the imperative is the same as the past form used with the second person pronoun. Some change their prefixes but it is unusual for singular forms

前加成分 n。如 az（[你]吃），aztɕin（[你们]吃）。

祈求式分两种：一种是说话者要求对方让第三者做某动作，表现形式是使第二人称命令式前加成分的声母颚化（如为零声母则加 j），如 jaz（[你]让[他]吃），jaztɕæ（[你]让[他们]吃）；一种是说话者要求对方让自己或自己这一方做某动作，表现形式是在命令式形式后加上后加成分 la（说话者一方为单数）或 liə:ɭ（说话者一方为复数），如 azla（[你]让[我]吃），azliəɭ（[你]让[我们]吃）。

禁止式是在动词现在时形式前增加前加成分 tɕa，如 tɕazən（[你]别吃），tɕaztɕin（[你们]别吃）。tɕa 的元音应与动词词根的元音和谐，如 ta（戴）—tɕa（别戴）。

否定式是在动词词根前加 ma。ma 加在动词未来时形式前表未来否定式，加在动词过去时形式的前加成分后表过去时否定式，如 maza（[我]没吃）。ma 的元音应与动词词根元音和谐，如 za（舀）—maza（不舀）—təmaza（没舀）。

以下是动词各种语气的表现形式：

确定语气是指动词所表示的动作行为为说话者所确定或亲见，所加成分按所强调的主语或宾语的人称或主语和宾语所表事物的领有者的人称分几种：强调第一人称时加后加成分 k，强调第二人称时加后加成分 sa，强调第三人称时加后加成分 w。例如：

　　　səzək（那头牛）吃了（我的菜）

　　　səzsan（那头牛）吃了（你的菜）

　　　səzew（那头牛）吃了（他的菜）

不确定语气是指动词所表示的动作行为为说话者所听说，不能肯定，所加成分可以按所强调的主语或宾语的人称或主语和宾语所表事物的领有者的人称分为以下几种：强调第一人称时

to add "n" as a prefix. For instance, in "az" (You [sing.] eat ) and in, "aztɕin" (You (pl.) eat).

The invocative form is divided into two types: the first form indicates that the speaker requires the listener to make the third person do something. This form palatalizes the initial consonant in the prefix of the second person imperative (in the case of a zero initial consonant, "j" is added), as in "jaz" (You ask him to eat), and "jaztɕe" (You ask them to eat). The second form indicates that the speaker requires the listener to make the speaker himself or people on the speaker's side do something. This form adds the suffix "la" (when one speaker is present) or "liə:ʎ" (when more than one speaker is present). For instance, "azla" (You ask me to eat) and "azliə:ʎ" (You ask us to eat).

The prohibitive is constructed by adding the prefix "tɕa" before verbs of present tense, such as "tɕazən" (You [sing.] don't eat.), and "tɕaztɕin" (You [pl.] don't eat). The vowel in "tɕa" should be harmonized with the vowel of the verbal root, such as "ta—tɕa" (wear—don't wear).

The negative is constructed by adding "ma" before the verbal root. If "ma" is added before verbs in the future tense, the negative future form is produced; if "ma" is placed after the prefix of the past form of verbs, then the negative past form is produced. The vowel in "ma" should be harmonized with the vowel of the verbal root, such as "za" (ladle) —"maza" (will not ladle)—"təmaza" (didn't ladle).

Below are the forms used to express various kinds of verbal moods.

The definite mood implies that the behavior expressed by the verb is confirmed or witnessed by the speaker. There are several kinds of affixes which agree with the person connected with the stressed subject or object, or the person of the owner of the subject or object. When the first person is stressed, the suffix "k" is added; when the second person is stressed, the suffix "sa" is added; when the third person is stressed, the suffix "w" is added. For example:

səzək (that cow surely) ate (my vegetables)

səzsan (that cow surely ) ate (your vegetables)

səzəw (that cow surely) ate (his vegetables)

The indefinite mood suggests that the speaker has only heard about what has been done and is not sure whether it's true or not. There are also several affixes which agree with the person of the stressed subject or object, or the person of the owner of the subject or object. When the first person is stressed,

加后加成分 wa，强调第二人称时加后加成分 wan，强调第三人称时加后加成分 wi。例如：

səzwa （那头牛）吃了（我的菜）

səzwan （那头牛）吃了（你的菜）

səzwi （那头牛）吃了（他的菜）

（6）形容词。形容词和动词的语法特征比较接近，相当多的常用形容词词根采用叠音形式，形容词的比较级形式是在形容词后加附加成分 s。

（7）副词。否定副词能插在前加成分和动词或形容词之间。副词在句子中还起关联作用。成对的副词在句子中互相呼应，形成一些特殊的句子格式。

（8）助词。助词比较丰富，有结构助词和语气助词两类。其中结构助词又分为限制助词、施动助词、受动助词、工具助词、比较助词、处所助词、从由助词等。结构助词用于名词、代词或名词性词组后，表示词与词、句子成分与句子成分之间的关系。有 gu（表施事或工具），ta（表处所），ʁa（表时间），jgu（表从由）等。例如：

qa　　χe　gu　Φa　　ja

我　　针（助词）　衣　缝　　　我用针缝衣服。

the:　ej　ʁa　　do Φu

他　一　夜（助词）跑 了　　　他在一个晚上跑了。

（9）连词。复句中有时使用部分汉语借词作连词。并列复句中一般不用连词连接主句和分句。

**3. 语序**

句子成分的基本次序是：主语—宾语—谓语。名词、代词作定语在中心语前面；形容词、数量词组作定语在中心语后；指示代词和量词或助词结合作定语，在中心语前后均可。修饰关系的语序一般是：名词（或人称代词）—被修饰语—形容词—数词（或指示代词）—量词。

qa　　stuaχa　dza:

我　　饭　　　吃　　　我要吃饭。

the suffix "wa" is added; when the second person is stressed, the suffix "wan" is added; when the third person is stressed, the suffix "wi" is added. For example:

səzwa    (that cow probably) ate (my vegetables)

səzwan   (that cow probably) ate (your vegetables)

səzwi    (that cow probably) ate (his vegetables)

(6) The grammatical features of adjectives are similar to those of verbs. A considerable number of common adjective roots use the form of repetition. The comparative degree of the adjective is expressed by adding a final "s".

(7) Negative adverbs can be inserted between the prefix and the verb or adjective. Adverbs also contribute to sentence cohesion. In addition, paired adverbs work together to form some particular sentence patterns.

(8) There are many auxiliary words and they can be divided into structural auxiliary and modal auxiliary. Types of structural auxiliary include finite auxiliary, agentive auxiliary, affected auxiliary, instrumental auxiliary, comparative auxiliary, locative auxiliary and causal auxiliary. When a structural auxiliary comes after a noun, pronoun or noun phrase, it indicates the relationship between words or between sentence components.

For example, "gu" (agentive or instrumental auxiliary), "ta" (locative auxiliary), "ʁa" (indicating time), "jgu" (causal auxiliary).

| qa | χe | gu | Φa | ja | |
|----|----|----|----|----|---|
| I | needle | (auxiliary) | clothes | sew | (I sew clothes with a needle.) |
| the: | ej | ʁa | | doΦu | |
| he | one | evening (auxiliary) | | escape | (One evening he escaped.) |

### 3) Word Order

The basic word order is: subject—object—predicate. Attributive nouns and pronouns come before the main part of the sentence whereas attributive adjectives and quantitative phrases are placed after the main part. When the demonstrative pronoun is combined with a quantifier or auxiliary word as an attributive, it can come either before or after the main part. Generally, the order of modifiers is: noun (or personal pronoun)—modified word—adjective—numeral (or demonstrative pronoun)—quantifier.

Examples:

| (1) qa | stuaχa | dza: | |
|--------|--------|------|---|
| I | dinner | eat | (I want to have dinner.) |

the:gu    qa    ma:    Φa    phʂiʂ    the:    khsepe haɹmaɹni
kantse  aχlu

他（助词）  我   妈妈   衣服  白   那    三件   悄悄地
干净      洗了

他把我妈妈的那三件衣服悄悄地洗干净了。

### 三、羌语的使用情况与使用场合①

羌语除阿坝藏族羌族自治州内的羌族使用外，还有绵阳地区的北川县和甘孜州的丹巴县的羌族使用，在四川全省有 16 万多人。此外，还有四万多的藏族居民（主要是黑水县藏族居民）不使用藏语而用羌语。羌语的具体使用情况是这样的：

（1）主要使用羌语的羌族地区有茂县、松潘县、汶川县及理县的山区。这里有大片的羌族聚居村寨，羌族居民一般都能比较熟练地使用羌语。

（2）羌、汉语交替使用，以使用汉语为主的地区有茂县、汶川县、松潘县和理县的公路沿线或城镇附近的聚居村寨。在这些地区，羌族居民在家庭或村寨中使用羌语，其中 40 岁以上的中年人和老年人运用羌语一般比较熟练；40 岁以下的青壮年和儿童中，不常出门的运用羌语比较熟练，常出门的就感到陌生，当中有些人只会听，不会说。但该地区的全体羌族人都能流利地使用汉语。

（3）黑水县境内自称"尔玛"的藏族居民都使用羌语，羌语是其唯一的交际工具。上个世纪 50 年代中期调查时黑水居民懂汉语的很少，到 80 年代才多起来。根据调查，黑水县使用羌语的藏族人中，只有少数人

---

① 羌语的使用情况与使用场合及羌族文字部分主要引用了徐平、徐丹著的《东方大族之谜》一书，知识出版社 2001 年版，第 96～98 页。

(2) the:gu qa ma: Φa phṣiṣ the: khsepe haɹmaɹni kantse aχlu

He (auxiliary) my mother clothes white those three silently clean wash

(He silently washed clean those three white garments of my mother's.)

In a sentence of two or more clauses, it is unnecessary to connect the main clause with the subordinate clause. Nevertheless, loanwords from Chinese are sometimes used as conjunctives in complex sentences.

## III. The Current Situation Regarding Spoken Qiang①

In addition to being spoken in the Aba Tibetan and Qiang Autonomous Prefecture, the Qiang language is also spoken by Qiang people living in the Mianyang area of Beichuan County and in Danba County in Ganzi Tibetan Autonomous Prefecture. There are altogether about 160,000 people speakers of the Qiang language throughout Sichuan Province. There are also more than 40,000 Tibetans (mainly in Heishui County) who speak Qiang instead of Tibetan. Specific details regarding the Qiang language use are as follows:

(1) The main regions where the Qiang is spoken include the counties of Mao, Songpan and Wenchuan and the mountainous areas of Li County. Qiang people inhabiting the villages of these regions are generally proficient in Qiang.

(2) In some areas, Qiang and Chinese are used interchangeably. In Mao, Wenchuan and Songpan counties and in villages near the main road through Li County, Chinese is more often spoken. In these areas, the people use Qiang in their villages or families. People aged forty or older are proficient in Qiang whereas among people under forty, those who spend more time in the villages can usually speak the Qiang language much more fluently than those who spend time away from the village. Some of the latter can understand but not speak Qiang. All the Qiang people in these areas can speak Chinese fluently.

(3) The Tibetans who call themselves "Erma" in Heishui County speak the Qiang language. A survey done in this area in the mid-1950s shows that few people at that time understood Chinese. The number has increased greatly since the 1980s. However, the Qiang language has continued to be their only means of communication. Investigations also show that only a few of those

---

① Relevant introductions, including the written language of the Qiang, are based on the book The *Mystery of the Great Eastern Nation* by Xu Ping and Xu Dan, p96-98.

因宗教活动或经商等原因学会了一点藏语。

（4）北川县和平武县的绝大部分羌族居民、丹巴县的大部分羌族居民、松潘县白羊乡的羌族居民、汶川和理县的城镇及公路两侧散居村寨里的羌族居民已不会使用羌语，而改用汉语。

羌语的使用场合是这样的：

（1）羌语在家庭中的使用：凡使用羌语的羌族居民或藏族居民，在家庭日常生活中均使用羌语交际。在茂、理、汶三县，羌族家庭中若有不懂羌语的客人在场时，一般不用羌语而使用汉语；松潘县的镇平、镇江、小姓等乡镇以及黑水地区，则不管有没有不懂羌语的客人在场，都使用羌语交流。操北部方言的藏族与羌族居民之间常互相通婚，他们使用羌语。

（2）羌语在集贸中的使用：松潘县、茂县、汶川县、理县的大片羌族聚居区，在本村寨或邻近村寨之间使用羌语，农村集市上也常使用羌语，但有其他民族的人在场时使用汉语。黑水县内无论村寨或乡镇的集市上，人们往往都使用羌语。

（3）羌语在公共场合的使用：茂县、松潘、汶川、理县等地的大片羌族聚居区，在乡镇以下的行政机关集会时，有些使用羌语；若有其他民族的人在场，则用汉语。黑水县境内不仅在大多数乡镇机关使用羌语，而且在县级机关的许多会议上也使用羌语；如有其他民族的人在场，一般配以口头翻译。企事业单位如医院、邮电所、贸易商店、车站等，通常使用汉语，但在彼此熟识的羌语使用者之间，普遍使用羌语。

（4）羌语在教育中的使用：上个世纪 80 年代以前，羌族没有与本民族语言相适应的文字，中、小学都用汉语教学。茂县赤不苏、沙坝等少数地区的部分小学，曾使用羌语辅助教学，即汉语老师先学习羌语，然后在教学中用羌语解释汉语课本中学生不易理解的难点，收到了较好的效果。目前，四川阿坝师范专科学校和四川威州民族师范学校等学校有专门从事教学和研究羌语的系科和机构。

Qiang-speaking Tibetans in Heishui County have learned a little Tibetan for religious or business reasons.

(4) In the counties of Beichuan, Pingwu, Danba, and in Songpan County's Baiyang Village and the villages near the main route through Wenchuan and Li counties, most Qiang people cannot speak Qiang. Chinese has become the language of daily use.

Situations where the Qiang language is used:

(1) In the family. People who can speak the Qiang language, whether Qiang or Tibetans, use Qiang in daily communication. In the counties of Mao, Li and Wenchuan, Qiang people speak Chinese if guests are present who don't understand the Qiang language. In Heishui County and some villages of Songpan County like Zhenping, Zhenjiang and Xiaoxing, Qiang people speak their own language whether guests understand it or not. Tibetan and Qiang speakers of the northern Qiang dialect often intermarry.

(2) In the market. Qiang people in Songpan, Mao, Wenchuan and Li counties speak the Qiang language in their own villages, neighboring villages and even markets but Chinese is used if people of other nationalities are present. Meanwhile in Heishui County, the Qiang language is used everywhere at any time.

(3) In public. In the Qiang inhabited areas of Mao, Songpan, Wenchuan and Li counties, Qiang is sometimes used at village administrative conferences. If people of other ethnic groups are present, Chinese will be used instead. However, in Heishui County, the Qiang language is used not only at village administrative conferences but also at some county-level administrative conferences. If people of other ethnic groups are present, interpreters are used. In hospitals, post and telecommunication offices, shops, and stations, people always use Chinese. However, among Qiang-speaking acquaintances Qiang is the standard form of communication.

(4) In education. Until the 1980s, the Qiang did not have their own written language, so Chinese was taught in elementary and middle schools. But some elementary schools in Chibusu and Shaba in Mao County have, in the past, successfully used a Qiang-assisted teaching method whereby Chinese teachers learn the Qiang language first and then use it to explain difficulties in Chinese texts. At present, Aba Normal Technological Academy and Weizhou Normal School for Nationalities in Sichuan Province have set up departments and organizations specially engaged in the teaching and research of the Qiang language.

茂县、汶川、理县、松潘的 100 多所小学和部分中学进行了羌汉双语教学，有专兼职羌文教师 320 多名。

（5）羌语在羌族宗教活动中的使用：羌族信奉原始宗教，宗教活动均由"释比"或"许"（ʂpi 或 ɵy，汉语称"端公"）主持。无论祭山、还愿、看病、驱鬼还是婚丧嫁娶等都要请"释比"。"释比"是最完整、最忠实的羌语使用者，他们保留了羌族古老的唱诗和传说，是羌族民间文化的传承人。因此可以说，在羌族地区的民族宗教活动中，全部使用羌语。

（6）羌语在文化活动中的使用：羌族地区各县歌舞团或文艺工作队公开演出时，有用羌语表演和报幕的。其中茂县歌舞团每年演出 50 场左右，羌语节目约占三分之一，题材大多反映羌族历史故事或现实生产生活的有关内容。另外，聚居区的乡镇广播站，也多用羌语广播当地的时事、通知、音乐节目等。

（7）羌语在法律行为中的使用：羌族地区的人民法院在聚居区进行民事或刑事调查时，多使用羌语进行询问或审讯。有的地区法院审理案件时，常常为不懂汉语的羌族当事人配备汉语翻译员。召开公审大会时，则使用汉语和羌语两种语言进行宣判。

## 四、羌族文字

20 世纪 80 年代以前，羌族一直没有与本民族语言相适应的文字。羌族聚居区的政府机关、学校教育等各方面都使用汉语。中华人民共和国成立以后，不少的羌族干部和群众都提出过创制羌族文字的要求。从 20 世纪 50 年代起，党和政府就对羌族语言的调查研究十分重视。中国社会科学院派出过民族语言调查第七工作队，阿坝州成立过民族语言文字研究室，对羌语进行过比较深入的调查研究。阿坝州民族语言文字研究室也做过

Over 100 elementary schools and some middle schools in Mao, Wenchuan, Li and Songpan counties have adopted the bilingual teaching of both Chinese and Qiang. Full-time and part-time teachers of the Qiang language amount to 320.

(5) In religious activities. The Qiang believe in primitive religion. All religious activities are presided over by the "Shibi" (ʂpi or ɵy, in Chinese "Duan Gong", i.e., Qiang priest), and these include mountain worshipping, fulfilling vows to the gods, curing diseases, dispelling ghosts, and performing weddings and funerals. Qiang priests have remained the most faithful speakers the Qiang language. They have preserved ancient Qiang songs, poems and legends and are the real inheritors and conveyors of Qiang folk culture. The Qiang language is used in all religious activities in the Qiang areas.

(6) In cultural activities. When the performing arts groups or literature and art groups of each county in the Qiang area put on a performance or display, Qiang is used in the performance and for the accompanying announcements. For example, Mao County's performing arts group gives about 50 shows every year and one third of the programs are performed in the Qiang language. These programs usually include stories about the history of the Qiang and about their daily lives. In addition, village broadcasting stations prefer to use the Qiang language to broadcast current affairs, announcements and musical programs.

(7) In legal cases. The People's Court in the Qiang area often uses the Qiang language during inquiries and trials in civil or criminal investigations. During lawsuits some local courts provide interpreters for Qiang litigants who don't understand Chinese, and the final judgment is pronounced in both Chinese and Qiang in public trials.

## IV. The Written Language of the Qiang

Prior to the 1980s the Qiang did not have a written form of language and Chinese characters were used in Qiang areas by government bodies, schools, etc. After the People's Republic of China was founded, many Qiang public officials and locals proposed the creation of a written language system for the Qiang. From the 1950s, the Communist Party and Chinese government have attached great importance to Qiang language research. At that time, the Chinese Academy of Social Sciences sent the No. 7 National Language Research Work Team to conduct in-depth research of the Qiang language. The National Languages Research Institute was also established in Aba Prefecture, trying to

为羌语创制拼音文字的尝试（以北部方言为基础，以麻窝话为基本音点）。后来由于种种原因，停止了这一工作。党的十一届三中全会以后，随着我国经济建设及改革开放的深入发展，羌族的多数群众和干部再次提出创制羌族文字的要求。根据党的民族政策，从羌族人民的实际愿望出发，四川省民族事务委员会（简称"省民委"）于 1984 年派出调查组，就羌语的分布、使用情况和羌族是否需要创制文字等问题进行了实地调查。1989 年 7 月，经省委省政府批准，省民委组建了"羌族拼音文字创制领导小组"，来统筹这一工作。经过 2 年的调查研究，以及培养羌族语言工作者，创制方案，进行教学试点等工作，完成了《羌族拼音文字方案》的创制。1991 年 10 月，省委省政府批准了这个方案，并按程序报国家民族事务委员会（简称"国家民委"）。国家民委于 1993 年 3 月对方案进行了专家鉴定，批准同意在羌族地区试行。经过十余年的试行，取得了明显成就。

有的学者认为，古羌人与华夏人共同创造了中华文化，现今的汉字也算是古羌人的文字。也有的学者认为西夏是羌人建立的国家，西夏有文字，也可算是羌族的文字。但是，根据"文字是语言的符号，是用来表述语言的"这一基本定义，汉文和西夏文均不能作为羌族的文字。因为从历史记载的事实来看，当代的羌族人只是古羌人众多支系中的一支，与历史上同华夏族融合的古羌人，以及建立西夏国的古羌人在文化的传承渊源上是有所不同的。两者不能混为一体。

新创制的羌族文字，选择了拉丁字母拼音形式，因为拼音文字比较科学、准确，易于印刷、书写，好学易懂，便于普及。经过周密的调查研究

set up an alphabetic writing system for the Qiang (based on the northern dialect of the Qiang and taking Mawo vernacular as the standard). Later, this project was stopped for various reasons.

With the further development of China's economy and continuing reform and opening-up after the Third Plenary Session of the 11th Central Committee of the Communist Party of China, Qiang people once again expressed a longing for their own written language. In accordance with policies on ethnic affairs set by the Party, and in consideration of the needs of the Qiang people, the Ethnic Affairs Commission of Sichuan Province sent out an investigation group in 1984 to examine the distribution and employment of the Qiang language and to find out if a written language system was really needed by the Qiang.

In July 1989, authorized by the provincial government, a working group for the creation of a Qiang alphabetic script was set up. In the next 2 years, the group carried out further surveys, trained Qiang language workers, put forward the first draft and conducted pilot teaching projects. Finally, the tentative design of the Qiang alphabetic writing scheme was finished. In October 1991, it was submitted to the State Ethnic Affairs Commission after being approved by the Sichuan provincial government. In March 1993, having been examined and approved by relevant experts, the State Ethnic Affairs Commission decided to test the writing system in the Qiang areas. Now, the system has been successfully in use for over 10 years.

Some scholars think that the ancient Qiang people and the Huaxia people jointly created Chinese culture, so the present Chinese characters could be regarded as characters of the ancient Qiang people. Other scholars think that the Xi Xia Dynasty was founded by the Qiang, so the characters of the Xi Xia Dynasty could also be regarded as Qiang characters. However, according to the basic definition that "characters are the symbol and carrier of language", neither Chinese nor Xi Xia characters should be seen as Qiang characters. Historical records tell us that the present Qiang people are only one of the many branches of the ancient Qiang. As far as their cultural origin is concerned, they are different not only from the ancient Qiang people who merged with Huaxia people but also from those who founded the Xi Xia Dynasty.

The newly created Qiang writing system uses a phonetic Latin alphabet form. The phonetic alphabet has been adopted because it is easy to print, write, learn, understand and popularize. In January 1990, after thorough research and

和对有代表性的音点反复讨论以后，1990 年元月，羌族的广大干部、知识分子和各地区、各方面的代表人士齐聚一堂，一致同意选北部方言的曲谷话，即曲谷土语作为设计拼音文字的基础土语。因为曲谷土语说的人多，使用人口比较集中，通行面比较广，而且羌语的语音保留得比较完整，语音的辐射面比较宽，能兼顾羌语的南部方言区和北部方言区。在选择曲谷话作为标准音点的同时，羌文创制者还学习和借鉴了国内其他少数民族创制拼音文字的经验和教训，从而少走了弯路，较快地完成了创制工作。

《羌族拼音文字方案》(初稿)包括 8 个条目和 4 个附录。该方案根据国际上公认的语音原则，系统地阐述了文字所表示的语音内容，即字母按照实际读音书写，词怎么念就怎么写。考虑到羌语是形态变化较为丰富的语言，在文字的处理上也适当照顾到形态变化。在少数情况下虽然实际读音发生了变化，但是拼写仍旧不变。

羌族拼音文字的创制及推广，必然对羌族地区政治、经济、文化的繁荣起到极大的推动作用，对于羌族文化的挖掘整理同样有很大的帮助。

（耿亚军　徐希平）

extensive discussion, Qiang cadres, intellectuals and representatives from different areas gathered together and unanimously agreed to take the Qugu vernacular of the northern dialect as the basis of the writing system. This is because the Qugu vernacular is spoken by a comparatively large number of Qiang people and can be widely understood. It also preserves the typical sounds of the Qiang language and can best represent both the northern and southern dialects. Taking the Qugu vernacular as the standard, the working group members have also drawn lessons from the creation of writing systems for other minority groups in China.

*The Alphabetic Writing System for the Qiang (First Draft)* includes 8 sections and 4 appendixes. In conformity with internationally recognized phonetic principles, the draft systematically sets forth the phonetic content expressed by the written letters, i.e., the letters are written in accordance with the actual pronunciation; how the word is read determines how it is written. The writing system also takes into consideration the many morphological changes in the Qiang language: the spelling remains consistent in spite of some phonetic changes.

The creation and popularization of the Qiang alphabetic writing system will undoubtedly play a positive role in the political, economic and cultural prosperity of  the various Qiang areas. It will also help in the further exploration of the Qiang culture.

( Translated by Jiang Jing, Chen Shuyu )

# 第四章　羌族文学

在长期的历史发展中，羌族人民创造了绚丽多彩的文学，主要表现在民间文学和书面文学两个方面。它们不仅是羌族文化中的一块瑰宝，也是中国各民族共同的精神财富。

## 一、民间文学

羌族民间文学作为世代传承的口头创作，是羌族文学中最基础和最重要的部分，在羌族民间有着广阔肥沃的社会土壤和深厚的群众基础。羌族民间文学内容丰富，题材广泛，体裁多样，基本上可以分为神话、传说、故事、歌谣（包括史诗）、寓言和童话，许多作品有着较高的思想性和艺术性。

羌族民间文学除神话、传说之外，绝大部分作品都是对生活的直接反映，这些作品具有朴素的历史真实性。大多数作品的思想都是对先民们伟大功绩的肯定和赞颂。另外，作品还注重直接陈述事理。凡所叙述，都是劳动人民的乡土话，朴素自然，生动活泼，具有浓厚的生活气息。

### （一）神话

羌族神话是羌族早期的民间文学，按其内容可分为八类，即开天辟地神话，人类起源神话，自然及其变化神话，动、植物神话，图腾、祖先神话，洪水、干旱和大火神话，文化起源神话，神性英雄神话等。这些神话的共同特征是：① 具有鲜明的地域特色；② 与现今残存的原始心理、宗教信仰保持着不同程度的联系；③ 以反映原始先民与自然斗争的神话为主体；④ 以幻想的折光形象地反映现实并进行审美评价。

# CHAPTER FOUR   THE LITERATURE OF THE QIANG

Over their long history, the Qiang people have created a wealth of folk and written literature. This literature is a treasure trove not just for the Qiang people but for all of China's ethnic groups.

## I. Folk Literature

Folk literature, passed on orally from generation to generation, plays the most fundamental and significant role in the literature of the Qiang and is deeply rooted in the social background into which they were born. The folk literature of the Qiang possesses rich content, covers wide-ranging subjects and comes in various genres. These can be classified into myths, legends, stories, folk songs (including epics), fables and fairy tales. Many of the works display a high level of ideology and artistry.

Apart from the myths and legends, most of the works in Qiang folk literature directly reflect the realities of life. They are of great value in terms of historical authenticity, with most of them extolling their ancestors' great achievements. Narrated in the simple, natural language of common laborers, these works are also characterized by a rational clarity, with factual explanations and vivid descriptions of everyday life.

### 1. Myths

Myths are one of the earliest forms of Qiang folk literature. They can be divided according to content into eight categories: the creation of the world; the origin of mankind; nature and its transformation; animals and plants; totems and ancestors; floods, droughts and fire; the origin of culture; and god-like heroes. The myths generally ① have distinct regional features; ② are connected to varying degrees with primeval thinking and religious beliefs; ③ mainly depict the struggles of the ancient people against nature; and ④ reflect reality and extol beauty through a prism of fantasy.

　　羌族开天辟地类神话较多，其中以《开天辟地》《狗是大地的母舅》《盘古出世开天地》等较为著名。这些神话，是羌民对自然崇拜的产物，是对自然神秘力量的幻象。

　　关于人类起源的神话则从不同角度叙述了人类的起源。如《羊角花的来历》《猴人变人》《人是咋个来的》等。

　　《羊角花的来历》讲述，在远古的时候，宇宙一团昏黑，没有天地和万物。天神阿爸木比塔叫神公木巴西造天，神母如补西造地，又造了日月星辰和万物。大地造好以后，需要人来掌管，木比塔就用羊角花（即杜鹃树）的树干，照着自己的模样，用刀削成了九对小木人，并把他们放在一个地坑里，用石板盖上。第一个戊日揭开石板看时，小木人会眨眼睛了；第二个戊日揭开石板看时，小木人会摇头甩手了；到了第三个戊日，阿爸木比塔刚刚把石板揭开，小木人便一溜烟地跑了出来，见风便长，一下子就变成了大人。从此，世上有了人类。

　　羌族神话还对自然及其变化的原因进行了朴素的解释，如《山沟和平坝的来历》和《白公鸡的故事》说是因为烧了癞蛤蟆皮、白公鸡皮而引起了地表的变化。如《太阳》《月亮》说，太阳是个女人，月亮是个男人。羌族关于自然及其变化的神话大多是以妇女为主角，这无疑是羌族母系社会延续时间较长的一种反映，更是对女性劳动的颂歌。

　　植物神话，侧重于讲述粮食种子的来源。如《粮食的来历和丢失》《五谷的来历》就是较有代表性的作品。据《粮食的来历和丢失》描述，是羌族先民丹巴协惹从天庭盗回了粮食种子，从此人间才有了粮食和蔬菜。

Many Qiang myths concern the creation of world, such as the well-known works of *The Creation of Heaven and Earth, Dog—the Maternal Uncle of Earth, The Birth of Pan Gu and his Creation of Heaven and Earth*. These myths, imagined fantasies about the mysterious power of nature, are the product of the Qiang people's activities in the worship of nature.

The myths regarding the origin of mankind describe the origin of human beings from different aspects, such as *The Origin of the Ram's Horn Flower, From Ape Man to Human*, and *How Men Came into Being*.

According to *The Origin of the Ram's Horn Flower*, the universe was nothing but darkness in remote antiquity. Father Mubita, the god of heaven, commanded the god Mubaxi to create the sky and the goddess Rubuxi to build the land. Later, the sun, the moon, the stars and all things on earth were created. To govern these creations, Mubita made nine pairs of little wooden people, carved in his own image from the trunk of ram's horn tree (the azalea tree). Then he put the carved people into a hole in the ground and covered them with a flagstone. On the first Wu day (Wu means the fifth of the ten Heavenly Stems which are used in combination with the twelve Earthly Branches to designate years, months, days and hours in traditional Chinese astronomy), when the flagstone was lifted, the little people were able to blink their eyes. On the second Wu day, the couples began to shake their heads and swing their arms. On the third Wu day, Father Mubita was just removing the flagstone when the wooden people darted out, and the moment they saw the wind they immediately grew into full-sized human beings. From then on, there were humans in the world.

The myths of the Qiang also present simple explanations about nature and the reasons behind its transformation. Two related works, *The Origin of Valleys and Plains* and *The Tale of the White Rooster* state that changes to the earth's surface were caused by the burning either of a toad-skin or of the skin of a white rooster. In the myths *The Sun* and *The Moon*, the sun is portrayed as a woman and the moon as a man. Most of these myths about nature and its changes have women in the leading roles, which reflects the relatively long duration of Qiang matriarchal society and also extols the hard work of Qiang females.

Myths about plants lay particular emphasis on the origin of grain seed, as seen in representative works such as *The Origin and Loss of Grain* and *The Origin of the Five Food Crops*. According to the tale of *The Origin and Loss of Grain*, grain originated from the grain seeds that were stolen from heaven by an ancestor called Danbaxiere. Thenceforth, grains and vegetables began to grow

植物神话证明了羌民自我意识的成长和羌族历史的发展。

在图腾、祖先神话和神性英雄神话中，《角角神的故事》《霞芝姑娘盗水》具有一定的代表性。这两个神话分别讲述了角角神的来历与作用，以及人间没有水，霞芝姑娘就把天水放到了人间等故事情节。

羌地还流传着主题相似，但各具特色的洪水、干旱和大火神话。这些神话叙述了天灾灭绝人类，幸免的兄妹二人配婚，再度繁衍人类的故事。洪水神话最有代表性的是《洪水滔天》，干旱、大火神话有《兄妹射日治人烟》《大火以后的人类》等。

文化起源神话，表现了羌民的探索精神和美好的幻想。代表作有《燃比娃盗火》《阿巴补摩》等。《燃比娃盗火》讲述了人间没有火，燃比娃从天上盗来了火种的故事；《阿巴补摩》则说人们病后没有医药，备受疾病的折磨，阿巴补摩便采集常见的草、虫为人治病。

羌族神话，反映了羌民征服大自然的无畏精神和坚强意志，歌颂了原始先民们艰苦创业这一伟大的主题。

### （二）史诗与叙事长诗

羌族历史悠久，在其发展过程中，产生了许多有关本民族的历史与文化的史诗和神话叙事长诗。羌族史诗与叙事长诗是羌族先民们集体意愿的表现和智慧的结晶，对羌族后世文学从内容到艺术都产生了深远的影响。

史诗《羌戈大战》，神话叙事长诗《木姐珠与斗安珠》《人神分居的起源》是影响最大的作品，也是羌族民间文学的代表作品。

《羌戈大战》（异文《嘎尔都》《羌人与戈基人斗争的故事》属同一主题）叙述了羌族先民迁到岷江上游后与早已在此定居的戈基人战争的故事。

on earth. These myths reveal the Qiang's growing sense of self-awareness and their historical development.

Among the myths about totems, ancestors and god-like heroes, *The Tale of the Jiaojiao God*, and *Lady Xiazhi Steals the Water* are most representative. The former describes the origin of the *Jiaojiao God* and his duties and the latter talks about Lady Xiazhi diverting water from heaven to the earth when there was no water in the world.

Sharing similar general ideas while keeping their own distinctive features, the myths relating to floods, droughts and fires have spread extensively among the Qiang areas. These stories tell of the extinction of men after natural catastrophes and how a surviving brother and sister then married to start a new circle of life. The myths about floods, droughts and fires are separately pictured in *Great Water Flooding the Sky*, *Brother and Sister Shoot the Sun and Restore Life to Earth*, and *Human Beings after the Fire*.

The spirit of discovery and the wonderful imagination of the Qiang people are conveyed in the myths about cultural origin, which are represented in *Boy Ranbi Steals the Fire* and *Ababumo*. The first of these talks about a boy named Ranbi who stole tinder from heaven to bring fire to people on earth, and the second concerns Ababumo's collecting of herbs and insects to heal people when they suffered from diseases and did not have any medication.

The myths of the Qiang are all on a grand theme and eulogize the Qiang ancestors' efforts to conquer nature. Through them the strong-mindedness and fearlessness of the Qiang are vividly presented.

## 2. Long Narrative Poems (Epic)

Many historical and mythical epic poems emerged during the long history of the Qiang - a testimony to their collective wisdom and aspirations and a great influence on the content and artistry of later Qiang literature.

The epic *The Wars of the Qiang and the Ge* and two long mythical narrative poems, *Mu Jiezhu and Dou Anzhu* and *How Gods Came to Live Apart From Men*, are the most influential works as well as representatives in Qiang folk literature.

*The Wars of the Qiang and the Ge* describes the battles between the ancient Qiang people, after their migration to the upper reaches of Min River, and the native habitants, the Geji people. (This same theme is also seen in *Gaerdu* and in *The Story of the Battle between the Qiang People and the Geji People*.) The

史诗长达 600 余行，分"序歌"、"羊皮鼓的来源"、"大雪山的来源"、"羌戈相遇"、"找寻神牛"、"羌戈大战"、"重建家园"七部分。它以白描的手法，生动地再现了羌族先民迁到岷江上游定居的艰苦历程和英勇斗争的历史真实，讴歌了羌族先民的勇敢和智慧。

史诗《羌戈大战》语言生动活泼、朴素自然，具有羌族独特的风貌，显示出人类童年时代的文学所特有的魅力。整部作品，包含着浓厚的崇神思想，具有世俗的性质，充满了人间生活气息。《羌戈大战》是人们从民族学、历史学、宗教学等角度来研究羌族历史文化的宝贵资料。

羌族的神话叙事长诗，是继史诗之后，在神话和歌谣的基础上形成的新的文学样式，《木姐珠与斗安珠》就是一部流传最广、影响最大的作品。它用诗的语言叙述了一个神话故事，生动、形象地展示出经受考验的婚姻的特征，我们可以从中透视神话与原始宗教的亲密关系及羌族的婚姻形态。

神话叙事长诗《木姐珠与斗安珠》(异文《木姐珠与燃比娃》)描述了羌族青年与仙女恋爱的故事。大意是：天神的聪明、美丽的三女儿木姐珠私自下凡，爱上了勤劳、善良、诚实、勇敢的羌族牧童斗安珠。天神知道后大怒，准备害死斗安珠。勇敢的斗安珠在聪明的木姐珠的帮助下，三破天神提出的难题，终于获得了天神的允诺，与木姐珠结为夫妻。他俩在离别天庭后，双双来到羌寨，用勤劳的双手修建房屋、开荒种地，过上了幸福美满的生活。全诗共分"倔强公主"、"牧羊少年"、"龙池巧遇"、"赠发定情"、"大胆求婚"、"三破难题"、"火后余生"、"再次求婚"、"险遭毒计"和"创造

epic includes seven parts, namely, "Overture", "The Origin of the Sheepskin Drum", "The Origin of Great Snow Mountain", "The First Encounter between the Qiang and the Ge", "In Search of the Divine Cattle", "The Battle between the Qiang and the Ge", and "Rebuilding the Homelands", containing more than 600 lines in total. Recounting the hardships of the early Qiang people's migration and settlement in a vivid and straightforward way, the epic sings the praises of the ancestors' bravery, wisdom and heroic struggles in history.

The epic, with its vivid and simple language, demonstrates the unique style of the Qiang as well as the special charms of literature from early times. The whole work is pervaded with a strong sense of god worship, but also with the earthy flavor of common customs and daily life. It provides valuable material for the study of Qiang history and culture from ethnological, historical and religious perspectives.

Long mythical narrative poems, which emerged after the historical epic, formed a new literary style based on myths and folk songs, and these are best represented by the most popular and renowned work *Mu Jiezhu and Dou Anzhu*. This is a vivid, poetic account of a mythical story which describes the tests and trials of getting married. It reveals the close relationship between myths and primitive religion as well as introducing the marriage customs of Qiang people.

The long mythical narrative poem, *Mu Jiezhu and Dou Anzhu* (also called *Mu Jiezhu and Boy Ranbi*) describes a love story between an immortal maiden and a young Qiang man. Mu Jiezhu, the third daughter of the god of heaven, was a very clever and pretty immortal, who once descended to earth without her father's permission and fell in love with a kindhearted, honest, hard-working and chivalrous shepherd boy named Dou Anzhu. When her father heard about this, he was furious and planned to kill the shepherd boy. However, with the help of clever Mu Jiezhu, brave Dou Anzhu successfully overcame three difficult tasks set by the god of heaven, and gained his approval of their marriage.

Later, after leaving heaven, the couple settled down in a Qiang village, where they built houses with their own hands, turned wasteland into farmland and lived happily ever after. The poem is divided into ten parts, namely, "Willful Princess", "Shepherd Youth", "Encounter at Dragon Pool", "Falling in Love at Zengfa", "Bold Proposal", "Overcoming Three Obstacles", "Survival after the Fire", "Re-Proposal", "Escaping from the Trap", and "Making

幸福"等十个部分。长诗始终给人以无法超越的美的享受。

下面引用《木姐珠与斗安珠·创造幸福》中的一节：

我要用手把人间容貌改，我要用心血把大地浇灌。我要叫山山水水听人话，我要把人神界限全改变。

喜鹊筑巢辛勤衔百草，蚂蚁打洞群力日夜忙。木姐珠和斗安珠，为幸福哪怕汗水淌。

石砌楼房根基稳，三块白石供房顶。中间一层人居住，房脚下面养畜禽。

山坡地高种青稞，河坝地沃种玉米。高山牧草发茂盛，正好养马放牛羊。

从此羌人学会种庄稼，牛羊成群放满山。广袤平原尽羌属，子孙繁衍大发展。

金秋带来了丰收的喜悦，漫山遍野滚动着金浪。青稞小麦结籽累累，禽畜成群一片兴旺景象。

神话叙事长诗《人神分居的起源》(《美布和智拉朵》)，由"序歌"、"智拉朵"、"美布"、"盘歌"、"求婚"、"灶神上疏"、"回娘家"、"老鸹林"、"喜鹊坝"、"蜘蛛皮"、"蚂蚁湾"、"对话"、"尾声"等 13 个部分组成。通过天神的公主与羌人首领的儿子的爱情婚姻故事，反映了人与大自然的斗争和人在斗争中的主动地位，是一曲斗争和劳动创造的赞歌。

叙事长诗《赤机格布》反映了羌族人民热爱和平，反对非正义战争。长诗充分表现出羌族人民维护团结的优秀品德。

Happiness". From beginning to end this narrative poem brings sheer delight to its readers.

The following paragraphs are extracted from the final chapter "Making Happiness" from *Mu Jiezhu and Dou Anzhu*:

I will change the world with my own hands; I will devote my whole being to the earth. Let the mountains and waters be at my command and I will narrow the gap between man and gods.

The magpies busy themselves collecting grasses to build their nests; the ants are busy day and night, working together to dig their burrows. Mu Jiezhu and Dou Anzhu work together towards happiness with the sweat of their brow.

Stone houses stand firm on their solid foundations, with three white stones on the roof in the place of sacrifice. The family lives on the middle floor with the domestic animals down below.

Highland barley grows high on the mountainsides while corn occupies the fertile riverbank. The lush high mountain pastures are perfect for raising horse, sheep and cattle.

From that time on, the Qiang people farmed and herded cattle and sheep all over the mountains. The broad plains belonged to the Qiang and their descendants multiplied and prospered.

The golden autumn brings the joy of an abundant harvest with golden waves rippling across hill and dale. Wave upon wave of seed-bearing highland barley and wheat, and poultry and livestock in large number paint a picture of prosperity.

The long mythical narrative poem *How Gods Came to Live Apart From Men* (*Mei Bu And Zhi Laduo*) has thirteen chapters: "Overture", "Zhi Laduo", "Mei Bu", "Song of Dishes", "Proposal", "Honoring the Kitchen God", "Returning to the Maternal Family", "Crow Forest", "Magpie Land", "Spider Skin", "Ant Bay", "Conversation", and "The End". Recounting the story of love and marriage between the daughter of a god and the son of a Qiang tribal chief, the poem reflects man's fight against nature as well as man's initiative during the struggle. The poem is a eulogy to the struggle, hard work and ingenuity of the Qiang people.

Another long mythical narrative poem called *Chiji Gebu* is a heart cry reflecting the Qiang people's love of peace and their rejection of unjustified wars. It contains a strong expression of their excellent moral character and of how highly they prize their ethnic solidarity.

风俗长诗《说亲词》《喜事歌》《哭嫁歌》《丧葬词》等作品，形象地反映了羌族的传统风俗和羌民的愿望与追求，以及他们在宗教、道德等方面的基本观念。这些长诗运用了拟人化和重叠反复等手法，语言朴实，比喻生动，富于哲理。

（三）传说

羌族民间传说一般以一定的历史事件和历史人物的活动、风土人情为背景，用舒展的想象的翅膀，借助艺术的夸张去编组故事，刻画人物，进行广泛概括，揭示事物的本质，具有较高的艺术性和思想性。

羌族的传说主要有《石纽投胎》《洗儿池血石》《禹床》《望崇山》《采药山》《禹背岭》《大禹王的故事》《夏禹王治水》《夏禹王的传说》《李白拜禹穴》等。这些都是羌族人民世代相传且不可磨灭的精神财富。其中，大禹的传说是羌族民间文学宝库中一颗璀璨的明珠，它生动地叙述了大禹生于西羌和大禹在羌族地区留下的珍贵遗迹和神奇传闻。

地方传说：有的反映了羌族先民征服大自然的斗争，如《勒夏的故事》；有的赞颂了古代先民的高尚品德和智慧，如《鬼打石》；有的反映了对民族和阶级压迫的反抗和斗争，如《太子坟》。

动植物的传说：主要讲述了羌族地区常见的一些动物、植物的起源（包括动、植物的习性与特征），如《玉花姑娘》《红嘴鸟的传说》《狡猾的娃沙》《桂桂阳》《犏牛羊豹子》《荞麦的来历》等。《玉花姑娘》揭示了爱情悲剧的实质，赞颂了人民的斗争精神；《狡猾的娃沙》歌颂了劳动和勤劳，批判狡诈坏思想。植物传说

Long poems about folk customs such as *The Matchmaker's Words*, *A Song for Joyous Occasions*, *Song of the Weeping Bride* and *Funeral Words* vividly reflect the Qiang people's dreams, aspirations and traditional customs as well as their basic attitudes towards religion and morality. These poems use devices of personification, repetition, vivid metaphor and simple language, and are rich in philosophy.

### 3. Legends

Folk legends of the Qiang are usually based on specific historical events, on the activities of historical figures, and on local customs. The Qiang organize their plots and draw their characters with great imagination and artistic embellishment. Against a broad background, the essential nature of things is brought into clear focus, revealing high levels of ideological thought and artistic quality.

As a beautiful pearl in the treasure house of Qiang folk literature, legends about Da Yu vividly describe Da Yu's birth among the Western Qiang, his legendary deeds, and his valuable legacy. Many well-known legends, such as *Reincarnation at Shiniu*, *The Blood Stone in the Baby Bathing Pool*, *Yu's Bed*, *Mount Wangchong*, *The Herb-collecting Mountain*, *Yu Moves the Mountain*, *The Tale of King Yu the Great*, *King Yu of Xia Controls the Floods*, *The Legend of King Yu of Xia*, and *Li Bai's Visit to the House of Yu*, all embody the indelible spiritual wealth passed by the Qiang from generation to generation.

Legends connected with local places record the Qiang ancestors' fight against natural disasters, as in *The Story of Le Xia*. Others commend their ancestors' great virtue and wisdom, such as *The Ghost Knocking on the Stone,* and some, such as *The Prince's Tomb,* describe the Qiang people's resistance to and fight against racial and class oppression,.

The legends related to fauna and flora mainly cover the origin of some typical plants and animals of the Qiang region (including their habits and characteristics). They include *Lady Jade Flower*, *The Legend of the Red-billed Bird*, *Crafty Wa Sha*, *Gui Gui Yang*, *The Yak, the Sheep and the Leopard*, and *The Origin of Highland Barley*. *Lady Jade Flower* tells a tragic love story, lauding the people's fighting spirits; *Crafty Wa Sha* extols labor and industriousness while criticizing craftiness. The legends about plants and animals show

表现着不同历史阶段的人对植物的感知和认识，有的批评了以己之长比人之短的习惯，有的揭露封建伦理道德造成的悲剧等。

龙与蛇的传说：这类传说覆盖了整个羌族地区，每个村寨各有说法。如反映人与自然作斗争的龙的传说《龙池斗宝》《神龙斗道士》《龙赤海的传说》等。关于爱情婚姻方面的龙的传说，有三类：一是龙爱恋羌女并与之结为夫妻的，如《牙萨姐》；二是在人和龙的爱情故事中穿插社会斗争，如《映红寨的兰巴吉》；三是龙王逼迫羌女为妻的，如《黄三姑娘》。这类传说，都是以美丽的羌女嫁龙为妻为主要线索。反映人与蛇的关系的传说有《蛇大哥》《端午节的来历》等。

风俗传说：通过与节日、信仰、服饰有关的故事，反映羌族古老的历史及多方面的社会生活，是羌族人民认识社会、历史的重要艺术手段。风俗传说可以分为四类：一是节日民俗传说，如《吊狗节》；二是人生礼仪民俗传说，如《嫁女的来历》；三是服饰民俗传说，如《同心帕》《云云鞋的传说》等；四是民间游艺民俗传说，如《羌笛的来历》《口弦的来历》。

以释比为主要人物的传说：以讲述释比所具有的神奇法术或与道士、喇嘛比法时，总是释比胜利等为基本内容，具有浓厚的宗教色彩。

有反映羌民的灵魂现象及物我混同观念的"毒药猫"的传说，等等。

people's perception and knowledge of plants in different historical periods and from different angles. Some of the legends criticize the habit of comparing one's own strong points with others' weak points; and others expose tragedies caused by feudal ethics.

Legends about dragons and snakes spread over the whole Qiang area, with variations from village to village. Some dragon legends describe man's struggles against nature, such as *The Magic Weapons Battle in the Dragon Pool*, *The Battle between the Divine Dragon and the Taoist Priest*, and *The Legend of Red Dragon Lake*. Dragon legends concerning love and marriage are classified into three types: the first type describes the dragon falling in love with a Qiang girl and their subsequent marriage, as in *Sister Yasa*; the second type weaves social struggles into a love story between humans and dragons, as in *Lan Baji from Yinghong Village;* the last type relates how a Qiang girl is forced by the Dragon King to be his wife, as in *Lady Huang San*. The main thread of these legends focuses on the marriage between beautiful Qiang girls and dragons. Legends that reflect the relationship between humans and snakes are represented in works such as *Brother Snake* and *The Origin of the Dragon Boat Festival*.

Legends about Qiang customs, including festivals, religious beliefs, dress and personal adornment, recount many aspects of the Qiang's long history and colorful social lives. They are regarded as an important artistic medium for Qiang people to learn about their society and history. There are four types of legends about customs: ① festival legends, such as *The Dog Hanging Festival*; ② legends about social etiquette, such as *The Origin of Giving A Daughter in Marriage*; ③ legends about dress and personal adornment, such as *The Handkerchief of Unified Hearts* and *The Legend of the Yunyun Shoes*; and ④ legends about folk entertainment, such as *The Origin of the Qiang Flute*, and *The Origin of the Mouth Harp*.

The legends in which the Shibi is the main character tell about the Shibi's mysterious magic arts and his magic power contests with Taoist priests and Buddhist lamas. Since the Shibi always wins in such legends, they inevitably convey a strong religious sense.

There are also Qiang legends about the "poisonous cat" which deal with spiritual phenomena and the shadowy area between the physical body and the soul.

还有许多近现代历史事件、人物的传说，如《黑虎将军》《熊贵血染下五寨》《刘钒开盐井》等，都具有浓郁的地方特色，反映了一些地方的史实。

红军在羌族地区与羌族人民团结战斗，战胜敌人的史实，也产生了许多动人的传说，构成了羌族现代民间文学中传说的重要内容。如《红军碉》《夜袭赤陡坡》等。

（四）歌谣

羌族民间歌谣，具有浓厚的地方特色和民族特色。独特的民族印证和强烈的情感色彩，通过歌谣的形式表达出来。这些歌谣唱出了美好理想，抒发了哀乐之情。歌谣题材广泛，语言朴素、生动自然，潇洒流利，散发着清新的泥土气息。歌词多为四个音节或七个音节一句：或见物生情，即兴唱来，自成一格；或即兴而唱，边想边唱，无拘无束。有的悠扬优美，有的高亢嘹亮，有的活泼诙谐，有的缠绵婉转，十分动人。其中以劳动歌和习俗歌最有代表性。在羌族文学作品中，歌谣在数量上占有一定的优势。

《戈西莫》《打猎歌》《修房造屋歌》《采茶歌》等劳动歌谣勾勒出一幅幅生动的劳动画卷。羌族新时期的劳动歌，在曲调形式上，还继承传统劳动歌的特色，但内容更加充实、清晰、鲜明，反映了羌民当家做主的主人翁精神和劳动创造物质财富的雄心壮志，如《改土战士出早工》《庄稼成熟了》等。

《郭郭围》《婚礼开坛祝酒歌》《造屋歌》等礼仪习俗歌更是丰富多彩。以婚歌来说，有《说亲词》《催亲歌》；有姑娘出嫁前夕，由出嫁姑娘与众姐妹唱的《嫁女歌》《新娘歌》《离娘调》等；新娘到男家后，

A great number of the legends deal with people and events in modern history, such as *General Black Tiger*, *Bleeding Xiong Gui at Xiawu Village*, *Liu Fan Opens Up the Salt Well*, and so on. These are full of local character and give a glimpse of some local history.

Also, the Red Army's victory over the enemy in alliance with Qiang people, resulted in numerous moving legends which compose an important part of modern Qiang literature such as *Watchtower of the Red Army* and *Attacking Chidou Slope at Night*.

### 4. Folk Songs

Folk songs of the Qiang are rich in local character, ethnic color and strong emotion. Full of beautiful idealism, they express the Qiang people's joys and sorrows. The folk songs cover a wide range of topics, and are written in plain, lively, natural language, with an unrestrained fluidity and an earthy sense of connection to the land. The songs have four or seven syllables in each sentence and are sometimes sung with spontaneous improvisation at the sight of something particularly inspiring. Some of the songs are melodious, some sonorous, some lively, some humorous, and some are sentimental, sweet and moving. Of the various kinds of Qiang literature, folk songs are the most plentiful.

The most representative folk songs are those about work or customs. Work songs, such as *Ge Ximo*, *The Hunting Song*, *The House-building Song*, *The Tea Leaf Collecting Song*, all contain vivid depictions of laboring scenes. Modern work songs, while preserving the characteristics of traditional work songs, are clearer and richer in content. *The Land Reform Soldier Going to Work Early* and *The Crops Are Ripe* are examples of folk songs displaying the Qiang people's consciousness of being their own masters, and showing their aspirations of becoming prosperous through hard work.

Songs about customs, such as *Guo Guowei*, *Toasting Song upon Jug-opening at A Wedding*, and *The House-building Song,* are even richer and more colorful. There are marriage songs such as *Matchmaking Words* and *Hastening the Wedding*. Some of them are sung by the bride with her sisters before the wedding, such as *Marrying Off A Daughter*, *Song of the Bride* and *Leaving the Bride's Mother*. Others are performed during the banquet after the

男家正宴时有《过礼歌》《赞新娘》《赞新郎》《铺床歌》等。这些歌谣语言生动感人，令人难以忘怀。如《离娘调》唱道：

横搭彩棚好绑猪，猪儿一声我一声。猪儿声声滴眼泪，猪儿没得我伤心。猪儿伤心要被杀，小妹伤心要嫁人。

丧歌是伴随丧葬礼仪的歌。有吊丧者唱的《吊亡人歌》；有子女痛哭老人的《痛别歌》；有缅怀亡者的《悼歌》；有出葬时唱的《出葬歌》，下葬时唱的《安葬歌》；还有释比做法事唱的《丧葬词》《招魂歌》等。这些歌或赞颂死者生前功德，或安慰亡灵。

可以说，在羌族修房造屋、婚娶丧葬等重大礼仪活动中，做每一件事都有歌声相伴，并且自成体系，内容十分丰富。

时政歌则反映了羌族劳动人民在旧社会对政治生活的态度，抨击了地主阶级等对劳动人民的残酷剥削。有的表达了羌族人民在政治上的理想、在生活上的愿望以及不屈不挠的奋斗精神；有的表现了羌族人民对黑暗势力的反抗精神和对自身解放的渴望。《羌民苦》《烈火要向地主烧》《当兵就要当红军》等，是较有影响的作品。羌族新时政歌主要是歌颂性的颂歌，有的歌颂共产党、毛主席的，如《党是羌民大救星》等；有的歌颂民主改革的，如《自己有了田和地》等。

情歌在歌谣中数量最多，艺术性和思想性都较高。这些情歌表达了男女相爱的悲欢离合，极富生活气息。如《妹十八来郎十八》：

妹十八来郎十八，对着青天把誓发。郎有二心遭雷打，妹有二心双眼瞎。

还有《情哥做事没计才》：

bride's arrival at her husband's home, such as *Presenting the Betrothal Gifts*, *Praising the Bride*, *Praising the Groom*, *Preparing the Bed*, etc. The vivid and moving language of these songs makes them particularly memorable. The following is taken from *Leaving the Bride's Mother*:

The decorated tent has been put up and the pig is bound for slaughter. My cries blend with the squeals of the pig. The pig grieves over being slaughtered, but nothing is sadder than leaving my mother to get married.

Funeral songs accompany funeral rituals. *Song for Mourning the Departed* is sung by people offering their condolences to the dead; *Song of A Lamentable Departure* is sung by the bereaved sons and daughters to their parents; *An Elegy* is sung to cherish the memory of the dead; *The Funeral Song* is performed during the funeral and *The Burying Song* during the burial; *Funeral Speech* and *Song of Calling Back the Spirits* are sung by the Shibi as he carries out the funeral rites. All these songs either praise the achievements of the dead or comfort their souls.

In fact, every important ceremonial activity such as house building, weddings or funerals, is accompanied by songs. And for each activity there are songs rich in content and fit for the occasion.

Songs about political issues lash out at the landlord class for their exploitation of the laborers, reflecting the Qiang attitude to political affairs in the past. Some of the songs voice the Qiang people's political ideals, testifying to their aspirations and indomitable fighting spirits; others express their resistance against powers of darkness and their longing for freedom. Influential works include *The Bitter Life of the Qiang People*, *Let Our Anger Burn towards the Landlords*, and *Joining the Red Army*.

New political songs of the Qiang are mainly paeans of praise. Some admire the Communist Party and Chairman Mao, such as *The Communist Party—Liberator of the Qiang People*; some show appreciation of democratic reform, such as *Having Our Own Farmlands*.

Love songs constitute the largest category of folk songs. Containing a high level of ideology and artistry, these love songs express the sorrows and joys of lovers and they resonate with the richness of life, as in *I Am 18, So Are You*:

I am 18, so are you, we pledge our loyalty beneath the blue sky.

If you fall in love with a another girl, let lightening strike you,

If I give my heart to another man, let my eyes be blind.

*My Poor Darling Man* is another love song:

情妹住在山梁上，走拢门前九道墙。喂的狗儿像老虎，叫我咋个能拢场。

情哥做事没计才，回家烧个馍馍来。狗儿咬你馍馍打，狗吃馍馍你就来。

羌族新情歌，反映新社会、新思想、新风尚，更重要的是把个人爱情与祖国大家庭的建设事业联系起来，如《大大方方送一张》《我爱情哥劳动好》等。

在羌族的歌谣中，民谣的数量较少，以对农时农事和某一历史时期社会现实状况的反映为主要内容。如描述新中国成立前北川一帮土匪打劫的民谣：

到了曹山坡，本钱摸一摸；过了旧关岭，本钱才得稳；过了凉风垭，才得见爹妈。

## （五）民间故事

羌族民间故事是羌族民间文学又一重要组成部分。其中幻想故事、动物故事、鬼狐精怪故事、生活故事、机智故事、寓言故事等，在内容和形式上都有较多的现实性和较好的艺术性，具有羌族独特的风格。

幻想故事内容丰富，既有灵怪故事，如《姐妹俩》，又有如《肉坨坨里的儿子》的怪孩子故事，此外还有变形故事、神奇宝物故事、兄弟故事等。幻想故事运用想象和夸张，有感人的描绘，具有丰富的象征性与审美性。

生活故事概括起来有长工斗地主故事，如《财主和长工》，有反抗旧礼教的爱情婚姻故事，如《成成门和阿拉扎吉》，此外还有傻女婿故事、机智故事等。羌族生活故事包含了丰富多彩的内容，且手法多样化，选材得体，生活气息浓厚。

My beloved girl lives on the mountain range, and it's as if I must get through nine walls before reaching her door. Her dog is as strong as a tiger, so how can I reach her?

Be smart, my poor darling man, take a steamed bun with you. When the dog bites you, just throw him the bun, and then you can come to me because the dog will eat the bun.

The newer Qiang love songs reflect China's new society, new thoughts, and new fashions, and in particular, they relate personal romantic love to the cause of building the new motherland. The most typical ones are *A Bounteous Gift*, and *My Beloved Man's Hard Work*.

Among the Qiang folk songs there are relatively few ballads, and these mainly introduce farm activities during farming seasons and the social reality of certain historical periods. One example describes thefts by bandits in the Beichuan area before 1949. The song goes:

You should be careful of the money you carry when you get to Caoshan Slope; after passing Jiuguan Mountain, you can be sure of the safety of your money; having passed through Liangfeng Pass, you can be sure of the safety of your life, and only then can you meet your parents.

## 5. Folk Stories

Folk stories are an important part of the folk literature of the Qiang and they include tales of fantasy, animals, ghosts and demons, life and humor, as well as allegorical stories. In both content and form, they demonstrate a high level of realism and artistry, in a unique Qiang style.

Fantasies cover various topics, such as the elf story of *Two Sisters*, and the story about a strange child, called *Child in the Meat Lump*. In addition, there are stories about deformation, miraculous treasures, brothers, etc. Using imagination and hyperbole, these fantastical stories are rich in symbolism, and present us with touching portrayals and a deep appreciation of beauty.

Briefly outlining stories about life, they include stories of struggles between laborers and landlords, such as *The Rich Landlord and the Long-term Hired Laborer*; stories about love and marriage, such as *Cheng Chengmen and Ala Zhaji*, which show a rejection of feudal ethics, stories about silly sons-in-law and other witty stories. These stories are rich in content, diverse in style and the topics are very aptly selected, presenting a vivid picture of the real life of the Qiang people.

羌族寓言蕴含诙谐情趣和幽默感，具有刚健清新与机智锋利的特色。主要表现在：形体短小，寓意鲜明，语言朴实，现实性强。羌族笑话的主要特色是：嘲讽笑话与生活故事紧密联系，幽默笑话与诙谐笑话相映成趣。

## 二、书面文学

羌族的书面文学，从某种意义上讲，创作的历史悠久，且随时代变迁有很强的地域性和跳跃性，同时受中原文化的影响较深。

但是，在深入探讨羌族书面文学之前，我们首先要指明，由于"羌"是一个较为宽泛的民族概念，其内部分支众多，不同的羌族支系之间存在很大的差异。就地域而言，岷江上游的羌族书面文学是这一地域文化特殊的产物，它与当地的风土人情、文化传统有着密切的联系，并且主要是清代及其以后的文学创作。而岷江上游之外的古代羌人，虽在书面文学创作上发轫较早，但与岷江上游这块土地没有直接的内在联系。不过，这些作品仍是整个羌族书面文学的组成部分。

### 1. 西晋以前的羌人书面创作

西晋以前（约公元前 572 年—公元 264 年），流传的书面作品数量较少，但价值较高。根据现有的文史资料看，可以说最迟在春秋中叶，古羌人就已经出现了书面文学作品。如作为抒愤劝喻的《青蝇》，其作者当为春秋时姜氏戎的首领。它有着浓郁的先秦民族的风味，是目前见到的最早的羌族书面诗作。另外还有抒情述怀的组歌《白狼歌》。这个时期的诗歌之作，多为四言诗，这与羌族本身的古歌创作的语言特点有关。

Qiang allegories are witty and humorous, noted for their clarity, wisdom and tartness. They are characterized by brevity, clear morality, plain words and strong realism. Qiang jokes are distinctive in their satirizing of real life stories and their interplay of humor and wit.

## II. Written Literature

In a larger sense, the written literature of the Qiang has been produced over a long period within which times of change and migration have resulted both in strong regional influences and in periods of non-productivity. It has also been strongly influenced by the culture of central China.

However, care must be taken over the term "Qiang" as it refers to both the present-day Qiang of the upper Min area, and to various Qiang tribal groupings throughout history. Thus, some written literature referred to as Qiang is from Sichuan's upper Min area and some is from other Qiang regions and groups of earlier times. The Qiang literature of the Min area is closely linked to local customs and traditions, and all Qiang written literature from the Qing dynasty onwards has been produced in this region, but the term "Qiang written literature" must also include the literary works from earlier times, places and Qiang peoples. For this reason it is necessary to take a brief look at its historical development and look at its style and characteristics.

### 1. Written Literature before the Western Jin Dynasty (572 BC— 264 AD)

Works from this period are small in quantity but significant in value. According to literary and historical materials, the written literature of the ancient Qiang emerged in the middle of the Spring and Autumn Period. The poem *Blue Fly*, authored by the chief of the Rong tribe of the Jiang during the Spring and Autumn Period, is the earliest known written work of the Qiang. Characterized by its ancient pre-Qin style, the poem expresses anger, encouragement and persuasion. Another typical literary work of the time is the highly emotional suite of songs called *Song of the White Wolf*. Works produced during this period were usually written with lines of four words, which was the characteristic style of ancient Qiang song composition.

### 2. 后秦时期的羌人书面创作

约公元 384 年至 417 年，随着姚氏羌人的崛起，以及后秦政权的建立，书面创作也出现了一度的蓬勃兴旺。主要有《琅琊王歌词》和《钜鹿公主歌词》。它们以新的汉歌诗体，丰富了羌族书面文学样式。迄今为止，《琅琊王歌词》是最早的羌族书面五言诗作，而《钜鹿公主歌词》则是最早的羌族书面七言诗作。它们以雄浑刚健的文风和写时抒意的精神，与其他少数民族诗作交相辉映，为繁荣诗歌艺术园地作出了贡献。在这一时期，还出现了姚兴这样的散文作者，作品有《与僧迁等书》《通三世》等。后秦的佛经翻译对书面文学创作也产生了积极的作用。

### 3. 西夏时期的羌人书面创作

公元 1038 年至 1227 年，主要有散文创作、书面诗作、碑文创作等。这一时期的书面创作意义深远，不仅是因为创作了诸多的羌族作品，而且还在于它为羌族书面创作在元代的进一步发展和兴盛奠定了坚实的基础。

### 4. 西夏羌人遗民的书面创作

这里还要特别提一下西夏羌人遗民的书面创作情况。这一时期的作品主要是诗和诗文。涌现了一大批作者，如诗文大家余阙，诗人张雄飞、昂吉和王翰。此外，还有斡玉伦徒、完泽、买住等人。

### 5. 清代至新中国成立初期的羌族书面文学创作

这一时期以诗歌和散文为主，有揭露、抨击黑暗社会现实的作品，描写山川风物和个人生活的作品，以及反映羌族民间生活和民俗信仰的作品。这一时期的创作取得了较大发展，一是涌现了一批羌族作者，如"嘉庆高氏五子"，

## 2. Written Works during the Later Qin Period (384 AD—417 AD)

With the increasing power of the Yao tribe of the Qiang and the establishment of the state of the Later Qin, written works flourished. Two representative works, *Poem of King Langya* and *Poem of Princess Julu*, brought new Han poetic forms into Qiang written literature. According to records, the *Poem of King Langya* is the earliest Qiang poem of a style with five characters to a line, while the *Poem of Princess Julu* is the earliest with seven characters to a line. They use a firm literary style to convey ideas and historical events, resonating with other ethnic minority works, and contributing to the broader field of Chinese poetry. This period also witnessed the works by prose writers such as Yao Xing, including *Letters to Seng Qian and Others* and *Through Three Generations*. The translation of Buddhist scriptures in the Later Qin period also actively influenced the written literature of that era.

## 3. Written Works during the Western Xia Period (1038 AD—1227 AD)

Works in this period mainly consisted of essays, written poems and tablet inscriptions. These works are of great significance because many were created by the Qiang, laying a solid foundation for the further development and prosperity of Qiang written literature during the Yuan Dynasty.

## 4. Written Works by Descendants of the Western Xia Qiang People

We would like also to mention some literary works of the descendants of Western Xia Qiang people. These literary works include poems and poetic prose by such outstanding poets and writers as Yu Que, Zhang Xiongfei, Ang Ji, Wang Han, Woyuluntu, Wan Ze and Mai Zhu.

## 5. Writtenz Works from the Qing Dynasty until the Early Stages of the People's Republic of China

The literature of this time mainly consists of poems and essays with three leading themes: exposure of social conditions; descriptions of local mountains and river scenery and tales of individual lives; and introductions to local customs, beliefs and Qiang daily life. This was a period of considerable literary development in three particular ways. Firstly, a number of new Qiang writers emerged, such as a group called the "Five Gaos of Jiaqing", composed of Gao

即高万选、高万崐、高吉安、高辉光、高辉斗等五人，代表作分别是《飞沙关》《过雁门观晴雪》《温凉泉》《汶阳八景咏》《七盘古道》。他们的共同特点是：立足于故乡之土，描绘山川，唱咏古迹，诗风淳朴，笔力道劲。二是开了羌族书面文学以诗歌形式来吟咏故乡山川的艺术先河，如赵成嘉的诗文作品《锁谷坪》《雁门关》等。三是这一时期的书面作品，大多具有浓厚的文学意味，少数作品在思想内容和艺术技巧上还达到了较高的水准，以高体全的无题诗为代表。

### 6. 当代状况

当代羌族书面文学创作形式十分丰富，散文、小说、诗歌以及电视文学剧本等体裁皆备。创作的题材更为广泛，涉及社会的许多方面，反映了新时代、新生活和人民新的精神风貌。

据现有资料，小说是历代羌族文学中所没有的体裁，在当代才出现。代表人物有谷运龙、叶星光、向世茂、蒋宗贵、吴刚、余德成、张翔礼、阙玉兰等。其中以谷运龙和叶星光成绩较为突出。谷运龙创作了多部作品，他的小说写普通人的遭遇，以反映时代的缩影，表现改革所带来的社会变迁和人们的精神面貌为基本倾向，立意新颖、意真情挚、笔法细腻。他的《飘逝的花瓣》曾于 1985 年获第二届全国少数民族文学创作二等奖，成为第一部获得全国性创作奖的羌族作者的小说作品。他的《家有半坑破烂鞋》，于 1992 年获得四川省首届少数民族优秀文学作品奖。叶星光的小说风格多变，笔法较灵活，既接受本民族文学的熏陶，保留自然天成、质朴浑厚的特色，

Wanxuan, Gao Wankun, Gao Ji'an, Gao Huiguang and Gao Huidou. Representative works of these writers include *Flying Sands Pass*, *Crossing Yanmen Pass on a Sunny Snowy Day*, *Hot and Cold Springs*, *Songs of Eight Scenes in Wen Yang* and *The Ancient Paths of Qi Pan*. The common characteristic of these works is that they are all rooted in the writer's native place, with lyrical descriptions of the mountains, rivers and ancient sites written in a simple yet powerful style. Secondly, a new Qiang literary style was initiated using a poetic form to describe the beauty of this native scenery, as seen in the poetic prose works, *Suo Valley Plain* and *Yan Men Pass,* by Zhao Chengjia. Thirdly, most of the works have a strong literary quality, bringing ethnic minority works to new levels in terms of ideas, content and artistic skills, as in the untitled poems composed by Gao Tiquan.

## 6. Modern Written Works

Contemporary Qiang literature takes various forms including essays, novels, poems and television plays. The themes of these creative works encompass a wider sphere, covering many aspects of the society. They reflect a new generation of Qiang people with a new way of life and new attitudes and approaches.

Novels are a new addition to Qiang written literature. Writers of this genre include Gu Yunlong, Ye Xingguang, Xiang Shimao, Jiang Zonggui, Wu Gang, Yu Decheng, Zhang Xiangli and Que Yulan. Among them, Gu Yunlong and Ye Xingguang are the most prominent. Gu Yunlong's novels are about ordinary people's experiences, mirroring changes wrought by national reforms, both in society and in people's mental outlook. Gu Yunlong has written many works, all of which are characterized by sincerity, innovative ideas and an exquisite descriptive style. His novel, *Drifting Petals*, was awarded second prize in the Second National Ethnic Minority Literature Competition in 1985. Thus he became the first Qiang author to win a national prize for a novel. Moreover, in 1992, he was awarded a prize for his work *Many Worn-out Shoes in My Home* at the first "Competition for Outstanding Ethnic Minority Literature" in Sichuan Province.

Ye Xingguang is a versatile author who writes using a variety of styles. On one hand, he makes full use of traditional Qiang literature, keeping the notion of a created natural world and writing in an honest, simple style. On the other hand,

又大胆采用一些现代小说的表现手法与结构模式。作品多运用综合开放、灵活变幻的手法，给人留下深刻的印象。1997年，发表了羌族第一部电影文学剧本《尔玛魂》。1998年，编写第一部羌族神话剧《木姐珠剪纸救百兽》。1996年，小说《情殇》获得全国路遥文学创作二等奖。1998年，他将历年的小说精选结集，以《神山·神树·神林》为题并出版，成为羌族文学史上仅见的两部小说集之一。

当代羌族散文创作有了很大进步，作者众多，内容丰富多彩，各具特色，从结构安排到叙事手法较为和谐的运用，都可见羌族作者已较为熟练地掌握了写作技艺，并以此反映羌族人民的生活，抒发健康的情感。如朱大录、谷运龙、梦非等多着力描摹故乡的风土人情、历史变迁和现实思考；罗子岚则长于对僻壤山野之民朴实心灵的刻绘；张善云有关九寨的科普旅游的系统介绍，堪称人与自然的颂歌。而其中以朱大录、张善云的散文成绩较为突出。朱大录的《羌寨椒林》在1981年全国首届少数民族文学评奖会上荣获散文创作奖，这是有史以来羌族作者第一次获得全国性文学创作奖。张善云的散文以其丰富的知识性而别具特色，他写的有关九寨的散文更是美不胜收，如《九寨红叶动心魄》、《九寨野草》、《林中奇观叶上珠》等。罗子岚的《没有回音的土地》和《沙滩上的黄昏》也别有风格。

当代羌族作者的诗歌创作基本上是新体诗，这也是新中国成立前羌族人所没有的。诗歌作者思维活跃，观念更新，视野更为广阔，多以一种强烈的使命感从事诗歌创作。其作品反映广泛的社会生活，更着重于本民族的历史文化与现实的思考，力图演绎古老羌族拼搏奋进的坎坷历程，表现其独特的心理素养和个性特征，

he boldly adopts the writing styles and structural patterns of modern novels with a wide-ranging open mind and great flexibility, making a profound impression on the reader. In 1997, Ye Xingguang published the first Qiang movie drama, *Spirit of Erma*. In 1998, he wrote the first Qiang mythological play, *Mu Jie Zhu's Paper-cuts?? Save One Hundred Animals*. His novel, *Dying Love*, won second prize in the Lu Yao National Literature Competition in 1996. In 1998, he published a selection of his earlier stories in the book trilogy *Sacred Mountain, Sacred Tree, Sacred Forest,* one of only two collections of short stories in Qiang literary history.

Contemporary Qiang prose has developed considerably. There are more writers and their works are rich and varied, each with their own distinctive features, displaying skilful structural organization and narrative techniques. In these accomplished works one can see the breadth and the emotional health that characterizes the lives of the Qiang. Writers such as Zhu Dalu, Gu Yunlong and Meng Fei give detailed descriptions of local conditions, customs and historical changes, as well as offering reflections on contemporary reality. Luo Zilan skillfully portrays the simple and honest nature of the people living in remote mountain areas whilst Zhang Shanyun's systematic introduction to travelling in Jiuzhaigou could be called a literary celebration of man and nature.

Among Qiang prose writers, Zhu Dalu and Zhang Shanyun are the most eminent. In 1981, Zhu Dalu's *Prickly Ash Woods in a Qiang Village*, was awarded the prose prize in the first National Minorities Literary Awards, becoming the first Qiang work to win a national award for literature. The uniqueness of Zhang Shanyun's writings lies in their profound knowledge and his essays about Jiuzhaigou are breathtakingly beautiful. These include works such as *The Soul-inspiring Red Leaves of Jiuzhai*, *The Grasslands of Jiuzhai*, *The Wonder of Dewdrops on Forest Leaves*. There are also some stylish works from Luo Zilan, such as *Lands without Echo* and *Dusk over the Sands*.

Modern Qiang poems are mainly in a new style. Contemporary poets, with new, dynamic ideas and extended horizons, have a strong sense of purpose in their poetry writing. Their poems provide a broad view of Qiang society and place greater stress on their own people's history and culture and on reflections about reality. They attempt to unravel the ups and downs of the ancient Qiang people's fierce struggle towards progress, bearing witness to the Qiang people's distinctive qualities of mind and character. They also describe the rethinking

进而抒写新的时代背景下深刻的反思与追求，以及对文明进步美好未来的憧憬。代表作家有李孝俊、何健、余耀明等。李孝俊于 1994 年 6 月将多年的诗作整理结集为《在这片星光下》。诗集共分为五个部分。整部诗集充分展示出羌族青年诗人满怀热忱，在生活的道路上曲折行进的心迹历程，也在一定程度上显示出新一代羌人珍视历史、热爱故乡而又思索命运、向往山外广阔天空的真实性灵与精神。何健的作品多为组诗形式，代表作有《山野的呼唤》《羌民篇》等。他的作品向人们展现了羌族的历史文化与纯朴秉性，刻画其倔强的灵魂。余耀明的作品以平淡质朴、富于民族特色而著称，如《羊皮鼓》《赠你一双云云鞋》《故乡》等。

羌族的文学，以其丰富多彩的内容和形式以及深厚的文化底蕴，显示出它独有的优点和特长，是中国文学浩瀚的历史长河中一颗璀璨的明珠。

（耿亚军　徐希平）

processes and new desires of the current generation and their expectation of cultural improvement and a prosperous future.

Representative poets include Li Xiaojun, He Jian, and Yu Yaoming. In June 1994, Li Xiaojun gathered various of his poems into a collection called *Under the Starlight*. Divided into five parts, the collection lays bare the thoughts and feelings of an earnest young Qiang poet in a life filled with ups and downs. To a certain extent it also highlights the true heart of the new Qiang generation in their esteem of history and love for their native place, their reflections on their destiny, and the desire for their life experience to extend into a wider world.

He Jian's works are mostly composed in sets of poems, such as *The Call of the Mountains*, and *Poems of the Qiang People*. His works describe the history and culture of the Qiang and their simple, honest character and resilient spirit.

Yu Yaoming's works are famous for their plain language and ethnic flavor. Examples include *The Sheepskin Drum*, *A Pair of Yunyun Shoes for You* and *Hometown*.

The literature of the Qiang, with its rich content, unique style and profound depths of cultural reality, is a distinctive part of national literature, flowing with other literary streams into the broad river of Chinese literary history.

( Translated by Dai Zhiyong, Chen Shuyu )

# 第五章　羌族的宗教信仰<sup>①</sup>

羌族是一个拥有悠久历史和古老文化的民族。在长期生产劳动与生活中，羌族人民不仅创造了巨大的物质和精神财富，而且还形成了具有自己民族特色的宗教信仰。

## 一、以天神为主神的多神信仰

古代的羌族由于对自然现象和天体的运行无法解释，对天灾人祸十分恐惧。他们认为世界上的万事万物都有灵魂、有生命，由此而产生了万物有灵的观念和自然崇拜等原始宗教文化并延续至今。这种宗教文化现象成为羌族文化中独具特色的重要组成部分。

羌族的宗教信仰至今还停留在巫术和灵气崇拜阶段，没有专门的宗教机构和组织。

### （一）多彩的诸神

羌族普遍保留着比较原始的宗教信仰，主要是自然崇拜，万物有灵；敬奉祖先，尊巫信鬼。

羌族崇拜信仰的神有数十种之多，按其性质和特点，大致可分为以下几类：

#### 1. 自然界诸神

在羌族的宗教观念中，自然界首先是他们崇拜的对象，自然界诸神主要包括天神、地神、火神、山神、树神、水神、羊神等。由于自然界中的天、地、山、水、树与羌民的生产和生活关系最为密切，因而成为他们自然崇拜的主要对象。按照羌族的原始宗教观念，在自然界的诸神中，天神居于主神的

---

① 在羌族宗教信仰中，羌语称羌族的祭司为"释比"。有些书中则称"端公"。后者是汉语对羌族祭司的称谓。本书采用前者。

112

# CHAPTER FIVE    RELIGIOUS BELIEFS OF THE QIANG①

As mentioned previously, the Qiang are a people with a long history and an ancient culture. Over time they have not only created material and spiritual wealth but have also formed their own distinctive religious beliefs.

## I. Polytheism: Belief in Many Gods with the God of Heaven as Greatest

Since ancient Qiang people could not explain certain natural phenomena and the movement of celestial bodies, they were extremely afraid of both natural and man-made disasters, and believed that everything in the world had its own life and spirit. In this way, primitive religious beliefs of animism and nature worship came into being and constitute a distinctive and important part of Qiang religious culture. Until today, shamanic arts and an atmosphere of mystery remain central to Qiang religious belief and they have no specially established religious structure or organization.

### 1. The Various Gods

Qiang people generally hold rather primitive religious beliefs, including nature worship, the belief that everything has a spirit, ancestor worship, and belief in the effectiveness of sorcery and the existence of ghosts.

The Qiang people worship and believe in many gods, which can be divided into the following types according to their different characteristics. The gods of nature constitute the first group. According to the Qiang, these are the most respected and revered and include the gods of heaven, earth, fire, mountains, trees and sheep. Since heaven, earth, fire, mountains, trees and sheep have the closest relationship with the lives and work of the Qiang in the natural world, the gods representing them have become the primary gods revered by the Qiang. In the original religious beliefs of the Qiang, the god of heaven is the highest

---

① Among religious beliefs of the Qiang, the Qiang priest is called "Shibi" in the Qiang language. In some works he is referred to by the Han term "Duangong" but we have chosen to use "Shibi."

地位，极为崇高，他是天地间万事万物的主宰，能祸佑人畜。其次是山神、火神、树神、水神、羊神等。

## 2. 地方神

除了普遍信仰的自然界诸神以外，羌族的各村寨还有各种彼此不同的地方神，大多数属自然崇拜性质。羌族诸神中，地方神构成一个庞大的系统，如每一个村寨的寨神和寨盘业主以及寨子附近山川自然物的神灵等。其中还有阴神、阳神等。村寨的碉堡也有碉神，因为它能使村寨里的人在外敌来临时得到保全，所以也应加以供奉。在羌族人民的宗教观念中，最初，由人有"灵魂"出发，推及外界事物，认为一切所在皆有精灵寄托与主宰，鬼神观念遂生。在以后的发展中，又将鬼与神分开了。于是众多的神中有了正神与邪神、善神与恶魔等区分。正神指那些有益于人的生命财产安全的神灵，即地方保护神；邪神指危害人畜的妖魔鬼怪，往往与人作祟。正神，如理县若达、佳山、西山等寨有松树神，乾溪寨有岩鹰神等。邪神，如理县星上纳瓦寨有田角怪藤神，木尔达寨有刺条坝子神，九子寨有岩神，等等。每一位正神均有相应的神话传说，邪神则没有。羌人每年请释比祭祀正神，祈求保佑；对于那些邪神，自每年的正月起至三月底期间，选择属猪、羊、龙、马四日，举行禳解，以期求得平安。

## 3. 祖先崇拜的诸神

第三类是祖先崇拜的诸神。一般供于家中，泛称家神。一般家中都供有人类祖先神木姐珠、斗安珠；家族奉祀的有男女祖宗神、男女保护神等。例如，有的人家堂屋正中神龛上供有三位神灵：中间是家神，已采用汉族的"天地君亲师"的写法；左侧是灶神；

god, in charge of everything in heaven and on earth, and with the power to bless or bring disaster on human beings and livestock. Below him are the gods of mountains, fire, trees, water and sheep.

In addition to these higher and more widely worshipped gods, there is a second group which includes different local gods worshipped in each Qiang village. These local gods form a large system, including the god of each village, the spirits of ownership of village as well as specific gods of mountains, rivers and other natural features near the village, and the gods of Yin and Yang. There is also a god of the watchtowers in the village, who is worshipped because such a god can protect the whole village when an enemy invades.

In early Qiang religious thinking, every human being had a spirit, and this concept then spread to everything in the external world having a spirit. The notion that things are controlled by spirits then extended to the concept of supernatural beings, and then to the existence of ghosts and deities. Hence, among the numerous deities there are righteous gods, and evil gods or demons. The righteous gods are those who protect people's life and property. These are local protector gods, such as the pine tree god in Ruoda, Jiashan and Xishan villages in Li County and the rock eagle god of Ganxi Village. The evil gods or demons are those who make mischief and do harm to people and livestock, such as the evil vine god of the field corners in Xingshangnawa village in Li County, the god of the thorny dam in Muerda Village, and the rock god in Jiuzi Village. Each righteous god has a corresponding mythical legend while the evil ones do not.

Every year, Qiang people ask the Shibi to offer sacrifices to the righteous gods and to pray for blessings. Regarding the evil gods, people hold rituals on Pig Day, Goat Day, Dragon Day and Horse Day (specially designated days during the first three month of the year) to exorcise evil and pray for peace.

The third group of gods consists of ancestral gods who are generally worshipped at home, hence the term "domestic gods". In an ordinary home the human-like Qiang ancestral gods, Mu Jiezhu and Dou Anzhu, are venerated and a family or clan will offer sacrifices to male and female ancestral gods and protector gods. For example, some families worship three different gods on the household shrine located in the middle of the main room. The family god is central, often represented by the Han-style couplet "Heaven, Land, Ruler, Parents and Teacher." On the left is the kitchen god while the

右侧是观音菩萨。每日早晚要向家神烧一次香，表示崇敬。有的地方还将仓神、门神或山神供于家中。家中有从事特殊行业的，还供有各自行业的祖师神。

在羌族的祖先崇拜中，大禹是深受羌民崇信的主要神灵之一。在羌族的许多地区，以大禹出生为主要内容的遗迹和传说，流传甚广，特别是今天北川县禹里羌族乡一带更为集中。主要传说有大禹在"石纽投胎"，以及"血石的来历"、"禹穴的来历"等。另外，在汶川、理县、松潘等地区的羌族民间，也都存在着类似的传说和遗迹。在羌族的思想观念中，大禹的遗迹尤其是石纽（大禹投胎之地）被认为是最圣洁的地方。羌民在远行的时候，带上这里的泥土，据说可以保佑平安。还有人认为，血石、禹穴等大禹遗迹具有生育的作用。每当妇女不孕时，在禹穴坐一坐或者捡一块血石都能使妇女怀孕，这种习俗至今还在流传。遇到旱涝灾害时，羌民要在释比的主持下，祈求禹王消灾免难，保佑万事平安。大禹遗迹被羌族视为神圣之地，具有崇高的宗教地位。

随着羌民族的变迁，其祖先崇拜的内容也复杂化了。例如，所有的民族英雄以及凡有功于民族者，羌族均视为神而予以崇拜，如建筑房屋神、石匠神、铁匠神、战争指示神等，均属此类。对于民族英雄的崇拜，还伴有相应的民间传说，比如汶川县克枯寨崇拜的龙山太子，他除暴安民，后来却被反动统治者谋杀了，羌人将其遗体埋在龙山顶上，世代崇祀。又如茂县黑虎等寨崇拜的黑虎将军，据说原是领导这一带羌民反抗清朝统治的起义首领，后因寡不敌众而遇害。

### 4. 图腾崇拜

羌族中残存着图腾崇拜的遗迹，较普遍的是羊图腾崇拜的遗迹。这主要表现在：据说羌族自称"尔咩"，"尔咩"与羊的叫声相近。传说在羌人与戈基人的战斗中，羌人均在颈部悬羊毛线作为标志，

Guanyin Bodhisattva is on the right. Every morning and evening, people burn joss sticks to show their respect. In some places, the gods of the storehouse, door and mountain are worshipped in the house too. People who engage in specific trades even make offerings to the founder of their profession.

Among the ancestors worshipped by the Qiang, Yu the Great is one of the most admired. Stories and legends about his birth, such *as Yu the Great's Reincarnation in Shiniu, The Origin of the Bloodstone*, and *The Origin of Yu Cave* spread throughout Qiang areas, especially in the area of Yuli Village of Beichuan County. Similar legends and historical traces also exist in the counties of Wenchuan, Li and Songpan. In Qiang people's minds, any historical traces linked to Yu the Great, including Shiniu, the place where Yu the Great was born, are regarded with the greatest veneration and reverence. When people are away from home, they take some clay of Shiniu with them to keep them safe and sound. In the eyes of the Qiang, the relics of the "bloodstone" and "Yu Cave" can help a woman to conceive. When a woman cannot conceive she either goes and sits in "Yu Cave" or picks up a "bloodstone". The custom still prevails to this day. Also, when drought or excessive rain occur, Qiang people hold ceremonies presided over by the Shibi and pray to Yu the Great to dispel disaster and suffering and keep everything safe.

With the historical changes and migrations of the Qiang, their ancestor worship became increasingly complex. For example, all ethnic heroes and any historical figures who have made great contributions are esteemed as gods. There are gods of architecture, stonecutting, iron-smithery and war. Veneration of national heroes is always accompanied by corresponding folklore. An example of this is the Dragon Mountain Prince worshipped by villagers of Keku in Wenchuan County. He strove for peace and against violence but was murdered by reactionary leaders. The Qiang buried him on top of Dragon Mountain and have held sacrificial ceremonies in his memory from generation to generation. Another example is General Black Tiger (Hei Hu) who is worshipped in Hei Hu and other villages in Mao County. He was the leader of an armed insurrection against the rule of Qing Dynasty, but his men were hopelessly outnumbered by the Qing troops and he was also killed.

Vestiges of totemism still remain among the Qiang, and the sheep totem is the most popular. The Qiang autonym of "Ermie" is said by some to be similar to the bleating sound made by sheep. In the legendary battle against the Geji people, the Qiang all wore a piece of wool round their necks as a symbol,

这实际上是模拟羊的形状。至今羌民在参加祭山大典时，还要由释比分别在他们的身上系上羊毛线，以示与羊同体。羌族在丧事中用羊作"死者替身"、"为灵魂引路"的习俗，以及各种祭典中杀了羊、撒羊血、不准吃羊肉，或烧成灰，或弃之野外等，可能都是原始社会的图腾崇拜遗迹。古代羌民曾以畜牧业为生，羊是牲畜中与羌民关系最密切的动物，因此有可能把羊当作与自己有着某种血缘关系的动物而奉为"图腾"，对其加以崇敬和保护是很自然的。

### 5. 鬼的观念

羌民还有鬼的观念，认为人有灵魂，死后继续存在，但成为鬼。并非所有的鬼都是祸害，只有凶死或夭亡人之鬼才会加害于人。对于人的灾祸、疾病，人们认为是那些鬼魅所为，但也不能得罪它们，而是要讨好、禳解。例如，有一种毒药鬼，被认为是人们致病的根源。被毒药鬼附身的人，老年女子称鬼婆，少年女子则称鬼婆娘，如是男子则称鬼男子。如遇到这种情况，就要求助于释比作法，驱鬼禳解。

羌族所信仰的本民族诸神，皆无庙宇，一般以用石头砌一小石塔，上面竖一块白石为象征。羌族信仰的神灵无一不与其生产、生活等息息相关。

### （二）祭山搜山为恩佑

对于那些保佑人们的善神（或谓正神），羌族人奉敬甚诚。以祭天神为最经常而以祭山神为最隆重。羌族人民世代生活在高山峡谷之间，岷山支系的九顶山、鹧鸪山便横贯羌族分布的地区。山和羌族人民的生活息息相关，人们从山上得到诸如粮食、木材、药材、

imitating the appearance of a sheep or goat. To this day, when Qiang people attend sacrificial mountain ceremonies, they ask the Shibi to tie a piece of wool on them to show that they are one in spirit with the sheep.

At funerals the Qiang use a sheep as a substitute for the deceased and the sheep is also believed to lead the way for the dead person's soul. At various ceremonies a sheep is killed, its blood is sprinkled and its meat cannot be eaten but is either burned or thrown out in the open countryside. These are possible customs that show vestiges of totemism. The ancient Qiang used to depend on animal husbandry for their livelihood and since sheep were more closely connected to the Qiang people than other domesticated animals, it is possible that they saw sheep as having a certain kindred relationship with them. It was a natural step from this to worshipping and protecting sheep and esteeming them as their totem.

Qiang people also believe in ghosts, believing that the soul lives on after death and becomes a ghost. Not all ghosts are harmful but the ghosts of those who are murdered or die young may bring evil on others. According to the Qiang, disasters and diseases are the doings of ghosts and demons who should never be offended. Instead, people should appease them and pray for misfortune to be averted. For example, a ghost named the "poisonous ghost" is regarded as the source of all diseases. Any old woman to whom the "poisonous ghost" is attached is called a ghost woman, and similarly any maiden is a ghost girl and any man a ghost man. Under such circumstances people seek the help of the Shibi who uses his magic rites to expel the evil spirit and avert misfortune.

There are no temples for the gods of the Qiang. The Qiang generally just build small stone towers and put a white stone on the top to symbolize the gods.

## 2. Sacrificial Mountain Worship and Seeking Blessings:

Qiang people devoutly respect and revere the righteous gods who protect them. Sacrificing to the god of heaven is the most common whereas sacrificing to the mountain god is the most ceremonious. For generations, Qiang people have lived among deep valleys and high mountains, including Mount Jiuding and Mount Zhegu of the Min Mountain range, which traverse the Qiang area. The lives of the Qiang are closely connected to these mountains, which provide them with various necessities of life such as grain, timber, medicinal herbs, wild

野兽、牲畜等各种生活资料。但是在人们无法驾驭自然力、无法正确认识自然与人的关系，不能保证生活资料稳定供给时，对山的虚幻的观念和认识就使羌人确信有山神存在，并且每年都要举行祭山的仪式，以报答山神的恩佑。祭山在羌人的宗教活动中是最被重视的，流行的一句谚语"皇帝祭祀，百姓祭山"，就说明了这一点。

雨水对于以农业耕作为主要生产方式的羌族人来说如人体命脉一般重要。故每值久旱不雨，就要举行大型的搜山求雨活动。若仍无成效，则在巫师带领下去附近最高的"神山"顶上求取木刻，组织群众集体拜神，敬酒献牲，许愿，并唱祈雨歌。汶川一些地方在祈雨时，还要举行一种"赶旱魃"的模拟巫术。首先由一人装扮成鬼怪"旱魃"形状，藏匿于树丛中，然后巫师率领众人，敲锣、呼喊，遍山进行搜寻。此人被寻出时，必须在前面奔走，巫师则率众在后面追赶，直至其精疲力竭被捉为止。这象征着旱魃已被赶走，甘露即可降临。

## 二、神秘的白石崇拜

羌族的神灵系统中，除火神以锅庄为代表、释比以猴头为代表外，其余诸神都以白石作为象征，这就是有名的白石崇拜。信仰万物有灵的羌族，在每家平顶房屋最高层的石塔顶上，一般都供奉着一块或几块白色的石英石，作为天神或诸种神灵的象征。这构成了羌族文化中一个独具特色的文化现象。

这种具有羌族特色的神的象征物 —— 石英石，与羌族的历史有关。传说羌族的先民曾有过一次大流亡，其中有一支羌族的先民

animals, and livestock. Back in the times when people couldn't control the forces of nature, when there was no way of accurately understanding man's relationship with the natural world, and when there was no reliable supply of life's necessities, imaginative notions about the mountains gave the Qiang a firm belief in the existence of the mountain god. Sacrificial mountain ceremonies are regularly held every year in return for the blessings of the mountain god. It is the most important religious activity of the Qiang, as shown by the common saying that "the emperor offers his sacrifices to the imperial ancestors whereas the common people offer their sacrifices to the mountain."

The Qiang primarily depend on agriculture. For them, rainwater is their lifeblood, so in seasons of drought, ceremonies are held on a large scale to pray for rainfall. If these are of no effect, the Shibi leads the people to the top of the highest "sacred mountain" near their village to beg for a wood-carved god bless. He then leads the people in collective worship, offering their oblations, making vows and singing their prayers for rain. In some places in Wenchuan County, when people pray for rain, they practice a kind of simulative sorcery called "driving away the drought demon". First, one person disguises himself as the drought demon and hides in the grove of trees. Then the sorcerer leads the rest of the people, beating gongs, shouting loudly, and searching for the "drought demon" all over the mountain. When he is found, the "drought demon" must run ahead, with the sorcerer and others in hot pursuit, until he is exhausted and caught. This symbolizes that the drought demon has been dispelled and rain should be on its way.

## II. Mysterious White Stone Worship (Symbols of Various Gods)

As indicated by the expression "white stone worship" all gods in the Qiang system of deities are symbolized by the white stone, except for the god of fire, which is represented by the iron fire place, and the ancestral god of the Shibi, represented by the head of a monkey. Qiang people, who believe that everything has a spirit, put one or several white quartz stones on top of the stone tower on their roof as a symbol of the god of heaven or other gods, and make offerings to them. This practice is a distinctive cultural phenomenon of the Qiang.

This use of the white stone (quartzite) is related to the legendary war between the Qiang and the Ge in Qiang history. It is said that the ancestors of the Qiang were once forced to leave their native land. Later, one of the branches

在此定居后，遇到了强大的敌人戈基人。双方交战前，羌民的领袖于梦
中得到神的启示，神指导他们用坚硬的木棍和白石块与戈基人作战，并
在颈上悬羊毛线作为标志。羌民依梦而行，果然战胜了戈基人得以安居。
后来为了报答神恩，但又不知神的具体形象，于是羌人商议用白石作为
天神的象征，供奉于每家房屋顶上，朝夕膜拜。从此，供奉白石和祭天
就成了羌人的传统习俗。

这种崇拜已经有很久的历史了。羌族人民在举行任何重大仪式时，
都必讲这段光荣历史。在释比祭神还愿时，也必须诵读这段历史。在供
奉神灵的地方，无论山上、地里、树林还是庙里、屋顶、火灶等处都供
以白石。其中，以供奉在屋顶上的白石代表最高的天神。每一家羌民的
屋顶正中，都供奉有白石一块或几块。如有供五块白石的，则一是天神，
一是分昼夜的神，一是地神，一是本地土主神，一是猎神，这些都是诸
神中最受崇敬的。

羌族最初以白石作为天神的象征，不仅供奉在每家的屋顶上，而且
也供奉在每一村寨附近的"神林"里。神林是一片葱郁的山林保护区，
严禁任何人砍伐。屋顶的白石是家祭的地方，而神林则是全寨公祭的场
所。后来，羌人又以白石作为一切神灵甚至祖先的象征进行崇拜。其实，
白石崇拜有广泛的崇拜内容，并不仅限于对一种自然石的崇拜，羌族的
白石崇拜实际上是一种灵物崇拜。它之所以受到崇拜，是因为它身上附
有神灵，代表了它本身形体所不具备的某种神奇力量，是对神灵的崇拜。

原始宗教中，对于神的形象大都是凭梦寐中所见而造的某一
意象，或以某种特殊的物体形状而作，甚至没有具体形象可言的神
灵，如衣角、体垢、昆虫、落叶、动物和人造物都可以作为神的形象的
代表，这是原始宗教"万物有灵"的体现。羌族原崇拜抽象的人类祖先
神、男性主宰神和女性主宰神，这三种神应都是祖先崇拜的某种形式，

settled down in today's Qiang area where they were confronted with a formidable enemy - the Geji people. Before the war started, the leader of the Qiang had a dream. He was instructed in the dream by a god that they should use hard sticks and white stones as their weapons and should tie a piece of wool round their neck as a symbol. The Qiang people followed these instructions and, sure enough, they defeated the Geji and settled down in peace. Afterwards, the Qiang people wanted to repay the god's kindness to them. As the god did not have a concrete image, they decided to use a white stone to symbolize him. They placed the white stone on their roof and offered daily sacrifices to it. Hence, it has become a traditional custom for Qiang people to venerate these white stones and to offer sacrifices to the god of heaven.

This kind of worship has a long history and recounting this particular period of glorious Qiang history has become an integral part of any important ceremony of the Qiang. When the Shibi makes sacrificial offerings and vows to the gods, he is required to chant this history. White stones can be seen wherever the gods are worshipped: on the land, on mountains, on roofs and towers and in kitchens and groves. The white stone on a roof represents the greatest god - the god of heaven. If there are five stones on the roof, one stands for the god of heaven, one for the god that distinguishes day and night, one for the god of land, one for the local god and the last for the god of hunting. These five gods are most respected and revered.

Initially, the white stone only symbolized the god of heaven. It was placed not only on the roof of the family house but also in the "sacred grove" of every village. The roof of the home was used for family offerings whereas the sacred grove, which is a protected area of verdant mountain forest where any felling of trees is forbidden, was where public ceremonies for the whole village were held. Later, the white stone came to symbolize all the gods and even the ancestors of the Qiang.

In primitive religion, images of gods are often created on the basis of dreams or in connection with special objects. Even the edge of garments, dirt on the skin, insects, fallen leaves, animals and artificial objects can be taken as symbols of gods, embodying the animistic belief that everything has a spirit. The human ancestral gods and male and female ruling gods of original Qiang worship are all abstract forms of ancestral worship, symbolized by the white

亦均以白石为表征，供奉于每户的二层正屋之中。

羌族对石头的崇拜实际起源于石头的工具和武器作用。而石头崇拜与羌族人的尚白习俗相结合，也就产生了羌人独特的白石崇拜现象。羌族"白石在，火就在"的观念和白石生火的事实，又使羌族的白石崇拜深深打上了火崇拜的烙印。白石生火，白石中居住着火神，这也就是火神的象征。同时，白石生火——一种事物产生另一种事物的事实，隐含着"生"的观念。所以，石头生火与人类生育观念相沟通，使白石在羌人的心目中具有生殖功能和阐释族源的功能。最终，白石成为各种神灵的象征，从而被供到羌家屋顶的塔子上和村寨外的神林中。几千年来，白石一直是羌族精神世界中一块光焰不灭的宝石。

## 三、地位崇高的释比

羌族宗教信仰的核心为万物有灵。羌人相信事物的变化和运动是受制于其内的灵性，这种灵性的神秘力量对人有利害关系，能招致吉凶福祸。在羌人历史舞台上出现的释比，便以其"超人"本领扮演了巫术师与领袖的角色，其言行能感召神灵，从而影响社稷民生。

### （一）释比法事

羌族的宗教中，与鬼神发生联系的是释比，羌语还有"许"、"诗谷"、"比"等叫法，为不同方言土语的音译变体。他是不脱离生产的宗教职业者。羌人认为释比是与羌人祖先一起从天上下凡的，在神道系统中法力很大，并能与神相通，还与恶魔打交道，所以，在羌族社会生活中占有重要的地位。在很长的时间内，他是羌民中最权威的文化人和知识集大成者，在人们的心目中享有崇高的地位和威信。他熟记本民族的历史

stone which is also venerated in the main room on the second floor of every family house.

The Qiang's conception that "where there is white stone, there is fire" and the fact that white stone can produce fire adds to it another profound significance: the worship of fire. The god of fire dwells within the stone, and the fire produced is a symbol of the god. One thing producing another also implies birth or reproduction, hence the Qiang belief in the white stone's reproductive function, which in their opinion can explain the origin of the Qiang.

As seen above, Qiang stone worship is connected to the stone's use as both a weapon and a tool. This, combined with the Qiang esteem for white, has developed into the unique phenomenon of white stone worship. It is essentially a kind of spirit worship. The reason why Qiang people worship the white stone is because gods and their supernatural power are thought to be attached to it. For thousands of years, the white stone has been the most important treasure in the spiritual world of the Qiang.

## III. The Shibi and his High Social Position

The core of Qiang religious beliefs is animism. Qiang people believe that everything is controlled in its changes and movements by the spirit within and the mysterious power of these spirits can bring either good fortune or disaster on people. The Shibi, with his "supernatural" abilities, plays the role of both shaman and leader in Qiang history. Since the Shibi can summon and influence the spirits, he is an influential figure in local society and in people's lives.

### 1. The Religious Ceremonies of the Shibi

In Qiang religious activities, the Shibi is the one who makes contact with both gods and ghosts. In the Qiang language, he is also called "Xu", "Shigu" and "Bi", which are transliterated variants of local dialects. Although the Shibi has a religious role, he also works like the rest of the villagers. The Qiang believe that, just like their ancestors, the Shibi originally came from heaven to earth, and with his great power in the spiritual realm and his ability to communicate with the gods and demons he is a very important figure in Qiang society. For a long time, he has been the most authoritative and knowledgeable intellectual and has enjoyed a high position and great prestige. The Shibi learns by heart the history

传说，能背诵各种神话故事等。他会念各种不成文的经咒，有一套"能显神通"的法器。因而，人们相信他有控制自然的本领，会呼风唤雨，繁殖牲畜与百谷，甚至人们"命运"的亨蹇，他亦有转移的能力。他又是医生，"能治"百病。这样，在自然力、社会力等的压迫之下，人们把自己的希望寄托在释比身上，想通过他求得神灵的保佑。所以，生产生活中的一切敬神、还愿、驱鬼、除秽、治病、送魂等活动以及婚姻丧事都由释比主持操办。因此，释比是羌人中的"祭司"、"魔术法师"和"医生"的综合人物。其报酬主要是玉米、小麦、猪肉、羊肉和鸡，还有钱。

释比在羌民中影响广泛，是羌民的精神领袖，而释比的法事活动则是其存在价值得以体现的主要方式。释比的法事活动，目前众多专家学者比较一致的看法是按对象分的三分法，即上（神事）、中（人事）、下（鬼事）三大类法事活动。从法事活动的广度方面和性质结合考虑，将其分为占卜测算、礼仪司祭、招魂迎财、驱邪送鬼四大类。

### 1. 占卜测算

在羌族的传统信仰民俗中，占卜是一种十分常见的巫术活动。占卜测算是其他法事活动的组成和前奏，也是一项独立的法事活动。在我国古代的甲骨文中就已有关于羌人占卜的历史记载。

羌族的占卜在种类上较为复杂，主要有：

（1）羊髀骨卜。是羌族古老的占卜法。所用的必须是羊髀骨，且须取自用以祭祀的羊身上。一般在羊宰祭后未烧煮前取骨。问卜者手持青稞向释比说明请求，然后由释比一面念经，一面取艾叶捻成小团，放在羊髀骨上烧灼，待炙出花纹后，释比根据纹路的长短、走向来判断吉凶祸福，以及应采取的对策。

of the Qiang and their legends and can recite all kinds of fairy tales, oral scriptures and incantations. He also has a set of ritual instruments which have magical powers. Consequently, people think that he has the ability to control the forces of nature, cause animals and crops to prosper, influence people's destiny and even to transform badness into goodness.

The Shibi is also a doctor who can "cure" all diseases. Under pressure from both natural and social forces, the Qiang people place their hope in the Shibi, wanting through him to obtain the blessings of the gods. Events such as worship of the gods, fulfilling of vows, driving away ghost spirits, purification, healing sickness, escorting the souls of the dead, as well as weddings and funerals, are all taken care of by the Shibi. He is, therefore, a combination of priest, sorcerer and doctor. As a reward for his services the Shibi is mainly given maize, wheat, pork, mutton, chicken, and also money.

The Shibi has extensive influence in Qiang society and is the people's spiritual leader. The religious ceremonies he carries out are the place where his value is most evident. According to the research of most scholars, there are three levels of ceremonies presided over by Shibi and they are classified as follows: upper (concerning gods), middle (concerning human affairs) and lower (concerning ghosts). They can also be divided into four different types of ceremony according to the nature of their purpose: divination, sacrificial rites, evoking the spirits to bring prosperity, and dispelling evil.

Divination is a common element in traditional Qiang belief and customs. It may be carried out as a prelude to or as part of other religious ceremonies or on its own. Ancient inscriptions on bones or tortoise shells record Qiang use of divination. Its diverse forms are listed below.

(1) Divination using the thighbone of a sheep. This is an ancient divination method of the Qiang. The thighbone from a sacrificial sheep must be used. The bones are usually removed from the sheep after it has been slaughtered but before it is burnt as a sacrifice. The person who wants a prediction holds some highland barley in his hand and explains his requests to the Shibi. Then, while chanting scriptures, the Shibi takes some leaves of the Chinese mugwort and moulds them into a small ball which is placed on the sheep's thighbone and burnt. When a pattern has emerged on the bone as a result of the leaves burning, the Shibi divines good or bad fortune according to the length of the lines and assesses what measures should be taken in response. This method is often used

此多用以卜运气、病因、行人的祸福。

（2）青稞卜。又称"麦卦"，为汶川县等地羌族释比所常用，主要是占卜诸神的意愿和全寨乡民未来的吉凶。

（3）柏木卜。为常用的占卜术，功能是：① 卜算神路，了解神灵旨意；② 卜算释比师路，便于在弄清师路的基础上跳神；③ 卜算释比的猴头神是否保佑释比做法事。

（4）吊白狗卜。用白狗占卜，测算当年能否丰收。如茂县土门一带的羌族，将一活着的狗吊起来，如果白狗七天七夜不死，则认为是丰收之年；不然，就认为是灾年。

羌族的占卜多种多样，还有羊扇骨卜、羊毛线卜、立水柱子、鸡嘴卦、鸡蛋卜、手卜、水卜等，难以尽数。

流传于羌族民间的占卜，有以下几个特点：① 问卜频繁，事事行占；② 卜法不同，用途各异；③ 这种古老的传统占卜与羊的关系密切。占卜的长期流存还与其自身的巫教功能有关，是人们某些行为的依据和指南，同时还具有一定的心理影响功能。

### 2. 礼仪司祭

礼仪司祭则包括：① 成年冠礼；② 婚嫁；③ 丧葬；④ 许愿还愿，如家庭平安愿、病人求愈愿等。

### 3. 驱邪送鬼

驱邪送鬼是指请释比把患者身上和家中的灾厄病痛、邪魔鬼怪清除出去或使之脱身，大体上分为形形色色的治病巫术魔法和一命填一命的救命替代法事。

### 4. 招魂迎财

招魂迎财的特点主要是希望把善的招回来，或招回某物使某事致善，如招地财、招牛财、招魂等。

to predict luck and to divine the cause of disease and the fortune or misfortune of people who are away from home.

(2) Divination with highland barley, also called "wheat divination". This is mainly popular in Wenchuan County. This kind of divination is used to predict the will of the gods and the future good or ill luck of the whole village.

(3) Divination using cypress branches. This is frequently used and has three functions: to divine the ways of the gods and understand their will; to divine the ways of the Shibi's first ancestor and get a clear understanding of how the Shibi's sacred dance should be performed; to see whether the Shibi's activities are blessed by the god of the monkey head.

(4) Divination by hanging a white dog. This method is used to predict whether or not there will be a good harvest. For example, Qiang people in the Tumen area of Mao County hang a live dog for seven days. If the dog is still alive, they believe they'll have a good harvest but if it has died they believe they will have a bad year.

The Qiang have numerous other divination methods, such as divination using sheep ribs, sheep wool, using sticks and a bowl of water, chicken beaks, eggs, people's hands, water divination and various others. General features of divination among the Qiang people include the following: ① it is a frequent practice related to almost every aspect of daily life; ② different methods of divination have different purposes; ③ traditional Qiang divination relates closely to the sheep. The continued existence of divination is connected to its instructive function, guiding people's behavior and, to some extent, also influencing them psychologically.

Sacrificial rites conducted by the Shibi include manhood ceremonies, marriage ceremonies, funeral ceremonies, and making and redeeming vows to the gods to pray for the safety of the family and recovery of patients.

Exorcising evil refers to a practice whereby the Shibi is asked to dispel diseases, misfortunes and evil powers from people or their houses. In general, the practice takes two forms: one is to use various magic arts to cure sickness; the other is a ceremony where the life of an animal is used as a substitution to save the life of a person.

Evoking the spirits is a practice aimed at bringing in wealth and general prosperity to the family. It includes practices by the Shibi to evoke the good spirits, the god of the land, and the ox king.

（二）释比的传承方式

释比由师徒制产生，无经文，一切咒语均由释比口传。收徒人数不限。传授时，多在晚上举行，既是劳作闲暇之时，又可增加其神秘色彩。学习通常需 3 至 5 年，能背诵与应用一切经咒并熟悉一切仪式后，即可举行"谢师礼"而正式"毕业"了。届时，徒弟要宴请师傅，邀请本寨及邻村释比出席谢师仪式——盖卦，并赠师傅鞋袜衣服等物作酬报，而师傅也赠徒弟法器一套，让其独立应约行术。

释比的法器，包括一切法事活动中所用之物，是释比演示仪式从而与神鬼发生关系的法宝。释比视其为圣物，无故不可乱动，忌他人触摸。

释比在法事活动中大多是下着白裙，上穿羊皮背心。有的释比还披豹皮，头戴猴皮帽。释比使用的法器主要是羊皮鼓，直径约 45 厘米，在诵经时用。据说最早的释比是在神猴引导下学得法术取到经书的，当时的经文写在白桦皮上。释比取经归来时，疲倦入睡，经书被一白羊食尽，从此羌族人就没有经书，也没有文字。此时又有一金丝猴告诉释比，若将白羊杀死，独自将其肉吃下，并以皮作鼓，每敲一下，便能忆起经书的一句话。从此，释比在诵经时必须敲羊皮鼓。

释比所用法器还有木制神杖，上刻有鬼王头，下包铁皮，专用于做

## 2. How The Role of Shibi Is Passed On

The Shibi is selected by a system of master and apprentice. Since there are no written texts, the entire tradition is taught by oral instruction. There is no limit to the number of apprentices under one Shibi. Instruction is generally in the evening, which adds to the air of mystery and is also when people have finished work. The learning process usually lasts for three to five years. When the apprentice can memorize and apply religious scriptures correctly and has become familiar with all rituals, he holds a ceremony called a "gaigua" to thank his master and to formally announce his graduation. During the ritual, the apprentice entertains his master at a banquet and presents footwear and clothes as gifts to him. In return, the master gives his apprentice a set of ritual instruments, signifying that the apprentice is qualified to perform sorcery independently. Other Shibi in the village and from other villages are also invited to attend this ceremony.

The instruments of the Shibi, including all the tools used in every ceremony, are the religious materials by which the Shibi contacts ghosts and gods. They are regarded by the Shibi as sacred, only to be used in the correct way and not to be handled by others.

During rituals the Shibi generally wears a sheepskin waistcoat and white skirt. Some Shibi wear a monkey-skin hat and a leopard-skin over their shoulders. The major instrument used by Shibi when he chants scriptures is a sheepskin drum about 45cm in diameter. It is said that the earliest Shibi mastered magic and acquired religious scriptures under the direction of a divine monkey. At that time the scriptures were written on white birch bark. As the Shibi was bringing the scriptures back to his people, he grew weary and fell asleep. While he slept, the scriptures were eaten by a white sheep and since then the Qiang have had no written language or scriptures. However, just then another golden monkey came and told the Shibi that if he killed the sheep, ate its meat and made a drum out of its skin, then with every beat of the drum, he would remember a piece of scripture. It is for this reason that the Shibi must beat a drum when chanting scriptures.

There are also other instruments. A sacred wooden stick, with a ghost king head carved at the top and a covering of iron sheeting on the lower part, is used

驱鬼法事；师刀，长尺余，亦用以驱鬼；铜铸法铃，诵经念咒时使用；骨质白色念珠，作法时挂在颈上；金丝猴头，释比作法时供奉的神物。另外还有皮口袋等。各种法器上都系着一些兽毛、羊角、铜铁片等物，在撞击时能发出声音，配合诵经念咒，造成神秘的气氛。

### （三）释比经典

羌族释比在各种宗教仪式上做法事的时候都要吟唱经典。这些经典不仅是羌族人民世世代代集体智慧的结晶，更是羌族悠久的历史文化遗产的传播载体。在历史上，羌族并没有形成独立的哲学、文学、艺术、宗教等，而只是浑然一体的社会意识，释比经典便是这种社会意识的总结。所以，它具有较强的概括社会生活的能力，塑造了一系列鲜明的人物形象，在结构安排上显示出了较高的艺术水平，具有较高的文学和艺术性。释比经典可归类为上中下坛三个部分，因法事性质不同，演唱的经典也不同。一般说来，上坛是神事，包括序经和正经。中坛为人事，下坛是鬼事。神话传说和释比经典是羌族主要的"史志"资料，释比经典不仅反映出丰富的社会内容和历史内容，也为历史学、民族学的研究提供了重要材料，堪称一部生动的百科全书。

释比经典是靠口耳相传、口传心授的方法而代代相承的。释比吟唱的经典往往叙说种种宗教仪式的进行过程和风俗习惯的来历、内容等，成为民俗信仰的重要载体，同时担负着解释风俗习惯的来历的任务。这些经典，内容丰富，形象鲜明，生活气息浓厚。在羌族释比的经典中，还非常明显地表现了一种阴阳相对的哲学思想，具体表现在将大自然中的一切都视为有性别的，雌雄结合、阴阳相配，产生万物。

in rituals to expel ghosts. The Shibi's knife, usually more than 30 cm long, is also used to drive away ghosts. A copper bell is used when chanting scriptures and incantations. When the Shibi performs his magic arts he wears a string of white prayer beads made of bone around his neck. The head of a golden monkey is venerated as a sacred article. A leather bag is also one of Shibi's instruments. Animals' hair, sheep's horns and pieces of iron and copper are tied to the various instruments, so that they make a noise when struck, accompanying the Shibi's chanting and helping to create a mysterious atmosphere.

### 3. The Oral Texts Of The Shibi:

The Shibi sings these oral texts when he performs his rituals in various religious ceremonies. They are not only the fruit of the collective wisdom of the Qiang but have also handed down the legacy of their long history and culture. Historically, philosophy, literature, art, and religion have been an integral part of Qiang social consciousness rather than developing as independent subjects and this social consciousness is summarized in the oral texts of the Shibi. This means they give a good outline of Qiang society, portraying a distinctive series of characters and images and displaying a high level of literary and artistic skill.

The texts of the Shibi can be divided into three parts. The first part, the upper altar, deals with matters of the gods. It contains a preface and the main text. The second part, called the middle altar, deals with human affairs. The last part, called the lower altar, deals with things relating to ghosts. The Shibi sings different parts of the oral texts according to the different nature of the ceremonies. This material is a vivid and encyclopedic representation of Qiang society and history and is an important contribution to historical and ethnographic research.

The Shibi's oral texts have been handed down from generation to generation. They often describe the procedure of various religious rites and the nature and origin of local customs. They play an important role both in passing on information about Qiang customs and beliefs and in explaining the origins of various Qiang traditions. All the oral texts are closely related to people's lives and are rich in content and distinctive in form. They also clearly display the philosophical idea of Yin and Yang opposites, attributing everything in the natural world with a male or female identity and creating a balanced Yin and Yang universe.

## 四、各种各样的禁忌

由于羌族的宗教观念中认为鬼神无处不在，主宰人们的凶吉福祸，因此，羌民在生活中为了避凶趋吉而形成各种禁忌。

### （一）禁忌的大致类别

（1）生活禁忌。① 居室内的禁忌。如禁止戴草帽打雨伞进屋，不得将脚朝向神龛，不准在神龛上挂衣服，不准在屋内吐痰、杀生，不能在屋内随意打洞等。每年农历正月下旬，要请释比做法事，禳解上一年所犯禁忌的罪过。② 婚姻禁忌。如羌族有的地方有同姓乃至同村寨不婚之禁忌，新娘在被背出娘家大门后，禁止回头看等。③ 生育禁忌。如生小孩后，最忌生人进屋，有的要在门上挂红色旗子以示禁止生人入内。小孩平时挂铜镜，帽上钉海螺壳，禁生人触动。产妇在小孩满月之前，不准外出，不得进入灶房。如果家畜中羊、牛等下犊后于门槛束一捆木棒，数目与所生牲畜数同，表示禁忌生人进入，认为生人入内会踩断母畜奶汁。④ 丧葬禁忌。如在丧葬中，给死者穿上六件衣服，在嘴内放金子、银子、猪肉、菜叶等，衣袋中还放释比开的"路票"，让灵魂能安然到达阴间世界。凡凶死者举行火葬，火化日期与时辰不能与家中任何人的生日及时辰相同，如相同则此人应到高处躲避起来，认为在死者之上就可以转凶为吉。凡老人死，家人一定为他宰羊一只，为其魂引路，并在羊的内腔中找出怀疑受伤的地方，以决定老人病伤的所在。然后请别人吃此羊的肉，家属都不能吃。

## IV. Various Historical Taboos

In Qiang religious beliefs, ghosts and gods exist everywhere and can dominate human fate. To avoid misfortune and encourage good luck, the Qiang have established various taboos which can be divided roughly into the following kinds:

### 1) Taboos of Life

(1) Indoor taboos. The following are forbidden in the house: wearing a straw-hat; holding an umbrella; putting one's feet towards or hanging clothes on the household shrine; spitting; killing living things. During the last ten days of the first lunar month, the Shibi is invited to perform rituals praying for the gods to forgive people's sins in breaking these taboos over the past year.

(2) Marriage taboos. Men and women who have the same family name or come from the same village are not allowed to marry. When the bride leaves the door of her family home, she must not look back.

(3) Birth taboos. When a baby is born, strangers must not enter the room. Some families hang a red flag at the door to warn strangers not to enter. A copper mirror is usually hung around the baby's neck and the baby wears a hat decorated with spiral seashells. Strangers mustn't touch the baby. After a woman has given birth to a baby, she is not allowed to enter the kitchen or go outside until the baby is one month old. The presence of strangers is also unwelcome when domestic animals such as sheep and cattle give birth. The Qiang think that the presence of a stranger will cause the animals to stop milking, so they tie a bundle of sticks corresponding to the number of new-born animals at the threshold to show that strangers shouldn't approach.

(4) Funeral taboos. For funerals, people dress the dead in six items of clothing and put gold, silver, pork and vegetables in their mouths. They also put a "travel ticket" issued by the Shibi in the dead person's pocket so that the soul can arrive safely in the afterworld. People who die a violent death are cremated and the chosen date must not be on the birthday of any family member. If by chance the date of cremation is on a family member's birthday, that person should hide in a high place, thereby turning bad luck into good. When an old person dies, his family will slaughter a goat to lead the way for the soul of the dead. The family then dissects the goat to discover why the person has died. People outside the bereaved family are invited to eat the meat of the goat. If a

如死者是坠崖而死，家里人一定要为他请释比来招魂，并将一只羊从死者坠崖处丢下崖，作为"替死魂"。如果这只羊未死，并跑回家来，则认为大不吉利，还会有第二人在这里摔死。家有病故的人，则要在其下葬五天后，才能与外人来往。⑤ 年节禁忌。如每逢羌历年，羌族全寨都要停止生产劳动。此外，还有其他一些生活禁忌，如在吃饭时、出行时、生病时的禁忌等。

（2）生产禁忌。例如：惊蛰和逢戊日不得下田耕耘，因戊属土，耕耘会犯土不利。忌砍伐神林用以修房。打猎时，忌用黄叶盖头，等等。

（3）祭祀禁忌。例如：凡请释比为病人驱鬼，外人不得入内。每年 3 月 12 日，羌寨里要宰一只羊供神，以祈求土地菩萨保佑丰收。并且忌路一天，禁止过往行人进寨。这天称为"青苗会"。

（4）释比在履行与鬼神打交道的职责时所要遵守的禁忌。例如：在举行大型祭祀活动中，要提前一个月忌吃葱、蒜之类的食物。做法事前，必须要洗手、沐浴。法器忌他人触摸。在祭祀正神时，忌使用法杖等。

### （二）禁忌的口传依据

羌族民间禁忌的产生与传承，是与一定的口传依据连在一起的。根据禁忌的口传依据特点，可以将其分为两个类别：① 抽象的简洁言辞，是指用来解释和说明某一禁忌的口传依据在表达上显得较为抽象简洁，大多只是对禁忌的原因作大致的勾勒，使人感觉到其危险所在，而不做进一步的细说。② 形象的民间文学，

person falls down a cliff and dies, the Shibi is invited to call back his soul and to throw a goat down the cliff from the same spot as a substitute soul or scapegoat. If the goat survives and runs home, it is considered to be an ominous indication that a second person will fall down the same cliff and die. If a person dies of illness, his family must not have contact with others until five days after the funeral.

(5) Festival taboos. Everyone in the village must stop work during the Qiang New Year Festival. There are also certain taboos which must be observed when eating, traveling or during illness.

### 2) Production Taboos

No agricultural work is done on Waking Insects Day (the third solar term, usually early in the third lunar month) or on the Wu days (the fifth of ten Heavenly Stems which combine with the twelve Earthly Branches to designate years, months, days and hours in traditional Chinese astronomy). Since the "Wu" heavenly stem is related to the earth, it is seen as unlucky to work on the soil these days. Also, tree felling for house building is forbidden in the sacred grove and hunters must not use yellow leaves to cover their heads when hunting.

### 3) Sacrificial Taboos

When the Shibi is invited to exorcise ghosts from a sick person, outsiders are not allowed to enter the room. On March 12th a goat is slaughtered in the village and the people ask the god of the land to bless their crops. All roads and paths are closed and no one is allowed to enter the village. This day is called "Green Seedling Festival".

### 4) Taboos Observed By The Shibi When Communicating With The Spirit World

One month prior to any large-scale sacrificial ceremonies he must not eat things like garlic and onion. Before the Shibi performs his rituals he must have a bath and wash his hands. No one else may touch his ritual instruments. Also when offering sacrifices to the highest god, he should not use the sacred rod.

Qiang folk taboos are produced and transmitted orally in two different ways: firstly by means of simple, abstract expressions, explaining and illustrating the reasons for the taboo and the dangers of breaking it, without going into much detail; and secondly, explaining the taboos through folk literature,

是指用来解释和说明某一禁忌的口传依据是一则民间故事、传说，或是羌族某一宗教经典中的片断。

### （三）禁忌的特点

羌族的民间禁忌作为一种特殊的文化现象，具有以下几个特点：① 与信仰有关的禁忌较多。从禁忌中反映出来的思想特质看，羌族的民间禁忌主要源于宗教思想的影响和对生活经验的总结。② 原始宗教的色彩较为浓厚，主要表现为与自然崇拜有关的禁忌多，原始多神信仰的特质明显。③ 与象征意义有关的禁忌事项较多。作为一种特殊的民俗古规，禁忌在社会生活中具有影响和约束人们行为的作用，可以维护社会秩序。而在民俗生活中，禁忌的宗教功能主要表现在信仰可以通过一定的禁忌行为来表达他们对于神明的虔诚与敬畏。

道教是羌族宗教信仰的一个重要组成部分。尽管佛教、藏传佛教以及西方的天主教、基督教等都在羌族地区流传，但是始终没有影响羌民对本民族宗教的信仰。

羌族几千年的文明，蕴含着具有羌族特色的宗教信仰，这使其成为中华民族文化百花园中的一枝奇葩。

（耿亚军　王康）

such as folk stories and legends, or through sections of the Shibi's oral texts.

Qiang taboos have various culturally distinctive characteristics. Firstly, many of them are influenced by religious beliefs and related thought patterns as well as general life experience. Secondly, they are closely related to primitive religion with many of relating to worship of nature and primitive polytheism. Thirdly, a great number of taboos have symbolic significance. As a kind of ancient folk law, social taboos serve to influence and restrain people's behavior, thus protecting social order, whilst religious taboos are mainly a means for the Qiang to express their devotion to and reverence for the gods

Daoism comprises another important part of Qiang religious beliefs. Although Buddhism, Tibetan Buddhism, and western Catholicism and Christianity have spread in Qiang areas, this has not influenced Qiang adherence to their own religious beliefs.

(Translated by Dai Zhiyong, Chen Shuyu)

# 第六章　羌族音乐

　　羌族人民勤劳勇敢，能歌善舞。羌族传统音乐是羌族人民在漫长的历史发展进程中集体智慧的艺术结晶。古老质朴的羌族音乐不仅是羌族人民的重要文化遗产，也是中华民族艺术史上的优秀篇章。羌族音乐可归纳到民间音乐类别之中。

## 一、羌族民歌

　　由于没有本民族的文字，羌族民歌靠世代口授心承而延续下来。加之羌语的地方方言较多，部分民歌有的已经没有人能够完全懂得其意义。现今流传下来的民歌主要是演唱本民族的历史和礼仪的，且保留着原始古朴的风貌。千百年来，羌族的民歌经过无数歌手、释比的加工创造，其曲调越来越完善丰富。

### （一）劳动歌

　　劳动歌曲是生产劳动过程中用歌声激发和鼓舞劳动者的生产热情，起指挥生产、协调动作、振奋精神作用的民歌。羌民在一起打场脱粒、抬石、扛木时常有这类歌曲伴随，男女轮番齐唱，气氛热烈，如茂县黑虎乡的《啊，拉山觉》。

啊，拉山觉（行板略快　有力地）

（齐唱）啊　啊拉山觉，啊米收基　牧 勒（哦），山觉呃，拉一呃（索　呃）。

歌词译意：一起来呀，一起干！

# CHAPTER SIX    MUSIC OF THE QIANG

The Qiang are excellent singers and dancers. As a form of historical, collective wisdom, the traditional music of the Qiang has become one of their most important cultural heritages and, furthermore, a fine chapter in the history of Chinese art. Generally speaking, the music of the Qiang can be placed in the category of folk music.

## Ⅰ. Folk Songs of the Qiang

Because the Qiang language has no written form, the folk songs of the Qiang have depended for their survival on oral transmission from generation to generation. However, due to the diverse local dialects, some of the songs have become very hard to understand. The songs surviving today are mainly about Qiang national history and cultural practices and have preserved the simplicity of their original style. Under the influence of numerous Qiang singers and Shibi over hundreds of years, the melodies of these folk songs have been greatly enriched and improved.

### 1. Work Songs

Work songs are sung to direct the work and bring harmony as people labor together, inspiring the workers and giving them fresh enthusiasm. The work done by the Qiang, such as threshing grain, shifting stones and carrying wood, is often accompanied by these kinds of songs, sung in unison by the men and women in turn, creating a lively atmosphere. "Ah, La Shan Jue" from Heihu Village, Mao County is a typical song of this kind.

**Ah, La Shan Jue ( tempo: brisk, powerful )**

（齐唱）啊　啊拉山觉，啊米收基　牧　勒（哦），　山觉呃，　拉一呃（索　　呃）。

Main idea of the song: Come on, let's work together!

在收割青稞、小麦及除草劳动时，他们又以舒缓的节奏唱另一种劳动歌，如《约约》。

**约约（行板　强弱拍分明）**

以上劳动歌曲通俗上口、易学易记，类似汉族地区的劳动号子。不同之处只是旋律音调的呼号特征不如劳动号子那么明显，主要演唱形式是对唱或齐唱，而不是一领众和。

从其反映的生活内容、音乐结构形式和表现风格等方面看，这类民歌似是羌民族由游牧转向农耕初期的产物。劳动歌词由"咳、嘞、哟、嗬、咿、哦"等衬词构成。它至今仍保持着旋律简洁、节奏鲜明、结构短小、集体性强和紧密伴随生产劳动而生存与发展等特点。

（二）山歌

"汉民唱歌，爱唱盘古开天地；藏民唱歌，爱唱纳里西其；羌民唱歌，爱唱纳吉纳娜。"（羌族民歌手语）"纳吉纳娜"，羌族北部方言，意为

When Qiang farmers are harvesting the highland barley or wheat, or weeding the land, they prefer to sing songs in a moderately slow tempo, such as the song "Yue Yue".

**Yue Yue（tempo: with distinct downbeat and upbeat）**

The lyrics of the song contain no exact meaning but the rhythm is intended to re-energize the workers and increase enjoyment and enthusiasm.

The work songs mentioned above are popular and easy to learn and memorize. They are similar to working songs in Han culture, the exception being that the tone and melody of the "call to work" are not as clear as in the Han songs, and they are mainly sung in unison or antiphonally, rather than with one person leading.

A look at the content of the lyrics and the structural form and style of the music, quickly reveals that these folk songs are the result of early changes in Qiang lifestyle from nomadism to farming. The lyrics of the work songs are composed with interjections such as "hai", "le", "yo", "he", "yi", and "oh" etc. Until today these work songs of the Qiang have preserved their distinctive features: simple melodies, distinct rhythms, brevity of structure, and a close relationship with collective labor.

## 2. Mountain Songs

"When the Han people sing, they love to sing about Pan Gu's creation of the universe (Chinese mythology); when Tibetans sing, they love to sing about Na Li Xi Qi; when the Qiang sing, they love to sing about Na Ji Na Na." "Na Ji Na Na" is an expression in northern Qiang meaning "the song of our

"我们祖先的歌"。这类歌曲多依据特定的自然环境借物抒情，表达对美好生活的向往和追求。当羌民在放牧或农耕时，常以"纳吉纳娜，纳玛尤西，尤西惹纳，惹拉扎沙"四句四言体固定格式的歌起兴，并随之引出一系列内容丰富的歌词。此四句词有深刻的内涵，其译意为"纳吉纳娜的歌，我们不能不唱啊！唱起它吧，不要忘了自己的祖先"。因此，《纳吉纳娜》被当成山歌这一民间歌曲体裁的代名词。它是羌民族在长期社会生活中以统一语言、统一地域、统一经济生活和表现在统一文化上的统一心理气质而产生的，并作为一个乐种将羌民族的传统音乐文化延续至今。歌声中表达的思想感情古朴深沉，演唱表情自然舒畅，具有强烈的民族自尊意识。

### 纳 吉 纳 娜（慢板 追忆地）

纳　吉里纳呀娜（呃），　　　　　纳　　玛那尤　西，
哦　布尔拉索　罗，　　　　　　　哦　切纳拉索　波，

拉尤　西拉惹　（罗　　　呀拉），
拉罗　扎拉哦　（扎　　　呀拉），

惹　拉里扎　呀沙（呃），
惹　玛那拉塔　尕　哦。

### （三）叙事歌

羌族叙事歌是在羌民烧火做饭的火塘旁或一定集体活动中配合演唱的民歌。表演时，众人席地围坐成圈，圈内置当地人喜欢的"咂酒"，边饮酒，边由年长的人演唱，用以教化后代。歌唱内容常为讲述本民族英雄名人生平事迹、追忆历史、颂扬祖辈的功德、赞美山川景物等。演唱形式以齐唱为主。

forefathers". This kind of song is often set in a particular natural environment, using metaphor to express feelings, conveying a longing for and pursuit of a happy life. When the Qiang are grazing livestock or farming, they often start singing "Na Ji Na Na, Na Ma You Xi, You Xi Re Na, Re Na Zha Sha", a fixed four-word-a-line quatrain which can precede a whole series of richly creative lyrics. These four lines are rich in connotation. They can be translated as "The song of our forefathers, the song we must always sing! Sing it aloud, and never forget our forefathers." Consequently, "Na Ji Na Na" has become synonymous with the mountain song genre in Qiang folk music. The music stems from the mentality and common culture of the Qiang, a product of shared language, locality, economy, and lifestyle, and has become a special music genre carrying forward the traditions of the Qiang. The thoughts and feelings expressed in the singing of these songs are simple yet profound, with the singers conveying a natural, carefree spirit and a strong sense of ethnic self-esteem.

**Na Ji Na Na (slow, retrospective)**

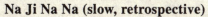

## 3. Ballads

Qiang ballads are usually sung at the fireplace where dinner is cooked or at particular group activities. When they are sung, people often sit in a circle on the ground, with their favored sucking wine in the center, and as they drink the wine, one of the elders sings, using the songs to teach the younger ones about their culture. These ballads, sung in unison, recount glorious stories of Qiang heroes, evoking the past, eulogizing the deeds of their forefathers, and extolling the beauty of the mountains and rivers.

如《穿阿旺特》，是一首歌唱传说中的羌族部落英雄旺特的生平事迹的叙事歌。歌词共有数十段。据称，旺特出生于茂县三龙乡的麻黄寨。他在清朝统治初期领导羌民反抗当地土司和封建王朝的欺压盘剥，提出废除世袭的土司制，实行改土归流。可是，斗争不幸被镇压，旺特壮烈就义。事后，他便作为羌族历史上的民族英雄被歌颂传唱。

### 穿阿旺特（慢板　追忆地）

纳　吉　纳娜　(哟　　哦)，　也日阿　姆　尤西　　(哟)，
日阿　冷　扎沙　(哟　　哦)，　也米　　出尔米色　　(哟)，

尤　　西日阿拉　(哟)　也)，　日阿　冷　扎沙　(哟)，
斯　　出尔惹色　(哟)　也)，　各　　古　回巴　(哟)，

(哟)　尤　西　(哟)　也　尤　　西　日阿拉 (哟)。
(哟)　尤　西　(哟)　也　尤　　西　日阿拉 (哟)。

歌词译意：这支歌哟忘不了，只有从头唱起来，许多往事，涌上心头。

叙事歌音乐节奏自由，速度徐缓，旋律音程多在一个八度内起伏上下，调式以商、徵居多，有时也出现徵—商调式的交替游移，一般一个乐句一气呵成而不再细分出乐节，通常使用混合节拍。这类歌曲大都集中在茂县沙坝区一带聚居的羌族中。

"Chuan Ah Wang Te", for example, is a ballad about the deeds done by Wang Te, a legendary hero of the Qiang tribes. The lyrics of the song are divided into many sections. It is said that Wang Te was born in a place called Mahuangzhai in Sanlong Village, Mao County. During the early Qing period, he led the Qiang people in resistance against the oppression and exploitation of the feudal system, under which they were ruled by local hereditary headmen, and proposed direct government rule instead. Unfortunately, the rebellion was suppressed and Wang Te was killed. Since then, the Qiang have remembered him as a hero, eulogizing him in song.

### Chuan Ah Wang Te (slow, retrospective)

纳　　吉　纳娜　（哟）　　哦），　也日阿　姆　尤西　　（哟），
日阿　冷　扎沙　（哟）　　哦），　也米　　出尔米色　　（哟），

尤　　西　日阿拉　（哟）　　也），　日阿　冷　　扎沙　（哟），
斯　　出尔惹　色　（哟）　　也），　各　　古　回巴　（哟），

（哟）　　尤　西　（哟）　也　　尤　　西　日阿拉（哟）。
（哟）　　尤　西　（哟）　也　　尤　　西　日阿拉（哟）。

Main idea of the song:

We cannot forget this song. We must sing it from the beginning and as we do, things of the past flood our minds and hearts.

Ballads are free in rhythm and slow in tempo, with the melody usually staying within one octave. The modes used are mainly Shang and Zhi (notes 2 and 5 in the Chinese pentatonic scale, equal to D and G in Western musical notation), and sometimes a combination of both. In general, the songs use mixed meters and each sentence flows freely without being divided into smaller parts. Most ballads are found among the Qiang who inhabit the Shaba area of Mao County.

147

（四）风俗歌

**1. 情歌**

反映羌族婚恋的歌曲，没有约定俗成的专用称谓。过去，羌族的婚姻是建立在包办基础上的，男女青年没有恋爱自由。为求得婚姻自由，诅咒包办婚姻制度，青年们就用歌声来宣泄内心的苦闷，倾吐对意中人的眷恋之情。于是，出现了情歌。

羌族民间相传，羌族族源是由纳吉和纳娜男女二人创始，羌人都是他们的后裔。所以，羌族民歌总是以"纳吉纳娜"作为歌头。

另外，有神话中仙女与凡人相配成婚，以后形成羌族某一部族支系的爱情神话传说。在释比的唱诵经文中就有叙述木姐珠和斗安珠婚姻结合过程的故事。用"纳吉纳娜"的唱词反映羌族男婚女嫁的情歌，在岷江上游的羌族北部方言区广泛流传。

《纳吉纳娜》的歌词共有 10 段，内容反映纳吉纳娜的相恋之情。由于他们的婚姻爱情经历了痛苦的煎熬，因此歌曲情调悲戚伤感。现今仅有个别羌族老人还能较完整地演唱此歌。

**纳 吉 纳 娜（行板　倾诉的）**

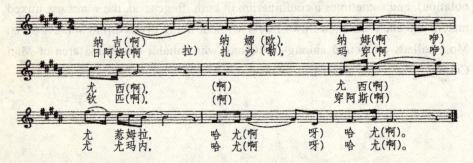

## 4. Songs About Customs

### 1) Love Songs

There is no set term for songs about love and marriage in Qiang culture. In the past, marriage was arranged by the parents and young people had no right to choose their loved ones. In their desire to choose their own partners and in their rejection of the arranged marriage system, young people would use songs to offload their sadness and pour out their feelings for their beloved. In this way, love songs came into being.

All such folk songs of the Qiang start singing with "Na Ji Na Na." This has to do with certain folktales, which record that the Qiang people are descendants of Na Ji and Na Na, the earliest ancestors of the Qiang.

Other folktales tell of the love story between an immortal maiden and a mortal man and this tale later became a romantic, mythical legend of certain Qiang sub-tribes. The classical texts sung from memory by the Shibi, for example, tell us how Mu Jie Zhu and Dou An Zhu fell in love with each other and got married. Singing "Na Ji Na Na" to imply the love between a man and a woman has become common practice in the northern Qiang area near the upper reaches of Min River.

The lyrics of the song "Na Ji Na Na" are divided into ten sections, describing the love between Na Ji and Na Na. Because they experienced pain and suffering in their relationship, the song generates a sad mood. Today only a few elderly Qiang people can sing this song in its entirety.

### Na Ji Na Na (slow, with feeling)

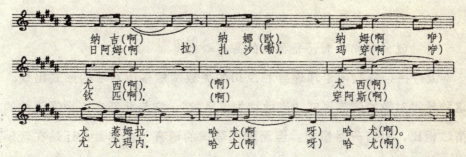

歌词译意：

　　唱起纳吉纳娜啊，想起他们哪，真伤心呀真伤心。

　　纳吉纳娜从头唱啊，唱起歌儿想起他们，真伤心呀真伤心。

　　有的羌族情歌，是在青年男女之间相互产生爱慕之情后，双方在山野或田间劳动时轻松愉快地吐露的各自的心声。如《尕斯支拉乌尔巴》，它反映了一对恋人由于爱情的滋润，生活再苦再累也情愿的欢愉心境。音乐旋律流畅，情意起伏张弛有致，呈现了欢快明朗的色彩。

### 尕 斯 支 拉 乌 尔 巴（中板）

歌词译意：

　　我唱起纳吉纳娜，青春年少，正是好时光。

　　我们都相爱啊，登再险的高山心也宽。

　　流行在杂谷脑河沿岸理县和汶川的羌族情歌多以对歌的形式出现。这种轮番对歌的演唱形式，当地称为"盘歌"。它与北部方言地区流传的情歌相比，别有一番情趣。但无论在歌词的语言、内容上，还是在音乐表现形式和风格上，羌族北部方言区流传的情歌才算得上地道的羌族传统歌曲。

Main idea of the song:

Singing Na Ji Na Na reminds me of their story, how sad it is!

From the moment I start singing Na Ji Na Na, I think of them, how sad it is!

Other love songs reveal the joyful emotions of the young men and women working in the mountains or fields after they have fallen in love with each other. "Ga Si Zhi La Wu Er Ba" is a typical song of this type in which two lovers, inspired by their love, live happily together in spite of all life's hardships. The melody is smooth and easy with a happy vitality, conveying affection amidst the ups and downs of life.

### Ga Si Zhi La Wu Er Ba (medium tempo)

Main idea of the song:

As I start to sing Na Ji Na Na, we are young, in the prime of youth.

Because we love each other, climbing rugged and dangerous mountains seems easy for us.

The love songs prevalent along the banks of the Zagunao River, in both Li County and Wenchuan County, are usually performed in an antiphonal style, which is called "Pan Ge" in local dialects. Compared with the love songs common in the northern part of the Qiang region, "Pan Ge" has a style of its own. However, in terms of lyrics and musical form and style the love songs of the northern Qiang area are the more typically representative of Qiang love songs.

## 2. 酒歌

"西忍木"是羌语北部方言,为"酒歌"之意,主要流传于茂县、黑水及松潘部分地区。

喝"咂酒"、唱酒歌是羌族习俗礼仪中不可缺少的音乐活动。羌族婚丧嫁娶、喜庆年节、修房造屋、请客迎宾,特别是宗教祭祀活动时,都要置数坛"咂酒"于神坛下或火塘边,先由年高德众的长者举行"开坛"仪式,敬请上界天神和下界诸神先行享用,而后人间凡民才可领受。这是一项庄重严肃的仪式规程。开坛词意为祈祷上天,祝福吉利,期盼神灵保佑。致词后,围坐火塘四周的人们按辈分大小依次轮番畅饮。酒过数巡,乘着酒兴,由一人引吭高歌,众人随节而合。

羌族素有"渴羌"之称,其豪饮放歌习俗,具有久远的历史。当今羌族酿酒,用青稞、小麦或玉米发酵后,封固于陶土坛器中,数日后即可饮用,醇香味美,称之"咂酒"。

"忍木拉·耸瓦"是羌语北部方言,意为"唱给客人的歌"。按羌族的习惯,亲朋贵客盈门,要先安排在"咂酒"坛边饮用"咂酒",由有身份的男女老年人面对客人演唱此歌,以示迎宾待客的礼节。表演时,男女分别呈半圆形列队,相互用小指扣着靠近身旁左右的歌者的腰带,用歌声表达对贵客尊重赞美之情。身体随歌声以悠缓节奏左右摆动,气氛隆重,仪态端庄。一段完,歌声暂停,男者肃立,女性则以十分优雅的体态双脚有力地踏击出一定的节奏,胯部往复转动,同时,速度加快,踏至客人前戛然而止,此时续唱劝酒歌。

### 2) Wine Songs

"Xi Ren Mu" means wine song in northern Qiang, and is a prevalent music form in Mao County, Heishui County and some parts of Songpan County.

Drinking sucking wine while singing wine songs is a central custom among the Qiang. At weddings, funerals, festivals, house building, feasts, and particularly in some religious activities, sealed jugs of wine are placed near the altar or fireplace. According to solemn ceremonial rules, an elder of great virtue and high prestige is invited to perform the ritual of "wine opening," respectfully inviting the gods of heaven and earth to enjoy the first taste before the ordinary people can partake. The Qiang believe that in this way they are blessed and protected by the gods and will have good fortune. After the elder delivers a speech, all the people sitting around the fireplace take turns to drink the wine, beginning with the most senior. In high spirits after several rounds of drinks, someone will launch into a song with the others following suit.

The Qiang are often called the "thirsty Qiang", and their custom of drinking to their utmost limit accompanied by enthusiastic singing has a long history. Today, the Qiang are well-known for their method of making alcohol, in which highland barley, wheat or maize is fermented and then sealed for days in earthen jugs before it is ready to serve. This flavorsome, special brew is called "sucking wine".

"Ren Mu La · Song Wa" means "the song dedicated to the guests" in northern Qiang. It is Qiang custom, when close friends or guests come to visit, for the guests to stand beside the wine jug and drink the sucking wine while the older male and female hosts stand facing them singing "Ren Mu La · Song Wa" to welcome them. During this performance, men and women line up in separate semicircles, each one holding the waistband of the person on either side of them with their little fingers. The ceremony expresses great respect for the guests. Amidst this ceremonious atmosphere, the singers sway from left to right in an elegant and dignified manner, following the leisurely rhythm of the music. When one section of the song is finished, men stand respectfully still, while the women gracefully stamp a particular rhythm with their feet, their hips moving back and forth, moving faster and faster until they stop abruptly in front of the guests, at which point everyone resumes singing the drinking song.

### 奎 拉 哦 忍

也拉罗　索梅罗　劳嘀
央，　嘀呀纳哈克呀嘞
噜　若，索奎拉哦嘀
哦嘀央，呃哈嘀罗鲁
呃，莫嗯索嘀莫索呃哦日阿纳。

歌词译意：歇息啦，喝口酒，舒心放量，牵起手来，唱歌又跳舞。

酒歌演唱以一领众和的形式为主，均由老人咏唱。歌中内容为颂扬先辈英雄、赞美山川景物、追忆民族迁徙历史及劝酒助兴。常依特定的起始词作即兴编创，以"咆"、"嗨"、"嘞"、"惹"四个单音节词起唱编词，它们的含义分别是："远客歇息"、"美酒为你洗尘"、"请舒心畅饮"、"感谢你光临"。这种真诚待客的情谊及歌唱语言，表现了羌民淳朴善良的优秀品质。

### （五）多声部民歌

羌族多声部民歌现保存并流传于岷江上游北部方言区的黑水县知木林和松潘县的小姓乡镇坪部分羌寨和茂县松坪沟、太平乡等地羌族居民中，它是羌族民间音乐宝库里近年发掘出来的艺术珍品。

知木林地区聚居着近千名着藏族服饰、说羌语的原始部族，他们自称为"阿尔麦"（"阿尔麦"即"羌人"之意，系羌语羌族称谓"尔玛"或

## Kui La Oh Ren

也 拉 罗 索 梅 罗 劳 嗬
央， 嗬 呀 纳 哈 克 呀 嘞
噜 若， 索 奎 拉 哦 嗬
哦 嗬 央， 呃 哈 嗬 罗 鲁
呃， 莫 嗯 索 嗬 莫 索 呃 哦 日 阿 纳。

Main idea of the song: Why not have a rest and drink some wine? Relax, take your fill; hand in hand let's sing and dance.

Wine songs are often sung with one person leading, usually an older person. The songs are mainly in praise of past heroes and of beautiful mountain and river scenery, recounting tales of their historical migrations, and urging people to drink and be merry. Although the lyrics are mostly improvised, wine songs usually start with singing four single-syllable words: "Pao", "Hai", "Le" and "Re", which respectively mean "have a rest, guests from afar", "we give you good wine of welcome", "please relax and drink your fill" and "thank you for coming". Such sincerity and friendliness truly reflects the kind, unsophisticated, and genuine qualities of the Qiang people.

## 5. Multivocal-part Songs

Qiang multivocal-part folk songs have been preserved and passed on in the northern dialect areas of the upper Min River in Hei Shui County's Zhimulin and Xiao Xing town in Songpan County, as well as in Mao County's Song Ping Gou and Tai Ping township. This valuable art form has only been discovered in recent years.

In the area of Zhimulin, there are nearly one thousand indigenous inhabitants who speak the Qiang language and wear Tibetan clothing and adornments. They call themselves "Ah Er Mai," which means "Qiang people" and is an alternative pronunciation for other Qiang autonyms "Erma" or

"日麦"的别音,故仍归属羌族)。这里的人们擅长演唱一种古老的二声部

民歌,这种二声部民歌常出现在劳动生活、结婚仪式和舞蹈的伴唱中,它

有独特的表现形式和演唱风格。如《果塔纳玛》,就是一支反映民族迁徙和

歌唱历史渊源的二声部民歌。

## 果 塔 纳 玛(男声二部重唱)

"Ri Mai," indicating that they are also Qiang. People in this area excel in performing an ancient folksong with two-part harmony that can be heard at weddings, as a dance accompaniment or accompanying daily work. It is a unique form of performance and singing style. The song "Guo Ta Na Ma", for instance, is a folk song duet about the migration of the Qiang people and their historical origin.

### Guo Ta Na Ma (duet of male voices)

歌词译意：

唱的迁徙歌啊，遥远的地方传来，打从"巴士古"地方走，一天又一天；

祖辈创造的歌，早有高低两种音，是阿泰最先唱。

当两个人一起唱类似上例民歌《果塔纳玛》时，民间歌手有"一个唱细点，一个唱粗点，要有底脚"之说，他们对自己演唱方法的要求是"要唱得两头平，中间鼓"。这里的"细"是"高"之意，"粗"是"低"之意，"要有底脚"就是要唱出低声部。"两头平，中间鼓"是说同音起唱同音终止，曲中则可分开声部进行。从《果塔纳玛》可以看出，歌曲旋律的进行明显反映出下方声部音高位置确是低于上声部，形成由同音开始到二度音程为主、再回到同音的第一乐句。当歌曲继续往下发展时，上下两声部中出现了具有推动力效果的二、三度音程为主的二部和声，随后同在同度长音上作上声方小三度颤动歌唱，末了同时结束于主音。其演唱效果真是形象地达到了"两头平，中间鼓"的艺术要求。

## （六）祭祀、庆典歌

"吉农吉刹"，是羌族祭祀山神、庆贺丰收等活动中所演唱的风俗歌的总称。每逢上述活动，羌民们都要在其寨前搭一彩棚，上悬刀枪子弹以示驱赶镇压邪魔。全寨青壮年男子身穿花衣裳，彩色腰带上别一支两尺余长的油竹竿，内插三根野鸡翎在寨外聚集，老人们也着新衣一道前往各户祝贺，家家杀牛羊，饮"咂酒"，歌舞娱乐活动穿插其中，持续数日。此间，"吉农吉刹"一般演唱两套曲目，甲套共 12 首，

Main idea of the song:

We sing a song of travels from afar, coming from a place called "Ba Shi Gu" we moved on day after day.

The song of our ancestors, pitched both high and low; it is Atai who first sang the song.

When two singers perform folksongs similar to "Guo Ta Na Ma", they must adhere to the saying that "one should sing the song thin whereas the other should sing it thick and there should be a foot at the bottom". The two vocal parts should also be "flat at both ends with a swell in the middle." Here "thin" means in a high pitch; "thick" means in a low pitch; "a foot at the bottom" means the bass part should be dominant; and "flat ends with a swell in the middle" means the two singers should start and finish the song in unison while the rest of the song is performed in parts". Take the song "Guo Na Ta Ma" as an example. In the first sentence of the song, the two singers start on the same note and then move to a two-note interval harmony where the second vocal part is pitched lower than the first before returning to the first note together. As the song develops a powerfully surging two-part harmony appears with intervals mainly of seconds and thirds, after which a prolonged note is sung together and the upper part then sings a vibrato minor third above the lower part. Finally, both vocal parts end on the principal note. This wonderfully demonstrates the artistic requirement of "flat ends with a swell in the middle".

## 6. Sacrifice and Celebration Songs:

"Ji Nong Ji Sha" is the general term for songs performed when offering sacrifices to the gods or celebrating a plentiful harvest. On these occasions, the Qiang usually put up decorated tents in their villages and hang up knives, guns and bullets to indicate the expelling of demons and evil spirits. All the young men gather outside the village wearing decorated clothing with oiled bamboo tubes stuck in their colorful waistbands. The bamboo tubes are usually more than 70 centimeters long and have three pheasant feathers inserted in them. The older people, wearing new clothes, visit every family to wish them well. In each family, cattle and sheep are slaughtered, people drink sucking wine, and singing, dancing and recreational activities continue for several days. During this time, two sets of "Ji Nong Ji Sha" are often performed. The first set includes twelve songs with a steady, smooth melody,

由十几位50岁以上的老人坐唱，一领众和，前后呼应，曲调平稳。乙套十三四首，边唱边跳，载歌载舞，节奏鲜明，旋律流畅、简洁。

### （七）请神歌

羌族地区每逢重大节庆、婚期喜宴、生日祝寿、新房上梁或落成，都要举行群体性的请神仪式。仪式以对神灵的呼唤开始："哦索，呀！呃，呃，呃……"场面壮观，充满浓厚的宗教色彩。

呼唤声后，接唱请神歌《基哦索》。

### 基哦索（中速）

**歌词译意：** 天神啊，大神！求你保佑啊，大神！

在边唱边舞过程中，不时地插入阵阵呼唤和吆喝声。仪式完后，情绪陡变，歌唱内容转至节庆、婚宴或祝寿活动的欢快主题，如赞美新郎新娘人品、才貌，祝福主人世代人财兴旺、安居乐业等，内容非常丰富，形式古朴清新，风格独特，整个活动充满浓厚的生活气息。这种以礼仪程式与民间歌舞音乐来表现社会习俗的传统文化方式，在羌族人民的精神生活中，至今仍占有重要的位置。这些曲调音域宽广，声音粗犷，旋律优美，

performed by a seated group of people, usually around fifty years old or older. One of the singers leads, echoed by the others. The second set includes about thirteen or fourteen brisk songs with an easy melody, which are performed joyfully and accompanied by dancing.

### 7. God-Calling Songs

During important festivals, wedding feasts, birthday celebrations, when putting the main beam of a house in place or on completion of a house, the Qiang always hold ceremonies calling on the gods. The ceremonies begin with people crying out to the gods, "Oh, suo, ya! Eh, eh, eh..." It is a spectacular scene permeated with a strong religious aura.

Everyone then starts singing the song "Ji Oh Suo".

**Ji Oh Suo (slow)**

（哦）　基哦索　基哦索　基哦　索，　索　基哦　

索　嘀，　（哦）　基哦索　尤米　基哦　索　

基哦　索　嘀基哦索。　哦嘶！　呀　欧！

Main idea of the song: Oh, god of heaven, the greatest, please bless me, O great god!

The singing of this song is usually interspersed with dancing accompanied by people's cries. After the religious ceremony, the mood suddenly changes and the songs turn to celebratory themes such as festival celebrations, wedding feasts or birthday congratulations. This may include praising the bridegroom and bride's moral attributes, abilities and good looks or wishing future peace and blessing on the hosts and their descendants. The content of these songs is exceptionally rich and yet simple and pure in form and unique in style. The whole event resonates with the richness of daily life.

To this day, this kind of traditional culture, as seen in the customary rituals and folk singing and dancing, plays an important role in the life of the Qiang. These broad-ranging songs, with their uninhibited vocals, beautiful melodies,

感情奔放，豪壮有力，颇具民族风味，成为羌族音乐不可分割的部分。

## 二、羌族民间舞蹈

羌民无论是欢庆丰收、节日聚会、婚娶丧葬，还是祭礼活动，都喜欢用歌舞的形式来表达他们的思想感情。他们的舞蹈动作一般以脚部、腿部动作为主，动作粗犷豪放、朴实，模拟性强，是直接从客观生活中吸取而创造出来的直观艺术形态。

### （一）萨朗

又称跳锅庄。"萨朗"系羌语北部方言对"歌舞"的称谓，意即又歌又舞。它是羌民最喜爱，也是最常见的一种反映喜庆或悲痛的自娱性舞蹈。

"萨朗"主要用于欢度年节、喜庆丰收、婚丧嫁娶等场合。表演时，在场院里或火塘边男前女后站成圆圈或弧形，人们饮酒欢歌，酒后即手拉手围着火塘起舞。舞蹈时男女各成一行或混合而围成一个圆圈，由能歌善舞者手持串铃领头，男子齐唱一段（或一乐句），女子复唱一遍后一同起舞。不用伴奏乐器而用徒歌形式，曲前和句前常加一拍或半拍起始音。速度由慢至快，跳至激烈处，领舞者带头突然加快舞步并变换基本动作。句尾插入吆喝声。曲毕，饮"咂酒"助兴。少顷，另一曲起，……通宵达旦，热烈欢乐。

"萨朗"的内容以表现自然崇拜和民间风俗居多。尽管根据表演场合和舞蹈风格特色的差异可分"忧事萨朗"和"喜庆萨朗"两类，但是"忧事萨朗"与"喜庆萨朗"的歌曲和舞蹈动作都基本相同。如跳衣角舞时，男性双手持长衫前摆两角，女性持围腰两角，围成各种队形，或圆圈，或一字长阵，或两排对舞……舞者边舞边唱，动作缓慢。

unrestrained emotion and energy, and their ethnic flavor, constitute an indispensable part of the music of the Qiang.

## II. Folk Dances of the Qiang

Whether they are celebrating an abundant harvest, gathering for a festival, attending a wedding or funeral, or a sacrificial ceremony, the Qiang always like to express their thoughts and feelings through singing and dancing. The lower body movements are most important in the dancing and the steps are simple, unconstrained, and easy to follow. The dance choreography is often drawn directly from observations of daily life.

### 1. Sa Lang

The word "Sa Lang" in northern Qiang means to sing and dance at the same time. It is also called the "Guozhuang". The Sa Lang is a favorite dance and a common form of self-entertainment for the Qiang, reflecting both joys and sorrows.

The "Sa Lang" is performed at harvest celebrations, festivals, holidays, weddings, and funerals. It is danced with a circle or an arc of men in front and women behind, either in an open space or around a fire pit. After drinking and merry singing, people dance around the fire holding hands. As they dance, the men and women each form a line or blend together in a circle, with the best singer shaking some bells and leading the way. The men sing something in unison, the women repeat it and then the dancing starts. The music is sung a cappella and is often started with a beat or half a beat before the singing commences. The music moves from slow to fast as the lead dancer suddenly quickens his pace and changes to another set of dancing steps. Each song ends with the singers giving a shout and everybody drinks more wine to liven things up. A few minutes later, another song begins and they dance joyfully through the night.

Most "Sa Lang" are connected with local customs or with Qiang beliefs. There are two kinds of "Sa Lang", one for happy occasions and one for sad and both with much the same dance movements. For example, while dancing, the men hold the front corners of their long garments and the women hold the two sides of their aprons. As they slowly dance and sing they create various formations as they move between circles and lines.

（二）席步蹴

"席步蹴"系羌语南部方言，意为"酒席歌舞"。又称"约布补"或"索达席"。主要流传于汶川县的龙溪和理县的通化、薛城一带。

"席步蹴"是羌族人民在婚丧嫁娶、节日欢庆及农事劳作后的自娱性舞蹈。"席步蹴"和"萨朗"是在同一文化环境和氛围中产生、发展，并长期共同生存的艺术形式，其表演形式与"萨朗"类似。因此，就整个表现方法和表演的过程与行式来说，二者是基本一致的。不同之处在于"席步蹴"是在室内表演，且舞步深沉有力。

（三）祭祀舞（巫舞）

又称释比舞，是一种祭祀性舞蹈。释比作法时，头戴金丝猴皮帽，帽上插野鸡翎，并挂各色纸符，说唱结合，边舞边跳：时而摇动法刀轻腿漫步，悠闲自如；时而挥舞法杖，铿锵有力，威风凛凛；时而敲击羊皮鼓，轻松灵活；时而挥动令牌，神秘莫测。舞蹈时，随着所念咒语和羊皮鼓的节奏，时快时慢，回旋跳跃。

作法毕，接羊皮鼓舞。领舞者左肩扛神像木棍，右手持盘铃击节，后面跟随着皮鼓舞队。舞蹈路线是先曲线，后圆圈，舞步古朴刚健，鼓声粗犷豪放，民族风格甚浓。

（四）皮鼓舞

又称羊皮鼓舞、铃鼓舞。羌族信奉原始宗教，常有宗教祭祀活动的祭祀舞（巫舞）表演。这类活动，羌语北部方言称为"侧拜举·苏得萨"，南部方言称为"莫恩纳萨"。

### 2. Xi Bu Cu

"Xi Bu Cu" in southern Qiang means feast dancing. It is also called "Yue Bu Bu" or "Suo Da Xi". This kind of dance prevails in the Longxi area of Wenchuan and in Tonghua and Xuecheng in Li County.

"Xi Bu Cu" is also performed during festival celebrations, weddings, funerals, and when farm work is finished. As an art form, both "Xi Bu Cu" and "Sa Lang" originated and developed in the same cultural environment, so they are similar in style. However, they are slightly different in that "Xi Bu Cu" is performed indoors and with heavier dancing steps.

### 3. A Dance for Offering Sacrifices (Shaman Dance)

The sorcery dance, a dance of sacrificial rites, is also known as the Shibi dance or the Shaman dance. When the Shibi or Shaman is practicing his ritual arts, he wears a golden monkey fur cap decorated with pheasant feathers and paper shapes of various colors while he sings, dances, and recites incantations. At times he waves his ritual knife, moving smoothly with slow, light steps. At other times he brandishes his magic cane in an awe-inspiring fashion. Sometimes he beats lightly and skillfully on his sheepskin drum, and other times he waves his spirit tablet with an air of mystery. The dancing is performed either fast or slow according to the rhythm of the incantations and drum beating, with the dancers whirling and leaping.

The Shaman's rituals are followed by a sheepskin drum dance. The lead dancer carries a "sacred rod" on his left shoulder, while beating time with a shallow bell in his right hand. He is followed by a group of sheepskin drum dancers who dance in a curve before moving into a circle. The dance steps are simple and energetic, and the drumbeats are bold and unconstrained. All in all, this kind of dance has a strong ethnic feel to it.

### 4. The Drum Dance

The drum dance is also known as the sheepskin drum dance or bell drum dance. The Qiang have primitive religious beliefs and often perform a sacrificial dance (Shaman dance) as part of their sacrificial rites. This kind of religious activity is called "Ce Bai Ju • Su De Sa" in northern Qiang and "Mo En Na Sa" in southern Qiang.

每逢喜庆之日，羌寨的男女老少都要身着盛装，举行皮鼓舞会。有单人舞、双人舞、集体舞等形式。舞者头包白色云云帕，身穿长毛羊皮褂，脚穿云云鞋，左手举起单面皮鼓，右手持小木棒敲击，在唢呐、铜铃等乐器的伴奏下翩翩起舞。

集体性皮鼓舞由一释比领舞。释比装束与巫舞相似，还有三名响铃手，头戴有红飘带、兽颌骨的法冠，左肩扛着插有五彩纸旗和彩纸棍的麦草把，手握铜质响铃。击鼓手数名，身穿自织长过膝盖的麻皮衫，外罩一件羊皮短褂，脚着布鞋或草鞋，腿裹羊毛织成的毡子绑腿，腰束桃花织带，左手执羊皮鼓，右手握鼓槌，排成两行纵队，跟随领舞者和响铃手的节奏而起舞。

舞者起舞时，领舞者慢慢举起神棍，然后向天空一挥，响铃手跟随其后举铃摇动三下，众鼓手即随之放声呐喊。突然，领舞者收回神棍，转体。铃鼓手一声长啸，腾空而起，铃鼓声由缓变急，由疏而密。接近尾声时，铃鼓之声由急转缓，舞者由快而慢，逐渐至停止。

（五）跳盔甲

羌语称作"克西叽·忽苏得〔忍〕"，又叫铠甲舞，是一种古老的祭礼性舞蹈。舞者人数不定，身穿生牛皮制作的铠甲，头戴插野鸡翎和麦秆的头盔或毡帽，腰束红布腰带，手执长矛、长剑、短刀或尖刀，身背弓箭。数人中有一两支猎枪，队形成单行呈长蛇阵。在领头者的带领下，擂起大鼓，吹响牛角，发出"嗬哈！嗬哈！"的吆喝声。舞蹈开始时先跳圈，然后排成两阵。长弩飞舞，肩上的铜铃伴着舞者有节奏的呐喊和武器的碰撞声，铿锵有力。

At happy events, young and old alike put on their colorful festive garments and have a drum dance party at which there are solo dances, dances with just two people, and group dances. The dancers wear shaggy sheepskin waistcoats, Yunyun shoes, and white Yunyun scarves wound like turbans around their heads. Holding up single-sided drums in their left hands and beating them with short wooden sticks, they gracefully start to dance, accompanied by the suona (a trumpet-like wind instrument) and bells.

A Shibi, or Shaman, whose costume is similar to that worn in the sorcery dance, leads the group dances. Three bell players, wearing headgear made from an animal jawbone and decorated with red ribbons, hold copper bells and carry straw brooms on their shoulders which are decorated with colorful paper flags and small paper sticks. The drummers, of whom there are several, wear long, home-made, hemp garments which reach below the knee, short unlined sheepskin waistcoats, cloth shoes or straw sandals, woolen felt puttees and waistbands embroidered with peach blossom. With the drums in their left hands and drumsticks in their right hands, they form two lines and dance to the rhythm of the lead dancer and the bell players.

While dancing, the lead dancer slowly raises the "magic stick" and waves it in the air. Then the bell players hold up the bells and ring them three times as the drummers give a loud shout. Suddenly, the lead dancer draws back the stick and turns around. The bell players and drummers let out a long cry which fills the air, the noise of the drums and bells intensifies in a grand crescendo, and then, as the song draws to a close, the performers slow down and gradually come to a halt.

## 5. The Armor Dance

Also called "Ke Xi Ji · Hu Su De (Ren)" in Qiang, the armor dance is an ancient sacrificial offering dance. The dancers (any number) wear rawhide armor, helmets or felt caps decorated with pheasant feathers and wheat stalks, and red waistbands. They carry spears, long swords, and daggers or sharp knives. All of them carry bows and arrows on their back and one or two have a hunting gun. The dancers stand in single-file battle formation, and, following the leader, they beat their drums, give a blast of the ox horn and cry out with a loud "Ho ha!" Starting off in a circle they then move to form two battle lines. As their raised bows dance in the air, the bells on their shoulders ring to the rhythm of the dancers' cries and the clanging of the weapons. The songs accompanying

跳盔甲舞的歌词内容为或诉说羌人祖先的业绩，或叙述与其他部族的战争历史。

### （六）巴绒舞

羌语音译，即古老之意，是在领歌节时跳的舞蹈。尤以茂县赤不苏一带最为盛行。舞者均为女性，排列次序依年龄而分前后，队首为领舞者。领舞者起歌后，众人随之合唱且起舞，并由领舞者指挥变换歌曲、动作和队形。歌舞由缓而急，队形不断变化。在舞蹈之前，还要由老年人（女性）致辞、敬酒。

### （七）哈日舞

亦称"呃日"。羌语意为"我们要进行练兵演习"，属出征前誓师的军事舞蹈。

哈日在出征前的"议话坪"表演。由各羌寨的羌民自带武器聚于部落三角形旗帜下，先歌后舞。舞蹈动作简单，伴一呼一应的吼声，不断变化队形，并随呼喊声晃动武器，或面对面冲向场中，作对打等动作。一段舞完，歌声又起，歌毕，舞又起，如此反复进行。最后，晃动武器，与欢呼声交织成一体，将舞蹈推向高潮。哈日场面壮观、气势浑雄，是古代羌人在出师前誓师、操练，祈求必胜，提高士气和战斗力的舞蹈。

在羌族的民间舞蹈中，也有一些与汉族民间舞蹈相似的东西，如舞龙、跑旱船等。羌族文艺工作者还创作出了一大批具有民族特色和时代气息的舞蹈作品，有许多是对民间舞蹈的继承与发扬。

## 三、羌族民间古戏

羌戏，羌语称"刺喇"或"喻哦"。它脱胎于原始的傩舞，并处于傩舞向戏剧过渡的阶段，具有较为明显的傩戏性质。其内容与情节较为单纯简朴，与羌民的信仰活动密切相连。

the armor dance usually recount great ancestral deeds or the history of wars between the Qiang and other tribes.

### 6. Ba Rong

"Ba Rong", a transliteration from the Qiang language, means antiquity. Most common in the Chibusu area of Mao County, this dance serves to open the singing and dancing. Before the dance starts, an older woman makes a speech and proposes a toast. The dancers are all women and they line up according to their age, with the lead dancer at the head of the line. When she begins to sing, the others join in and begin to dance. The singing and dancing moves from slow to fast and the formation keeps changing, all under the direction of the lead dancer.

### 7. The Ha Ri Dance

The Ha Ri is also called "Er Ri" which, in Qiang, indicates troop maneuvers. It is a military dance for making a communal pledge before going into battle. Before the dance, people from different villages bring their own weapons, gather under the triangular flag of the tribe, and sing. When the dance begins, the dance steps are simple, with the dancers constantly changing formation. Echoing each other's shouts, they wave their weapons in the air and surge towards the center or fight each other in pairs as if against imaginary enemies. The dancing is interspersed with further rounds of singing and finally brought to a climactic end with joyful shouts and weapons waved high in the air. The great momentum and magnificent spectacle of the Ha Ri made it a powerful dance, strengthening the morale and military prowess of the ancient Qiang as they made their pledges and asked for victory before going to war.

Some Qiang folk dances are similar to those of the Han, such as the dragon dance and the boat dance. Also, many Qiang artists nowadays have created numerous modern dances with ethnic characteristics, continuing and developing local folk dancing traditions.

### Ⅲ. Ancient Qiang Opera

Qiang opera is called "Ci La" or "Yu Ou" in the Qiang language. It originates from an ancient "Nuo" dance used to drive away pestilence and was a transitional stage from this dance to operas performed on the same theme. The plots are usually simple and the content relates closely to Qiang religious activities.

羌戏的戏种，主要有与信仰活动相关的"释比戏"、英武悲壮的"武士戏"、古朴粗犷的"寨子戏"和喜庆欢快的"花灯戏"。这些戏在演出时，有南北两大方言系统。

### 1. 释比戏

释比戏是由释比的宗教祭祀舞蹈——傩舞演变而来的，与其他戏种相比，起源稍早。其主内容为祭神、敬神、还愿，如祈求神灵保佑平安，或祝愿死者灵魂早升天界，或消邪避灾解除人间苦难等。演出时，有台词、唱词、曲调和舞蹈，并有羌笛、口弦、唢呐、羊皮鼓、铜锣等乐器伴奏。演唱者也有特定的服饰道具。释比戏在本质上属于释比祭祀神灵、祈求、还愿的法事活动。释比戏的唱词和对白内容较为丰富，多为演绎本民族的历史与神话传说，如《木姐珠与斗安珠》《羌戈大战》等，它实际上是本民族史诗、神话传说的简单戏剧化。由于释比戏的主题内容较为固定，而内容又家喻户晓，加之演唱时皆用羌语，而羌族又没有本民族文字，所以释比戏没有书面的剧本流传。

### 2. 武士戏

武士戏反映的是古代战争生活和羌族大迁徙的历史。故事情节较为单调，如表现某地羌族遭外来侵略而报仇的故事。内容悲壮勇猛，对白简单、不固定，多是由表演者根据自己所了解的某段历史传说故事而加以自由发挥。其演员皆为自愿者，临时组织，以自娱自乐为主。

### 3. 寨子戏

寨子戏由各寨自己组织演唱，是一种自娱性的文化活动。有简单的用汉字写成的剧本，如汶川一带流行的《木姐珠剪纸救百兽》《斗旱魃》等。寨子戏在人物性格塑造、故事情节等方面都还处于十分粗犷的阶段，其表演动作和戏中的对白也不规范。释比是剧本的编写者，又是表演活动的组织者和主要演员。

### 4. 花灯戏

花灯戏主要表现的是羌民对理想生活的向往和安宁生活的渴求。花灯戏起源于北川坝底许家湾（"许家湾花灯"在这一带最为著名），

Basically there are four kinds of Qiang operas: the Shibi opera relating to religious activities, the solemn and inspiring warrior opera, the simple, straightforward village opera, and the festive lantern opera. They are generally performed in either northern or southern Qiang dialects.

(1) The Shibi opera has a longer history than the others and, deriving from the "Nuo" dance, is mainly about venerating and sacrificing to the gods and fulfilling vows to the gods, such as praying for blessing, asking that the souls of the departed go speedily to heaven, and asking for deliverance from evil, hardship and disasters. There are spoken lines, librettos, tunes, and dances in the performances. Accompaniment is provided by musical instruments such as the Qiang flute, mouth harp, suona, sheepskin drum, and gong and the performers have special costumes and stage props.

Shibi opera essentially belongs to the sacrificial rituals of the Shibi, including sacrificial offerings, prayers, and the redeeming of vows. The rich librettos and dialogues of Shibi opera are mainly simplified versions of the history, myths, and legends of the Qiang, such as *Mu Jie Zhu and Dou An Zhu* and *The Battle of the Qiang and the Ge*. The main content of Shibi opera changes little and is widely known to every Qiang family. Because it is performed in Qiang and the Qiang do not have their own written language, Shibi opera is not passed on in any written form.

(2) Warrior opera recounts war and migrations in ancient Qiang history. The plot themes are relatively limited, with simple yet stirring portrayals of the bold revenge of the Qiang on invading tribes. The actors are given free rein to improvise according to their understanding and knowledge of the legends. The actors are all volunteers who gather spontaneously and perform mainly for their own entertainment.

(3) Village opera is organized in different villages as a form of self-entertainment. There are some simple opera scripts written in Chinese characters such as those in Wenchuan for *Mu Jie Zhu Cuts Paper to Save One Hundred Animals* and *Fighting the Drought Demon*. It is the Shibi who writes the script, organizes the opera, and acts as the lead actor. Village opera is still at a fairly basic level in terms of character development and plot design.

(4) Lantern opera mainly expresses the Qiang's yearning for happiness and peace. It is popular in the Tumen River area, adjacent to Beichuan and Mao County. The most famous lantern opera is called *The Lantern of Xu Village*

主要流传于北川与茂县毗连的土门河一带。据说羌族花灯戏吸收了川剧的特色而逐步发展为具有本民族特色的花灯戏。表演者手中皆持一灯笼。每年正月初一至二月初为表演时间。一般由 9 至 12 人表演一些本民族的传统故事，如《木姐珠下凡》《白花山》等。花灯戏把戏剧的抒情、叙事和舞蹈的节奏结合起来，以表现和刻画人物的性格与矛盾冲突。曲调主要有《表花名》《十指尖尖把门开》《枝枝花儿开》等。在表演时根据不同的剧情，将不同的词套入不同的曲词之中。伴奏乐器主要有锣鼓、唢呐、笛子等。每曲的前面都有由乐器演奏的一段引子，曲调优美，较有独立性，节奏比较规整。

## 四、羌族民间乐器

### （一）羌 笛

羌笛又名"双管竖笛"，系竹制簧管乐器。早期的羌笛是单管，在西汉或更早发展成为双管。双管更加完善，成为中国民族乐器中的著名乐器。现代的羌笛，羌语称"切勒"（俗称"须须"），是一种六声阶（每管有六个音孔）的双管双簧竖笛，长 15～20 厘米，形似长筷，粗如小指，双管并列。羌笛选材考究，制作精巧。用当地特产的多年生箭竹（俗称油竹），选择杆直、筒圆、节长，而且头尾粗细比较均匀，竹肉不薄不厚，质地坚韧，纤维细致，不易开裂。每年入冬前将油竹砍回，待其干透后，将外层削成方柱形，经过反复打磨使其光滑，截成长 15～20 厘米的管身。两管并列，用细线于头、中、尾三处各缠一圈捆牢。每管之上各开六孔，孔距相等，两管之管头各插竹簧一片即成。

which originated in Xu Village in Beichuan County. Lantern opera is said to have borrowed many characteristics of Sichuan opera and has gradually developed into a unique Qiang art form. It often takes place between the first day of the lunar year and the early part of the second month, and is performed by nine to twelve actors, each holding a lantern.

The plot is often based on traditional Qiang stories such as *Mu Jie Zhu Descends to Earth* and *The Mountain of White Flowers*. A combination of emotional expression, narration and dance rhythms is used to express the personalities of the characters and the conflicts between them. The melodies in lantern opera include *Naming the Flowers*, *Opening .the Door with Ten Fingertips*, *The Blossoming of the Branches*, and others. Depending on the plot of the opera, different lines are combined with different melodies accompanied by gongs, drums, suonas, and flutes. Before each song, an instrumental prelude is performed which is a relatively independent piece with a regular beat and an attractive melody.

## IV. Musical Instruments of the Qiang

### 1. The Qiang Flute

The Qiang flute is also called the "two-pipe vertical flute" and is a reed instrument made of bamboo. Originally the Qiang flute had only a single pipe. It was not until the Western Han Dynasty or slightly earlier that it changed into two pipes and became a famous ethnic musical instrument in China. The modern Qiang flute, called "Qie Le" in Qiang and also often called "Xu Xu", consists of two adjacent vertical pipes, each with a reed and six finger holes, able to produce six musical notes. The flute is between fifteen and twenty centimeters long, rather like long chopsticks, with the diameter of each pipe roughly the size of one's little finger.

The flute is exquisitely made from carefully selected material, using only a special local plant called perennial arrow bamboo (also called "oil bamboo"). This must be straight and round with long even sections, not too thick or thin, and tensile but not easily split. The bamboo is collected each year before winter and once it is thoroughly dried the outer layer is squared off before being repeatedly polished and cut into short tubes. Two such tubes are placed side by side and firmly tied together at both ends and in the middle. With six equidistant finger holes drilled in each tube and a bamboo reed inserted in the top of each tube, the Qiang flute is then complete.

也有在笛管上涂上油、腊的，使之经久耐用。或刻上花纹，在笛梢吊两根红绸带，古朴美观。笛管顶部有簧嘴，嘴长 3~4 厘米，内径粗约 0.5 厘米。整管约等距开六孔，六孔笛筒音为 "sol"（G），孔音序 "la（A）、si（B）、do（C）、re（D）、mi（E）、fa（F）"，"si"（＝bB）音偏低，"fa"（＝#F）音偏高，不能超吹。用 "鼓腮换气法" 吹奏，双管发等音，量弱质柔，其声清澈、纤细，音域不宽，却悠扬婉转。早为文人墨客所重视，唐诗宋词中屡见羌笛、羌管的咏叹。

## （二）口　弦

口弦是羌地广为流行的乐器之一，羌语称 "俄罗"。是用外皮较厚、柔韧性很强的油竹削制成约 10 厘米长叶片，内刻 7 厘米左右细长簧舌（分单、双簧舌），弦的两端系着结实的细麻线。演奏时，只要将弦片放在上、下嘴唇之间，左手握住短柄，抖动叶片，右手牵动细绳，再变化舌头的位置和口形，让气流有序地放出，即能奏出优美动听的曲调。

在羌族民间，口弦的弹奏者以中青年或老年妇女为主。

口弦，给羌民特别是羌族男女的爱情生活增添了色彩。他们在约会中，不仅一奏一唱尽情欢乐，而且还创作出许多丰富多彩的口弦乐曲。如《出嫁曲》，即表达了羌族姑娘出嫁时那种悲喜交加的感情。而《丧曲》，则表达了对死者的悲悼之情。《苦曲》更是表现了在旧社会包办婚姻下妇女的痛苦和对婚姻的不满。而《吆羊曲》《撵山放狗曲》等则表现了羌民在劳动、狩猎时的欢愉心情。

Some flutes are rubbed with oil or wax to make them last longer and some are adorned with two red ribbons or carved with attractive patterns to make the flute more beautiful. The reed mouthpieces are about 3 ~ 4 cm long with an inner diameter of 0.5 cm. The flute's musical range is limited. The notes of the six finger holes, in the key of G (sol), are A (la), B (ti), C (do), D (re), E (mi) and F (fa). Because the holes are evenly spaced the B (ti) is a bit flat and the F (fa) is a bit sharp. The notes of the six finger holes, in the key of G, are A, B$^b$, C, D, E and F$^{\#}$] The pipes are played with air from the cheeks and both pipes have the same pitch, producing a sweet, clear, melodious tone. The Qiang flute was frequently mentioned in famous poems as far back as the Tang and Song Dynasties about a thousand years ago.

## 2. The Mouth Harp

The mouth harp (or mouth string), which is called "Er Luo" in Qiang, is also a very popular musical instrument for the Qiang people. To make a mouth harp, strong, thick-skinned, pliable oil bamboo is sliced into flat pieces about 10 centimeters long. Then a slim blade of seven centimeters long is carved inside (sometimes two blades). A strong string is then attached through each end of the instrument. The mouth harp is placed between the lips, held in the left hand by a small handle and shaken, while the right hand pulls the string. Attractive tunes can be produced by adjusting the position of the tongue and the shape of the mouth to control the airflow. The mouth harp is mostly played by young and middle-aged people and older women.

A particular feature of the mouth harp is that it adds color to the love lives of the young people. When they are dating each other, they not only enjoy themselves by singing and playing the mouth harp but also by creating a variety of rich and colorful mouth harp melodies. The song *Wedding Music*, for example, expresses the mixed feeling of happiness and sadness of the Qiang girl before she gets married. *Funeral Music* expresses condolences and mourning for the dead. *Bitter Music* expresses women's suffering and their dissatisfaction with the old system of arranged marriages. *Shepherd Music* and *Hunting with Dogs in the Mountains* express the happy mood of the Qiang people when they are working and hunting.

### （三）羊皮鼓

羊皮鼓，羌语称"日武"，也有称"侧拜举"，是释比法事活动中不可缺少的法器。羊皮鼓用羊皮绷制而成，单面皮鼓，直径一般在 45 厘米左右，无固定高音，声音浑厚，并配以盘铃（法铃）。盘铃摇动时发出明朗碰击声，和鼓点节奏组合成纯节奏型的打击音乐。演奏技巧有单击鼓面、鼓边和混合敲击三种。鼓点以反复单一节奏型为主。

### （四）盘铃

盘铃为羌族宗教仪式中的摇击乐器，又名"响盘"，形似碟盘而得名，羌语称"枯鲁"。响铜制，上部呈乳状，下部喇叭口外翻，直径约三寸，乳状体顶部有一小孔，内系舌锤，外接铃柄。演奏时，摇动铃铛，使舌锤与盘体碰撞发声，音色清亮柔脆。一般同羊皮鼓合用于祭祀舞（巫舞），可一人单独操作（左右手各持一个），也可由击鼓者兼奏。兼奏时，左手握鼓柄和盘铃，节奏与羊皮鼓点同。

### （五）脚盆鼓

脚盆鼓为木制鼓框，羊皮绷制鼓面，鼓面直径约 40 厘米，鼓底直径约 35 厘米，形如脚盆，故有"脚盆鼓"之称。演奏时用一对木制鼓槌敲打。

除上述乐器外，羌族民间还有唢呐、锣、鼓、钹、镲等吹打乐器，常用于婚丧嫁娶场合或转山敬神等宗教祭祀活动。

羌族音乐，伴随着民族的生存和斗争，并随时代的变迁和进步，逐渐形成完整而系统的表现形态和独特的艺术风格。同时，在与其他民族艺术长期相互借鉴、吸收和交融中得到充实、提高。今天，这些优美动听的山歌民谣、多姿多彩的民间舞蹈、丰富的古戏和原始古朴的民族器乐艺术，成为羌民族文明历史的不朽象征。

（耿亚军　徐希平）

### 3. The Sheepskin Drum

The sheepskin drum, called "Ri Wu" or "Ce Bai Ju" in Qiang, is an indispensable ritual instrument of the Shibi. It is made of tightly stretched sheepskin with a diameter of about 45cm. The drum has a variable high pitch and is played along with the shallow bell. The deep, mellow sound of the drum and the metallic tone of the bell blend to create a skillful, rhythmic kind of percussion music. The drumbeat is mainly a single repetitive beat, made either by beating the face of the drum, or the side, or both together.

### 4. The Shallow Bell

The shallow bell, shaped like a small inverted shallow dish, is a kind of musical instrument used at religious rituals. The Qiang people call it "Kulu". Made of copper, its under side is similar to the base of a wind instrument with a diameter of about 10cm. A short cord threaded through a hole in the top of the bell connects a tiny hammer inside the bell with a handle on top. When the bell is shaken by the handle, the tiny hammer strikes the inside surface producing a clear, light ringing sound. It is often performed with the sheepskin drum during dances on religious occasions. Sometimes it is played by one person with a bell in each hand, and sometimes by the drummer with his left hand holding both the drum and the bell, resulting in identical bell and drum rhythms.

### 5. Foot Basin Drum

The foot basin drum has a wooden frame with sheepskin stretched tightly across the top. The diameter of the drum face is about 40cm while the base is about 35cm. It looks like a foot basin used by the Qiang people and is usually played with a wooden drumstick.

Besides the instruments mentioned above, many other wind and percussion instruments, such as the Suona, Gong, cymbals, and small cymbals are used for weddings, funerals, mountain god festivals and other religious rituals.

The music of the Qiang has accompanied the survival and struggle of the Qiang people through centuries of change and development, gradually forming a complete and systematic form of artistic expression with its own distinctive style. At the same time, it has been greatly enhanced by contact with other types of folk art in China. Today, the melodious folk songs, colorful folk dances, entertaining operas and ancient musical instrument artistry, have become the immortal symbols of the history and civilization of the Qiang.

(Translated by Dao Zhiyong, Chen Shuyu)

# 第七章　羌族的节日庆典

羌族的节日，除了大年（春节）、清明、端午、中秋等与汉族大致相同外，还有"羌历年"、"祭山会"、"牛王会"、"领歌节"等富有民族特色的节日。兹分述如下：

## 一、羌历年

羌历年羌语称为"日美吉"，意为羌族的好日子、节庆日或过年日。羌历年是羌族最为隆重的传统节日，是羌族在粮食归仓后祭祀祖先和神灵，向神还旧愿、许新愿的重大节日。《隋书》记载，苏毗羌人"岁初以人祭，或用猕猴，祭毕入山视之"。可见其来历久远，且有浓厚的宗教色彩。古代氐羌人用十月历法（把一年分成十个月），十月初一被认定是一年之始，所以这个节日有送旧迎新之意。因地理条件不同，物候各异，所以，各地过羌历年的具体日期不一，仪式亦略有区别。改革开放以后，由羌族主要聚居地茂县、汶川、理县、松潘、北川的羌族代表在广泛征求各地羌民意见的基础上，共同商定将每年的农历十月初一日作为羌族过年的节日，羌历年的节期一般为三至五天。

年节的集体习俗与活动是男女老少着新装在家团聚，不出远门，不下地劳动，不上山砍柴、打猎，家家户户要祭祀供在白石堆上的牛羊头骨：

## CHAPTER SEVEN    FESTIVALS OF THE QIANG

The Qiang have a number of festivals. Some are similar to those in Chinese Han culture such as Spring Festival, Tomb-sweeping Day, Dragon Boat Festival and Mid-autumn Festival. Others are unique to the Qiang such as their New Year Festival, Mountain Sacrifice Festival, Ox King Festival and Song-leading Festival.

### I. New Year Festival

In the Qiang language, New Year's Day is called "Rimeiji" which means an auspicious day, feast day or New Year celebration day of the Qiang. The New Year Festival, celebrated after their crops have been harvested and stored, is the most important festival in Qiang tradition, during which Qiang people offer sacrifices to their ancestors and the gods, fulfilling old vows to the gods and make new ones. The *History of the Sui Dynasty* records that the Supi Qiang people "offered human beings or macaques as sacrifices to the gods at the beginning of the year, and then entered the mountain to observe the day." One can see that the festival has a long history and is strongly religious.

The calendar of the ancient Qiang people of the Di tribe was divided into ten months, with the first day of the tenth lunar month being the beginning of their new year, when they see out the old and welcome the new. Due to varying geographic and climatic conditions in different places, the New Year Festival was held on different days from community to community with slightly different forms of ceremony. As reforms brought greater openness in China, representatives from the major Qiang counties of Mao, Wenchuan, Li, Songpan and Beichuan sought local Qiang opinion and decided to make the first day of the tenth lunar month the official New Year Festival of the Qiang. The festival usually lasts for three to five days.

According to custom, during the New Year Festival all family members gather together in the home, wearing new clothes. Nobody should be far away from home, nor should people farm in the fields, climb mountains to collect firewood, or hunt. Every family should also offer the heads of the sacrificed

神灵的象征。并根据自古相传的天神木比塔的指点，在祭品上涂上颜色，再将祭品放在火塘上，或带到神林处在集体歌舞后吃用并互相赠送分享。每寨在神林前杀牛宰羊祭天，并将血洒在白石塔上，将牛羊的头供奉在白石塔上。祭毕，由四名男子抬着白石神（一块白石作为神的象征）遍游全寨，然后每人分得一份牛羊肉回家过节。年节期间，羌族青年男子还穿上新衣，腰系彩带并插上三根野鸡翎，组成载歌载舞的队伍到各家贺年。

年节的宴会又称"收成酒"。农历十月初一，家家户户在房顶的"勒克西"（即"勒夏"）前焚柏枝敬神。用荞麦面做成半月形的肉馅大蒸饼，用面粉做成牛、羊、鸡、马等形状的馍馍，作为祭品祭祀祖先与诸神。然后合家饮酒，吃早已准备的猪膘佳肴，跳萨朗舞。次日亲戚邻里互请吃饭、饮"咂酒"、唱歌跳舞。茂县维城、雅都一带过羌历年时，如本寨当年无成年人死亡，还要在墙上涂白色的"卐"字以表示庆祝之意。

## 二、祭山会

祭山会又称祭天会、山神会、塔子会、山王会等，它是羌族祭祀天神、山神（地神），祈求保佑六畜兴旺、五谷丰登、地方太平的大典。

cattle and sheep on a pile of white stones: a symbol of the gods. It is also believed that the god Mubita, in ancient times, advised that the sacrificial offering should be daubed with some color and placed on the fireplace or taken to the sacred grove. After singing and dancing together, the worshippers eat the sacrifices and later the leftovers are divided and shared.

In every village, people slaughter cattle and goats in front of the village's sacred grove and offer them to heaven. The blood of the sacrifices is sprinkled on the small white rock tower and the heads of the cattle and goats are placed on the tower too. When the sacrificial ceremony finishes, four men parade the white stone god (actually a white stone used as to symbolize the god) throughout the village. After that, each of the four men is given a piece of beef and lamb and returns home to continue the celebration. During the festival, young Qiang men also wear new clothes, tie three pheasant feathers to their waists with colored ribbons, and pay New Year calls on every family with singing and dancing.

The banquet held during the New Year Festival is called "Harvest Wine". On the first day of the tenth lunar month, every family burns some cypress branches in front of the "Lekexi" (i.e. "Lexia" is it the small tower with a white stone on it) on the roof to worship the gods. People use buckwheat flour to make half-moon shaped turnovers filled with meat, and use flour to make steamed bread in the shape of cattle, sheep, chickens, horses and other animals as offerings to their gods and ancestors. Then the whole family drinks wine, enjoys the prepared delicacies and performs the Sa Lang dance. The next day, relatives and neighbors invite one another to eat, drink sucking wine, and to sing and dance together. When the Qiang New Year is celebrated in the areas of Weicheng and Yadu in Mao County, people paint the auspicious character "卐" in white on the wall if no adult of the village has died during the year.

## II. The Sacrificial Mountain Festival

This festival is also called the Sacrificing to Heaven Festival, the Mountain God Festival, the Tower Festival, and the Mountain King Festival. It is a grand ceremony in which Qiang people worship the god of heaven and the god of mountains (land), and pray for peace, health, and a prosperous year with good crops and livestock. The book *History of the Northern Dynasty: History of the*

《北史·宕昌传》记载，宕昌羌人"三年一相聚，杀牛羊以祭天"。可见其由来久远。

因羌族地区各地农事季节不同或因古代分别属于不同部落，祭天会并无统一的时间，一般以村寨为单位或几寨联合举行，地点都在村寨附近的"神树林"。羌寨附近的山上有一座高约2米的石塔，塔顶放置几块白石，分别代表天神、山神、树神等，石塔周围有一片受到保护的茂盛的松柏、青杠树林，俗称神林或神树林，塔前的空地俗称神树坪，祭山会就在这里举行。

祭山会的仪式和内容比较复杂。大概说来，参加者必须是每户的成年男子，丧家和有产妇的人家不得参加。会首由每家每户轮流担任，负责祭山会的组织和筹备工作。祭祀仪式一般由当地的释比（巫师）主持。会首准备好一切祭品，其中主要的是一头黑色公羊，一只红公鸡，以及酒、肉、粮食、馍馍、香、蜡、纸钱等。释比头戴猴皮帽，腰悬法刀，颈悬骨质的白珠一串，手持响盘、巴郎鼓、羊皮鼓；徒弟执其他法器紧随后面。另一人执挂有纸旗和飘带的杉杆祖神（即祖神的象征）。参加祭祀的人则尾随他们。释比敲响羊皮鼓，手拄人头形法杖，在各种响器声中，一行人走进会场——神树坪。仪式开始：释比在塔前燃香点烛，陈设祭品，向神敬酒，唱《开坛解秽词》，燃烧柏香一堆，参加祭祀的人和黑羊从柏香上跨过，一切祭品、法器都在柏香上薰一遍，表示洁净，以便迎神祭神，这是祭祀的准备阶段。

*Dangchang* records that the Dangchang Qiang people "had a reunion every three years and slaughtered cattle and sheep to worship heaven", which shows the long history of the festival.

There is no uniform date for holding such a ceremony, due to the fact that different Qiang areas have different farming seasons and different historical tribal origins. Usually one village or several villages together hold the ceremony at the "sacred grove" near the village. On the mountain near the village there is a stone tower about 2 meters high, on top of which are placed several white stones representing the god of heaven, the mountain god, the tree god, etc. The stone tower is surrounded by a protected, sacred grove of pine, cypress, and Qinggang trees. The open space in front of the tower, where the Sacrificial Mountain Festival is held, is called the sacred tree glade.

The ceremony is quite complicated. Generally speaking, the participants include only adult men from each household. Any bereaved family or family with pregnant women is not allowed to take part. Families take turns to chair the ceremony each year and shoulder the responsibility for its preparation and organization. Usually a local Shibi presides over the ceremony. The chairman prepares all the sacrifices including a black ram, a red rooster, wine, meat, grain, steamed buns, incense, candles, and paper money. Then the Shibi appears, wearing a monkey fur cap, his ritual knife at his waist and a string of white bone beads around his neck. In his hands he holds a dish which resonates like the rim of a wineglass, a sheepskin drum and a Balang drum and he is followed by his apprentice carrying other instruments.

Another man carries a wooden rod (the symbol of the ancestors) on which paper flags and streamers are hung, and the other worshippers bring up the rear. The Shibi beats the sheepskin drum and leans on his ritual staff, the top of which may be shaped like a man's head. Accompanied by the sounds of the musical instruments, all the participants enter the meeting place—the sacred tree glade.

The ceremony begins as follows: the Shibi burns incense and lights candles in front of the tower, sets out the sacrificial offerings, proposes a toast to the gods, and sings the *Jug Opening and Purification Song*. Then the participants and the black goat must step over the burning pile of cypress branches so that the sacrificial offerings and the ritual instruments are made fragrant — symbolizing cleansing so that the gods can be welcomed. This is the preparatory stage of the ceremony.

祭祀正式进行：释比念还愿词，禀报神灵前来还愿之意，祈求天神太依支和热阿红保佑人畜平安、庄稼丰收。接着释比唱《开天辟地词》，唱祈颂山神史诗，再唱以羊替罪词，请天神、山神歆领享用。边唱边用青稞枝从羊头抹到羊尾，并将几颗青稞籽塞进羊耳，向羊和鸡浇三次水。鸡、羊因受冷水刺激颤抖三次，即表示神已领受，此时众人欢呼不已。随即杀羊并放鸡归山，将羊角置于塔顶，羊皮赠给释比，羊肉当场煮熟分给各家。唱完以羊替罪词，释比再唱《消灾免祸经》《长寿永生经》《丰收词》等古歌。随后向神灵求青稞种，此时，释比也有比较复杂的演唱：一面敲鼓，一面诵经咒，越唱越快，鼓声也相应越敲越急促，突然释比翻转羊皮鼓，单手托起，耸身一跃，就听到青稞籽飞入鼓内轻声咚咚作响……众人相应欢呼跳跃，赞美释比本领高强，祭祀活动达到高潮。释比唱请鸟兽吃祭品词，唱赞扬会首和寨民的古歌，大家席地而从，向释比敬献酒肉，然后共同饮酒唱歌作乐。

最后由释比唱祭山会结束词，并由释比带头，众人尾随其后，绕石塔载歌载舞三圈（俗称转山），确定下次会首后散会回寨。

在不同的地区，祭山会还有吊狗祭山、杀鸡祭山、杀牛祭山等习俗。其仪式与活动内容与上述大致相同，只是主要祭品不同而已。

The ceremony formally begins with the Shibi chanting words about the fulfilling of vows, informing the gods of people's willingness to redeem their vows, and asking the gods of heaven, Tai Yi Zhi and Re Ah Hong for a prosperous year with good crops and livestock. After that, the Shibi sings "The Creation of the World", an epic extolling the mountain god, and then the chant about the goat being a substitute for people's wrong-doings, inviting the gods of heaven and of the mountains to enjoy the sacrifices. As he chants, the Shibi wipes the ram from head to tail with highland barley stalks, stuffs several highland barley seeds into its ears, and sprinkles cold water three times on both the ram and the rooster. The ram and rooster shake each time with the shock of the cold water, which shows that the gods have accepted the sacrifices.

Now all the worshippers are jubilant. They immediately slaughter the ram and set the rooster free. They place the ram's horn on the top of the tower, give the sheepskin to the Shibi as a gift, cook the ram and share out the meat. When the "Scapegoat Chant' is finished, the Shibi begins to sing some ancient chants such as "Avoiding Misfortunes", "Longevity and Immortality" and "Abundant Harvest". Then, in a particularly complicated ritual, he petitions the gods for some highland barley seed. As he beats the drum and chants, the rhythm gets quicker and quicker until, suddenly, the Shibi flips the drum over, holds it up on the palm of one hand and as he leaps in the air the rat-a-tat-tat sound of barley seeds flying into the drum can be heard. All the participants cheer and jump for joy, praising the Shibi for his extraordinary abilities, and with this the ceremony reaches its climax. The Shibi then sings an invitation to the birds and beasts to share the sacrifices, as well as some ancient songs praising the chairman of the ceremony and the villagers. Everyone sits on the ground and respectfully offers wine and meat to the Shibi. Afterwards, they drink wine, sing, and make merry.

Finally, the Shibi sings the closing chant, leading the worshippers three times around the stone tower singing and dancing (this is called circling the mountain). After selecting the chairman for the next festival, the ceremony is over and people return to their village.

In different places, there are other customs for the Sacrificial Mountain Festival, such as hanging a dog or slaughtering a rooster or an ox. The procedures are basically the same as those above, just with a different sacrificial offering.

### 三、牛王会

牛王会又称"牛节"。时间为农历十月初一日，与羌历年节同一天，据说这一天是牛神（即牛王）的生日。牛神或称牛王菩萨，羌语称为"八渣瑟"。

牛王会来源于对牛的崇拜，这是羌族一种十分古老的习俗。在羌族地区，人们常称牛为"衣食父母"，羌族歌谣唱道："牛儿一生苦不尽，人间衣食不离牛。"《牛节歌》唱道："十月到了……一村一山，一寨一山，阴面阳面，都耕种完毕，……咦，一年中很辛苦，水冻了，山冻了，一冬不耕歇息了。"质朴的歌谣充满了对耕牛的关爱之情。所以，当牲畜有病疫时，羌区南部地方盛行招牛财的习俗，即请释比向牛王神通报，祈求它保佑牲畜祛病免灾。据说牛王是家畜的保护神，家家神龛上一般都要供奉牛王神，常年祭祀。每年农历正月二十日，要到释比处领一张印有图案的符纸，贴在牲畜圈的柱子上。过去羌族一般不吃耕牛肉，耕牛死后埋葬，埋葬处称为牛坟。埋牛之前，将牛皮剥下挂在树上，意为解脱牛的辛苦，让牛转世投胎变人。还要把牛角供在屋顶或神树坪的石塔上。

牛节一般是与羌历年一起过，一般是到牛王庙烧香、点蜡、烧纸钱，祭品是鸡、羊各一只，以祈求牛王菩萨保佑耕牛平安，六畜兴旺。全寨耕牛休息一天，还要给牛喂面馍馍、玉米馍馍。有些地区做一些太阳形、月亮形的馍馍挂在牛角上，然后将牛从圈中放出，任其自由悠闲地过节。

## III. The Ox King Festival

The Ox King Festival is also called the "Ox Festival". Like the Qiang New Year, this festival is celebrated on the first day of the tenth lunar month and is said to be the birthday of the god of oxen (the ox king), also called the ox king bodhisattva. In Qiang it is called "Bazhase".

The Ox King Festival comes from the worship of oxen, an ancient Qiang custom. In Qiang areas, people often call oxen their livelihood or their "food and clothing parents". Just as the folk song goes, "the life of oxen is endlessly bitter; people depend on the ox for their food and clothing." The "Ox King Festival Song" says, "the tenth month is here...all the farm work is finished on the mountainsides. After a year of hard work the streams and mountains are frozen and it's time to rest for the winter." This simple ballad shows the Qiang people's loving care for their cattle. When domesticated cattle fall ill, the Shibi is asked to tell the ox god and request him to heal and protect the animals, a custom called "Zhaoniucai" (prospering the livestock) which prevails in southern Qiang areas. It is said that the ox king is the tutelary god of domesticated animals and in every family, year in and year out, the ox king is worshipped at the household shrine. On the twentieth day of the first lunar month, everyone gets a paper printed with magic markings from the Shibi, which is then pasted on a post of the animal pen to keep the animals healthy.

In the past, the Qiang people generally did not eat the meat of plow oxen but would bury them when they died in what was called the ox tomb. Before the ox is buried it is skinned and the skin is hung in a tree, signifying freeing the ox from its hard toil and enabling it to be reincarnated in human form. The horns are placed on the roof of the house or on the stone tower in the sacred tree glade.

The Ox King Festival is always celebrated alongside the New Year Festival. People go to the Ox King Temple to light candles and burn joss sticks and paper money. Then they offer sacrifices, usually a chicken or a sheep, to the ox king bodhisattva and pray for the protection and prosperity of their plow oxen and other domestic animals. On this day, every plow ox in the village must rest and they are fed with steamed buns made of flour or corn. In some areas, pieces of dough in the shape of the sun and moon are hung on the cattle's horns. The cattle are then released from their pens and allowed to roam freely for the day.

187

### 四、领歌节

领歌节是羌族妇女的节日，羌语称"瓦尔窝足"，意为领歌会，又有农历五月初五的含义。主要流行在茂县、北川一带，时间为每年农历的五月五日，实际是从初三日开始，欢庆三天。

领歌节的来历：据说从前在曲谷西湖寨的山上海子边，来了一位美丽、善良、聪明的萨朗姐（后来习称萨朗神）。五月初五这天，她总要围着海子唱歌跳舞。清脆的歌声和婀娜的舞姿使羌民着了迷，情不自禁地跟着她学习。狠毒的头人想霸占萨朗，她坚决不从，被头人害死。悲痛的人们将她的遗体放在用羊角花（即杜鹃花）堆成的祭堆上火化，并在那里砌了专门用来祭祀萨朗女神的石塔，从此那里就被叫做"萨朗梁子"。每年羊角花开的时候，妇女们就到那里唱歌跳舞，久而久之就形成了"领歌节"。

每年农历五月初三，先由寨里几个妇女到山上的塔子（神林）处去祭祀女神"萨朗"（一说"明珠"或"入米珠"），向女神请示节日唱什么歌。次日全寨妇女不分老少，都由一位能歌善舞的年长女子领头，大家穿上艳丽的民族服装，收拾打扮，集合列队，载歌载舞挨家挨户去祝贺节日。主人用好酒好菜热情款待来祝贺节日的妇女。祝贺完毕，全寨妇女再集中到空地上欢歌劲舞，尽情地欢庆三天。

羌族妇女平时非常辛苦，操持家务，下地劳动，终年忙碌。领歌节期间，她们完全休息，所有的事情都由丈夫和儿子去做。领歌节是真正意义上的羌族妇女节。

（陈蜀玉　陈华新）

## IV. The Song-leading Festival

The Song-leading Festival ("Waerwozu" in Qiang) is a festival for Qiang women. It is named for the fifth day of the fifth lunar month, but actually starts on the third day of the month and lasts for three days. This festival is found mainly in the counties of Mao and Beichuan.

Legend has it that, once upon a time, a beautiful, kind-hearted, and clever girl called Sa Lang (later known as Goddess Sa Lang) went to the mountain lake of West Lake Village in Qugu. On the fifth day of the fifth lunar month, she would always sing and dance round the lake. The Qiang people were captivated by her clear voice and graceful dancing and were eager to learn from her. The ruthless village headman wanted to have her by force but she resisted him and, in the end, he killed her. The grieving villagers cremated her body on a pile of ram's horn flowers (azaleas) and then built a stone tower for sacrifices to Goddess Sa Lang, from which time on the place was called "Sa Lang Liangzi". Every year when the ram's horn flowers blossom, women would go there to sing and dance and this gradually became the "Song-leading Festival."

On the third day of the fifth lunar month every year, several women from the village go to the tower on the mountain (in the sacred grove) to offer sacrifices to Goddess Sa Lang (also called "Rumizhu" or "Mingzhi") and ask her about songs to sing for the festival. Then, on the next day, led by an older woman who is a particularly skilled performer, all the women in the village don their most festive clothing and, in a line, sing and dance from house to house, offering festive greetings to the other villagers, who present them with good food and wine. After the celebration, all the women in the village gather together in the open, singing and dancing to their hearts' content for three days.

Qiang women are usually busy with farming and managing household chores. During the Song-leading Festival, they have the chance to have a complete break while their husbands or sons take care of the chores. This festival is, in its truest sense, the Qiang Women's Day.

( Translated by Dai Zhiyong, Chen Shuyu )

# 第八章　羌族的衣食住行

## 一、衣　饰

羌族衣饰具有浓厚的民族特色与地域特色。《北史·宕昌传》有云：宕昌羌人"皆衣裘褐"。道光《茂州志·风俗》载："其服饰男毡帽，女编发，以布缠头，冬夏皆衣毡，妇女能自织。"据《汶川县志》，汶川一带羌族"妇女织麻，淳俗犹在"。《石泉县志·番俗》也记载北川羌人"女子剃头留细辫"，"地不产木棉，衣毡子，辟麻为布，极厚……女能织毯"。

1950 年以后，羌族地区大都没有了家庭的手工纺织业，衣着有较大改变。现代羌族男子头包白色、青色或黑色头帕，身穿过膝长衫，腿裹牛羊毛制作或麻织的绑腿，脚穿布鞋、胶鞋或草鞋，束腰带。腰带上系吊刀、皮裹兜子和火镰（打火工具，包括一块铁片和一块打火石，铁片即火镰）。喜庆日子都喜欢穿云云鞋。羌族妇女一般喜戴银制的头簪、耳环和手镯，头戴头帕。头帕因地域和季节不同其折叠方式和颜色有所不同。理县木卡、茂县曲谷一带盛行"一片瓦"头帕，即头顶叠瓦片状的青布，有的绣有花朵等图案或缀有银饰物。茂县、回龙、三龙、白溪、洼底等乡羌族妇女冬季戴绣有图案的四方头帕，

# CHAPTER EIGHT   CLOTHING, FOOD, SHELTER, AND TRANSPORTATION

## I. Clothing

Qiang clothing is ethnically and regionally distinctive. *The History of the Northern Dynasty: the History of the Dangchang* says that the ancient Dangchang Qiang people "all wore clothing made from animal pelts or coarse cloth". *The Annals of Mao Prefecture: Social Customs* in the Daoguang era (1821—1850 AD) record that "men usually wore felt hats while women braided their hair and wore a kind of cloth turban. Garments of woolen fabric were worn in all seasons and the women did their own weaving". *The Annals of Wenchuan County* say that around Wenchuan the Qiang "women still preserve the tradition of weaving hemp". *The Annals of Shiquan County* (today's Beichuan County)*: Social Customs* notes that "local Qiang women wore their hair in slender plaits; the land did not produce silk cotton, so people wore woolen fabric and made cloth with hemp. The cloth was extremely thick...women also wove blankets".

Since 1950, very few Qiang make their own textiles at home so their clothing has changed considerably. Nowadays men wear white, blue, or black turbans, knee-length gowns and a kind of narrow cummerbund. Puttees made of ox hair, wool or linen are usually wrapped around their legs from ankle to knee. They also wear cloth or rubber shoes or straw sandals. A knife, a leather pouch, and a set of tools used to make a fire comprising a flint and a small flat piece of iron, are tied to their waistbands. On festival days, they like to wear Yunyun shoes.

Qiang women in general prefer silver hairpins, earrings, and bracelets. Many women wear head-cloths. Depending on the region and season, these are of different colors and styles. In Muka in Li County and Qugu in Mao County, most of the women wear tile-shaped head-coverings of blue cloth on the crown of their heads. Some of these are ornamented with silver pieces while others are embroidered with beautiful designs such as flowers. In Mao County, women from the villages of Huilong, Sanlong, Baixi and Wadi wear square

春秋戴绣花头帕。黑虎乡羌族妇女以白布帕包头，帕头在脑后自然下垂，俗称"万年孝"。年轻姑娘节庆日戴彩色绣花头帕……总之，头饰的花样颇多。女子身穿曳至脚背的长衫，腰系绣花的围腰（即围裙）和飘带，外着羊皮褂。

特别值得一提的是羊皮褂和云云鞋。羊皮褂男女都喜欢穿，可防寒遮雨，劳动休息时可当坐垫。云云鞋形似小船，鞋尖微翘，鞋面绣有彩色云纹图案，或用彩色布在鞋面上剪贴成云纹图案再锁边子。传说古代羌人迁到岷江上游，遇到当地戈基人的反抗。羌人屡战屡败，受到神的启示，登云云鞋驾云奔逃，并用白石和棍棒反攻，终于打败了用麻秆和雪团作武器的戈基人。也有专家认为此说有误。但是，无论如何，在羌人的传统观念中，云云鞋是吉祥鞋，也是青年男女爱情的信物。羌族民歌唱道："送哥一双云云鞋，情哥穿上爱不爱？鞋是情妹亲手做，金钱银钱换不来。……"

## 二、饮 食

羌族居住在岷江上游的崇山峻岭之中，地瘠土薄，农业条件较差，这就决定了羌族人民的生活比较艰苦。但羌族的饮食习俗，仍然丰富而具有多样性和民族特色。

羌族的传统主食为玉米、洋芋（马铃薯）、荞麦、小麦、青稞和大米等。平时一日三餐，农忙时有一日四、五餐的，

head-coverings embroidered with decorative patterns in the winter and head-coverings with embroidered flower design in the spring. The women of Hei Hu Village wear a turban of white cloth with a piece hanging down at the back of the head. These are usually pinned at the back of the head and are called "wan-nian-xiao" (eternal filial piety). Young Qiang women wear brightly colored embroidered head-coverings during festivals and, in general, Qiang women often wear full-length gowns and embroidered aprons with broad embroidered ties hanging down behind. Over their gowns, they wear sheepskin vests.

The sheepskin vest and Yunyun shoes are particularly worth mentioning. Both men and women favor sheepskin waistcoats because they keep out the cold and the rain and can be used as a cushion during work breaks. Yunyun shoes are boat-shaped with slightly upturned toes. The uppers are embroidered or appliquéd with colorful cloud-like designs. Legend has it that when the ancient Qiang moved southwards to the upper reaches of the Min River, they encountered resistance from the native Geji people. Although the Qiang lost the initial battles, they received divine instruction that they should wear yunyun shoes in order to run with the clouds under their feet and they should counterattack with white stones and sticks. In the end, the Qiang won the battle against the Geji people, who only had hemp stalks and snowballs for weapons. Some experts would say this is not necessarily true but whatever the case, the Qiang traditionally see Yunyun shoes as a symbol of good luck and they are also a token of love between a man and a woman. As these lines from a Qiang folk song say, "My darling man, this pair of yunyun shoes is a gift for you, do you like them? They are made with my own hands and worth more than gold or silver…"

## II. Food

The Qiang live in steep, mountainous areas of the upper reaches of the Min River where soil is meager and farming conditions are poor. As a result, the Qiang lead a rather hard life. Nonetheless, their food shows great variety and particular ethnic features.

The typical staple foods of the Qiang include corn, potatoes, buckwheat, wheat, highland barley and rice. Usually every family has three meals a day although in the busy summer farming period there might be four or five meals a

冬闲时节也有一日两餐的。玉米最常见的烹煮方法：做成玉米面粥或"搅团"、玉米馍、玉米蒸蒸。也可以将玉米面拌和大米蒸熟，以玉米面为主的俗称"金裹银"，以大米为主的俗称"银裹金"。麦面荞面加工成面条。为适应打猎、放牧或外出做工需要，可将青稞、小麦、荞面加工成炒面。洋芋不但当粮做主食，也当蔬菜，其做法更是多种多样。

羌族的副食有肉食品和蔬菜等。肉食品有猪、羊、牛、牦牛和鸡等家畜家禽，而以猪肉加工做成的猪膘最具特色。年节时杀猪，将猪肉割成条块腌制后，吊在锅庄（火塘）上熏一段时间，到半干时移至通风处。这种猪肉很像四川的腊肉，羌族地区称为猪膘。风干后可随时切割一块煮熟食用。蔬菜主要有圆根菜、萝卜、白菜、豌豆、胡豆，以及当地各种各样的野菜等。豆类制成品有豆腐、凉粉等。酸菜是羌族饮食结构中的主要菜类，有燠酸菜和酸菜两种。食用方法是略炒、凉拌或烧成酸菜汤。调味品主要有花椒、辣椒以及姜、葱、蒜、盐、酱、味精等。可以用酸菜汤做酸菜荞面、酸菜搅团和酸菜糍粑等食物，都别有风味。

羌族居住在山区，山高林密，有取不尽、吃不完的山珍野味。肉食有野猪、麂子、野鸡、竹鸡、刺猪等。山菜有椿芽、蕨菜、薇菜、马齿苋、山药、泡参、鱼腥草、野葱等。各种菌类更是名贵的山珍。这些山珍野味极大地丰富了羌族人民的膳食。

羌族的饮品主要是酒和茶。"咂酒"是最富有民族特色的饮料。羌族男女老少都饮"咂酒"，羌区有"宁可三日无菜，不可一日无酒"的谚语。用青稞、小麦、大麦或玉米装入甑子蒸熟后，拌入酒曲，放进坛内发酵数日，即酿成酒。饮用时启坛注入开水，

day and only two meals a day in the winter farming period. There are several cooking methods: the Qiang often make cornmeal porridge or "jiaotuan", toasted corn buns and steamed corn buns. They also steam cornmeal mixed with rice. If this contains more corn, it earns the vivid description of "silver wrapped in gold" and if rice is the greater amount, it is called "gold wrapped in silver". Noodles are often made with wheat flour and buckwheat flour. Those who go out hunting, herding and laboring, often take with them fried noodles made from wheat and barley. Potatoes can also be eaten as a staple or as a vegetable, so there are diverse methods for cooking them.

Non-staple Qiang food includes meat products such as pork, mutton, beef, yak and chicken. Of these, their fat pork is the most distinctive. When the New Year comes, the Qiang slaughter a pig and cut its meat into large strips which are rubbed with salt and then hung over the fire pit to be smoked for a while. When these strips are semi-dry, they are moved to a ventilated place. This kind of pork product, called "fat pork" by the Qiang, is very similar to Sichuan bacon. It is convenient because it can be cut and cooked at any time.

There is a wide range of vegetables including cabbage, turnips, Chinese cabbage, peas, lima beans, bean products like tofu and bean jelly and various wild edible greens. Pickled Chinese cabbage is one of the main Qiang dishes. There are two kinds of pickled cabbage, namely, toasted pickled cabbage and ordinary pickled cabbage. It can either be slightly stir-fried, used in soup or served cold with a dressing. The main flavorings used are "huajiao" (prickly ash), chili pepper, ginger, shallots, garlic, salt, soy sauce, and MSG (monosodium glutamate). The pickled cabbage soup is sometimes combined with buckwheat noodles, porridge or glutinous rice paste to make other local dishes.

The Qiang live in mountainous areas. In these lofty mountains and thick forests there are almost inexhaustible sources of wild food. This includes meat products such as wild boar, muntjac, pheasant, bamboo partridge, and porcupine. It also includes edible wild greens such as Chinese toon buds, tender bracken leaves, bush vetches, purslane, Chinese yams, ladybell roots, cordate houttuynia (a fishy-smelling grass), wild shallots, and various rare fungi. These wild delicacies have greatly enriched the Qiang diet.

The main beverages of the Qiang are wine and tea. Sucking wine is a local Qiang specialty. Men and women of all ages drink sucking wine. A proverb indicates its importance, "better three days without dishes than a day without wine". To make the wine, highland barley, wheat, barley and corn are first steamed in a distilling utensil. Then they are mixed with distiller's yeast and sealed in earthen jugs and after a few days of fermentation the wine is ready. When the wine is to be drunk, boiled water is poured into the jug and thin

插上细竹管吸吮，吸完后再注入凉开水，饮到淡而无味时作罢。饮"咂酒"还有一定的礼仪。无论是节日、婚嫁、祝寿、婴儿满月，或是日常饮酒，都要先由年龄最长者致开坛词。开坛词因聚会的性质不同而有不同的内容，但一般都有对神灵的赞颂、对本民族英雄的歌颂、对祖先业绩的追述以及对主人的恭维和对客人的欢迎等。开坛人一边致开坛词，一边将竹管插入坛内蘸三滴酒洒向空中，表示向天地神灵和祖先致敬。然后才按年龄辈分饮酒，再互相敬酒，唱酒歌，跳锅庄，直至尽欢而散。酒歌有对唱、轮唱或多声部合唱等形式。轮唱内容丰富，故事性强，故亦称"酒戏"。此外，还有婚礼酒歌、寿礼酒歌、祭祀酒歌等。

茶叶也是羌族人民生活的必需品，饮茶者最喜欢炒青和晒青。茶叶还是葬礼中入殓的必备之物。

## 三、居　住

羌族居住的碉楼和庄房也极具民族和地域特色。其建筑工艺另有专题论述，这里只略谈一下与居住民俗有关的问题。

早在 2 000 多年以前，羌族人就以其精湛的建筑技艺著称于世。据《后汉书·南蛮西南夷传》，羌人"皆依山居止，垒石为室，高者至十余丈，

bamboo tubes are inserted to suck the wine. After the wine has all been sucked up, more boiled water is added until the wine has lost its flavor.

Specific etiquette is attached to drinking sucking wine. On the occasion of festivals, marriages, birthday celebrations and even on ordinary days, the wine can only be drunk after the oldest person has finished delivering a jug-opening speech. The contents of the speech vary with different kinds of gatherings but in most cases the speaker extols the gods, speaks in praise of Qiang heroes, narrates the great deeds of the Qiang ancestors, compliments the host and welcomes the guests. As he delivers the jug-opening speech, the old man opens the jug, dips a bamboo tube in the wine and then sprinkles three drops of wine skywards as a tribute to the ancestors and the gods of heaven and earth. Only then do others start to drink the wine and this is done according to their age and family position. They propose toasts to each other, sing wine songs and dance to their heart's content. The wine songs can either be antiphonal in style or sung as a round or as a multi-voice-part chorus. The rounds are rich in content, often telling a story, and are therefore also known as "wine play". In addition, there are wine songs for weddings, birthday parties and sacrificial rites.

Tea is a necessity in Qiang daily life and two kinds of tea are most favored by the Qiang, namely, "chaoqing" (made from tealeaves dried by stir-frying) and "shaiqing" (made from tealeaves dried in the sun). At funerals, the Qiang even put tea in the coffin to be buried with the deceased.

## III. Buildings

Qiang structures, including watchtowers and houses, are also ethnically and regionally distinctive. Since their architectural features have been discussed in a previous chapter, the focus here is on some housing customs.

As early as over two thousand years ago, the Qiang were famed for their masterly architectural techniques. *The History of the Later Han Dynasty: Minorities in the Southwest* states that the Qiang "lived in the mountains and built stone houses, which could be as tall as ten 'zhangs' (33 meters). These

为邛笼"。"邛笼"即古时羌语的音译词，意为碉楼。明顾炎武《天下郡国利病书》载："威、茂，古冉駹地，垒石为碉以居，如浮屠（佛塔）数重，门内以辑木上下，货藏于上，人居于中，畜圈于下，高至二三丈者谓之鸡笼，十余丈者谓之碉。"

碉楼主要用来抵御敌患，平时不用，一有敌情，羌民就携带武器据碉楼守御。碉楼多建筑在依山扼水的险要处或村寨的中央，呈六角形或八角形，高十余丈，十三四层。

庄房即羌民住宅，又称碉房。羌民一般三五十户聚居成一个寨子，主要分布在高山、半山或河谷台地上有饮用水和便于生产、自卫的地方。庄房一般分为三层或二层，底层为牲畜厩和用于堆放杂草。中层为居住用房，除寝室外，正中一间设有锅庄，即火塘，靠墙处设神龛供奉神灵。这里也是家庭会客和举行婚嫁丧葬等礼仪活动的地方。上层用来贮藏粮食等重要物资。房顶则主要用于打粮、晒粮。在房顶四角和靠山一边中间，还用片石砌一高约一米的塔形小石龛，放置一块或数块白石，羌语称为"窝露匹"或"纳克西"，为家庭祭祀天神、山神的地方。

建房造屋是羌民生活中的大事，有比较隆重的礼仪和丰富的民俗内涵。建房之前要请释比开地，确定设门处和神龛安放处。完工时要请释比择

tall houses were called Qionglong." The term "Qionglong" is a transliteration of the ancient Qiang term for watchtower. *The Strengths and Weaknesses of the Various Regions of the Realm*, written by Gu Yanwu in the Ming Dynasty, records that "in Wei and Mao, the area of the ancient Ranmang, the people lived in watchtowers built with stones, which, like Buddhist pagodas, had several stories. The dwellers used logs with steps cut into them to climb up and down. Goods were stored in the upper levels and the living quarters were in the middle with the livestock down below. The houses as tall as two or three 'zhangs' were called Jilong, while the houses more than ten 'zhangs' high were called 'diao'."

These watchtowers were mostly used to guard against enemies and so were not used in times of peace. If enemies approached, the Qiang people would take their weapons and defend from the watchtowers. The watchtowers are always situated at strategic passes or in the middle of the villages. They are mainly hexagonal or octagonal in design, more than 30 meters high, with thirteen or fourteen stories.

The Qiang live in villages of thirty to fifty households. The villages are often located on mountain ridges, mountainsides or in river valleys, in places where they can work the land, acquire water and defend themselves. As mentioned above, the house usually has two or three floors. The first floor is for livestock and fodder. The second floor, with several bedrooms around a central main room, is for living. This is also the place where the family entertains guests and holds weddings, funerals and other rites. A fire pit called the "Guozhuang" is located in the main room. A household shrine is placed against the wall of the main room for worship and to make offerings to the gods. The third floor is for the storage of crops and valuable goods. The roof of the house is used for threshing and drying grain. On the side nearest the mountain, the family use pieces of stone to build a one-meter tall, tower-shaped shrine, on which are placed one or several white stones to worship the gods of heaven and mountains. This rooftop shrine is called "Woloupi" or "Nakexi" in the Qiang language.

House building is an important event among the Qiang and is accompanied by solemn ritual of a rich Qiang flavor. Before a house is built, the Shibi is always invited to check the site and decide the location of the doors and the household shrine. When the building is completed, the Shibi will choose an

吉日良辰举行落成典礼。这天房主人要宴请家族亲戚邻居朋友，由母舅主持一切礼仪。在举行仪式时，木匠要吟唱许多歌谣，并要带上馍馍、核桃和硬币或小额纸币从房梁上抛下。抛三块馍馍给主人用衣袍接住，意为招财。其余则抛撒给前来庆贺的人，称为丢钱包子。还要用一只红公鸡将其鸡冠掐烂以血祭诸神。木匠吟唱的多是赞颂此地风水好，居住此地定会人丁兴旺、多福多寿以及感谢神灵的歌词。新房建好后，还要在房顶上立杉杆（作神的象征）供天神，并要请释比做法事。

## 四、交 通

羌族地区山高坡陡，沟深谷狭，两寨之间鸡犬相闻，对唱山歌如在对面，而往来交通却异常困难。所以，羌族的民谣唱道："上山如上天，下山脚杆软。两面喊得应，走路要半天。"旧时羌区所谓"官道"，只不过是沿着河谷、攀缘悬崖绝壁开凿山岩修成的羊肠小道。行人仰望只见"一线天"，俯视峭壁下的河流像一匹起伏翻飞的白绸。为提醒行人注意安全，沿途竖有"下马岩"、"上马岩"、"上轿石"等标记。在"难于上青天"的崇山峻岭深谷峭壁中交通往来、勤劳勇敢、充满智慧的羌族人民，

auspicious day and time to hold a house dedication ceremony. Relatives, friends, and neighbors are invited to enjoy the feast prepared by the owner of the new house. The ceremony is presided over by a maternal uncle of the family. During the ceremony, the carpenter sings many ballads and tosses steamed bread rolls (momo), walnuts and coins or low-value paper money from the main roof beam. If the house owner succeeds in catching three of the "momo" in the skirt of his garment it's a sign that he will be wealthy. The other things dispersed by the carpenter are caught by the guests who have come to celebrate and this custom is known as "tossing money dumplings" (diu qian baozi).

Added to this, a red rooster with its cockscomb cut off is offered as a blood sacrifice to the gods. The songs performed by the carpenter generally praise the auspicious location of the house, wish the inhabitants happiness, longevity and a flourishing family, and express gratitude to the gods. After the new house is built, a staff made of Chinese fir is placed on the roof as a symbol of deity, sacrifices are offered to the god of heaven, and the Shibi is invited to conduct a ritual ceremony.

## IV. Transportation

The Qiang live in rugged mountains and deep valleys. The crowing of roosters and barking of dogs in one village can be clearly heard in the next one. The antiphonal singing of mountain songs between two villages is performed as if face-to-face. Nevertheless, transportation between different villages is extremely difficult. As this Qiang ballad says: "climbing the mountains is like climbing to heaven, going down the mountains makes your legs shaky; and although we can have a conversation across the valley, it takes us half a day to reach each other."

In the past, the so-called highways in Qiang areas were just narrow footpaths winding along the river, climbing the mountainside or cut into the cliff face. Anyone who walks along these paths can see just a sliver of sky above them and the white thread of the rushing river down below. To remind people of the dangerous conditions, signs have been set up along the way advising people where to mount or dismount from their horses or take a sedan chair. The difficult terrain means that in many places neither vehicles nor horses can be used so the Qiang are very accustomed to carrying large loads on their own backs. To facilitate travel through this mountainous countryside the Qiang have

创造了栈道、溜索、索桥等交通设施，战胜了天险，堪称人间奇迹。

## 1. 栈道

栈道又叫阁道、复道，羌族地区和秦蜀古道千百年来都采用这种交通设施。据《四川通志》载，栈道"即古秦汉制也，缘崖凿孔插木为桥，铺以木板，覆以土，傍置栏护之"。实际上，开凿栈道的历史应早在秦汉以前上千百年的殷商时期。先民在长期的实践中发明了开凿栈道的有效方法：先用火烧岩石，再泼冷水。这可以使崖壁岩石在冷热巨变之中崩裂，从而加快了开凿岩壁修建栈道的进度。

## 2. 溜索

溜索又称溜筒、绳渡，是羌区一种渡过深谷湍急河流的古老方法。分平溜和陡溜两种。平溜为一条横跨大体持平的两岩的溜索；陡溜为两条溜索取倾斜之势横跨两岸，又称鸳鸯索。《康輶纪行》记载："松潘、茂州之地，江水险急，既不可舟，又难施桥，于两岸凿石鼻，以索系其中。往南者北绳稍高，往北者南绳稍高。手足循索处皆有木筒，缘之护手易达。"溜索不但渡人，也渡背缚行李者，甚至牛羊或其他较大之物也可借以渡过。

devised various structures such as plank roads, sliding ropes and suspension bridges.

## 1. Plank Roads

The plank road is a form of transportation which has been used in Qiang areas for over two thousand years, beginning in the ancient Qin and Han dynasties. *The General Annals of Sichuan* record that the plank road "was used in the ancient Qin and Han dynasties. To build the plank roads, holes were chiseled in the cliffs, then logs were inserted in the holes, and planks were placed on the logs. After that, the planks were covered with mud and guardrails were installed on both sides for protection". In fact, plank roads were first built as early as the Yin and Shang Dynasties, over one thousand years before Qin and Han dynasties. Over the years an effective method of chiseling holes in rocks was developed whereby the rocks were first heated and then cold water was poured on them. The quick change of temperature caused the rocks to split, which increased the speed at which the plank roads could be built.

## 2. Sliding Ropes

The slide rope is an old method of crossing rapid rivers. There are two kinds of sliding ropes: horizontal and sloping. The horizontal rope reaches from bank to bank and is roughly level. The sloping rope refers to two slanting ropes where the momentum produced by the incline helps people across the river. These are also known as "yuan-yang" meaning a pair of mandarin ducks or an affectionate couple. *The Travel Notes of Kangyou* record that "in the areas of Songpan and Mao Prefecture, where the rivers are particularly rapid, boats are impossible and bridges difficult to build, so holes were chiseled in the rocks on both banks of the river to which were attached two thick ropes that spanned the river. To cross the river southward the rope with the higher northern end would be used, and vice versa to travel northward. There were always wooden tubes at both ends of the ropes which protected people's hands and provided an easier passage".

These sliding ropes can be utilized to transport not only individuals but also people with heavy loads, and even cattle, sheep or other large items. The wooden tube is made by carving a round section of log into two halves, hollowing them out and then tying them together firmly around the rope. The

这里所说木筒，又称为溜壳，即将一节尺许可以双手把持的圆木剖为两半，挖空合于溜索上，再把两半绑牢。渡河者将皮带或绳索束在腰部，再把自己挂在溜索上，然后手持溜壳，手拉足推，滑向对岸。这是一种很惊险的渡河办法，但千百年来羌族人民已经习以为常。

### 3. 索桥

索桥又称绳桥，古称笮，笮系羌语音译。据说古羌人中一支名笮的部落发明了索桥，它可能是在溜索的基础上形成的。索桥的建造：先在水中立两桥柱当桥墩，再在桥柱上架横梁，在横梁上密布竹绲，竹绲两端系于两岸；再在竹绲上面铺木板，两旁用竹索或藤条编成网状的护栏以保证安全。

羌族地区山高涧深，水流湍急，架桥确实不易，所以普遍使用溜索和索桥。但溜索和索桥惊险而不安全，于是，充满智慧和创造力的羌族人民发明修建了"弓弓桥"，它又称木拱桥或交桥。先在河两岸用石头砌成坚固牢实的桥墩基础。然后在两岸分头施工，都在桥墩上平铺圆木若干条（以设计的桥面宽度为准），铺一层压砌一层平整的石块，再在上面铺第二层圆木……层层如此铺砌压石，但每层均向河心伸出五六尺，最后两岸压砌的圆木合龙交汇。再在上面铺一层圆木，两端各搭在两岸交接的圆木上，并在上面铺上树枝，覆上泥土，加以平整夯实，成为桥面。最后，在两旁修建护栏。一座平稳壮观的弓弓桥便建成了。弓弓桥不但使行人感觉安全舒适，而且解决了较大跨度的湍急河流上的渡河问题，实在是山区建桥史上一个伟大的创举。

山路陡峭险窄，渡河尤其艰危，不但无法使用车马，连肩挑也不可能，因此，千百年来羌族人民养成了背负物品的习惯。

（陈蜀玉　陈华新）

section of tube is usually about 30 centimeters long and can be gripped with both hands. Anyone who crosses the river should first secure himself to the sliding rope with a belt or rope, then grip the tube and gradually slide towards the opposite bank, with hands pulling and feet pushing. It is indeed a dangerous way to cross rivers but over the centuries it has become a normal part of life for the Qiang.

## 3. Suspension Bridges

The suspension bridge is also called a rope bridge. In ancient times, it was called zuo, which is a transliteration from the Qiang language, because it is said that the Zuo tribe of the Qiang people built the first rope bridges. The bridge was probably created on the basis of the sliding rope. To build a suspension bridge, two pillars are first secured in the water as piers. Then, crossbeams are placed on the pillars and densely covered with thick bamboo ropes whose ends are fixed to both river banks. After that, wooden planks are placed on the bamboo ropes and more bamboo or rattan ropes are woven to form guardrails along each side of the bridge.

The high mountains, deep valleys, and rapid rivers in Qiang areas make bridge building difficult so the hazardous sliding ropes and suspension bridges are widely used. However, the Qiang have also invented a wooden arch bridge. To build such a bridge, solid stone foundations are laid on both sides of the river as a base for the piers. The construction work is done separately from both sides. Round logs are placed on the piers in precise accordance with the planned width of the bridge floor, and on these are laid a level layer of flat stone rocks and then a further layer of logs. Each layer extends about two meters towards the center of the river until the last two layers from either side of the river reach each other. Afterwards, more logs are added to the joint section in the middle of the bridge. Tree branches and clay are used to cover the logs and are then leveled off to form the bridge floor. Once guardrails are built on both sides, this sturdy and spectacular arch bridge is complete. It not only ensures people's safety but also solves the problem of crossing wide and rushing waters, a true wonder of engineering in the history of bridge-building in mountainous areas.

( Translated by Dai Zhiyong, Chen Shuyu )

# 第九章　羌族的生产生活

## 一、农业耕作与守护

羌族居住在山区，山多地少，土地薄瘠，艰苦的生产条件和生存环境，决定了他们的农业生产方式、生产特征与习俗。

山地的农作物以玉米为主，其次为青稞、小麦、荞麦、土豆，还有芝麻、烤菸（即烟）等经济作物。其他副业为花椒、核桃、苹果及药材等。玉米和土豆等高产作物是在清代才先后传入的。山区的农业生产工具主要是适应土薄碎石多的山锄、瓜米子锄（形如瓜子、尖嘴）和鸭嘴铧（头圆而宽）、鸡嘴铧（头尖而窄）等。耕地普遍使用传统的"二牛抬扛"法。1950 年以后，羌民生产工具和技术都逐渐获得很大改进与提高，并学会增施化肥与农药，使羌区农业劳动生产率和粮食产量有显著的提高。

羌族地区流行着丰富的农谚，如："破五（农历正月初五）捡石头"，"误了一年春，十年理不伸"，"种地莫要巧，深耕细作好"，"打鱼不在浅滩，麦子不种高山"，"立秋无雨使人忧，地里庄稼一半收"，"春旱不算干，秋旱断炊烟"，等等。这些农谚总结概括了山区的生产经验和物候知识。

由于生产、生活的艰难和对丰收的渴望，羌族人民在 1950 年以前，有的地方在四月播种时，还要请释比作法诵经，举行比较隆重复杂的祭祀活动。

# CHAPTER NINE   AGRICULTURE AND LIFE STYLE OF THE QIANG

## I. Agricultural Cultivation and Protection

The Qiang dwell in mountainous areas with infertile soil and little cultivable land. The difficult living environment and poor productive conditions have determined the forms, characteristics and customs of the local agriculture.

The main crop in these mountainous areas is maize, followed by cash crops such as highland barley, wheat, buckwheat, potatoes, sesame and tobacco. In addition, the Qiang also grow walnuts, apples, medicinal herbs and a spicy condiment called "huajiao" or prickly ash. Corn and potatoes, which have high yields, were only introduced to the area during the Qing Dynasty. Farming tools, suited to the thin, rocky soil in the mountainous areas, mainly include a sunflower seed-shaped hoe with a sharp end, a duckbill-shaped spade with a broad, round end, and a chicken bill-shaped spade with a narrow, sharp end. The traditional way of plowing with a pair of oxen is still widely used. Since 1950, farming tools and techniques have gradually been greatly improved and chemical fertilizers and pesticides used, which has tremendously enhanced the efficiency and productivity of Qiang agriculture.

There are many popular farmers' proverbs in Qiang areas, such as "pick up the stones on the fifth day of the first lunar month"; "a spring without cultivation, a decade without yield"; "no pain in cultivation, no gain in produce"; "even as one doesn't fish in the shallows, so crop cultivation on the high mountains is useless"; "no rain at the beginning of autumn results in lower crop yields and dissatisfaction among the people"; "autumn drought is grievous and will halve the harvest"; and "spring drought is not serious but autumn drought brings hunger". Qiang climatic knowledge and agricultural experience in the mountain areas are summarized in these proverbs.

Because of the hardships of their daily lives and the desire for a good harvest, some people would ask the Shibi to perform some solemn sacrificial rites before seed-sowing in the fourth lunar month. Offerings would be made to

祭祀青苗土地神和青稞神（谷神），祈求神灵保佑，使当年获得丰收。

羌族地区以坡地为主，可耕地多被茂密的森林区隔，野兽出没无常，成群的熊和野猪为害最大。庄稼出苗以后，就要辛勤守护，直到成熟收获到家，才算完结。羌族人民要在庄稼地四周搭起草棚，带上猎枪，日夜巡逻守护庄稼，驱赶野猪、熊、刺猬、山鼠、乌鸦、野鸡等禽兽。天黑时还要在田地适当的地方燃起篝火以威吓野兽。……1950年以前，羌民除了辛勤守护庄稼，驱赶野兽，也借助巫术，希望通过神灵的力量来驱赶野兽。这种活动羌语称为"热扯"，意即"撵野兽"。每年秋收以后还大愿时，羌族都要请释比做法事驱除农害，这种活动也有隆重的仪式以及复杂的内容和程序。法事在凌晨天未亮时开始进行。释比在神树林中念诵驱赶鸟兽的古歌，唱毕停止击鼓。这时一个青年抱一只公鸡，另几个青年举着火把在前引路，释比尾随其后，边走边唱古歌"热扯"，走遍村村寨寨和田间地块。边走边呼唤地名，众人随声应和吆喝，表示已把鸟兽赶尽。最后杀鸡，用鸡血祭神，并把鸡血洒在预先做好的小白纸旗上。天渐亮后，各家把小旗插在自己的庄稼地里，把鸡肉煮熟，让每人吃一小点，表示鸟兽已被大家煮吃了，绝迹了。这表明羌民对神灵的虔诚和对驱除农害争取丰收的渴望。这也是旧时代山区农业生产力落后的一种反映。

the gods of the highland barley and areas with green shoots, asking them for protection, blessing and a plentiful harvest. This practice lasted till 1950.

The Qiang areas consist mainly of sloping terrain with most of the cultivable land divided by thick forest from which wild animals, particularly bear and wild boar, emerge and damage the crops. In the past, once the seedlings had sprouted, Qiang farmers would laboriously safeguard them until they were harvested, building thatched shacks around the fields to protect the crops from wild animals such as boars, bears, hedgehogs, marmots, crows and pheasants. At night camp-fires were built to scare away the beasts.

Prior to 1950, besides going to such great lengths to protect their crops, some Qiang would also resort to sorcery in the hope that spiritual forces would keep the wild animals off their farms. This was called "Re che" in the Qiang language, meaning "to drive away wild animals". When redeeming vows to the gods after the autumn harvest, the Qiang would invite the Shibi to carry out complex, ceremonious ritual procedures to drive out injurious insects and harmful beasts. Usually the ceremony would begin before dawn at the sacred grove near the village, with the Shibi reciting ancient songs for expelling birds and beasts. This was accompanied by a drum being beaten. Then a young man holding a rooster and several others holding torches would lead the way with the Shibi following behind. Together they would walk through the villages and fields singing the "Re che". As they went they would call out the names of the places they passed and people would call back to them, echoing the place names, which indicated that all birds and beasts had been expelled from these places.

In the end, the rooster would be killed, its blood offered to the gods and also some of its blood sprinkled on some small white paper flags which had been prepared earlier. As daybreak came, these flags were placed on the farmland of every household, after which the villagers would cook the rooster and give everyone a small piece. The eating of the rooster symbolized that birds and beasts had all been completely dispelled. The activities mentioned above are an indication of Qiang piety towards the gods and of their persistent struggle for a good harvest. To a certain degree, they also reflect the low agricultural productivity of Qiang mountain areas in the past.

## 二、饲养牲畜与狩猎

许慎《说文解字》有云："羌，西戎牧羊人也。"范晔《后汉书·西羌传》也记载：古代羌人之地"滨于赐支，至乎河首，绵地千里"，"所居无常，依随水草。地少五谷，以产牧为业"。这说明古代羌人居住在河湟地区，是依随水草的游牧民族，以牧放羊群为主要生产而辅以粗耕的农业。后来古羌人的一支迁移至岷江上游，与原住居民冉駹逐渐融合，开始定居生活，农业逐渐成为主要产业，而传统的畜牧便转产为重要的副业。

近代羌族地区的畜牧业以养羊、牛、猪为主。靠近汉族地区以养猪为主，靠近藏族地区仍以养牛（或牦牛）为第一位。养羊一般成群牧放，晚上赶回关在碉房（住房）底层的圈栏内。也有在山上牧地搭建圈栏，白天放牧，晚上赶回圈栏的。牧羊人则带上猎枪，住在羊圈旁的草棚内守护羊群。牧羊本是古羌人的主要产业，羊在羌族生活中至今占有重要地位，羌人对羊怀有特殊的感情。所以，每逢重大节日，仍要祭祀牛王菩萨和羊神。还有一首广为流传的《放羊歌》："正月放羊是新春，早放羊，早起身，羊儿吆喝前面走，露水打湿脚后跟。二月放羊是春分，遍地草儿绿茵茵。羊儿不吃山中树，爱吃地上草青青……"歌词从正月一直唱到腊月，历数放羊的欢乐与艰辛，也流露出牧羊人对羊儿的感情。

羌民饲养黄牛主要是解决旱田耕地的问题。这大概也是迁徙定居于岷江上游以从事农耕为主要产业之后的事情。新中国成立前，

## II. Raising Livestock and Hunting

Xu Shen's book, *Shuowen Jiezi (Explaining Simple and Analyzing Compound Characters)*, says, "Qiang are shepherds who belong to the Western Rong living in the northwest". In *The History of the Later Han Dynasty: the History of the West Qiang*, Fan Ye states that the habitat of the ancient Qiang was "situated close to the Cizhi River, extending to the headstream of the river and covering a distance of thousands of miles", "the Qiang had no fixed settlement, going wherever there was water and grasslands, and due to the lack of cultivable land, they were dependent on animal herding for their livelihood". This shows that the ancient Qiang, who lived in the Hehuang region, were a nomadic people for whom raising sheep was a primary occupation, supplemented by some crude agriculture. Later, a branch of the ancient Qiang moved to the upper reaches of the Min River and intermarried with the native Ranmang people. Having thus settled down, crop cultivation gradually became the primary focus of these Qiang, with traditional stock-raising as an important subsidiary.

Nowadays sheep, cattle, and pigs constitute the main livestock of the Qiang. In places adjacent to Han areas, mainly pigs are raised. In places close to the Tibetan areas, cattle (or yak) are the primary livestock. Sheep are usually pastured in flocks and kept at night in pens on the lower floor of the Qiang houses. Pens are also built on the mountain pasture areas so that the sheep can graze during the day and be rounded up and penned in at night. In such a case, shepherds with hunting rifles will live in thatched shacks beside the pens to protect the sheep.

Raising sheep was the principal occupation of the ancient Qiang and sheep still play an important role and hold a special place in the lives of the Qiang today. During important festivals, sacrifices are offered to the god of sheep and the ox king Bodhisattva. There is also a widely known "Shepherd's Song" which says, "Herding sheep in the first month of the lunar year and spring is on its way. Up early to herd the sheep, the sheep run ahead bleating while the dew dampens my heels. Herding sheep in the second month, the spring equinox is here, green grass covers the land, the sheep eat the tasty grass rather than the trees on the mountains..." The song goes through the year describing the shepherd's life, listing the joys and hardships of herding sheep and revealing a particular tenderness for sheep in the Qiang.

Cattle are raised by the Qiang mainly to plow the dry farmland. This probably began after the ancient Qiang settled down round the upper reaches of the Min River and engaged principally in crop cultivation. Before

羌族没有吃耕牛的习惯，认为牛和人一样辛劳一生，应该受到尊重。死后埋葬，有固定的牛坟，不许践踏。农历十月初一牛王会，要举行隆重的祭祀活动，前面已作专门叙述。

养猪是为了解决肉食和增加经济收入，近年已成为许多家庭的主要副业，所以羌区有"穷不丢猪，富不丢书"的谚语。

羌族还有一项重要的副业是狩猎。《打猎歌》（节译）唱道："我生来就是打猎的，不是吃人奶而是吃狗奶长大的。我刚满月就像狗一样笑了，我刚满三个月就会像狗一样坐着，刚满七个月就生出了一对狗牙，满十二岁梦都梦见打猎。"这首歌充满幽默浪漫的情调，表现了这位自幼与猎狗为伴的天生猎人对狩猎的热爱和着迷。

在羌族地区的不同地方，流传着许多不同的关于狩猎的习俗和充满神奇浪漫色彩的故事。北部方言区以农历正月十七日为狩猎节，相传这一天狩猎获取猎物的多少将预示着当年狩猎运气的好坏。这天，年满30岁的男女都要带着兽形馍馍和猎枪上山打猎。打猎结束，众猎手将各自带的馍馍排列起来，一边念咒语，一边射击……妇女到了中午则将自己的兽形馍馍放在适当的地方，用石块或砍刀将其"击毙"，然后食用。未成年人这天也要用箭射击或用刀"砍杀"象征性的猎物（兽形馍馍），将"头"献给长者，然后食用。

另一些羌寨在狩猎节这天还要举行"苏月"活动，即用兽形馍馍做靶子，举行射击比赛，射中即被视为当年狩猎必有好收获的兆头。这些当是古代羌人狩猎生活的遗俗，它反映了古羌人对狩猎极其重视以及男女老少都要参与狩猎技能演练的史实。

羌区还有许多有关狩猎的民间故事。理县羌族供奉猎神"混牟策"。相传他是猎人的师傅，法力高强，发明了安放绳套捕捉野兽的方法，

1949, the Qiang did not use their plowing oxen for food. They believed that cattle, like people, toiled hard their whole lives and should be granted due respect. They were buried in their own grave, on which people were not allowed to tread. On the first day of the tenth lunar month, the day of the Ox King Festival, solemn sacrificial activities are still held, as mentioned in previous chapters.

Pigs are raised to increase income and provide the Qiang with meat products. In recent years this has become an important sideline for many families. A Qiang proverb says, " the poor closely guard their pigs while the rich closely guard their books".

Hunting is also one of the key subsidiary occupations of the Qiang. One hunting song says, "I was born to hunt. I grew up drinking the milk of dogs instead of my mother's milk. At one month old, I smiled a dog's smile; at three months old, I could sit up as a dog sits up; at seven months old, a pair of canines grew in my mouth. When I was twelve years old, my dreams were all about hunting". The humor and passion of this song expresses the love and enthusiasm of a born hunter who has grown up with his hunting dog for a companion.

There are a large number of hunting customs and related legendary and romantic stories. In northern Qiang areas, the seventeenth day of the first lunar month is the "Hunting Festival". Legend has it that the number of animals hunted on that day predicts the luck of hunters for the whole year. Thus, on that day, men and women aged over thirty go hunting in the mountains, taking with them small pieces of dough in the shape of animals, which symbolize hunting quarry. After hunting, the hunters line up all the dough animals and shoot at them while chanting ritual chants. At midday, the women put their dough animals in a suitable place and use stones or chopping knives to "kill them" before eating them. Before any children eat these dough animals, they should also "kill" them with arrows or knives and then cut off the dough heads and offer them to the elder family members.

During the Hunting Festival in some other villages a shooting competition called "Su Yue" is held, in which dough animals are used as targets. Those who hit the target are seen as portents of good hunting during the coming year. This traditional activity indicates the great importance the ancient Qiang, young and old alike, attached to hunting.

Among the many hunting stories, tales about "Hun Mou Ce" abound in Li County where he is widely worshipped. Legend has it that "Hun Mou Ce" was a master hunter, skilled in magic arts, who invented a method of catching

有一次竟套住了山神。后来山神变成老虎把他吃掉了。因此，他被供奉为猎神。北川、茂县一带的羌族供奉梅山神。相传梅山是一位能干的女猎手，她出猎从未空手而归，所以被猎人尊奉为猎神。一次，她在与老虎搏斗中不幸牺牲。搏斗时老虎把她的衣服撕成破片，衣不蔽体，所以梅山神像多为木雕裸体，并被供奉在较为隐蔽之处。在捕猎无望时，猎人便盘腿而坐，口诵《雷公诀》《梅山咒》，裸体施行法术，祈求梅山女神将野兽驱入陷阱或绳套之中。

羌族人称猎人为"吊路子"或"打路子"。猎人称血为"染子"，称狗为"豹子"。在他们中间流传着许多狩猎的歌谣，如《獐子谣》："吊路子，做啥子，安索子，套獐子。安索要懂得几下子，看清脚印'花点子'，树干擦痒'滚杆子'，屙屎撒尿'撒豆子'……"这生动地总结了追踪捕猎獐子的经验。羌族成年男性大多既是生产好手，又是狩猎能人，他们不但枪法好，还会安绳套，安弩刀、弩箭，安置千斤闸，施行圈猎（即预设栏圈在猛兽出没的地方，放进羊兔等小动物作诱饵，引诱猛兽进圈，触动机关而被关住）等多种多样的办法。这些都是羌族先民世代积累起来的宝贵经验。但安放弩刀弩箭因容易误伤进山的行人，已被禁止使用。

## 三、其他副业

羌族人民还从事其他几种重要的副业，即家庭手工纺织、挖药材和采摘核桃花椒。纺织是新中国成立以前羌民全家人口穿戴的唯一来源，挖药材和采摘核桃花椒则是羌民重要的经济来源之一。

绩麻，织麻布、毪子和绑腿以及纺毛线是羌族妇女除了农牧业生产之外的又一繁重的手工劳动。《女人苦》（节译）唱道："四月放羊四月八，白天放羊夜绩麻。白天放羊一大群，黑了绩麻到五更。手拿麻线直间哭，

animals by laying a noose and once even captured the god of the mountains. "Hun Mou Ce" is thus esteemed as the hunting god by the Qiang. The Qiang living around Beichuan County and Mao County worship the goddess Meishan. It is said that she was a skilled huntress who never came back without quarry, so she is revered as the goddess of hunting. She gave her life in a fight with a tiger. During the fighting, her clothes were torn from her body by the tiger and for this reason woodcarving images of her are often nude and are therefore situated in secluded places. When a hunter has despaired of finding any prey, he may take his clothes off, sit down cross-legged and recite the rhyming "Thunder God formula" and the "Meishan incantation" beseeching the goddess Meishan to drive animals into his trap or noose.

Qiang people call hunters "noose-hunters" and hunters use the term "dye" for blood and "leopard" for dogs. Many ballads about hunting center on these themes, such as the River Deer Ballad, which says, "Noose-hunter, what are you doing? I am placing a noose to capture river deer. To place the noose you must know what to look for: the shape of their hoof marks; the traces left when they rub themselves against the tree trunks; and their pea-like droppings..." Qiang men are not only good marksmen but are also good at setting nooses, shooting blades and arrows from crossbows, laying a trap with a heavy kind of hoisting jack, and also building enclosures which shut automatically when touched and are baited with small animals such as sheep or rabbits to entice wild animals into them. Over the years the Qiang have accumulated much valuable hunting experience. However, since the blades and arrows shot from crossbows may accidentally hurt other people on the mountains, their use has now been forbidden.

## III. Additional Occupations

The Qiang also have several other important occupations, including spinning and weaving, digging for medicinal herbs, and picking walnuts and huajiao (prickly ash). Spinning and weaving were the only sources of clothing for the whole family before liberation. Digging medicinal herbs and picking walnuts and huajiao remain important financial supplements for the Qiang and they are abundant enough to be sold in other parts of China

Besides agriculture and animal husbandry, Qiang women are also occupied with the demanding work of spinning and weaving hemp, spinning wool and making woolen fabric and puttees. The song "The Hardship of Women" says, "On the eighth day of the fourth lunar month, I have to herd sheep in the daytime and spin hemp at night. There are so many sheep to herd, and then my spinning lasts almost till dawn. Holding the threads in my hands, I cannot help

公婆说要用秤称。隔壁二嫂心不忍，隔墙递了麻一捆。"《放羊歌》唱道：
"四月放羊早绩麻，绩得粗来公婆骂。绩得细来眼睛花，苦女子气得没办
法。"这些民歌是羌族妇女艰辛生活的真实写照。她们从事的原始手工纺
织，工效低，劳动强度大，异常辛苦。以绩麻为例，妇女吊麻线时，一
边用牙齿撕麻，一边用右手拉抻纤维，左手则拧转纺锤纺线。一件麻布
衫用的麻线，一般需用几个月才能纺成。

　　由于羌族妇女在家庭和本族社会生活中的重要地位和作用，她们比
较受到尊重，而且在羌族的神灵谱系中也列有女性祖宗神、女当家神和
媳妇神等。这是羌族文化中一种特有的现象。

　　挖药材是羌族的传统副业之一。羌区的深山密林盛产虫草、贝母、
羌活、党参等名贵药材。采药人一般被称为"药夫子"，他们在深山
临时搭建的草棚则被称为"药棚子"。他们准备好吃的和其他必需品
后结伴进山，行前要请释比占卜，选择吉日，按照"七不出门八不
归"的习俗，忌讳逢"七"的日子进山。到山里选定搭建草棚之地
后也要燃木香或香蜡纸钱、杀公鸡祭山神，向神灵许愿，祈求保佑。
采药季节一般是五六月挖虫草、贝母，六七月挖羌活。《采药歌》"五
月草莓红满山，正是虫草冒尖尖。不管官大和贫贱，都要低头斜眼看。

crying. My husband's parents say they will weigh how much I've spun. My sister-in-law next door, unable to bear this, secretly passes me a bundle of threads." "The Sheep Herding Song" says, "Herding sheep in the fourth lunar month, I start my spinning early. If the thread I spin is too thick, my husband's parents may criticize me; if the thread I spin is too thin, I will strain my eyes. Poor me, what can I do?" These folk songs are a true portrayal of the hardships of Qiang women. Their spinning and weaving is done by hand, a primitive way that is labor intensive and low in efficiency. Take the spinning as an example: when the women hang up the hemp threads, they rip them with their teeth and use their right hands to stretch the fiber while turning the spindle with their left hands. It usually takes several months to spin enough thread for a hemp robe.

Because Qiang women have an important function and position in their homes and in society, they are very respected. There are also female ancestral gods, female gods of domestic affairs, and a daughter-in-law god. This is a very distinctive Qiang phenomenon.

Collecting medicinal herbs is another traditional occupation of the Qiang. The remote mountains and thick forests in Qiang areas are teeming with many rare medicinal materials such as Chinese caterpillar fungi (cordyceps), fritillary, Qianghuo (notopterygium root), and Dangshen (codonopsis pilosula). Those who search for these herbs are known as medicine "masters", implying a knowledge of the art and the temporary thatched shacks which they build in remote mountain areas are called "medicine shacks". The herb diggers usually go to the mountains together, taking prepared food and other necessities with them. Before they set out, the Shibi is invited to practice divination and choose an auspicious date which must accord with the custom of "not going out on any date with a seven in it and not coming back on any date containing an eight". Once in the mountains, the herb diggers select a site to build their thatched shed and then burn fragrant wood or incense sticks, candles and paper money. They slaughter a rooster as a sacrifice to the god of the mountains, making vows in return for the blessing of the gods.

The best time for digging Chinese caterpillar fungi and fritillaries is in May and June, whereas the best time for digging qianghuo is in June and July. As the "Herb-collecting Song" goes, "In the fifth month, when the whole mountain is covered with red strawberries, it's time for the Chinese caterpillar fungi to sprout and everyone from high official to poor peasant goes cross-eyed looking

不论亲疏和里外，等你只有七八天。贝母开花吊灯笼，六月热天正伏中。二指锄头（小尖锄）手握紧，一锄一颗莫放空"，道出了采药的经验和季节。

挖药材一般是个人或两人分散行动。羌族存在"万物有灵"的观念，还有"男山"、"女山"之分，不但事事要小心谨慎以免触犯神灵，还要针对不同性别的山采取不同的祭祀方法。

羌族地区特产丰富，以药材、核桃、花椒为外销大宗。羌族民歌唱道："高山竹兜嫩悠悠，砍回家中编背篼。背篼编得宽又大，八斗粮食装得下。背篼编得牢又牢，背了核桃背花椒。"羌区山高路险，交通困难，进出物资全靠人背或牲口驮运。在许多栈道险段，只能依靠人背。从羌区背运出药材、核桃、花椒等土特产，再从外地背运回茶叶和日用百货。羌族称这种运输为"背背子"，称从事这种运输的人为"背子客"。"背子客"背负沉重的货物，攀缘悬崖峭壁上的崎岖栈道，一不小心就会坠落深谷。所以他们出发前要做充分的准备，检查好自己的背运工具"背篼"、"背架"、"T"字形的"拐爬子"（行走爬坡杵路和帮助保持平衡）等。特别重要的还要请释比做法事，祈求沿途的山神保佑。羌族认为，神灵如同人间的寨首一样，一山一寨、一水一地都有专管的神灵。释比做法事请神时，要一一呼喊"背子客"所经过的主要山、水、寨的神灵名，祭祀许愿。"背子客"平安顺利返回后要祭神还愿。

羌族中的"背子客"冒着生命危险从事艰危的背运工作，这在他们的心灵上留下了酸苦恐惧的烙印，所以羌区流行着这样的谚语："宁做三年牛，不下一回坝。"下坝指从羌区背货翻越崇山峻岭下到成都平原。

（陈蜀玉　陈华新）

218

for them. Then it's only seven or eight days until the hottest part of the sixth month by which time the fritillaries will have blossomed bright like lanterns. Gripping the finger-sized hoe, each scoop yields a reward."

Herb diggers usually work in ones or twos when actually digging. The Qiang not only hold that "everything has a spirit" but also that mountains can be male or female. As a result, herb diggers are very careful not to offend the gods, even adopting different sacrificial rituals according to the gender of the mountain.

A Qiang folk song says, "Tender bamboo grows well in the high mountains; I cut some to weave a basket. The basket I make is large enough for eighty liters of grain; the basket I weave is strong enough to carry my huajiao and walnuts." In the high mountains and on the rugged paths of the Qiang areas, travel is so difficult that goods and materials have to be transported in and out on people's backs or by animal and on some dangerous plank road sections even animals cannot be used. Local products such as medicinal herbs, walnuts, and huajiao are transported out of Qiang areas while tea and various everyday articles are brought in. The Qiang call this kind of transport "back-carrying" and those who transport the goods in this manner are called "back-carriers". Carrying their heavy loads they travel the rugged cliff paths where a moment of carelessness may result in a fall to the valley below. Thus these "back-carriers" have to prepare well before setting off, thoroughly checking their back baskets, carrying frames, and T-shaped walking sticks (to aid in walking and keeping balance).

As an important part of the preparation, the Shibi is invited to perform his rituals and pray for the protection and blessing of the mountain gods as the carriers travel. The Qiang believe that, just as the human world is ordered, so every mountain, village, river, and piece of land is administered by a god. During his rituals, the Shibi calls out the names of the gods who administer the main mountains, rivers, and villages along the route of the "back-carriers", worshipping and making vows to them. If the "back-carriers" return safely, they are expected to offer sacrifices and fulfil their vows to the gods. These Qiang "back-carriers" risk their lives doing such dangerous work, something which can create fear and unhappiness in their lives. A common Qiang proverb says, "I'd rather be an ox for three years than make one trip down to the plain" (i.e. carry goods across the mountains to the Chengdu area).

( Translated by Dai Zhiyong, Chen Shuyu )

# 第十章　羌族的家庭与社团

## 一、家庭和姓氏

羌族的家族是羌族社会的基本组织。一般都是直系亲属同居，成员限于祖孙三代，而以父母和子女两代同居者居多。多子的家庭在儿子成婚后便分居另立门户，父母身边最后留下幺儿同居养老送终。羌族人每家都有神龛供奉祖先和其他众神，儿子分居后神灵也要从老房子"分家"到儿子的新居去。对神灵也有新老的观念，老房子的神灵资历最高，分家后逢年过节互相拜年时是以神的资历高低决定拜年的次序。因老房神"大"，所以，兄长也总是到弟弟家拜年。拜年的本质是拜家神（祖先神）。分居时新房子的火种也要从老房子分出来。

家庭实行父系家长制，父死子继，无子家庭可招婿入赘，继承家业。女性基本处于被支配的地位，但妇女在生产劳动中有着重要的地位，家庭决定重大事情仍要征询她们的意见。

近代以来，羌族家庭基本是一夫一妻制。婚姻讲究门当户对，个别地方还存在父母包办，早婚，近亲（姑舅表兄妹）优先，以及兄死弟娶寡嫂、弟丧兄纳弟妇等习俗。

羌族的姓氏，《后汉书·西羌传》载："其俗，氏族无定，或以父名

# CHAPTER TEN    QIANG FAMILY AND SOCIETY

## I. Family and Surname

The family is the basic unit of Qiang society. Grandparents, parents and children often live together under one roof, although many homes consist of just two generations: the parents and children. If a family has more than one child, the older children will move out of the parental home after marriage but the youngest son will stay with his parents to care for them in their old age.

In every Qiang family there is a household shrine where ancestors and gods are worshipped. When the children move out from their parents' home, some of these gods are taken with them to the new home. The gods who stay in the old house are higher in rank than those who leave, the latter being considered as "juniors". Worship of the household ancestral gods is central to the offering of New Year greetings and the seniority of the gods influences who calls on who on New Year's Day or on other festivals. This means that the older brothers always visit the youngest brother's home (i.e. the parental home) at these times. When the children move to their new homes, burning cinders are taken from the fireplace of the old house and brought into the new house.

Qiang families have a patriarchal system. When the father dies, the son assumes his position. If the family has no son, the daughter's husband will marry into the family home and inherit the family property. Women are basically in a subservient position but because they are such an integral part of family labor and income, they are always involved in important family decisions.

Today, Qiang marriages are generally monogamous and emphasis is often placed on the bride and groom being socially and economically well- matched. However, practices still exist like parentally-arranged marriages, early marriage, a preference for marriage between close relatives (cousins), and a widow marrying her brother-in-law.

Regarding Qiang surnames, *The History of the Later Han Dynasty: the History of the Western Qiang* says that "the Qiang custom was either to have no fixed clan or that a tribe would be named after the father's given name and the

母姓为种（部落）号。"由此发展为一种父子连名制，在历史上曾实行过
很长的时期。

岷江和涪江上游的羌族几乎都有自己祖传的小房名。这些小房名逐
渐演化成今日羌族的姓氏。如毛耳志、何必志、何我勺、罗志保等小房
名（见理县龙溪寨的《火魂碑》及《回龙寺钟铭》），后来就逐渐用它们
的第一字（或音）改成相应的汉姓毛、何、罗等。这种情况在汉代即已
开始，以后历朝的羌族人中都有这样用自己的小房名的第一个字改成汉
姓的。历史上还有立过战功的羌人被封建王朝或官员赐予汉姓的。羌族
支系繁多，改姓的时代也大多不可考，因此，羌族的姓氏并不像汉族那
样有明确的可以稽查的谱系和辈分。

近现代的羌族人一般是根据父母的愿望取名，并且大多有两个名，
一为释比所取，一为家庭长辈所取。赘婿则必须随妻改姓，而将其本姓
附在妻姓之后，中间加一个有吉祥含义的字即成他的姓名。赘婿的子女
可随母姓，多子女的也可以分别随父母的姓。

## 二、母舅的特殊地位

羌族谚语说："天上的雷公，地上的母舅。亲不过小母舅，大不过大
母舅。"这充分显示了羌族社会控制方面的特色。虽然羌族社会结构主要
是以父系血缘关系组建起来的，但社会控制主要依靠母系的血缘关系，
母系血缘关系中的舅舅在羌族社会中具有特殊的地位。亲族与家族以母
舅、姑父、叔伯、姨父为主，称为"四大亲戚"，而其中的母舅享有最
大的权力。

mother's surname." In this way an enduring system developed in which there was a link between the given names of father and son.

Qiang living near the upper reaches of the Min and Fu rivers almost all have their own ancestral name. Over time, these names have gradually evolved into the surnames used by the Qiang today. For instance, the ancestral names of Mao Er Zhi, He Bi Zhi, He Wo Shao and Luo Zhi (e.g. on the "Fire Spirit Stele" and the "Huilong Temple Inscription" in Li County's Longxi Village) have been changed to the corresponding Han surnames of Mao, He and Luo by taking only the first syllable (or character). This practice was begun back in the Han Dynasty and over the centuries Qiang people have used this same method, forming a Han surname from the first character of their ancestral name. Historically, some Qiang who made significant military contributions had Han surnames bestowed on them by officials or by the imperial court. As the Qiang have numerous branches, it is almost impossible to know when these name changes happened and for this reason, unlike the Han, the Qiang do not have easily traceable genealogies.

In modern times, Qiang children are usually named according to their parents' wishes and most people have two names, one given by the Shibi and one given by an elder member of the family. A son-in-law who lives in the home of his wife's parents must adopt her family name, placing his own family name last and choosing an auspicious character as a middle name, thus creating a full name. His child usually takes his wife's family name but if he has several children they can be named after either his or his wife's family name.

## II. The Special Status of Maternal Uncles

A Qiang proverb says, "In the heavens there's the god of thunder, and on earth there's the maternal uncle. Mother's younger brother is closest to us but her oldest brother is the most respected." Although the main social structures of the Qiang are established on the basis of patriarchal bloodlines, their society functions through matriarchal influence. Connected through the matriarchal bloodline, maternal uncles hold a special position in Qiang society. Within a Qiang family network, the mother's brother, father's sister's husband, paternal uncles and husbands of maternal aunts are seen as "the four major relatives", and of these the maternal uncle has the greatest authority.

在羌族人的家庭生活中，母舅充当着特殊而重要的角色，在决定儿女婚姻，修房造屋时释比选择地基、神龛和大门的位置的最后裁定等重大事项上，都由母舅做出具有权威性的决定。在婚娶宴上，母舅和新娘的哥哥、弟弟（即小舅子）要吃压席酒——第一轮筵席之后撤去残余的菜肴，再上第二轮酒菜继续畅饮。

在羌族的丧事礼仪中，老人去世，孝子要派专人到母舅家报丧。母舅家来吊丧，孝子要到大门外迎接，跪在门外道路两旁。这时，由专人端着木盘，内放酒肉为众母舅洗尘；负责接待的"支客司"带领众孝子唱《迎舅歌》，在场的其他人则随声帮腔。孝子再向母舅禀报死者生病、请释比驱鬼治病以及后事安排等情况，待母舅认可后才能下葬。

《后汉书·西羌传》有羌人"贵妇人党母族"的记载，今天羌族地区母舅居于特殊地位当是这种古俗的遗风。

## 三、体现原始民主制的议话坪

议话坪羌语称"尔母孜巴"。辛亥革命以前每个村寨都有议话坪，部分偏远村寨议话坪制一直延续到新中国成立前夕。现在虽不存在议话坪会议这种形式，但遇有重大事情仍有召集大家集体讨论、共同参与解决的风俗。历史文献记载了党项羌人的议事制度，近代羌区还保存着的议话坪会议制度，当是古羌人原始民主制的遗俗。议话制是羌族文化中社会伦理道德、法律的重要组成部分，议话的决定有着规范人们行为、

In Qiang daily life, the mother's brother has the final say in many significant matters, such as the marriages of his nieces and nephews and the Shibi's choice of location to erect new houses, main entrances, and household altars. During wedding feasts, the maternal uncles and the bride's brothers stay to enjoy a second round of food and wine after the dishes of the first round have been cleared away.

Qiang funeral protocol requires the bereaved sons to send someone to inform the maternal uncle of a family death. When the maternal uncles come with their families to pay their condolences, the bereaved sons welcome them by kneeling on both sides of the path outside the main door. Then a person is assigned to offer the maternal uncles a wooden tray of wine and meat as a sign of welcome. The son in charge of receiving these guests leads the other bereaved sons in singing "Welcoming the Mother's Brothers" and anyone else present also joins in. After this, the bereaved son reports to the mother's brothers about how the deceased fell sick, how the Shibi was asked to exorcise the spirits and treat the illness, and what has been done regarding funeral arrangements. Without the maternal uncle's permission, the dead can not be buried.

*The History of the Later Han Dynasty: the History of the Western Qiang* records that "the Qiang esteem females and favor the maternal line." The special social status accorded to maternal uncles today is possibly linked to this ancient custom.

### III. "Yihuaping": A Reflection of Primitive Democracy

"Yihuaping" literally refers to public ground where important matters are discussed. In the Qiang language, it is called "ermuziba". Before the revolution in 1911, every village had its own public discussion ground. In some remote villages, this system lasted until 1949. Although the system no longer exists in its earlier form, the Qiang still come together and solve problems collectively when facing important matters. Historical documents record that the Dangxiang Qiang customarily had public discussion about matters of importance and it is thought that the more recent public discussion ground can be traced back to this original democratic system of the ancient Qiang. This discussion system is an indispensable part of Qiang law, morality and social ethics, and decisions made in this way regulate people's behavior,

定夺是非、管理社会生活的约束作用。

过去的议话坪是检阅羌丁武装、推选寨首、练武、决定是否出兵打仗等重大事务的地方。近现代则主要是制定、公布乡规民约，解决纠纷和封山育林等公共事务，也包括传统的推选寨首等事项。一般每年或每两年开会一次，会首任期长至七八年。如有重大事件需经议话坪会议讨论决定，则由寨首临时通知。参加议话评会议的为成年男子，人人都有发言权。一经议定的事项即具有法律的性质，全寨或参与议事作决定的其他各寨都必须遵守。例如，新中国成立前理县桃坪乡增头寨每年 7 月 5 日召开议话坪会议，寨首召集全寨各家主事男子开会。按惯例杀一只鸡，将鸡血洒在纸旗上。然后将纸旗插在田地和森林中，将鸡吊在树上，警示众寨民如有触犯寨规民约者，将像这只鸡一样死去。之后如有违犯者，则根据情节予以罚款或给予其他相应的处罚。羌区其他各寨的议事坪会议作出的决定莫不如此具有法律的效力。

## 四、尊老爱幼团结互助

尊老爱幼是羌族人民优良的传统美德。孝敬长辈、尊重年长者，慈爱幼儿、关心晚辈，同情和帮助残疾孤弱的人，都是羌族社会普遍的公德。一般重大礼仪活动都由年长者主持；对年老者，即使是辈分高的人对年长的晚辈仍须十分尊重。在新中国成立前，即使是地方上的保甲长、团总之类的豪绅，对年长者也都很敬重。

团结、友爱、互助是羌族道德观念的又一体现。维护村寨和本民族的共同利益

decide right and wrong, and set social restraints on Qiang society.

In the past, this discussion ground was also a public place where Qiang soldiers were inspected, village heads were elected, combat training was carried out, and decisions about whether or not to dispatch troops were made. More recently, it has been the place for formulating and announcing village regulations, resolving disputes, and discussing other public affairs, such as the closing of hillside areas to encourage afforestation. It is also where matters take place such as the traditional election of the village head, who serves a seven or eight-year term. These public meetings are convened once every one or two years. In circumstances where urgent discussion is necessary, the village head is empowered to give notice of a meeting. Participants in the discussion are adult men and every one has the right to speak. Once a decision is made it acts as the law of the village and must be obeyed by all villagers.

Prior to 1949, the head of Zengtou Village in Li County's Taoping Township would convene a public discussion every year on July 5th, attended by the heads of every household in the village. Usual practice was for a chicken to be slaughtered and paper flags to be sprinkled with the blood of the chicken. Then the flags would be erected on farmland or in the forest and the chicken would be hung up on the branch of a tree as a warning that anyone who violated village regulations would die like the chicken. After this, if someone did break the regulations, he would be fined or punished in a way appropriate to the circumstances. Decisions made in other Qiang villages by this system of public discussion also serve as local law.

## IV. Respect for the Old, Love for Children, and Mutual Cooperation

Respecting older family members, being kind to children and having a sympathetic attitude towards the disabled, orphaned or weak are traditional values and important attributes of Qiang society. In most cases, important rituals and activities are presided over by elders in the community. Someone of high social position should still show extreme respect to those older than himself. Before 1949, local and sometimes fairly ruthless people of high social status, like the village headman, would still show respect for their elders.

Harmony, friendliness and helping others are central tenets of Qiang society. Upholding the common interests of the Qiang people and their villages

是羌民共同的生活和言行的准则。羌区流行着这样的谚语："修建新房，大家帮忙"，"新婚喜事，亲朋帮忙"，"农忙大事，全寨帮忙"。农忙季节，羌民邻里间自来便习惯于结成不太固定的互助集体：或互相换工（即商定双方以工顶工），或用工一方请有空的邻居志愿帮忙。若有修房、婚娶、丧葬等事，主人只管伙食，来帮助者有好吃好，无好吃孬，从不计较；需要桌凳碗筷等用品，大家都热情主动送来……

在一些接近藏区的地方，还有不少羌、藏、汉族杂居的村寨，羌、藏、汉等民族团结、友爱、互助也形成传统。在一首羌族民歌《修雕房》中唱道："羌汉藏三兄弟相聚在羌山上，是要为羌人修房屋。汉民搬石，藏民拌泥，羌人砌墙。汗水流在一起，笑声飞在一起，劲使在一起。……新房落成，羌家主人宴宾客，汉藏兄弟请上座……感谢汉藏兄弟的帮忙。"

（陈蜀玉　陈华新）

is the norm in both word and deed for the Qiang, as evidenced in these popular local sayings: "Everyone helps with building a new house"; "Friends and relatives help at weddings"; "At important events or in the busy farming season, the whole village pitches in". In busy farming seasons, Qiang neighbors are accustomed to forming a team and helping each other out. They may exchange labor or if someone is free they will just volunteer to help. When houses are built or major activities like weddings and funerals are held, Qiang people are happy to offer help. The host just has to provide food for everyone and the helpers don't mind whether the dishes are plain or rich fare. If extra tables, benches, bowls or chopsticks are needed, neighbors happily lend theirs.

In some villages adjacent to Tibetan regions, Qiang, Han and Tibetans live together and ethnic unity and friendly cooperation are customary. A Qiang folk song called "Building a Qiang House" says, "Three young men, a Qiang, a Han and a Tibetan, gather together on a Qiang mountain to build a house for the Qiang. The Han carries the stones, the Tibetan mixes the mud and the Qiang lad lays the bricks. Their sweat blends together, their laughter rises to the skies, and their shared effort unites them... the house is now finished, the Qiang host holds a feast with many guests. My Han and Tibetan brothers, please take the seats of honor...thank you, my brothers, for your help."

( Translated by Dai Zhiyong, Chen Shuyu )

# 第十一章  羌族的相关习俗和
# 婚礼与葬礼

## 一、亲友社交的礼仪习俗

羌族人重情义，讲友好，注重礼尚往来。走亲访友、宾客往来，客人到门要轻声招呼，主人听声要热情迎接。主人没有回应，不能贸然进屋，否则会被认为不礼貌。主人家里有产妇或病人须"忌门"，即客人不但不能进入大门，还要立即有礼貌地退出离去。客人被迎请进屋，主人请客人坐下，献上烟、茶，并亲自将烟点燃。如来客是主人的长辈或年长者，则要请他坐在靠神龛的一方。客人在主人家不能乱窜，尤其不能进入卧室和主人闺女的住房。若发生这种情况，会被视为越轨，终身受到公众的耻笑。客人送的礼物，主人谦让一番后要接过来放在日常存放重要物品的房间，以示对客人的尊重。

招待客人，羌族一般用山珍野味、土产土味，荤素搭配。特别讲究劝酒，一般饮"咂酒"、白酒。无论客人是否喜欢，都要接受主人三杯敬酒。若推辞不喝，会被误认为嫌酒菜不好。饮酒之前要先诵开坛词或敬酒歌。客人越善饮，主人越高兴，或划拳，或唱酒歌，或围绕锅庄跳舞，直至尽欢而散。

# CHAPTER ELEVEN    QIANG CUSTOMS AND CEREMONIES

## I . Customs when Receiving Relatives and Friends

The Qiang people place great emphasis on hospitality and friendliness, adhering to the convention that "courtesy demands reciprocity" in social intercourse.

When visiting friends or relatives, a guest should call a greeting from the doorway, but not too loudly. Upon hearing the greeting, the host should come and warmly welcome the guest. If there is no response from the host, the guest should not enter the house as this may be considered impolite. If there is a woman in bed due to childbirth or a person is ill in the host family, the guest will not be invited in and should promptly and politely take his leave. If the guest is welcomed into the house, the host will offer him a seat, give him tea and a cigarette, which the host will light for him. If the guest is an older relative of the host or simply an older person, he should be invited to sit near the household shrine. The guest should not wander freely into other rooms, especially the bedrooms and in particular the master bedroom. This is considered highly offensive and such behavior may be ridiculed for years to come. As to gifts brought by the guest, it is customary for the host to decline them at first to show his modesty but then to accept them. The gifts should be placed in a room where important things are usually kept so as to show respect for the guest.

The Qiang often entertain guests with local specialties and delicacies of various kinds, including both meat and vegetable dishes. It is their tradition to ply the guest with alcohol, which is usually sucking wine or clear liquor. When toasted by the host, the guest, whether he likes the drink or not, should drink at least three cups of wine. Any refusal to drink could be misread by the host as dislike of the food and drink he has provided. Before drinking starts, the "Jug Opening Speech" is recited or the "Toasting Song" is sung. The more the guest drinks, the happier the host is. While drinking, people play the finger-guessing game (a drinking game often played at feasts), sing drinking songs, or dance

有的地方还有一些特殊的习俗，如黑水茂县一带的羌族，客人临门要鸣枪相迎。进屋后要请客人坐在锅庄上方，并捧出"咂酒"招待。

客人临走时要和主人告别，不能不辞而别。客人若家境较差，主人可赠送一定的物品。然后互约他日到家做客，主客依依惜别。

## 二、人生礼仪习俗

羌族人一生有繁多的礼仪和相关的习俗。这些礼俗反映了本民族社会和信仰的特征，是羌族文化的重要组成部分。

### （一）生育礼俗

#### 1. 求子

羌族信仰女神"娘娘菩萨"或"三星娘娘"，据说由她主宰生育并保佑女性和婴儿平安降生。农历三月三日或三月二十日，已婚妇女要带上祭品到娘娘庙去赶"娘娘会"，祈求早生贵子或祈求保佑自己顺产（已怀孕者）及儿女平安成长（已生子女者）。羌区有自古相传的"打儿窝"，它是村寨附近一个据说有生殖功能的岩壁洞穴。求子者到洞穴下口念求子的祈祷词，然后向洞穴中投掷石子，如已投中即被认为神灵应允生育。松潘、北川等县都有著名的"打儿窝"，北川县的禹穴沟尤具神话色彩。相传北川禹里乡禹穴沟是大禹出生之地，禹穴沟内有禹穴、剖儿坪、洗儿池、血石等大禹遗迹。当地羌民深信，凡不育妇女只要到此坐一坐、睡一夜或捡一块石头在手，都可实现怀孕生子的愿望，且不会出现难产。

around the fire pit. In some places in Heishui and Mao County there are other special customs, for example, firing rifles into the air to welcome the guest. The guest is invited to take the "seat of honor" in front of the fire pit.

When it's time to leave, the guest must bid farewell to the host and not leave without saying goodbye. If the guest's family is quite poor, the host will give him some gifts. Then they will arrange a time for a reciprocal visit and reluctantly part from each other.

## II. General Etiquette

The Qiang have various etiquette-related customs which are an important part of their culture, reflecting distinctive features of their society and their beliefs.

### 1. Birth customs

#### 1) Praying for a child

The Qiang people believe in the "Goddess Bodhisattva" or "Three-star Goddess", who is said to be in charge of human procreation and to have the power to bless and protect pregnant women and their babies. On March 3rd or March 20th of each lunar year, married women take their sacrificial offerings to the temple of the goddess, where childless women pray to soon have a son, pregnant women ask for a smooth delivery, and those who are already mothers pray for their children to grow up safe and sound.

In the Qiang area, an ancient tradition has been handed down of a cave in the cliffs near the village which has special power to enable women to conceive. Those who long for a child recite their prayers at the mouth of the cave and then throw stones into the cave. If the stones hit the target, it means the gods will allow the wife of the family to conceive a baby. The counties of Songpan and Beichuan have well-known caves of this kind, with that of Yu Cave Gully (Yuxuegou) in Beichuan being particularly mysterious and impressive. Yu Cave Gully, which is located in Yuli township, is said to have been the birthplace of Yu the Great, the reputed founder of the Xia Dynasty. Many relics attributed to Yu are found in Yu Cave Gully including Yu Cave, the "Baby-washing pool," and the "Blood Stone". Local Qiang firmly believe that any childless woman only has to sit in the cave or sleep a night there or pick up and hold a stone in the cave to conceive and have a safe delivery.

汶川绵虒一带还有另一种求子习俗：新婚之家于次年正月将舞狮队或舞龙灯的迎至家中堂屋舞狮或舞龙，狮或龙口中吐出预先准备的用红纸或红布包的核桃，叫做"红宝"；主人跪地致谢后，将"红宝"供在神龛上，期盼早生贵子。

### 2. 怀孕

妇女怀孕后若出现呕吐等妊娠反应，要请释比做安胎法事，并要在房顶上撑一把伞，据说可以避免鬼怪闯入，惊动胎儿，以免发生流产、早产或婴儿死亡等不幸事情。妇女怀孕后，在家庭中的地位也有所提高，家中人要处处予以照顾。孕妇自己也要小心谨慎，严守禁忌，以免触怒神灵，因孕妇身体被视为不洁之躯。临产前数日，娘家要送去婴儿衣帽、鞋袜和鸡蛋、糯米、红糖等物品，俗称"送催生"。有的人家还按相传的古俗，在临产前敲落木盆的盆底，或把铁锅从灶上取下，认为这样能使产妇顺产。

### 3. 分娩

新中国成立前，羌族妇女分娩多在牛羊圈内，没有助产，常以石块割断脐带或以牙咬断脐带。若胎盘不下来，就让产妇坐在一个高凳上，以热水烫其臀部。新中国成立后，革除了这些陋习，但妇女仍不得在供神的屋内生产。婴儿出生后，屋里要挂铜镜或玻璃镜，帽子上要钉贝壳饰品，认为能辟邪除魔。孩子出生后第一个来到产妇家的人谓之"逢生"，主人要煮醪糟鸡蛋

In the Miansi area of Wenchuan County there is another custom related to asking for a child. In the first month of the lunar year, following the wedding of a newly-married couple, a team of dancers is invited to perform the lion dance or the dragon lantern dance in the main room of their home. During the performance, the lion or the dragon spits out a "red treasure", a walnut wrapped in red paper or red cloth. After the host has knelt down to express his thanks, the "red treasure" is placed as an offering on the household shrine, and the family waits expectantly for the wife to conceive and bear a child.

### 2) Pregnancy

If a woman experiences vomiting during pregnancy, the Shibi is invited to perform rituals to prevent a miscarriage. The family will also open an umbrella on the roof of the house, which is said to prevent the intrusion of evil spirits which may disturb the unborn child and bring misfortune such as a miscarriage, premature delivery, or stillbirth. After a woman becomes pregnant, her status in the family is elevated and everyone in the house must give her preferential treatment. Pregnant women themselves are also careful to observe certain taboos so as not to offend the gods because the body of a pregnant woman is regarded spiritually as "unclean". When a woman is about to give birth, her parents will send some baby clothing, including hat, shoes and socks,  and some eggs, glutinous rice, and brown sugar—gifts said to hasten delivery. Some families even follow the old tradition of knocking out the bottom of a wooden basin or removing the iron wok from the kitchen range. It is believed that the woman will have an easy birth if these customs are observed.

### 3) Childbirth

Before 1949, most Qiang women gave birth to their babies unaided in cattle or sheep pens, where they would cut the umbilical cord with stones or even with their teeth. If the placenta did not come out, the woman would sit on a tall stool and hot water would be poured on her buttocks. After 1949, these old customs were abandoned. However, women are still not allowed to give birth to babies in any room where sacrifices are offered to the gods. After a baby is delivered, bronze or glass mirrors are often hung in the rooms and the baby's woolen hats are often decorated with shell ornaments to ward off evil spirits. The first guest to visit the newborn baby's family is welcomed warmly by the host and may be given eggs cooked in fermented

热情招待"逢生"的客人;"逢生"的人则要说些吉祥的祝愿话语。羌族认为"逢生"以女婴逢男性来客、男婴逢女性来客为最好,还认为小孩今后长大成人的性格、脾气等都与"逢生"的人的秉性、脾气以及进入产妇家时的情绪等有密切的关系。

**4. 婴幼儿成长期的礼俗和禁忌**

婴儿出生后,亲朋好友和邻居们要送鸡蛋、鸡、猪膘等食品,谓之"送祝米";产妇娘家更要送礼物。第三天要扯些草药煎成药汤给婴儿洗澡,叫做"洗三"。洗澡水不得乱泼,以免污秽神灵招致灾祸。新中国成立前,若生下畸形婴儿,要请释比来做法事,叫做"赶野仙"。据说这种"怪胎"是"野仙"作怪形成的;请释比做了法事以后就不会再生"怪胎"了。婴儿满月后产妇要将其抱出来给亲友和邻人抚摸观看;大家要说些吉利、恭维的话表示祝福,叫做"讨喜"。婴儿取名一般也在满月那天进行。这天要请近亲或邻居家的五至八岁的小孩来家玩耍,并准备三个"人形馍馍"和一坛"咂酒"(或白酒)。由婴儿的父亲或族中的长辈,或最年长的人命名,称为小名。命名后将馍馍和酒分给请来的孩子们吃。旧时有的还要请释比根据婴儿的生辰八字来命名,叫做大名。以后每年农历的正月十二日或二十四日要带孩子去敬神,祈求神灵保佑孩子健康成长。若孩子八字恶,生身父母难以带好,就要拜继给别人而称自己的父母为叔伯、姨姑。旧时还有把孩子拜给古树或大石的习俗,其做法是用红纸写成拜帖,

glutinous wine. In return, the guest is expected to utter some auspicious wishes for the baby. The Qiang consider it auspicious for the first guest of a baby boy to be female and that of a baby girl to be male. It is also believed that the temperament of the "first guest" and their mood when they make this first visit is closely connected with the future character and disposition of the child.

### 4) Customs and Taboos During Infancy

After a baby is born, relatives and friends of the family send gifts of eggs, chicken, and pork fat, with the mother's parents giving the greater amount. On the third day after birth, a liquid of medicinal herbs is made and the baby is bathed in it. After the bath, the liquid must not just be thrown on the ground as this would be regarded as a sinful action against the gods and could attract misfortune. Before 1949, the Shibi was always invited to perform his rituals if a malformed baby was delivered. This practice was called "driving away Ye Xian"—the demon considered responsible for such births—and it was believed that the ritual would prevent the demon from causing future birth deformities.

When a baby is one month old, the mother usually carries the baby outside so that relatives, friends and neighbors can see and touch him or her and everyone expresses their compliments and best wishes for the baby. Naming of the baby also usually takes place on this day. According to tradition, all five to eight year-old children of close relatives or neighbors are invited to come and play at the baby's house. The family of the baby prepare a jug of sucking wine or some liquor and three steamed buns shaped like people. Once the child has been named by either its father or one of the clan elders or the oldest family member, all the children present are invited to share the buns and wine. The name given in this case is an informal name. In old times, some families invited the Shibi to name the baby according to the birth date characters used in fortune telling and this would be a formal name.

From then on, on January 12th or 24th of the lunar calendar, the parents take the child every year to worship the gods, praying for continued health and blessing in the child's future life. If the birth date characters predict misfortune and it is difficult for the natural parents to raise the child well, the child is adopted and raised by other people and refers to his real parents as his uncle or aunt. Previously, there was even the custom of having the child "adopted" by an old tree or a large rock. In this ritual an "adoption" letter was written on a piece

贴在树上或石上，然后点香烧纸，磕头作揖（行拜继礼），并另取一名。小孩出天花要请释比做法事；小孩受到意外的惊吓生病，也要请释比做法事招魂。

羌族的生育礼俗，折射出羌人千百年来在生产力低下和缺乏生育保健卫生保障的条件下对子孙繁衍的强烈愿望以及为本民族种姓延续而艰苦奋斗的历史。

（二）成年礼仪——冠礼

冠礼是羌族男子人生的一个新起点。行冠礼的时间一般在男子12岁（又说18岁或16岁）。冠礼仪式由释比主持。先由释比打扫房屋禳除不祥，然后正式举行仪式。释比向天神献祭品（鸡或羊）。诸亲族围火塘而坐，受冠礼者着新衣冠。释比手持杉杆向神灵跪下，杉杆顶端有纸制人类始祖像。释比拜祭天神、山神等神灵。受冠礼人亦向人类始祖神跪下，此时另一位释比手持始祖的赠礼——白公羊毛和五色布条，围系在受冠礼者的颈上，以表示始祖的关怀和命根有系。之后释比唱诵与冠礼有关的经典，再由族长或年长者唱诵叙述羌族历史的史诗，祭祀家神，至此冠礼完成。

举行成年冠礼在不同的地方还有一些不同的做法。在茂县、北川等地的一些羌寨，成年冠礼不在家里专门举行，而是在一年一度的全寨或联寨的祭山还大愿时一并举行。祭山仪式之后，释比在神树林的石塔处边转边唱诵记述羌族历史的史诗《木姐珠与斗安珠》《羌戈大战》等，并给受冠礼者系上羊毛线，在他的额上抹一点猪油，

238

of red paper and stuck to the tree or stone, incense and paper were burned and people kowtowed, after which a new name was chosen for the child. If a child suffers smallpox or becomes sick as the result of an unexpected shock, the Shibi is invited to practice his rituals to appeal to the soul.

The birth customs of the Qiang reflect their strong desire for large healthy families despite centuries of low childbirth rates and poor hygiene when giving birth. They also tell part of the story of the Qiang people's struggle for survival and the continuance of their ethnic group.

## 2. The Coming-of-age Ceremony

The manhood ceremony marks a new starting point in a Qiang boy's life and is usually held when the boy turns 12 (or sometimes 16 or 18). The ceremony is presided over by the Shibi. Before the ceremony is formally initiated, the Shibi cleanses the house to avert any misfortune. Then he offers sacrifices (a chicken or sheep) to the god of heaven. All the members of the same clan sit around the fireplace and the boy who is the object of the ceremony wears a new hat and new clothes. When all these preparations have been made, the Shibi kneels down facing the shrine, holding a wooden staff to the top of which is stuck a paper ancestral image. He then offers sacrifices to the god of heaven and the mountain god. The boy, who is the focal point of the ceremony, should also kneel and worship towards the ancestral gods. At the same time, another Shibi holds a gift from the ancestors—some wool from a white ram and ribbons of various colors—which are placed around the boy's neck to show the care of the ancestors and their close connection with his life. To end the ceremony, the Shibi sings some texts relating to the manhood ceremony and the elders of the clan recite the epic history of the Qiang and offer sacrifices to the ancestors.

The manhood ceremony is conducted differently in different places. In some villages in the area of Mao and Beichuan Counties, the ceremony is held not at home but as part of the annual sacrificial mountain ceremony attended by everyone from the village or associated villages. After the sacrificial mountain ceremony, the Shibi recites some epics about the glorious history of the Qiang in front of the stone tower in the sacred grove. These include "Mu Jie Zhu and Dou An Zhu" and "The Great Battle of the Qiang and Ge". Then a length of sheep's wool is tied to the boy and some lard is smeared on his forehead to

以表示命根有系，天神保佑。当晚受冠礼者还要在自家屋顶祭仓神等神灵，由他的母亲主祭。北川有的羌寨举行成年男子冠礼的仪式时，还要进行一种请冠郎神的民俗活动。其做法是在石板上涂一层黄泥浆，泥浆上放一桶水，由受冠礼的人将水桶提起来。若石板和水桶一齐被提起脱离地面，则被视为一生有好运，能办成大事。

行冠礼后的男子被视为成年人，有资格独立行事，公开参加社交活动，享有成年人的权利和义务，并被公认为正式的社会成员。

（三）婚制习俗

羌族的婚姻形式基本上是一夫一妻。羌族中至今流传着许多关于婚制的歌谣和传说。《婚礼歌》唱道："自古男女皆婚配，此制本是木姐兴，所有规矩她制定，后人不得有减增。一代一代传下来，祖先古规须遵行。"俄巴巴瑟女神被认为是管理人间婚姻的大神。传说木比塔造人后，看到人间胡乱婚配很生气，便叫俄巴巴瑟女神专管人间的婚配大事。俄巴巴瑟的哥哥是专管人间投生之事的大神，在他的帮助下，俄巴巴瑟把投生凡间的男女在天庭时便配好对。俄巴巴瑟住在神与人交界的山上的杜鹃花丛中，她从天庭带来许多羊角，让每个投生人间的人男左女右各取一只羊角，采一束杜鹃花下山投生。于是到人间投生的人，不论天涯海角，总要配双成对，结为夫妻。至今羌族仍称羊角花（杜鹃花）为"俄司拉巴"，把订婚称为"插花"。

羌族民间文学作品中有许多关于兄妹成婚繁衍人类的传说，这反映了远古

indicate his connection with his ancestors and the blessing and protection of the god of heaven. That evening, a sacrificial ceremony presided over by the boy's mother is also held on the roof of the boy's house to worship the god of the store house and other gods. In some villages in Beichuan County, during the manhood ceremony, a bucket of water is placed on a flagstone covered with mud. The boy is asked to lift up the bucket and if the flagstone sticks to the bucket and doesn't fall, he is considered to be a lucky man with a successful future. This activity is called "inviting the god of manhood".

Once a young boy has experienced the manhood ceremony he is formally regarded as an adult and has full independence to take part in public and social activities. He also enjoys the full rights and duties of an adult and is recognized as a formal member of the society.

### 3. Marriage System

Qiang marriages are generally monogamous. Many ballads and legends about marriage still prevail. "The Wedding Song", for example, says that "The system of men marrying women was set up by Mu Jie in ancient times. She established all the rules and later generations should neither add to nor detract from them. Passed down from generation to generation, these rules of our ancestor must be obeyed." In Qiang mythology, the goddess Er Ba Ba Se is said to be in charge of marriage. After the god Mu Bi Ta had created humans, he was very upset that people were marrying or pairing off so casually. So he asked Er Ba Ba Se to take charge and bring order to the situation. Er Ba Ba Se's brother was the god in charge of humans coming to earth. With his help, every man and woman was paired in heaven before coming to earth. Er Ba Ba Se was believed to live among clusters of azaleas on the mountain that marks the boundary between gods and human beings. She gathered many ram's horns from the court of heaven and with men on the right and women on the left, they had to each take a ram's horn and a bunch of azaleas before coming down the mountain to the world of humans. From then on, these couples were destined to be married, no matter how far apart they happened to be. This is why the Qiang people use the term "Er Si La Ba" for the azalea (also known as the ram's horn flower) and becoming engaged is known as "the dividing of the flowers".

In Qiang folk literature, there are many legends about sisters marrying brothers and their offspring multiplying, reflecting the historical reality in

时期群婚、血缘婚的历史真实。《后汉书·西羌传》有云："其俗，氏族无定，或以父名母姓为种号，十二世纪后相与婚姻。"这说明早在 2 000 多年前已确立了一夫一妻的族外婚制。据上述传说，那时已把这种一夫一妻的族外婚制视为天神制定的不可违反的婚制。

古代羌人种类繁多，分布地域很广，经济发展水平不同，其婚姻形式也不尽一致。生活在今岷江、涪江上游的羌族，母系制延续时间较长。直到近代，入赘婚仍是他们的主要婚姻形式之一。《汶川县志》记载：1912 至 1949 年，"赘婿之风，亦极盛行"。羌族释比的经典也说："古今婚姻大不同，不同之处说根由，从前羌人男出嫁，男子入赘女子家。"入赘婚本人可以做主。女方系处女，一切仪式都要举行，只是男家不出财礼，女家给男家送礼。入赘者要改名换姓，跟女家同姓，还要给女家写赘约，规定入赘后男子要履行的义务和职责。

新中国成立前，多实行包办强迫的封建买卖婚姻。幼年时即由父母请人测字，合婚，然后举行订婚仪式。择婚有严格的等级界限，讲究门当户对和亲上加亲。在结婚年龄上盛行早婚。一般是男的 7 至 10 岁，女的 12 至 18 岁，往往是女大于男。有一首羌族民歌辛辣地讽刺了这种现象："十八姐儿三岁郎，夜夜把你抱上床。睡到半夜摸奶吃，是你老婆不是娘。

antiquity of communal marriage and marriage between blood relatives. *The History of the Later Han: History of the Western Qiang* says that "in Qiang custom, clans were not clearly defined and they either took their clan name from the father's personal name or from the mother's family name. After the twelfth century AD, there was intermarriage between clans". This illustrates that the system of monogamous marriage beyond the clan was established more than two thousand years ago, and, by the time of the legend above, it was already regarded as an inviolable system laid down by the god of heaven.

The ancient Qiang people were distributed over a very wide area in a variety of groups. They had varying levels of economic development and their forms of marriage also differed. Among those Qiang people who lived near the upper reaches of the Min and Fu Rivers, matriarchy prevailed for a long time. Until recent times, the main form of marriage was still for the husband to marry into the wife's family. *The Wenchuan County Annals* from 1912 to 1949 say that "there was a prevailing trend of a son-in-law marrying into his wife's family". Shibi texts also say that "marriage in the past differed greatly from today in that the Qiang man used to marry into his wife's household and live together with his in-laws". The husband and the wife can decide whether or not to have this kind of marriage. If the wife is a virgin, all the usual wedding rituals are carried out, except that the husband's parents don't provide betrothal gifts and the wife's family presents a gift of money to the husband's parents. The husband takes his wife's family name and signs a contract with the wife's family, stipulating the commitments and responsibilities he should fulfill after marriage.

Before 1949, mercenary marriages were often arranged by the parents. While the children were still young, their parents would have the characters of their names analyzed and if a boy and girl were found to be compatible, a betrothal ceremony was held. There were strict rules as to who could marry whom, with particular emphasis on social and economic equality and preference given to family connections. Marriages at an early age were quite common at that time. It was not unusual for a boy to marry between the ages of seven and ten. Girls were usually older—between twelve and eighteen. One rather caustic, satirical Qiang folk song says, "We are an eighteen-year-old wife and a three-year-old husband; I carry you to bed in my arms every night; at midnight you want to suck, but I am your wife and not your mother; if there was no

不是堂上公婆在，你当儿子我当娘。"缔结婚姻，男家还要给女家很多财礼。那时流行着这样的谚语："养女不发狠（不多要财礼），烧起锅儿等（等着受穷）。"这便是真实的写照。

在新社会，随着羌族社会的进步与经济的发展，历史上形成的许多不良习俗已逐步革除。婚姻已成为自主婚姻。

### （四）婚礼习俗

在羌族的人生礼仪中，婚姻被看得很重要，因而有很复杂的婚礼习俗，要经过开口酒、订婚酒、报期酒、开坛酒、搭棚酒、女花夜、正宴、回门等一系列程序。

开口酒。羌族一般是男方主动向女方求婚。男方备上"水礼"请"红爷"（即媒人）向女方求婚。女方家长认可后即收下"水礼"，将女儿的生辰八字写在"庚书"上交给"红爷"，带回男家。男家即请释比测算双方的八字是否相合，谓之"合婚"。如八字相合，即择日由"红爷"将女方的庚书送回女家，表明婚事已成。这时男家要给女家送一些礼物，到女家吃"开口酒"。吃"开口酒"时，双方主要是明确双方的关系并且商定吃订婚酒的日期。

订婚酒。由男女双方同时分别举行。男方准备酒肉宴请家门亲戚，告知订婚之事，同时请释比做法事，祈求神灵保佑这对未来的夫妇平安幸福。女方也同样宴请家门亲戚，告知这桩婚事。吃了订婚酒，

mother-in-law, you could be my son and I am your mother." In that era, when two people got married, the husband's family was usually required to give many gifts to the wife's family, as this popular saying shows, "If you raise a daughter and don't push for plentiful betrothal gifts from her husband's family, a poor life lies ahead of you."

Nowadays, with social progress and economic development, the custom of early marriage has been abolished among the Qiang, as have many other traditional practices, and young people are now free to choose their own spouse.

## 4. Weddings

Marriage plays a role of the highest value in Qiang society and consequently there are quite complicated wedding customs. The traditional village form of marriage is characterized by a series of rituals such as the "proposal wine", "engagement wine", "wedding date announcement wine", "jug opening wine", "erecting the wedding canopy wine", "the bride's wedding eve", "the formal wedding banquet" and "returning to wife's home".

A proposal of marriage is generally initiated by the man's family, which prepares a gift of food and wine to be taken by a matchmaker to convey the proposal to the woman's family. If the head of the woman's family approves and accepts the gifts, he will then write down the exact year, month, day, and hour of the daughter's birth and give this to the matchmaker to pass to the man's family. The man's family then invites the Shibi to calculate whether the couple's birth dates are well-matched. If they are, a date will immediately be chosen by the matchmaker, who sends the woman's birth details back to her family, indicating that an agreement has been made. The man's family then gives some gifts to the woman's family and visits their home to drink to the proposal. The two families drinking together set a seal on the relationship between them and also the time when the date of the engagement celebration is arranged.

The engagement-toasting ritual is held separately and simultaneously in the homes of the future bride and bridegroom. The man's family holds a banquet at which the relatives are informed of the engagement and the Shibi is invited to perform his rituals, asking for blessings of peace and happiness on the future couple. Similarly, the woman's family invites relatives to attend a banquet and informs everybody of the engagement. These engagement celebrations mean

婚事算正式定下了，以后每逢节日和女方父母生日，定了亲的女婿都要带着礼物去送节日礼、拜年或祝寿。

报期酒。一般由男方请释比按男女的生辰八字，择定吉利的婚期并向女方通报。届时男家备办米、面条、酒及衣服、围腰、鞋袜等物，由"红爷"和男家亲戚送去女家。女家宴请家门亲戚听取婚期的通报，并商谈有关嫁女的具体事宜，包括送亲人员、索要财礼数额品种等，即时告知"红爷"。这次宴客叫做报期酒或大订酒。婚期定后，男女双方都要做许多的准备。

开坛酒。一般在婚期的前几天，男女两家都要分别请家族和亲戚中有威望的人来吃开坛酒，商议婚礼的操办事宜并选定襄帮执事人员，其中最主要的是总管。整个婚礼事务由总管负责，下设各种执事人员。

搭棚酒。在男家婚期的前两天，要在家门口适当的地方搭一小棚当做"礼房"，作为众宾客送礼的处所。这时要请四大亲戚（姑父、母舅、姨父、伯叔）和襄帮人员吃搭棚酒。

女花夜。女花夜是女家婚礼的正期。众亲友前来送礼、吃喜酒，主人要盛情款待。客人们在宴会上跳喜庆萨朗舞，晚上要坐歌堂，欢乐通宵。

出嫁的姑娘是女花夜的中心人物。当晚她先拜家神，后拜众亲戚和众襄帮执事人员。拜神拜客毕，要让司礼人员将姑娘数年来做的云云鞋

that the marriage is formally confirmed and henceforth, on festivals and on his parents-in-laws' birthdays, the future son-in-law visits his fiancée's home to offer gifts or birthday congratulations.

The next step in the process is deciding on a date for the wedding ceremony. The man's family invites the Shibi to select an auspicious day for the wedding according to the birth date characters and the woman's family is informed of the decision. In due course, the man's family will prepare gifts of rice, noodles, wine, clothing, aprons, shoes, and socks, which are taken to the woman's family by the matchmaker and the man's relatives. At that time, the bride's family prepares a banquet and invites the relatives of the bride to inform them of the wedding date. Together they discuss all the details of the wedding, such as who will accompany the bride to the bridegroom's home on the wedding day and how many and what kinds of wedding gifts they should ask for. All of this is then told to the matchmaker. This is the "wedding date announcement celebration", after which both households make preparations for the wedding.

The "jug-opening ceremony" is held a few days before the wedding. Both households separately invite relatives of high standing to their respective homes where they share a jug-opening feast and discuss wedding arrangements and who will be responsible for what. The person in charge of the wedding arrangements is the main organizer and under his leadership various people are assigned various tasks.

Two days before the wedding, the bridegroom's household puts up a shelter or canopy on the open ground in front of their house, which serves as a "gift room" for presents brought by the guests. Four important relatives of the groom (his paternal aunt's husband, his mother's older brother, his maternal aunt's husband, and his father's brother) and the wedding attendants are then invited to join in drinking the "canopy toast".

The bride's wedding eve is the beginning of the celebration in the bride's family. All the friends and relatives of the bride bring gifts to the bride's house and are welcomed most hospitably by the host to share in the bridal feast. The guests dance a joyful, celebratory "Sa Lang" and sing deep into the night.

The bride is the center of attention on her wedding eve. On that evening, she first worships the household ancestors and then expresses gratitude to her relatives and all those assisting at the wedding for their great help. She then asks the master of ceremonies to present gifts of Yunyun shoes, which she has

分别赠送亲戚和长辈。同时，出嫁的姑娘还要唱答谢亲戚长辈的歌。最后，司礼人请父母出堂接受女儿的叩拜。

女花夜的第二天早上，即新娘的出嫁日。早宴之后，女家堂屋的神龛前摆设酒菜，祭祀神灵，由房族中的长辈念诵新娘离家敬神词，祝愿神灵保佑她吉祥如意，万事顺遂。随后父亲敬神，新娘放声哭嫁，执事人员则将嫁妆送出门外……母舅最后高声祝福新娘，并以敬神的青稞、麦子和米等撒向新娘，新娘则在送亲人员的簇拥下由其弟背负着离家。

正宴。这是男家娶媳妇的最隆重的礼仪。正宴的前一天，男家要派"接亲客"包括"红爷"、"引姑"和相关执事人员多至一二十人去女家迎亲，并给女家送去丰厚的礼物，如新娘穿的衣服和女方办酒宴所需的烟、酒、米、肉等物，这称为"过礼"或"接亲礼"。接亲客到女家时还要送开门钱、下马钱、进门钱等；女家的父母和四大亲戚则要到门外迎接。接亲客进屋后将礼品放在神龛前的桌子上，男方由"红爷"致"接亲词"，女方致"答谢词"，同时燃放鞭炮或鸣放猎枪，表示欢迎。

新娘离开娘家出门时放礼炮三响，燃放鞭炮，唢呐齐奏，由新娘的兄弟轮流背她上马或上轿。当新娘和迎亲送亲的队伍到达男家时，男家的亲族和四大亲戚要在门外迎接，并给女方的送亲客敬礼，鸣放鞭炮和铁炮三响。

made, to relatives and senior family members. And she sings songs of gratitude to them. Lastly, she kowtows to her parents who are invited by the master of ceremonies to sit in the main room of the house.

The following morning is the wedding day. After an early morning feast, food and drink are presented in front of the family altar in the main room of the bride's house as a ritual sacrificial offering to the gods. Senior clan members recite lines about the bride's departure, asking the gods to bless and protect her and give her a good life. After this, the father of the bride also worships the gods, the attendants carry the bride's trousseau out of the door, and the bride wails loudly to show how sad she is to be leaving her family. Finally, in a loud voice, the bride's maternal uncle blesses the bride and scatters over her head highland barley, barley, and rice, which have been offered to the gods. As the bride's dear ones gather round in farewell, her younger brother carries her from the house on his back.

The formal banquet is the most important wedding ritual. On the preceding day, the groom's family sends up to twenty people to the bride's home to fetch the bride. This entourage usually consists of the matchmaker, bridal attendants and other wedding assistants. They present generous wedding gifts to the bride's family, including beautiful clothes for the bride and cigarettes, wine, rice and meat that are needed to prepare the banquet at the bride's house. It is also customary for them to tip the people who open the door for them, those who help them dismount from their horses, and those who allow them into the house. Before entering the house, they are greeted warmly by the four important relatives and the bride's parents and once they are inside, they display the gifts prepared by the groom's family on the table in front of the household shrine. The matchmaker delivers a speech, receiving the bride on behalf of the groom's family, and this is followed by a representative of the bride's family giving a speech to express their gratitude. During this time, firecrackers are set off or hunting rifles fired into the air as a sign of welcome.

As the bride leaves her family home, a gun salute of three shots is fired, firecrackers are set off and suonas are played in unison. The bride's brothers take turns to carry her on their backs and place her on a sedan chair or on a waiting horse. When the bride and all her entourage arrive at the groom's house, relatives of the bridegroom, including the husbands of his maternal and paternal aunts and his parents' brothers, all meet the bride outside the home, extending a special greeting to those from the bride's family. Fire crackers, gun shots or

新娘到男家大门口时止步，由男家母舅或长辈搭上红盖头。这时释比在门前做"撵煞"的法事，向新娘头上撒些豌豆（或青稞），并念诵经咒，其词云："日吉时良，天地开张，新人到家，大吉大昌……东方一朵白云起，西方一朵紫云来，两朵彩云来相会，新郎新娘请进来。天无忌，地无忌……诸煞回避。"然后转身向堂屋中的两家主要亲戚和新郎父母道喜，说些恭喜主人大吉大利的话语。

这时新郎新娘在"引姑"的牵引下进入堂屋，点香师燃香点烛，陈设供神祭品，新郎新娘并立于神龛前。司礼依次高呼：先拜天地，再拜祖宗，后拜亲长父母。最后新郎亲手揭去新娘的盖头，夫妻对拜。拜亲长时双方母舅都要说些嘱咐的话。拜堂行礼完毕，司礼人还要说些吉祥如意的祝词，然后新郎新娘进入新房。

新郎新娘在新房短暂停留后，即出来敬神、拜客和举行谢"红爷"仪式。这时由司礼人员将新娘陪嫁带来的许多云云鞋按辈分分赠给男家众亲戚。新郎向新娘家送亲的母舅、兄妹等人敬酒点烟。接着司礼人代表男家唱《谢红爷》的歌词并赠送谢"红爷"的礼物。"红爷"收礼后唱歌答谢。

一切仪式完毕，才举行盛大的午宴，轮番款待众多的亲朋好友和邻里乡亲。当晚男家要举行坐歌堂活动，众宾朋围着火塘唱歌、跳舞。

even a small cannon may be set off at this time. The bride stops at the entrance of the groom's house for the groom's maternal uncle or an older family member to cover her head with a red veil. At this point the Shibi carries out a ritual to get rid of evil spirits, scattering peas (or highland barley) over the head of the bride and reciting incantations which say, "On this auspicious day, at this good time, witnessed by heaven and earth, the newlywed bride comes to her new home. What a blessed moment... a white cloud rises from the east while a purple cloud rises from the west; as the two clouds meet so the bride and the groom are joined together. Heaven and earth, please don't be jealous of the couple...and be gone, all you evil spirits". Then the Shibi turns to the parents of the groom and important relatives of both families seated in the main room, congratulating them and wishing the hosts good fortune and prosperity.

Following this, the bridegroom traditionally leads his bride into the main room where they stand before the household shrine and burn incense, light candles, and offer sacrifices. The master of ceremonies then instructs them in a loud voice to first bow to the gods in heaven and on earth, then to bow to their ancestors, and lastly to bow to their parents and elders. Finally, the groom unveils the bride and they bow to each other. When the newlyweds bow to their older relatives, the maternal uncles on both sides give them some advice about life. After this ritual, the master of ceremonies will offer some more good wishes to the couple and then they enter the bridal chamber.

After they have been in the bridal chamber for a short time, the newlyweds come out to worship the gods, honor the guests and hold a ceremony to express their gratitude to the matchmaker. Then those helping the wedding distribute many Yunyun shoes in the bride's dowry as gifts to the relatives of the groom, starting with the most senior. The groom proposes a toast to and light cigarettes for the maternal uncles and for the brothers and sisters of the bride who have accompanied her to the groom's home. Afterwards, a representative of the groom's family sings a song to express thanks to the matchmaker and presents gifts to him. Having accepted the gifts, the matchmaker reciprocates with a song expressing his appreciation for the kindness and hospitality of the hosts. Once these rituals are over, the relatives, neighbors, friends and villagers are in turn all treated to a grand lunchtime banquet. In the evening, the groom's family organizes a party and all the guests gather round the fire-pit to sing and dance.

第二天为"谢客日"。送亲客返回娘家。新婚夫妇备办礼物回娘家——俗称"回门"。新婚夫妇到女家"回门",也要举行隆重的敬神和拜女家亲戚、长辈的仪式,然后女家设宴款待女婿、女儿和众宾客。至此,男女两家的婚礼全部结束。

## (五)丧葬习俗

羌族一般都认识到"人既有生,也就有死"的自然法则,认为年满60岁的老人去世为喜,不满60岁死去为忧。丧葬的主要习俗如下:

(1)临死与入殓。临死前将其从卧室移至堂屋的床上,称为"换床",好让他的灵魂踏上西去回归"老家"(祖宗始居之地)的路程。家人将红纸包的茶叶、米粒、银子、金子等放入他(她)的口中作"盘缠"。断气后将他(她)移至火塘一侧净身更衣。周身冰凉后入殓,入殓时在棺材底撒上火塘灰,灰上印着若干酒杯口印,再铺纸钱并陈放尸体。尸体旁放其生前喜爱之物如拐棍、烟袋等殉葬品。还要放一把五寸长的小刀,一小瓦罐酒,一个烟袋。死者肩上挂一杂粮口袋,内盛五谷、纸钱灰、念经的路条等。

(2)报丧。人死后鸣枪三响,表示礼送亡魂,也是向村寨邻里报丧。同时,死者的儿子要立即向亲戚报丧,最重要的是先到母舅家

The next day is "thanking the guests day" and also the time for the bride's companions to return to the bride's former home. The newlyweds then prepare some gifts before making their customary first visit back to the wife's parents. This ritual includes solemn ceremonies in which the couple offer sacrifices to the gods and kowtow to the relatives and elders of the bride's family. After this, a banquet is served for the daughter, son-in-law and many guests and this brings to completion of all the rituals and ceremonies of the wedding.

## 5. Death

The Qiang generally recognize the natural law that "where there is life there is also death". They think that if a person dies when over sixty years old, he is considered to have died naturally but to die younger than sixty is considered a misfortune. The following are the main funeral customs of the Qiang.

### 1) Encoffining

When someone is dying, he will be moved from the bedroom to a bed in the main room of the house, according to the tradition of "changing beds". This is to help the soul of the dead set out on the journey westwards back "home" to where his ancestors originally lived. Once the person has died, family members put tea, rice grains, silver and gold, all wrapped in red paper, in his mouth to provide for the journey. The body is then placed on the ground beside the fire pit to be cleaned and given a change of clothing. After the corpse is completely cold, it is placed in a coffin. Prior to this, the floor of the coffin is scattered with paper money and ash from the fire pit, with images of drinking vessels traced in the ash. Some of the deceased's favorite items, such as his walking stick and tobacco pipe, are placed next to him as grave goods, as well as a knife, roughly 15cm long, and a small crock of wine. In addition, a bag is placed on his shoulders containing mixed grains, ash from paper money, and some scriptures to serve as a "travel permit" on the journey.

### 2) Announcing a Death

When a person dies, three shots are fired in the air as a farewell to the soul of the dead and to announce the death to people in the village. The son of the deceased immediately informs relatives of the death, going first to his maternal uncle's.

报丧。母舅闻讯后即备办吊唁的礼品，带着相关的亲戚一路号哭前来奔丧。到丧家后，死者的儿女要向母舅禀告死者病情和亡故、入殓的相关细节，回答母舅的询问，还要赞颂母舅的到来，表达感激之情。

（3）请释比做法事并查找死者的病因。丧家要请几个释比做法事。首先是入殓前由释比做法事念经，给死者净身、穿戴入殓。其次是在做法事前，由死者的长辈杀一只羊为死者引路，称"引路羊子"或"替罪羊"。杀羊前释比念经咒，并向羊耳里喷凉水，羊受惊浑身发抖，便认为是羊代替死者"认罪"了。再将羊剖开寻找"病因"，查看羊的各内脏，发现哪一部分不正常，便认为死者是这一部分脏器发生病变导致了死亡。再举行盛大、复杂的吊丧祭祀活动。释比做法事，身穿牛皮铠甲，戴皮帽扮铠甲神。相传铠甲神与守护神共八个人，故称"八大将军"。孝子孝女跪地，释比做法事，有的摇巴郎鼓和响盘，有的打羊皮鼓，舞蹈步子为万字格和八阵，来回跳跃，左右穿梭，高唱哀悼死者的歌……总之，做法事和祭祀的过程细节复杂，场面盛大而热闹。

（4）大夜。"大夜"与死者告别。葬礼之前的晚上称为"大夜"。在大夜，熄灭所有灯烛，只燃一麦草火把，揭开棺材，由母舅和亲属

On hearing the news, the maternal uncle prepares gifts of condolence, and then, with other relatives, hastens to the home of the deceased, wailing all the way. When the maternal uncle arrives, the bereaved sons and daughters report to him details concerning the illness, death and funeral preparations for the deceased. Having responded to the inquiries of the maternal uncle, the bereaved children express their gratitude to him for coming to help them.

### 3) Finding Out the Cause of Death

To follow the correct procedures and find out the cause of death, several Shibi are invited to perform their rituals. Before the body is placed in the coffin, the Shibi chants some scriptures, cleanses the body and puts fresh clothes on it. An older member of the bereaved family then slaughters a goat or sheep to lead the deceased on his journey and to serve as a "scapegoat" for him. Before the goat is slaughtered, the Shibi chants more scriptures and sprinkles cold water in the goat's ears. The goat is startled and its whole body trembles, which is seen as the goat becoming a substitute, bearing the guilt and sin of the dead. The goat is then slaughtered and cut open to discover the "cause of death". All the internal organs are carefully examined and if any organ is found to be abnormal, it is believed that the same organ in the body of the dead person was the source of his sickness and death.

A grand and complicated sacrificial ritual is then performed to mourn the deceased. While the Shibi carries out such rituals he wears a kind of leather armor and cap to disguise himself as the god of armor who, according to legend, is one of the eight protector gods, known as the "eight generals", who are believed to safeguard the souls of the dead. The mourning sons and daughters kneel on the ground while several Shibi perform their rituals. As they sing loud laments for the deceased, some of the Shibi shake their shallow bells and "Balanggu" (a small drum with a handle and clackers), some beat sheepskin drums, while others dance, leaping back and forth as their steps trace characters representing battle and long life. Such complicated and detailed rituals create an impressive and stirring spectacle.

### 4) Farewell Night

The evening before the actual funeral is when everyone bids farewell to the deceased. That evening, all lights and candles are extinguished except for a straw torch. The coffin is opened so the maternal uncle and other relatives can

看最后一眼亡人。然后盖棺，再点亮灯烛，举行一次祭奠。释比做法事，导引死者的灵魂走向墓地。

（5）火葬。火葬是羌族历史最悠久的葬俗。先秦古文献早有羌人实行火葬的记载。《旧唐书·党项传》载，唐代党项羌人"死则焚尸，名为火葬"。一个姓氏（即一个宗族）设一处火坟场，场内有一个"火坟坑"，坑上有一座小木屋，屋内供奉着本族历代祖先的神位。火葬时将小木屋移开，把棺木放到坑内，由亲儿子点火。这时释比做法事，送葬队伍鸣枪，家属和亲戚围坐号哭，唱丧歌，跳丧舞，饮丧酒。熄火后捡骨埋之。

（6）土葬。有研究认为，大约在清朝康熙、乾隆以后，受汉族的影响和官府的提倡，羌族逐渐实行土葬。羌人认为人有"三魂七魄"，人死后"魄"即散去，三个灵魂一个守自己的坟墓，一个留在家中受祭，暗中保佑其后人，另一个回到老祖宗的"老家"去与祖宗团聚。所以，在羌族的葬俗中不言葬，而只说"送"，火把引路，大刀开路，娘舅开路，释比做法事，通过释比的法力将死者的灵魂一一送到该去的地方。

丧家请阴阳先生择好墓地并挖好墓坑。出葬前夕举行悼念活动，唱丧歌，跳丧舞，释比做法事祈求亡魂保佑家人和村寨的安宁。凌晨

have a final look at the dead. Then the coffin is closed, all the lights and candles are lit and a memorial ceremony is held in which the Shibi performs rituals to lead the soul of the dead to the burial ground.

### 5) Cremation

Cremation is the oldest form of burial in Qiang history. Early records of Qiang use of cremation can be found in ancient pre-Qin documents. *The Old History of the Tang Dynasty* says that during the Tang Dynasty the Dangxiang Qiang "burned the deceased, which was known as fire-burial (cremation)". Usually those with the same surname and hence from the same clan are cremated and buried at the same burial site. At this site, a cremation hollow is dug and a small wooden house placed over it. In the wooden house, ancestral memorial tablets are displayed. As the cremation begins, the small wooden house is removed, the coffin is placed in the hollow, and the bereaved son lights the fire. Then the Shibi performs his rituals and people in the funeral procession fire their rifles in the air. Family members and relatives of the dead sit in a circle, wailing, singing funeral songs, dancing funeral dances, and drinking the funeral wine. Once the fire has died out, the bones of the dead are collected and buried.

### 6) Ground Burial

Some studies show that Qiang people gradually adopted ground burial in the later Qing Dynasty, under the influence of Han culture and with the encouragement of local government. The Qiang believe that people have "three souls and seven spirits". After a person dies, the spirits disperse but one of the souls stays to guard the grave, one stays at home to receive offerings and to bless and protect his descendants, and the third soul returns to the native place of his ancestors to be reunited with them. Consequently, rather than use the word "bury" in their death customs, Qiang people prefer to speak of seeing someone off. With a torch to guide the way, the help of a knife and the mother's brother to open the way ahead, and with the supernatural power of the Shibi and his rituals, the soul of the dead is seen off to its rightful place.

When a bereaved family decide on ground burial for the deceased, they invite a geomancer to choose a good grave site and dig the burial pit. On the evening before the burial, mourning activities are held, including singing and dancing, and the Shibi performs his rituals asking that the soul of the dead will bless and protect the family and the village. Before dawn the next day, the

出葬时释比和铠甲神在前，众孝子和亲戚送葬，把棺材抬往墓地。母舅在房顶为死者开路，释比做法事念经送葬，或唱或诵，配合着沉闷的鼓声和其他嘶鸣的乐器声，营造出一种送葬的悲痛气氛。走一段路要放一阵猎枪。棺材上要绑一只鸡（或随棺牵一只羊）以"避煞"。棺材入墓穴前释比杀鸡（或宰羊），把血绕墓穴淋一圈，表示为死者"买地"。棺材放入墓穴后先撒一点土即止，这时除孝子外送丧的人在墓穴周围唱丧歌，跳丧事锅庄。接着举行招魂仪式，由释比敬神祭神作法招魂。然后举行告别和追悼死者的仪式。最后丧家请释比、铠甲神、阴阳先生和众宾客吃早饭。早饭后众宾客散去，留下至亲和释比、铠甲神去垒坟。至此丧礼结束。

（陈蜀玉　陈华新）

bereaved children and other relatives of the dead lift the coffin to carry it to the graveyard and the Shibi and the "god of armor" head the funeral procession. From the roof of the house, the maternal uncle "opens the road" for the soul of the dead. As the procession moves towards the grave the Shibi performs his rituals, singing and reciting scriptures to a depressing drumbeat and the whining, high-pitched sounds of other musical instruments, all of which adds to the mournful atmosphere. Every now and then shots are fired along the route. A live chicken is tied on top of the coffin, or a sheep follows behind on a halter, to ward off evil spirits. Before the coffin is placed in the grave, the Shibi slaughters the chicken or   sheep and sprinkles its blood in a circle around the grave to indicate that this area has been "bought" for the deceased. Earth is then scattered on the coffin and all the people in the burial procession, except the bereaved sons and daughters, begin to sing the funeral song and perform the funeral dance around the grave. Following this, the Shibi carries out the ritual of calling back the spirit of the dead, offering worship and sacrificial offerings to the gods. Next is a ceremony of farewell to and mourning for the dead. Finally, the bereaved family provides breakfast for the Shibi, the god of armor, and all the guests, after which the guests return home leaving the Shibi, the god of armor, and close relatives to conclude the funeral by piling a mound up over the coffin.

( Translated by Dai Zhiyong, Chen Shuyu )

# CHAPITRE UN   HISTOIRE DES QIANG

Le peuple Qiang, dont on peut dater l'origine aux temps préhistoriques, est l'un des plus anciens peuples de Chine. Un grand nombre de traces écrites sur le peuple Qiang peuvent être trouvées dans les documents historiques relatifs à l'antiquité chinoise. L'œuvre principale de Xu Shen, *Shuowen Jiezi (Origin of Chinese Characters)*, nous donne une définition claire des Qiang: les Qiang sont ces bergers qui font partie du peuple des Rong de l'Ouest vivant dans le nord-ouest; le mot lui-même est divisé en deux termes, "gens" et "berger". Tous les documents sur l'antiquité voient les Qiang comme un peuple caractérisé par sa préoccupation de la vie du cheptel, spécialement dans l'élevage des moutons. Le livre *History of the Later Han Dynasty: the History of the West Qiang,* écrit par Fan Ye, dit que les Qiang vivent du commerce de l'élevage des moutons et de l'agriculture, ce qui indique que la principale industrie des Qiang à cette époque était l'élevage, complété de quelque forme primitive d'agriculture. Selon certaines découvertes archéologiques, des reliques d'anciens Chinois vivant à l'Age du Néolithique, il y a quatre ou cinq mille ans, ont été trouvées dans la vaste région comprise entre le Fleuve Huangshi, dans les provinces du Gansu et du Qinghai, à l'est, et les vallées des fleuves Jinghe et Weihe, dans la province du Shaanxi. Ces gens sont en fait les anciens Qiang. Le livre de Fan Yi dit aussi que les origines des Qiang se trouvent chez les San Miao, une branche de la famille des Jiang. Selon les légendes historiques, les San Miao formaient une tribu existant à l'époque où Shun, un monarque légendaire de l'ancienne Chine, était au pouvoir. L'un des ancêtres des San Miao est Jin Yun Shi, l'officier du gouvernement au service de Huangdi (l'Empereur Huang). Les gens de la tribu des San Miao, descendants de Yandi (l'Empereur Yan), font aussi partie de la famille Jiang. Donc, l'origine connue des Qiang de l'Ouest est la tribu des Jiang dont l'ancêtre est l'Empereur Yan.

Dans les temps reculés, l'élevage tirait sa source de la chasse, une tâche dont se chargeaient les hommes, alors que l'agriculture venait de la cueillette, une tâche dont se chargeaient les femmes. Dans la légende, la plupart des tribus Jiang étaient impliquées dans l'agriculture. La tribu des Gonggong était l'une des plus anciennes des Jiang, encore plus vieille que Shennong (le Dieu des Fermiers en Chine). La légende veut que 70 pour cent de la région habitée par les Gonggong était couverte d'eau, et seulement 30 pour cent était couverte de terre. Donc, les Gonggong vivaient à une époque de crues et dévouaient leur vie à la prévention des inondations, génération après génération. "La tribu des Gonggong dominait toute la Chine. Un fils de Gonggong, Houtu, pacifia ensuite le pays. Alors, tous les gens le vénérèrent comme Dieu de la Terre." (Book of Rites: *Sacrifice Offering*) Les descendants de la tribu des Gonggong assumaient la charge de "gestion de la terre", quand l'Empereur Huang était au pouvoir, et la charge de "contrôle de l'eau" quand Shaohao (le fils de l'Empereur Huang) lui succéda. Si Yue (quatre ducs de la tribu des Gonggong, sous l'Empereur Yu), qui étaient responsables des territoires du sud, du nord, de l'est et de l'ouest, aidaient aussi à la régulation des rivières et des cours d'eau. L'eau est la condition préalable à une première étape de la civilisation, et la base du développement d'une agriculture primitive. Ainsi, la tribu des Gonggong, des Jiang, était parmi les premières des anciens Qiang, avant même les ancêtres des Chinois, à choisir l'agriculture comme mode de vie. En ce sens, c'était la tribu Jiang des anciens Qiang qui inaugura la civilisation agricole de Chine.

De plus, les anciens Qiang sont l'un des peuples qui composent le peuple Huaxia, duquel le peuple Han provient. Selon *Guoyu*, une compilation d'anecdotes historiques, constituant le plus important ensemble de récits historiques de la Chine pré-impériale, "Shaodian épousa Youjiao et donna naissance à deux fils, Huangdi et Yandi. Huangdi grandit près de la Riviere Ji, tandis que Yandi grandit près du Fleuve Jiang. A cause de ces conjonctures différentes, Huangdi porta Ji comme nom de famille, tandis que Yandi porta Jiang comme tel". Tandis que la relation entre ces tribus Qiang, portant le même nom de famille, Jiang, devenait de plus en plus forte, ils émigrèrent à l'est en grand nombre. Il est dit dans le livre de *Lushi* que les Chiyou, de la tribu Banquan, dont l'ancêtre est Yandi, étaient experts dans la fabrication de cinq types d'armes, à savoir la dague, la lance, la hallebarde, la lance Qiu et la lance Yi. La fabrication des ces armes en métal montre le grand talent des Chiyou pour la réalisation des armes, aussi furent-ils vénérés par les générations futures comme Dieux des Armes; alors que Yu, le supposé fondateur de la dynastie Xia, les légendes le voient comme un descendant des Qiang. Sur la base de nombreux documents, écrits cinq cents ans après que Sima Qian ait écrit le livre *Historical Records: the Chronological Table of the Six States,* entre la dynastie Han et la dynastie Jin, Yu naquit à Shiniu, dans la terre des Qiang de l'Ouest, et était un descendant des Qiang. Par conséquent, certains érudits ont même conclu que les

Qiang constituaient la tribu dominante durant la dynastie Xia.

Aux temps préhistoriques, la tribu des anciens Qiang, appelée Jiang, vivant au nord-ouest de la Chine, ainsi que les Gonggong, les Yandi, les Chuyou et d'autres tribus, furent parmi les premières à venir en Chine centrale, et s'y mêlèrent à une tribu dirigée par Huangdi, après de nombreuses années d'association et d'intégration. Donc, il est clair que les anciens Qiang sont l'un des peuples qui composaient le peuple Huaxia, duquel naîtrait le peuple Han. En ce qui concerne ces anciennes tribus Qiang qui n'allèrent pas en Chine centrale, elles se dispersèrent dans les régions du Fleuve He Hang dans les provinces du Gansu et du Qinghai, et dans une partie de la province du Shaanxi. Elles continuèrent à rôder autour en nomades et étaient sous-développées. Leurs descendants devinrent plus tard ces Qiang vivant dans la région frontalière de l'Empire Shang. De nombreuses inscriptions ont ete trouvées sur des carapaces de tortue, relatant les vies des Qiang et leurs querelles de guerre avec la Dynastie Shang. Dorénavant, l'histoire des Qiang entrait dans une nouvelle ère avec les témoignages écrits.

Sous la Dynastie Shang, les Qiang et les Shang se faisaient toujours la guerre, et la plupart du temps, les Qiang étaient défaits. Le but d'une expédition punitive, pour la Dynastie Shang, était d'obtenir comme butin de guerre des Qiang, afin d'en faire des esclaves, et de les sacrifier. Des inscriptions vues sur des carapaces de tortue ou des os d'animaux, datant de la Dynastie Shang, indiquent que les Qiang étaient sacrifiés avec des animaux: cela pouvait être cinq esclaves Qiang avec trois bovins, ou trois esclaves Qiang et deux bovins. Le prix des esclaves Qiang, à cette époque, était même plus bas que celui d'un bovin. A coté de cela, les esclaves Qiang étaient parfois enterrés vivants avec les morts. Des données statistiques montrent qu'il y eut en tout 7750 esclaves Qiang utilisés en sacrifice, et plus de 5178 esclaves Qiang utilisés comme présents, dans les tombes.

Sous la Dynastie Zhou, les Qiang accroissèrent rapidement leur nombre et répandirent leur nom. Bien que la plupart d'entre eux vivaient dans le nord-ouest de la Chine, certains des Qiang réussirent à s'installer dans la Chine du centre. Apres la fondation de la Dynastie des Zhou de l'Ouest, la famille royale rencontra de grandes difficultés chez elle et à l'étranger. Pour consolider son pouvoir, la famille royale des Zhou continua à renforcer son alliance avec les Qiang. Certains aristocrates Qiang se virent offrir un poste officiel à la tête des états Shen, Lü et Xu, dans les vallées Jianghan et Huaihe. Le puissant état Qi fut fondé dans l'est pour supprimer les rébellions. D'autres états établis par les Zhou, avec des nobles Qiang

262

désignés à leur tête, incluent: Ji (désormais Shouguang dans la province du Shandong), Xiang (Huaiyuan dans la province de l'Anhui), Zhou (Anqiu dans la province du Shandong), Zhang (Dongping dans la province du Shandong), et Li (Suizhou dans la province du Hubei). Ces états étaient situés dans les régions frontalières du territoire Zhou, comme d'importantes garnisons, et formaient une sorte de défense naturelle contre les invasions étrangères. Dans les dernières années de la Dynastie des Zhou de l'Ouest, Youwang, le dernier empereur de la dynastie, accorda une faveur à Baosi, une de ses concubines impériales de l'état dirigé par la famille Si, et détrôna la Reine de Shenhou. Plus tard, le père de Shenhou, aristocrate Qiang et chef de l'état Shen, conspira avec Quan Rong et tua Youwang au pied de la Montagne Li. Plus tard, au cours de la cérémonie présidée par le père de Shenhou, Yijiu, le prince de la Couronne, fut intronisé Empereur sous le nom de Pingwang. Cependant, comme Quan Rong avait aussi envahi son territoire, l'Empereur Pingwang fut forcé de se déplacer à l'est, à Louyi. En raison de la fin de l'alliance entre les Zhou et les Qiang, la confusion régna au sein de la famille royale des Zhou, et finalement la dynastie vint à s'éteindre.

Le chef de l'etat Rong (un descendant des Si Yue), et les chefs des états Qi, Lü, Shen et Xu sont tous Qiang. Ces Qiang furent les premiers à venir dans la Chine centrale. Ensuite, ils devinrent   aristocrates, ducs ou seigneurs et se dirent Huaxia. En fait, il était largement admis, sous la Dynastie Zhou, que tous les peuples devaient attacher une grande importance, et se conformer, aux rites cérémoniaux et aux règles des Zhou, et adopter le mode de vie de la nation Huaxia. Un dicton populaire à cette époque disait: si la Chine adopte l'étiquette barbare, tous les Huaxia deviendront des barbares; si les barbares adoptent l'étiquette chinoise, alors, ils seront des Huaxia. En plus des Jiang du peuple Qiang qui s'étaient mêlés à la societé Huaxia, durant la Dynastie des Zhou de l'Ouest, d'autres Qiang fondèrent l'état Yiqu à l'Epoque des Printemps et des Automnes et durant la période des Royaumes Combattants, avec sa capitale située dans l'actuel comté Ning, dans la province du Gansu. Ils s'installèrent et construisirent des châteaux. Leur connaissance de l'agriculture était relativement à un haut niveau, et ils préféraient la cremation, pour perpétuer les traditions Qiang. Après cela, Qin détruisit l'état Yiqu et unifia le pays tout entier. La Dynastie Qin établit aussi le premier gouvernement impérial centralisé en Chine. Alors, les tribus de l'ouest de la Chine, la plupart d'entre elles Qiang, se mélangèrent graduellement au peuple Qin. Il est écrit dans le livre *History of the Later Han Dynasty: the History of the West Qiang*, que "il n'y eut pas d'envahisseurs venant de l'ouest depuis l'unification du pays".

Quand vint la Dynastie Han, les Qiang qui avaient dejà pénétré la Chine centrale s'entendaient bien avec les Han. Ceux qui n'étaient pas venu en Chine centrale, vivaient dans la région de Longxi et du Fleuve Huangshui, jusqu'au sud de la Grande Muraille, et s'étaient divisés en plusieurs tribus avec leur propre chef. Toutes ces tribus portaient différents noms et n'étaient pas dépendantes les unes des autres, c'est pourquoi elles s'attaquaient et se combattaient souvent. "Les plus puissants habituellement devenaient seigneurs et les faibles recherchaient leur protection." (*History of the Later Han Dynasty: the History of the West Qiang*) Depuis que la plupart des tribus étaient en transition, entre le dernier stade des tribus claniques des sociétés primitives, au commencement de la société hiérarchisée, ils se différenciaient des Qiang qui vivaient dans les états Qi, Lü Shen et Xu établis dans les premières années de la Dynastie Zhou. Parmi elles, les plus puissantes tribus Qiang étaient celles de Xianling et de Shaodang. Il y avait aussi les Zhong, Lejie, Beinan, Dangjian, Jian, Han, Qiedong, Shendi, Qianren, Laojie, Fengyang, Shanjie, Shaohe, Gongtang, Xiaogong, Funan, Dangtian, Wuwu, Lingwu, Dianna et Huangdi. Toutes se trouvaient dans la région comprenant les actuelles provinces du Gansu, du Qinghai, et du sud-ouest de celle du Shaanxi. A cette époque, les tribus Qiang s'engagèrent dans des conflits de différentes importance avec la Dynastie Han, et hésitaient entre se rebeller contre la Dynastie Han ou capituler. Toutefois, la plupart des tribus Qiang furent défaites et demandèrent allégeance. Elles furent éparpillées et se déplacèrent à l'intérieur pour s'installer dans des villages frontaliers de différents comtés. Ceux qui ne s'étaient pas rendus vivaient toujours au-delà de la Grande Muraille et furent appelés "Qiang de l'Extérieur".

Quand Wudi fut à la tête du pays, il renforça le pouvoir central de l'état, développa l'économie de la société, protégea les activités courantes dans le nord-ouest, et favorisa une communication amicale avec les pays des Régions de l'Ouest. Dans le but de ruiner tous les efforts entrepris par la Dynastie Han, les aristocrates Hun assemblèrent des forces avec des nobles Qiang, pillant les états voisins qui étaient sous la domination de la cour des Han. Dans de telles conditions, la Dynastie Han eut à envoyer des troupes, pour des expéditions punitives contre les rebelles, de nombreuses fois. Quand Xuandi gouverna, des tribus Qiang comme celle de Xianling se révoltèrent, assaillant des cités, tuant des officiels, attaquant la ville de Jincheng et anéantissant les armées Han. Alors Xuandi mobilisa le pays tout entier et envoya Zhao Chong Guo, un éminent général, pour renforcer l'armée Han. Xuandi promulga même le décret "tuer le coupable avec de grandes troupes" (*History of the Later Han Dynasty: Biography of Zhao Chong Guo*) et attribua de fortes récompenses aux Qiang qui assistèrent les troupes Han. Heureusement, la guerre prit fin en cinq mois. Pour consolider cette victoire et maintenir la paix dans les villages frontaliers du nord-ouest, la cour Han stationna ensuite des troupes de garnison, dégagea une étendue désertique, et fit pousser des céréales le long de la frontière.

Le gouvernement de la Dynastie Han créa des institutions d'administration et de gestion dans la région Qiang de l'ouest. D'abord, l'institution militaire de Xipingting (aujourd'hui la ville de Xining dans la province du Qinghai) fut établie. Ensuite, il y eut des comtés avec des magistrats comme chefs administratifs. Pour faire face à la situation spéciale de la région Qiang, "Shuguo Duwei", un officier militaire de confiance fut assigné pour se charger des "tribus aborigènes dociles et des minorités ethniques" (*History of the Later Han Dynasty: Annals of the Officials of All Ranks and Descriptions*). La plus importante fonction du gouvernement pour diriger la région des Qiang de l'ouest, était Officier Protecteur des Qiang, qui était en charge des affaires des Qiang, sur ordre impérial venant directement de la Dynastie Han. L'officier était aussi compétent pour régler des conflits au sein des tribus Qiang, pour servir d'intermédiaire lors de disputes entre Qiang et Han, pour patrouiller à certains moments pour connaître les épreuves et les difficultés des Qiang, pour envoyer des gens qui comprenaient leur langage, afin de récolter à temps les dernières informations sur eux, et donc d'être sur ses gardes à l'avance. A l'époque de la Dynastie des Han de l'Est, les Qiang menèrent trois révoltes de grande ampleur contre le gouvernement, en tout durant plus de soixante ans. Bien que les révoltes furent cruellement réprimées, elles frappèrent durement le règne de la cour Han, ce qui contribua au déclin et à la chute de la Dynastie des Han de l'Est. Il est ainsi dit dans le livre *History of the Later Han Dynasty: the History of the West Qiang* que: " l'ennemi fut presque mis à terre, le trône des Han, cependant, chuta".

De nombreuses tribus sous la Dynastie Han se trouvaient dans la vaste région des actuelles provinces du Xinjiang, du Tibet et de Mongolie Intérieure. A la même époque l'on trouvait d'autre tribus Qiang dans le sud-ouest, comme les Mao, Baima, Canlang et Baiyi. Parmi elles, les Qiang de la région de Ranmang vivaient dans les comtés de Wenchuan, Li et Mao, près des étendues supérieures du Fleuve Minjiang.

"C'est Wuding, un Empereur de la Dynastie Han, qui créa le comté de la Montagne Wen pour les minorités ethniques dans la région de Ranmang, dans la sixième année de son règne. Dans ce comté, il y avait six tribus Yi, sept tribus Qiang et neuf tribus Di... aussi ces gens venaient dans l'état de Shu, et travaillaient comme domestiques en hiver, pour éviter le climat froid. En été, ils retournaient dans les montagnes pour échapper à la chaleur." (*History of the Later Han Dynasty: Minorities in the Southwest*) Ils avaient de fréquents rapports avec les Han, et en étaient grandement influencés. La terre des Qiang était stérile, ils avaient donc une agriculture sous-développée et prospéraient grâce à l'élevage, spécialement de celui des yaks, et faisaient des tapis de feutre en laine, avec des poils de bœuf. Ils accumulèrent aussi des connaissances médicales uniques pour soigner les maladies. L'architecture des Qiang était particulière en ceci que les maisons étaient construites "en pierre à une hauteur de dix Zhangs" (le Zhang est une unité de longueur de la Chine ancienne, correspondant approximativement à 3,3 mètres). Ces architectures aux caractéristiques Qiang sont encore utilisées par eux aujourd'hui. En résumé, pendant la période de plus de quatre cents ans que la Dynastie Han domina, les interactions entre les Qiang et les Han furent grandement facilitées. De surcroît, et objectivement, quelques décisions politiques et mesures prises par la Dynastie Han permirent le développement de la société et de l'économie des Qiang, en même temps que la fusion des Han et des Qiang.

Dans les premières années du troisième siècle, la Dynastie des Han de l'Est s'effondra, et suivit la confrontation entre trois royaumes nommés Wei, Shu et Wu. La guerre, sur une longue période, détruisit l'ensemble de la productivité et prit de nombreuses vies. Pour augmenter le nombre de soldats et de travailleurs, tous les souverains des trois royaumes portèrent leur regard et prêtèrent attention aux minorités qui étaient autour. Les Qiang devinrent la première cible. Le Royaume de Wei et le Royaume de Jin, dans le nord de la Chine, attirèrent les minorités Hun, Jie, Di, Qiang et Xianbei à venir et vivre ensemble avec le peuple Han. Dans l'armée de Cao Cao, il y avait des soldats Hun, Wuhuan, Di, Qiang et d'autres peuples. Durant la guerre entre les royaumes de Wu et de Shu, les deux rivalisèrent sévèrement pour le recrutement de Qiang. Pendant la guerre entre le Royaume de Wu et celui de Shu, dans les régions du Yunnan et du Guizhou, la concurrence pour les groupes ethniques comme armées de recrutement fut aussi intense, le résultat fut que de plus en plus de minorités vinrent vivre avec les Han. Jusqu'à la période de la Dynastie des Jin de l'Ouest (de 265 à 317 après J.C.), les Qiang se trouvaient partout dans la plaine du Shaanxi. A cette époque, les personnes qui pensaient qu' "il y avait trop de minorités en Chine centrale" étaient assez puissantes et influentes, alors ils avancèrent la suggestion "être prudent vis-à-vis des minorités" (*History of Jin Dynasty: the History of Northern Minorities*). Par conséquence, les tensions entre les minorités ethniques et le peuple Han s'intensifièrent.

Dans la première année du règne de Huidi, sous la Dynastie Jin, les peuples Di et Qiang se soulevèrent dans la plaine centrale du Shaanxi, Qi Wan Nian du peuple Di s'intrônisa roi. Dans la quatrième année du règne de Huidi, Hao San des Hun se révolta. Plus tard, son fre, Hao Du Yuan fomenta lui aussi une révolte. Des officiels du gouvernement réalisèrent le danger et mirent en avant l'idée de "bannir les minorités", ce qui aboutit à conduire les peuples Qiang et Di en dehors de Chine centrale et les laissèrent retourner sur leurs terres natales. Comme résultat, la tension entre les minorités ethniques et les Han fut si intense qu'une révolte de grande ampleur provoquée par des réfugiés Han, Di et Qiang éclata.

Dans les dernières années de la Dynastie des Jin de l'Ouest, cinq peuples qui avaient précédemment émigré en Chine du centre, sous la Dynastie Han, se rebellèrent successivement contre la Dynastie Jin. Ils fondèrent seize différents états appelés dans l'histoire les "Seize Etats". Parmi eux, un noble Qiang nommé Yao Chang établit l'état de Hou Qin, et un noble Di, Fu Jian, établit l'état de Qian Qin. Les seize états gouvernèrent leurs régions indépendantes, dans le nord de la Chine, par la force des armes, attaquant les cités et pillant les villes. Le chaos causé par la guerre se poursuivit, et la famille royale de la Dynastie des Jin de l'Ouest eut à descendre vers le sud, se contentant de préserver sa souveraineté sur le sud du cours infieur du Fleuve Yangtze. Les ancêtres de Yao Chang, sous la Dynastie Han, étaient les chefs de la tribu de Shaodang des Qiang. Après l'établissement de l'état de Hou Qin, les souverains de la Famille Yao portèrent grand intéret au Confucianisme, et soutinrent que "personne parmi les minorités ethniques n'a jamais été assez compétent comme Empereur de Chine depuis l'antiquité, aussi devons-nous dépendre de la Dynastie Jin et la servir loyalement et de tout notre cœur" (*History of the Jin Dynasty: Chapter Sixteen*). Cela montre clairement la voie que les dirigeants de l'état de Hou Qin prirent, pour diriger les affaires d'état et montre l'influence de la culture Han sur les Yao. L'année 394 après J.C. fut le témoin de la mort de Yao Chang et de la succession de son fils, Yao Xing, sur le trône. En cette période, de grandes avancées furent accomplies par l'état de Hou Qin: il offrit l'amnestie et s'engagea auprès des réfugiés à réprimer les actes de

brualité commis par les Qiang et les Han; il libéra tous les civils de l'état qui étaient devenus esclaves à cause de la famine; il simplifia les lois et les règlements; il fit preuve de prudence en jugeant des affaires de justice; il fonda l'enseignement de la loi à Chang'an; il gratifia de promotions les officiels honnêtes et droits, tandis qu'il punissait la corruption avec la plus grande sévérité; il créa un système pour superviser les officiels du gouvernement, et leur offrit des promotions selon leurs capacités et leurs performances; il encouragea la croyance du Bouddhisme, fit relire et traduire plus de trois cents volumes de classiques bouddhiques à Chang'an. Dans les dernières années de Yao Xing, tous ses fils luttèrent pour le trône, ce qui aggrava les conflits internes. Après la mort de Yao Xing, Yao Hong lui succéda sur le trône. Durant son règne, des révoltes fomentées par les Qiang et les Hun, et des conflits au sein de la famille royale survinrent un à un. Par la suite, la ville de Chang'an fut capturée par les troupes Jin et Yao Hong fut tué. Ce fut la fin de l'état de Hou Qin, après une existence de trente et un ans.

A l'époque des Seize Etats, il y eut plusieurs régimes au nord-ouest de la région du Gansu et du Qinghai, comme ceux de Qian Liang, Hou Liang, Xi Qin, Nan Liang et Bei Liang. Les Qiang et d'autres minorités du nord-ouest de la Chine souffrirent des guerres sans fin et des désastres, et menèrent une vie tourmentée et instable. Plus tard, la tribu Tuoba du peuple Xianbei mit fin à l'existence des seize états, combattant chacun d'eux, et unifia le nord de la Chine avec l'établissement du régime Wei du nord. Par conséquent, les moyens d'existence des gens furent temporairement rétablis, et l'économie se développa. Cependant, les dirigeants Wei du Nord imposèrent une série de lois brutales pour réprimer son peuple. Quiconque conspirait contre l'état était décapité avec tous ses proches, même s'ils étaient innocents, sans considération du sexe ou de l'âge. Encore pire, telles propositions de lois criminelles augmentèrent continuellement: la liste des crimes qui devaient être punis de décapitation crût de cent quarante à deux cents trente cinq. Des plaintes sur le nombre croissant des taxes levées furent entendues partout. Durant la période des Wei du nord, des révoltes contre le gouvernement éclatèrent les unes après les autres. Les plus conséquentes furent la rébellion des 100 000 hommes menée par Gai Wu, et l'insurrection des Qiang et des Han menée par Mo Zhe et son fils. Ces révoltes durèrent cinq ans et firent définitivement chanceler le règne de la Dynastie des Wei du Nord. En conjugant leurs efforts dans la lutte, diverses minorités incluant les Qiang, les Di, les Hun et les Han réduisirent les écarts entre les groupes ethniques, et petit à petit, se fondirent ensemble.

La Dynastie du Nord et du Sud fut une intéressante période dans l'histoire chinoise: elle était politicalement instable, mais idéologiquement fertile; socialement turbulente, mais culturellement prospère. Dans la perspective de l'histoire des Qiang, les guerres fréquentes avaient transformé la terre de la Chine centrale en un champ de bataille où les dirigeants de différents peuples se battaient pour le trône. Cependant, les mêmes désastres et souffrances avaient permis une meilleure compréhension et une association entre les Qiang et les autres peuples chinois, ce qui accéléra le mélange des Qiang et des autres peuples et rendit l'intégration des autres minorités possibles. Premièrement, depuis la Dynastie des Han de l'Est, les Qiang et les autres minorités avaient émigré continuellement. Une partie des nomades Qiang devinrent paysans tournés vers l'agriculture. Ils changèrent leur mode de vie et, peu à peu, acceptèrent la culture de la Chine du centre. Deuxièmement, les fréquents conflits séparatistes et les communes révoltes avaient fortement unifié les Qiang avec les autres peuples. Les mêmes centres d'intérêt promurent la compréhension parmi les différents peuples. Troisièmement, le régime de la dynastie féodale releva continuellement les comtés administratifs, et nomma des nobles Qiang comme officiels, ce qui cassa dans une certaine mesure la structure fermée des organisations tribales, et força les classes supérieures Qiang à assimiler, de leur propre initiative, des aspects importants des autres peuples. De surcroît, le chaos et l'exil causés par la guerre et les migrations des Qiang et des autres peuples, spécialement des Han, avaient permis aux différentes minorités de mener progressivement les mêmes politique, voie économique et vie culturelle. Par ailleurs, la promotion de la culture Han, et la préconisation du Confucianisme, par les dirigeants Wei du Nord et de Hou Qin, contribuèrent à l'intégration des minorités Chinoises. Ainsi, nous pouvons dire que la période troublée des Dynasties du Nord et du Sud fut celle du développement et de l'union des différents peuples.

En 589, l'Empereur Wen, de la Dynastie Sui, réunifia le pays tout entier et mit fin à la situation de désunion et de chaos qui régnait depuis plusieurs siècles. Dans les premières années des Sui, l'Empereur Wen adopta de nombreuses mesures afin de gérer son régime. Sur le principe de "coexistence pacifique", il essaya de résoudre les problèmes des minorités d'une manière calme, et désapprouva l'emploi facile des armes. En ce qui concerne les Qiang, il exploita leurs aristocrates pour exécuter sa politique morale. Il créa aussi des comtés administratifs près du cours supérieur du Fleuve Minjiang, et dans l'aire entre les actuelles provinces du Gansu et du Sichuan. Bénéficiant des réformes introduites par son prédécesseur, le deuxième empereur de la Dynastie Sui, l'Empereur Yang, fonda le comté de la Montagne Wen, dans l'actuelle ville de Fengyi, du comté de Mao, administrant onze autres petits comtés. Le comté du Mont Wen était le plus grand dans le Sichuan à cette époque. En établissant des comtés administratifs, le pouvoir central consolida son gouvernement et son administration sur la région Qiang. En résumé, les sereines mesures prises par la Dynastie Sui ont produit des effets politiques favorables et ont apporté une stabilité sociale.

Comme la Dynastie Sui déclinait et que la Dynastie Tang s'affirmait, l'Empereur Taizong, le deuxième Empereur de la Dynastie Tang, ne tint plus le préjugé traditionnel "attacher de l'importance aux Han et regarder de haut les minorités", mais prôna des attitudes objectives envers les minorités parmi lesquelles les Qiang.Ceci est démontré dans les aspects suivants: premièrement, des mesures fortes, particulièrement des attaques militaires, furent prises contre ces puissantes tribus minoritaires qui mettaient en danger la sécurité du pays. L'on porta une attention particulière dans les régions frontalières à améliorer les équipements militaires, et à y augmenter les effectifs.. Deuxièmement, les chefs et les nobles des tribus minoritaires furent nommés gouverneurs militaires héréditairement. Troisièmement, le système de Jimi fut introduit pour les minorités ethniques à un niveau local. Sous un tel système, des préfectures de Jimi furent établies dans la région habitée des minorités. Dans chaque préfecture de Jimi, les Qiang pouvaient s'auto-déterminer totalement et n'avaient pas à payer d'impôts au gouvernement central. Politiquement, les préfectures de Jimi étaient sous l'autorité de la cour impériale. Enfin, une préfecture de Jimi était autorisée à changer son statut administratif en fonction des situations, ce qui pouvait la promouvoir en une préfecture régulière placée directement sous la juridiction de la cour impériale, ou transformée de préfecture régulière en préfecture de Jimi, dans le cas d'instabilité politique.

Au cours du septième siècle, il y eut un Royaume nommé Supi, au nord du Plateau Tibétain. Le Royaume de Supi était principalement composé de femmes Qiang. Comme il est dit dans le livre *History of the Sui Dyanasty: the History of the Kingdom of Women*, "Un Royaume situé au sud de la Montagne Verte avait une reine appelée Supi. Supi fut sur le trône pendant vingt ans alors que son époux n'était pas en charge des affaires d'état. Le seul métier que les hommes pouvaient prendre était celui de soldat. ... C'était la coutume pour les femmes de mépriser les hommes, et les femmes n'etaient pas jalouses du fait que les hommes pouvaient avoir plus d'une partenaire. Tous les hommes et les femmes du royaume peignaient

leurs visages de différentes couleurs et en changeaient plusieurs fois dans la journée." Le livre de *Tongdian* dit aussi, "Dans le royaume situé au sud de la MontagneVerte, tous les hommes portaient leurs cheveux décoiffés et toutes les femmes portaient leurs cheveux tressés. ... La plupart des femmes nobles disposaient de serviteurs mâles privés, mais les hommes n'étaient pas autorisés à avoir des servantes. Même une femme simple était maîtresse dans sa famille, avec plusieurs époux. Tous les enfants dans la famille portaient le nom de la mère." Le Moine Xuanzang mentionna aussi, dans son récit *A Journey to the West in Tang Dynasty*, que le modelage géographique du Royaume des Femmes de l'Ouest était "large d'ouest en est et étroit du nord au sud". "Il était situé à l'ouest du Royaume de Tubo, au sud du Royaume de Yutian et à l'est du Royaume de Sanboa (près du cours supérieur du Gange en Inde)". Il est écrit dans *New History of the Tang Dynasty: Biography of Supi*, que "les Supi étaient des Qiang. Plus tard, le royaume fut annexé au royaume de Tubo et renommé Sunbo". Ran Guang Rong écrit dans son livre *History of the Qiang* qu'en plus de Supi, il y avait un autre royaume dominé par des femmes Qiang et qui était aussi appelé Royaume des Femmes de l'Est, dans l'histoire. Dans le livre *The Old History of the Tang Dynasty: Biography of the Eastern Women Kingdom*, il est dit "les Qiang fondèrent le Royaume des Femmes de l'Est. Parcequ'il y avait déjà eu un Royaume des Femmes de l'Ouest, les Qiang nommèrent celui-ci Royaume des Femmes de l'Est. Traditionnellement, les femmes étaient en charge des affaires d'état dans une telle société. A l'est du royaume se trouvait la tribu Qiang Dangxiang, dans la préfecture Mao, au sud-est était la préfecture Ya". Toutes ces informations historiques sus-mentionnées prouvent qu'il y eut de nettes carcatéristiques d'une société matriarcale dans l'histoire des Qiang. Cela fournit des données de valeur pour l'étude du féminisme, relative au développement des femmes des minorités en Chine. En fait, les traditions du mari vivant avec la famille de sa femme et nommant les enfants d'après leur mère, se perpétuent comme avant dans la région des comtés de Li, Wen et Mao, dans la Préfecture Autonome d'Aba. Peut-être doit-il y avoir un rapport avec le Royaume des Femmes de l'Est, dans l'histoire.

Les traces de fusion et de séparation des minorités se trouvent toujours dans le développement et l'évolution de la langue. Le langage, l'un des traits majeurs caractérisant la communauté d'une nation, est relativement stable. En d'autres mots, il y a des connexions historiques inévitables parmi les divers langages d'une même famille linguistique.

Le tibétain et la langue des Qiang sont tous deux des branches de la famille linguistique Tibéto-Birmane. Une ancienne tribu des Qiang vécut, un temps, avec les aborigènes, sur le Plateau Tibétain, et constituèrent le peuple Tubo, sous la Dynastie Tang. Ensuite, les Tubo ingérèrent de nombreuses autres tribus Qiang, pas à pas, qui devinrent les Tibétains d'aujourd'hui. La langue Jingpo est aussi une branche de la famille linguistique Tibéto-Birmane. Les ancêtres de la minorité Jingpo émigrèrent vers le sud, depuis la Chaîne de la Montagne Transversale du Plateau Tibétain, et vécurent dans la région au nord de la préfecture de Dehong et à l'ouest du Fleuve Nujiang, sous la Dynastie Tang. Selon les coutumes des Jingpo, les vivants devaient accompagner l'âme des morts. Des recherches indiquent qu'après la mort des Jingpo, la route pour guider l'âme des morts mène aussi loin que la Montagne Kunlun. Ainsi, nous pouvons affirmer que les ancêtres des Jingpo vécurent un temps dans la région où les Fleuves Lancang et Nujiang prennent leur source, près du Plateau Qinghai-Tibet, où les anciens Qiang habitaient. La langue du peuple Yi a aussi été influencée par les anciens Qiang. Légende, littérature et histoire du peuple Yi, toutes nous disent que les ancêtres des Yi migrèrent des montagnes couvertes de neige, sur le plateau nord-ouest chinois, aux actuelles provinces du Sichuan et du Yunnan, pas à pas. La littérature des Han pourrait confirmer cela aussi. De nombreuses coutumes populaires des Yi, telles que porter des capes de feutre, prendre un ou deux caractères du nom du père pour baptiser son fils, et la crémation, sont très similaires de celles des Qiang . Le peuple Bai fut aussi une minorité issue des anciens Qiang. Les Bai étaient appelés Bo avant la Dynastie Han. "Les Bo sont des descendants des Qiang." (*Historical Records: Annotates of the Biography of Sima Xiangru*) Durant la Dynastie Han, Bo et Qiang, ou Bo et Di, étaient souvent considérés par les Han, comme ne faisant qu'un. En outre, les aïeux de nombreuses minorités ethniques comme les Hani, Naxi, Lisu et Tujia, étaient partiellement d'anciens Qiang. Il est manifeste que différentes branches des anciens Qiang se mélangèrent avec d'autres minorités, à diverses périodes de l'histoire, et selon différents contextes sociaux. Ainsi, beaucoup de nouvelles minorités se formèrent, ce qui expliqua comment les anciens Qiang évoluèrent d'un vaste groupe de tribus, à l'actuelle minorité de faible population.

Après que la Dynastie des Song fut fondée, les souverains de la Dynastie attachèrent une grande importance au développement de la culture et de l'éducation, plutôt qu'au renforcement de la présence militaire dans la région habitée par les Qiang. Ils soutenaient que "d'une part, s'ils dépêchent des troupes dans les régions

pauvres des minorités, tous les impôts sur la terre payés par les Han seront engloutis, et les gens simples de Chine centrale s'épuiseront; et que d'autre part, cela ne vaudrait pas la peine d'être fait, car ce ne le serait que pour ces minorités stupides!" (*History of the Song Dynasty: One of the Minorities*). En 1038 (la cinquième année du règne de l'Empereur Renzong), Yuan Hao, un descendant des Qiang de Dangxiang, fonda le Royaume des Xia de l'Ouest. Le royaume reprit la traditionnelle coiffure des Dangxiang Qiang, abandonna le nom de Li et Zhao, conféré par les dynasties Tang et Song, et adopta le traditionnel nom—Weiming. Furent prises aussi une série de mesures incluant l'établissement de systèmes de recrutement des officiels et des militaires, la création de leurs propres caractéristiques, uniformes et convenances formelles. Ainsi, un royaume complet fut établi, ce qui est un épisode significatif dans l'histoire des Qiang. En 1127, Genghis Khan, le conquérant mongol, annexa le Royaume des Xia de l'Ouest. Cette période du Royaume des Xia de l'Ouest, la plus prospère de l'histoire des Qiang, dura en tout 190 ans.

La Dynastie des Yuan fut fondée avec les Mongols comme principal corps constituant. Dans la dynastie féodale des Yuan, les préfectures de Jimi, en place depuis la Dynastie Tang dans les régions habitées par les Qiang, furent abolies. Au lieu de cela, des troupes furent stationnées et des patrouilles militaires furent mises en place pour assurer le prestige de l'armée et inspirer la crainte. De plus, les souverains de la Dynastie Yuan encouragèrent vigoureusement le Lamaisme. De nombreux temples furent construits dans la région habitée par les Qiang, aussi les Qiang furent grandement influencés par cette religion. Des gens renoncèrent même à leurs propres croyances et devinrent lamaistes. La Dynastie Yuan créa aussi la province administrative du Sichuan et le "Département de Xuanweishi sous tutelle du Ministère des Diverses Minorités" pour se charger des affaires des minorités.

Pendant la Dynastie Ming, à la période du milieu du quatorzième siècle, l'économie sociale des Qiang se développa davantage, et il y eut de plus en plus d'associations entre les différents peuples, ce qui permit l'établissement de relations politiques plus proches entre la région habitée par les Qiang et le gouvernement central. Le système de "Tusi" initié sous la Dynastie Yuan fut parfait sous la Dynastie Ming. Dans le système de Tusi, le gouvernement central décerna le titre de Tusi aux chefs de différentes tribus afin de s'occuper des affaires tribales. La position de Tusi était héréditaire. Un système tel que celui-ci était employé par la cour impériale pour diriger et administrer les minorités nationales. Dans les premières années de la Dynastie Ming, le Sichuan fut unifié, tous les chefs des tribus Qiang se rendirent l'un après l'autre. Après qu'ils se furent rendus et promirent allégeance à la cour impériale, le système de Tusi pût être executé. Autour de la région de l'actuelle Préfecture Autonome d'Aba, les Qiang furent menés par leurs Tusi pour construire des passages frontaliers, des forts, des tertres et des douves, qui garantirent la paix dans la région et le développement de la productivité.

Sous la Dynastie Qing, le système de Tusi fut aboli. A la place, la succession des chefs qui étaient en charge des affaires minoritaires ne fut plus héréditaire. Aux endroits où les Tusi gouvernaient auparavant, "Liuguan", le gouverneur local appointé par la cour impériale, leva des impôts, après avoir recompté les familles et mesuré les terres. Le système politique des minorités ethniques était le même que celui utilisé dans les autres régions Han. Une telle réforme fut d'abord mise en pratique au Yunnan, puis au Guizhou, au Guangxi et au Sichuan. Bien que la réforme dans la région Qiang du Sichuan avait déjà été amorcée dans les dernières années de la Dynastie Ming, cela ne fonctionnait pas totalement jusqu'à la dix-septième année du règne de Qianlong (1752 après J.C.). La réforme menée dans la région Qiang, non seulement consolida la mainmise de la Dynastie Qing sur les régions reculées, et stabilisa et unifia ce pays constitué de tant de différentes minorités, mais aussi rehaussa le niveau de l'économie et de la culture des groupes minoritaires. Cependant, la réforme, à cette époque, ne put être très complète. Des Tusi, dans des villages reculés, continuèrent à diriger les Qiang jusqu'à 1949.

Le premier octobre 1949, la République Populaire de Chine fut fondée. En décembre de la même année, Chengdu fut libérée. En janvier de l'année suivante, l'Armée Populaire de Libération Chinoise vint en force sur la terre des Qiang. Les régions rurales et urbaines dans les comtés de Wenchuan, Mao et Li furent successivement libérées. En 1958, les régions habitées des comtés de Mao, Wenchuan et Li furent renommées en District Autonome Qiang Maowen de Beichuan. En 1960, l'établissement administratif des comtés de Wenchuan et Li fut repris, tandis que le District Autonome Qiang Maowen continua d'administrer l'ancien comté de Mao. En 1987, la Préfecture Autonome Tibet Aba fut renommée Préfecture Autonome Tibet Aba et Qiang. Pendant ce temps, le District Autonome Qiang Maowen fut aboli et le comté de Mao fut repris. En 2003, le Conseil d'Etat de Chine approuva la création du District Autonome Qiang Beichuan, administrant l'ancien comté de Beichuan. Aujourd'hui, les Qiang du vingt-et-unième siècle ont tourné une nouvelle page de leur histoire,et progressent à grands pas dans les domaines culturels et du développement économique, grâce à leur intelligence et leur hardeur au travail.

## CHAPITRE DEUX    TOUR DE GUET DES QIANG

L'architecture des Qiang est particulière dans l'architecture des groupes minoritaires en Chine. Elle comprend des tours de guet, des maisons de pierre, des salles faites de bois et de terre, des résidences des magistrats (bureaux gouvernementaux des souverains d'alors), des hameaux, des ponts, et des chemins de planches le long des falaises. Des descriptions des logements des Ranmang d'il y a deux mille ans peuvent être trouvées dans *History of the Later Han Dynasty: Minorities in the Southwest*. Elles montrent qu' "ils vivaient sur les flancs des montagnes, construisaient leurs maisons avec des pierres et ces maisons pouvaient atteindre dix Zhangs" (le Zhang est une unité de longueur de la Chine ancienne, équivalant à 3,3 mètres). A cette époque, de tels logements étaient appelés "Qionglong", ce qui est la traduction de "tour de guet" dans la langue Qiang. Les tours de guet, qui sont les témoins de l'histoire des Qiang, représentent le mieux leur style architectural.

Des recherches de vestiges culturels, conduites dans la Préfecture Autonome Tibet Aba et Qiang, montrent que, en dehors des districts de Hongyuan, Ruoergai et Jiuzhaigou, dix des treize districts dans la préfecture ont des tours de guet. Quatre districts, Maerkang, Wenchuan, Li, et Mao, en possèdent le plus grand nombre. Comme trois des quatre districts susmentionnés correspondent à la zone d'habitation des Qiang, les tours de guet des Qiang se trouvent donc principalement dans la Préfecture Tibet Aba et Qiang.

Plusieurs explications peuvent être avancées sur l'apparition et le développement de ces tours. L'une d'elle est que les Qiang du nord-ouest, durant la Dynastie Han, migrèrent vers le sud le long de la vallée du Fleuve Minjiang, tandis que l'influence de la culture Han se propageait vers le nord, vers le fleuve, donc les guerres semblaient inévitables dans le corridor de Minjiang, où différentes minorités entraient souvent, et brutalement, en conflit. Aussi, les tours de guet devaient-elles apparaître.

Une autre opinion soutient que la construction des tours est en étroite relation avec la religion des Qiang et le rôle important joué par le Shibi (appelé aussi "Xu"; connu sous le nom de "Duangong" par les Han). Le Shibi est le chef spirituel des

Qiang, il a ainsi autorité suprême pour concevoir, dessiner et construire toute structure. Il croit que toute chose possède son propre esprit, pense la tour de guet (ou Qionglong) en tant que "palais du ciel", et considère le dieu de la pierre blanche comme le plus important des dieux. Donc, la construction des tours de guet et des maisons est vue comme le travail de mise en place des pierres blanches, et la manière de célébrer les dieux. Habituellement, cinq pierres blanches ensemble symbolisent les cinq dieux tutélaires du ciel, de la terre, de la montagne, des arbres (forêt) et du village (le monde de l'homme). La haute tour de guet peut emmener aisément les dieux tutélaires au plus près des cieux, comme une échelle ou une route qui mènerait au ciel. Ainsi, les sentiments religieux et les idées du Shibi se reportent-elles sur les tours de guet. De plus, par l'intermédiaire de la structure en forme de cône, ils sont projetés dans l'espace où les dieux du ciel, du feu et du soleil se trouvent.

A coté de cela, il y a aussi des Qiang , aujourd'hui, qui pensent que la fonction de leur tour de guet est identique à la tour Fengshui dans la culture Han, à savoir, servir comme symbole pour conserver un lieu sûr et préservé.

Quelque soit l'explication, les tours de guet restantes des régions habitées par les Qiang, constituent un irremplaçable trésor historique, technologique et artistique pour le monde. Comme exemple de configuration de l'espace particulier dans l'architecture locale en Chine, et même dans le monde entier, la tour de guet des Qiang révèle un sens de la création architecturale et un extraordinaire développement de la culture. Dans les villages, d'inhabituelles conditions de densité, de vision d'ensemble, de grandeur, d'art de la construction et de religiosité peuvent être appréciés.

Bien que les Tibétains aient aussi des tours de guet dispersées dans les régions où les anciens Ranmang, du groupe Qiang, vivaient, la plupart des tours de guet des Tibétains coéxistaient avec les résidences des magistrats et étaient construites compactes et hautes. La plus haute des tours de guet Tibétaines est la tour de 43,2 mètres de haut de Baishe, dans le district de Maerkang. Généralement, les tours de guet Tibétaines sont de plus de trente mètres de haut, et donnent l'impression que le propriétaire est très aisé, en plus d'un air officiel et religieux. Les tours de guet des Qiang, au contraire, n'avaient pas le même aspect officiel. Les tours de guet des Qiang qui restent aujourd'hui sont principalement de trente mètres de haut et sont de formes variées. Ces constructions sont relativement rudimentaires, mais vivantes, originales, différentes, et typiques. Le dessin des tours de guet des Qiang est différent de celui des tours Tibétaines, et les caractéristiques de la charpente plus visibles aussi. Malheureusement, par suite de tremblements de terre, de guerres et d'autres raisons, les tours de guet qui étaient de cinquante mètres de haut se sont toutes effondrées ou ont été démolies. Cela est vraiment dommage. En résumé, les tours de guet Qiang et Tibétaines résultent d'origines culturelles diverses, elles sont les réalisations spatiales de deux systèmes architecturaux complètement différents.

Les configurations intérieures et extérieures des tours de guet Qiang sont en relation directe avec leur environnement, ainsi nous pouvons identifier les tours en fonction de leur emplacement. Le résultat est que trois régions se distinguent, le district de Mao, le cours inférieur de la Rivière Zagunao et celui de la Rivière Qiangfeng. Dans la région du district de Mao, les villages de Heihu, Sanlong, Qugu, Baixi, Wadi et Weicheng sont des lieux où les tours de guet conservent toujours leur forme originale. Les tours ont quatre, six, huit, ou même treize côtés. Les intérieurs sont circulaires, carrés, hexagonaux ou octogonaux. Intérieurs et extérieurs sont tous deux convergents. Les toîts des tours sont plats et les ensembles sont de forme conique avec des côtés faisant de trois à six mètres chacun. Toutes ces tours furent construites en pierres tassées. Les hauteurs sont autour de vingt mètres, et l'épaisseur des murs, à leur pied, varie de soixante-dix centimètres à un mètre. Dans ces tours, la plupart des appartements sont privés, certains sont communs, et il se trouve aussi un hall d'entrée pour tous. La structure de l'intérieur de chaque tour est travaillée dans le bois et supportée par les murs. Les tours pouvaient compter jusqu'à treize étages, mais en ont la plupart du temps seulement trois ou quatre. Une échelle de troncs taillés en dents de scie, et supportant des planches, relie les étages. En dépit de leur apparence simple et spectaculaire, les aspects pratiques de solidité et de stabilité ont aussi été pris en considération lors de la construction des tours. Pour faire face aux tremblements de terre, le mur extérieur est de forme conique. Cette structure unique est appelée "Qianlengzi". Les tours de guet encore existantes ont subi la magnitude de 7,5 lors du tremblement de terre de Diexi en 1933.

Les tours de guet, autour du cours inférieur de la Rivière Zagunao, sont de plusieurs types, les traits les plus caractéristiques sont les suivants: ① la plupart des tours de guet adoptent une forme pyramidale avec une base rectangulaire; ② les murs des tours de guet sont faits de glaise, comme pour le groupe de tours du village de Buwa, dont la hauteur est comprise entre vingt et trente mètres; ③ les toîts des tours de guet sont en forme de chaise; ④ aux deux derniers étages, des poutres à section carrée ressortent des murs, afin que des observatoires puissent être construits, en posant des planches de bois sur les poutres. Pour ces tours de guet de Buwa, un "Dougong", un système de tasseaux dans les constructions Chinoises traditionnelles, est appliqué pour supporter les corniches du haut. De telles structures sont manifestement influencées par le style des maisons résidentielles. En conclusion, c'est un grand progrès que les tours de guet puissent concilier les aspects esthétiques et la fonction défensive.

En dehors des tours de guet du village de Qiangfeng, les autres de cette région ne peuvent être considérées comme typiquement Qiang, notamment celles autour de Caopo. Caopo est une région où Qiang et Tibétains vivent ensemble. Géographiquement, elle dépend de la région de Qiangfeng. Cependant, en raison de sa proximité avec la région où les Han résident, les tours de guet de Caopo, tout comme les tours sur les quais, sont de forme et de structure énormes. Le toît des tours ressemble à ceux des constructions Han. Et cette similitude entre les deux styles architecturaux, totalement différents, montre le fin mélange des deux cultures.

En ce qui concerne l'association tour-village, comme il y a deux sortes de configurations spatiales, les tours uniques et celles combinées avec des domiciles, chacune doit avoir sa propre raison d'être, mais il faut la concevoir en fonction du village. Les tours seules sont situées à des passages stratégiques d'un ou de plusieurs villages. Fondamentalement, elles sont publiques et servent d'yeux au village—le large panorama que l'on a depuis les tours peut être utilisé pour observer. En procurant de l'information aux villageois, elles jouent ainsi un rôle important dans la défense contre les attaques surprises, alors, provisoirement, elles peuvent être appelées tours d'observation. En fait, le nombre nécessaire de tours, dans un lieu, dépend de situations et d'environnement spécifiques. Par exemple, avant de pénétrer dans l'espace dégagé de Heihu, l'on doit passer par un col étroit et stratégique, dans une vallée. Ainsi, la tour de guet doit être construite sur un lieu visible de tous, depuis n'importe quel village dans la région de Heihu. Si des attaques se produisent, la vigie, sur la tour, peut alerter les villageois, pour qu'ils se préparent, en lançant des feux d'artifice ou un son fort. Par conséquent, les tours de guet étaient à l'origine situées au-delà du col stratégique de la vallée, ce qui veut dire que l'actuel Village du Général Yang a évolué en fonction de l'expansion des tours d'observation, d'une fonction militaire à une fonction d'habitation. Le groupe de tours à l'ouest de la Rivière Qugu, est situé sur une terrasse sur les contreforts d'une montagne. Le plateau est entouré par la montagne, en dehors d'un côté descendant en pente raide vers la vallée, au pied de la montagne. Comme la vallée est l'unique point d'accès au village, une tour seule et géante est construite au bord de la pente. Une telle tour devait avoir la meilleure vue sur la vallée, et aussi être visible par n'importe quel villageois depuis le sommet de la montagne. Des tours de guet similaires comprennent les tours de pierre du Village de Longshan, au sommet de la Montagne Buwa. Généralement, le critère d'emplacement d'une tour Qiang ou d'une tour Fengshui, dans la culture Han, sont, dans une certaine mesure, similaires. Toutefois, les deux types de tours diffèrent l'une de l'autre, en ceci que la tour de guet est principalement utilisée pour observer la position de l'ennemi. Bien que la tour des Qiang n'ait pas de rapport spatial direct avec les villages, sa forme de réalisation ressemble à celle de la tour Fengshui, au niveau de la relation mentale, à la différence que la tour de guet est "militaire" quand la tour Fengshui est "civile", que l'une est conçue pour la survie, quand l'autre est conçue pour l'amélioration de la vie. Un tel phénomène spatial influence directement la location des villages et la disposition de ses édifices. Le plus important principe est que chaque structure ait une vision sur la tour de guet publique, sans aucun objet entre pour bloquer la vue. Ainsi, quand nous analysons le cas de toutes les demeures du Village de Yingzui, dans la région de Heihu, qui sont situés sur une ligne le long d'une arête montagneuse, au lieu d'être éparpillés au hasard, nous croyons que la raison sous-jacente est qu'aucune demeure ne doit bloquer la vue entre la tour et une des demeures. A la suite d'une étude approfondie de tous les villages Qiang comprenant des tours de guet, nous ne trouvons aucune exception. A la suite de cela, de nouvelles données sont ajoutées entre le choix de l'environnement et la hauteur à laquelle on construit des maisons.

Un autre type de tour de guet unique est habituellement situé au centre d'un village, ou à une position appropriée autour. Différente des autres tours susmentionnées, ce type de tour sert non seulement comme tour d'observation, mais aussi comme abri et poste de défense après que l'ennemi ait envahi le village. Le nombre de villageois, les ressources financières et l'environnement du village sont les facteurs qui déterminent combien de tours doivent être bâties dans un village. Il y eut une fois jusqu'à quarante-huit tours tours dans le Village de Buwa. Dans le village de Qiangfeng, cependant, il n'y a qu'une tour. Comme pour les tours de guet construites dans des régions montagneuses, si la hauteur de la tour est accrûe d'un seul chi (une unité Chinoise de longueur, à peu près égale à 0,33 mètres), le champ de vision depuis la tour peut atteindre plusieurs li (une unité de longueur Chinoise, égale approximativement à 0,5 kilomètres) de plus. Par conséquent, la hauteur de la tour dépend des formes particulières du terrain et de l'environnement, ce qui explique pourquoi de si nombreuses tours de guet uniques, de villages Qiang, diffèrent les unes des autres, en hauteur. De telles tours de guet situées aux centres des villages, ou autour de ceux-ci, sont relativement proches des domiciles des villageois, dans la configuration spatiale. L'ensemble de ces tours crée une ambiance de forteresses et de puissance. A cause de leurs diverses hauteurs, des combinaisons de différentes tailles de murs, de la terre ou des pierres indifféremment utilisées, et du rude travail de construction, les tours de guet présentent une solennelle, sensationnelle et primitive sophistication, ainsi qu'une beauté héroïque. Le premier exemple de tour de guet seule, la tour d'observation, est loin des villages. Mais cette distance a été voulue, il y a une certaine cohérence dans cette configuration.

Si nous sommes autorisés à comparer la tour unique avec les tours du village, alors, le premier niveau de défense est la distance entre les deux, alors que le niveau suivant est le développement de la tour de guet vers une tour résidentielle. Ainsi, un autre type de configuration spatiale est né, qui est, une tour de guet-résidence. Cela pourrait être aussi appelé second niveau de défense, dans le système défensif des villages. En conséquence, le grandiose spectacle, dans un village ou une région, des tours de guet familiales, et de toutes ces tours et demeures, totalement différentes les unes des autres, peut être apprécié dans des régions habitées par les Qiang. La région autour du district de Mao, en particulier, témoigne en même temps des caractéristiques architecturales des tours privées de certaines familles, et des tours publiques de villageois. En outre, sont appréciables ici différents motifs, qui apparaissent sur les tours de guet et les demeures.

Un grand nombre de tours de guet-domicile sont concentrées dans le District de Mao, notamment dans les Villages de Qugu, Sanlong, Heihu, Baixi, Wadi, Chibusu, Weicheng, et dans d'autres villages autour de la vallée de la Rivière Heishui, où se trouve le cœur de la culture Qiang. Un petit nombre de tours-domicile sont éparpillées dans les villages autour du cours inférieur de la Rivière Zagunao, et un très petit nombre se trouve dans les villages près des routes gouvernementales de la Vallée du Fleuve Minjiang, dans les Districts de Songpan, Mao, Wenchuan et Guan. Les Qiang ont-ils été effrayés par les forces armées Han, toujours stationnées le long des routes ? Ce qui expliquerait que les bâtiments de défense seraient devenus dénués de sens. Ou peut-être que ces villages ont été tellement influencés par la culture Han qu'ils auraient peu à peu perdu leurs caractéristiques architecturales traditionnelles. La question vaut d'être posée. Quoiqu'il en soit, l'existence de toutes ces formes spatiales ne peut être accidentelle; des facteurs historiques et sociaux se cachent sûrement derrière.

Le rapport entre la tour de guet et la demeure est, vraisemblablement, le témoignage laissé dans l'architecture par les Qiang, envers l'economie agricole féodale. Et s'il se trouve encore des tours de défense dans les villages, cela peut s'expliquer par la coexistence de plusieurs systèmes. Ainsi, l'existence des tours de guet-domicile reflète, dans une certaine mesure, le développement de la micro-économie paysanne, et de la domination du système féodal de servage. Manifestement, c'est une étape rudimentaire à une époque ancienne. Contrairement au système féodal Han bien établi, le système de servage des Qiang ne crée aucune règle stricte, pour quelque forme d'architecture que ce soit, ce qui permet liberté et absence de limites dans l'innovation des tours-domicile des Qiang. Par conséquent, les extraordinaires plans des maisons, différentes les unes des autres, ont surgi de cette affinité entre domiciles et tours de guet. De telles idées soulignent principalement la priorité des domiciles et des lieux d'observation, ainsi les autres structures comme les chambres à coucher, les étables et les pièces pour les provisions sont arrangées aléatoirement. Cependant, c'est la composition des espaces premier et secondaire, bien définis, qui crée une atmosphère spatiale merveilleuse, avec la combinaison de grandeur et de petitesse, d'éparpillement et de densité, d'ampleur et d'étroitesse, d'ouverture et de fermeture, de ténèbre et de lumière. Un tel phénomène spatial mérite d'être souligné.

Pour ce qui est de la tour elle-même, il s'agit d'un système à la base structurel, supporté par ses murs. Que les murs soient faits de pierres, ou de terre, les rayons de l'espace intérieur restent habituellement de quatre mètres, et très peu de plus de cinq mètres, les poutres, parallèles, à chaque étage, et au sommet de la tour, sont posées horizontalement, d'un mur à l'autre, grâce aux trous creusés dans les murs, ce qui fait que les murs intérieurs et extérieurs portent tous deux le poids de la tour entière. A cause de la grande hauteur des murs, et du poids de la tour, la base du mur devait être épaisse, et le mur se rétrecir vers le sommet. Ainsi, les sommets de certaines tours de guet sont petits comme des balayettes. Les régions peuplées par les Qiang se trouvent dans une ceinture séismique, aussi une grande importance est accordée à la prévention des tremblements de terre. Pour assurer la stabilité de la tour, la base du mur doit être large, la base et le mur joints hermétiquement, la paroi

du mur s'amincir détage en étage, et les coins doivent être renforcés. La profondeur des fondations est déterminée par la dureté des pierres et de la terre. Néanmoins, à cause du terrain accidenté, certains murs de tours de guet sont construits sans bases, spécialement les murs à l'arrière des tours. Si l'on prend comme exemple la tour de guet du Village de Qiangfeng: le mur à l'arrière de la tour est taillé à même la paroi rocailleuse; alors que les autres murs ont encore des bases murales. Pour ce qui est de la paroi extérieure de la tour, sa partie basse a généralement une inclinaison plus marquée que celle du haut, ce qui vise à rabaisser le centre de gravité de la tour de guet et améliore la stabilité face aux renversements. C'est pourquoi vous pouvez remarquez que la paroi de la tour n'est pas droite, quand vous examinez son apparence. Afin d'améliorer encore la stabilité de la tour de guet dans la région autour du district de Mao, la paroi de l'espace mural est courbée et a une forme concave. Ainsi, les angles de tous les coins des murs ont été réduits, ce qui veut dire que les angles aux intersections des murs sont devenus plus aigus. Les Qiang appellent cette structure "Qianlengzi". Les tours de guet, ici, quelles soient quadrilatérales, hexagonales ou octogonales, ont toutes de telles structures. En fait, une telle structure est très similaire au dessin d'une tente, ce qui pourrait susciter l'idée qu'elle a été influencée par le style nomadique des anciens Qiang.

Les tours des Qiang sont habituellement construites étage par étage, quelles aient été construites en pierre ou en terre. Quand le premier étage est bâti, des poutres sont posées pour supporter le plancher. Ensuite commence la construction du deuxième étage, puis du troisième... Une fois qu'un étage est fini, l'intervalle de temps avec la construction de l'étage suivant doit être assez long pour permettre un séchage complet. Si la terre de la préparation est encore humide, ou si la terre et la pierre n'adhèrent pas totalement, la structure ne peut porter aucun poids, et l'étage supérieur pourrait s'écrouler. Ainsi ces constructions durent toujours de nombreuses années. Les constructions des toîts des diverses tours diffèrent légèrement d'un endroit à l'autre. Encore que dans une région, les constructions des toîts soient les mêmes. Le but général d'un toît d'une tour de guet est qu'il évacue l'eau. La procédure est de poser d'abord les poutres et les solives, ou du bois de chauffage, puis des branches d'arbre ou de bambou. Par dessus les branches, l'on met des herbes telle la gentiane. Après cela, une couche de boue mélangée à du sable est appliquée sur les herbes et aplatie pour former une surface inclinée pouvant évacuer l'eau. A la fin, une gouttière faite de tubes de bambou est installée à travers un trou creusé dans le mur afin d'évacuer l'eau.

Au sommet de la tour de guet, se trouve un escalier qui mène au toît de la tour, à travers un passage ouvert. Parfois, le passage est couvert d'un panneau de bois, ou d'un fin panneau de pierre. Comme il pleut rarement dans le nord-ouest de la Chine, le passage est généralement toujours ouvert. Les différents étages sont reliés entre eux par des échelles de troncs d'arbre. En de très rares occasions, la tour de guet ne possède pas de porte au rez-de-chaussée, ainsi, l'occupant doit entrer dans la tour grâce à une échelle menant au deuxième étage. Après qu'il ait pénétré dans sa tour-demeure, il en retire l'échelle pour plus de sécurité.

En fin de compte, avec leur structure unique, la tour de guet des Qiang, la demeure et le village forment ensemble une combinaison spatiale harmonieuse. L'architecture des Qiang, représentée par la tour de guet, reflète le dur labeur et la sagesse des Qiang. Par conséquent, la majestueuse et sophistiquée tour de guet est devenue un observatoire des développements culturels et des changements sociaux des Qiang. Aujourd'hui, certaines constructions du Village de Taoping, dans le District de Li, sont susceptibles d'entrer sur la liste des sites classés au Patrimoine Mondial, Culturel et Naturel de l'UNESCO (Organisation des Nations Unies pour l'Education, la Science et la Culture). Nous espérons qu'avec le développement de nos sociétés, la tour de guet des Qiang attirera l'attention du monde dans l'histoire de l'architecture.

## CHAPITRE TROIS    LE LANGAGE DES QIANG

Le langage des Qiang appartient à la branche tibéto-birmane de la famille sino-tibétaine. On ne letrouve plus que dans la forme parlée, sans les caractères correspondants. Il fallut attendre en 1949 pour que fût créé un système d'écriture alphabétique. Les Qiang ont pour habitude de l'appeler "Erma". En raison de leur histoire faite de migrations continuelles, il fut difficile d'améliorer et de rassembler les nombreux mots employés par les différentes tribus, ce qui débouche sur un phénomène linguistique spécial: dans la Vallée du Minjiang, des différences de prononciation peuvent être trouvées non seulement sur un large territoire, mais aussi dans de petites poches. Au sein même d'une seule montagne peuvent apparaître des variations dans la façon dont ils parlent. De telles divergences et diversités reflètent des obstacles de communication parmi les Qiang et les vives caractéristiques linguistiques régionales créées par leur passé mouvementé.

### I. Dialectes des Qiang

Après des décennies de recherches et d'études, les chercheurs spécialisés dans le langage des minorités, ont des informations soutenant la théorie que le langage des Qiang peut être divisé en deux branches: le dialecte du sud et celui du nord. Le dialecte du sud s'étend dans le comté de Wenchuan, la majeure partie du comté de Li et la région de Fengyi du comté de Mao. Le dialecte du nord est populaire dans la majeure partie des comtés de Heishui et de Mao, des secteurs d'habitation Qiang des comtés de Songpan, Pingwu et du Comté Autonome Qiang de Beichuan.

De grandes différences existent entre les dialectes du sud et du nord, principalement en phonétique, lexique et grammaire.

Phonétique: dans le dialecte du nord, les voyelles sont divisées en longues et courtes, rétroflexes et non rétroflexes. Il contient aussi d'abondantes consonnes composées, qui, avec les consonnes simples, créent de nombreux codas. Pour les tons, il n'y en a pas, excepté un léger dans le dialecte du nord. En ce qui concerne la formation des mots, il existe de grandes différences phonétiques dont les plus fréquentes sont: réduction, sonore, métathèse et alternance des consonnes; harmonie, muette, suppression et épenthèse de la voyelle. Tandis que dans le dialecte du sud

l'on trouve moins de consonnes composées, pas de voyelle rétroflexe et deux codas nasaux. Et seulement dans de rares endroits, les voyelles sont divisées en longues et courtes. Contrairement au dialecte du nord, celui du sud a différents tons servant principalement à distinguer la calligraphie plutôt que le sens des mots. De plus, il y a quelques signaux de changements phonétiques à pister dans le dialecte du sud.

Lexique: les dialectes du sud et du nord partagent à peu près le même lexique, dans lequel les mots hétérogènes occupent approximativement 10%. Le dialecte du sud est grandement influencé par le chinois phonétiquement, lexicalement et grammaticalement, tandis que celui du nord a peu de relations avec le chinois. Le tibétain touche à la fois les dialectes du sud et du nord jusqu'à une certaine mesure. Bien que certains mots sont prononcés différemment dans les dialectes du sud et du nord, des règles strictes de prononciation existent tout de même.

Grammaire: les différences grammaticales entre les dialectes du sud et du nord résident principalement dans des expressions grammaticales plus compliquées dans ce dernier, qui correspondent surtout à l'inflexion intérieure et à l'affixe. Les différences grammaticales entre les sous-branches du dialecte du nord sont moins visibles que celles du dialecte du sud. En termes de catégories grammaticales, les pronoms personnels dans le dialecte du sud ont des cas nominatifs et accusatifs, alors qu'un tel phénomène n'existe pas dans le dialecte du nord. Même pour la catégorie grammaticale similaire, les façons de s'exprimer dans les deux dialectes sont quelque peu différents. Prenons le verbe à l'impératif comme exemple, dans le dialecte du nord, il a huit préfixes,et ils sont toujours cohérents avec la direction manifestée par le verbe, alors qu'il n'en a qu'un dans le dialecte du sud.

Pour toutes les différences phonétiques et grammaticales, au sein d'une région dialectale, qui apparaissent, l'on divise plus loin plusieurs types de langages locaux[1]:

Six langages locaux dans le dialecte[2]du sud et leur distribution:

(1) Langage de Yanmen: village de Yanmen, comté de Wenchuan; Bachuan et Ligu du comté de Mao.

(2) Langage de Longxi: villages de Longxi et de keku du comté de Wenchuan;

---

[1] La division des langages locaux est basée d'après *Mystery of the Great Eastern Nation* par Xu Ping et Xu Dan, p92-93.

[2] Quelques érudits mettent les langages de Puxi et Muka ensemble et nomment celui-ci langage de Daqishan. Il est utilisé dans les villages de Puxi, Xuecheng, Ganbao, Nongjiale, Zagunao, Sanzhai du village de Muka, Wenshan du village de Tonghua, Muka, Jiuzi, Lielie, Shuitang et Shajin du village de Tonghua, quelques parties du village de Shangmeng et du village de Xiameng dans le comté de Li.

la région ouest du Minjiang à Weizhou.

(3) Langage de Mianchi: Mianchi, village de Caopo, Sanjiang et Yulong du comté de Wenchuan.

(4) Langage de Puxi: villages de Puxi et de Xuecheng du comté de Li; certaines parties des villages de Ganbao, Nongjiale et Zagunao; Sanzhai du village de Muka et Wenshan de celui de Tonghua.

(5) Langage de Muka: Muka, Jiuzi et Leilei dans le village de Mula du comté de Li; Shuitang et Shajin du village de Tonghua; et quelques parties des villages de Shangmeng et de Xiameng; de plus, la plupart des habitants du comté de Danba de la Préfecture Autonome Tibétaine Ganzi parlent aussi Muka.

(6) Langage de Taoping: villages de Taoping et de Tonghua du compté de Li.

Neuf Langages locaux dans le dialecte[①] du Nord et leur répartition:

(1) Zhenping: villages de Xiaoxing, Zhenping et Baiyang du comté de Songpan; villages; villages de Taiping, Songpinggou, Jiaochang et Shidaguan du comté de Mao.

(2) Qugu: villages de Qugu, Yadu, Weicheng, Wadi et Baixi du comté de Mao.

(3) Huilong: villages de Huilong, Sanlong, Shidaguan et la partie sud du village de Jiaochang du comté de Mao.

(4) Heihu: village de Heihu, Shuicaoping et Sujiaping du village de Feihong du comté de Mao.

(5) Weimen: villages de Goukou, Weimen et Yonghe du comté de Mao.

(6) Weigu: villages de Weigu, Musu, Luoduo, Longba, Shidiaolou, Seergu et Waboliangzi du comté de Heishui.

(7) Zhi Mulin: villages de Zhi Mulin, Wumushu, Ciba, quelques parties des villages de Qinglang et de Maizha du comté de Heishui.

(8) Mawo: villages de Mawo, Hongyan, Xier, Shuangliusuo et Zhawo du compté de Heishui.

(9) Luhua: Yangrong et Changde dans le village de Shashiduo du comté de Heishui, et d'autres lieux comme Zegai, Ergulu, Rela, Mierkua, Simei, Shanbangou, Luobajie et Zhugedu du comté de Heishui.

---

① Quelques érudits soutiennent qu'il n'y a que six types de langages locaux dans le dialecte du nord, i.e. les mentionnés ci-dessous langage de Zhenping, langage de Qugu, langage de Heihu, langage de Zhimulin, langage de Woma, langage de Luhua. Ils classent le langage de Weimen en langage de Heihu, mettent les langages de Huilong et de Weigu dans celui de Qugu.

## Ⅱ. Caractéristiques de base du langage des Qiang

### 1. Caractéristiques phonétiques

#### 1) Shengmu

Dans les langages de morphèmes monosyllabiques, tels les langages sinitiques (y compris le mandarin) et de nombreux langages tibéto-birmans, shengmu, le commencement d'une syllabe, se réfère à la première des deux parties qui forment la syllabe. La seconde partie est appelée Yunmu.

Il y a environ 40 consonnes simples shengmu dans chaque dialecte. En général, les consonnes occlusives et affriquées sont divisées en muettes, muettes aspirées et sonores en fonction des manières d'articuler. De plus, quatre différentes façons d'articuler donnent différentes sortes d'affriquées: apicales, rétroflexes, lamées et en plaçant la langue au centre. Il y aussi des occlusives et des fricatives produites par la luette. Le dialecte du nord a plus de 45 consonnes composées, bien plus que celui du sud. Dans un ou deux dialectes du sud, les consonnes composées ont même disparu. La plupart des consonnes composées se composent de deux parties, i.e. une consonne cardinale plus une pré-consonne ou post-consonne. Un faible nombre se scindent en trois parties. Dans le cas du langage de Qugu, une sous-branche du dialecte du nord, il y a 42 consonnes shengmu simples et 49 consonnes shengmu composées, chacune comprenant deux parties; tandis que le langage de Yanmen dans le dialecte du sud a 41 consonnes shengmu simples et 18 consonnes shengmu composées dont les structures sont aussi de deux parties.

(1) Consonne shengmu simple (Figure 1).

Figure 1　Consonne shengmu simple

| Façons d'articulation / Endroits d'articulation | | | bilabial | apex avant | apex central | apex arrière | lame | lame avant | base | luette | glotte |
|---|---|---|---|---|---|---|---|---|---|---|---|
| apical | aphone | non-aspiré | p | | t | | | | k | q | (ʔ) |
| | | aspiré | ph | | th | | | | kh | qh | |
| | exprimé | non-aspiré | b | | d | | | | g | | |
| affrique | aphone | non-aspiré | | ts | | tʂ | tʃ | tɕ | | | |
| | | aspirated | | tsh | | tʂh | tʃh | tɕh | | | |
| | exprimé | non-aspiré | | dz | | dʐ | dʒ | dʑ | | | |
| fricative | aphone | | f | S | ɬ | ʂ | | ɕ | x | χ | h |
| | exprimé | | | z | | ʐ | | ʑ | ɣ | ʁ | ɦ |
| | nasal | | m | | n | | | ȵ | ŋ | | |
| | lateral | | | | l | | | | | | |
| | trill | | | | r | | | | | | |
| | semi-finale-voyelle | | w | | | ɻ | | j | | | |

Notes:

① Occlusives apicales et affriquées sont labialisées avant la première Yunmu "u". A côté de cela, une légère vibrante roulée prendra place si le courant d'air est très fort, comme dans tuə (porter).

② "l" est prononcé "ɬ" quand la pré-consonne "x" apparît, comme dans xli (moelle).

③ "j" et "w" peuvent apparaître soit à la fin, soit au début d'une syllabe, et leur prononciation est plutôt comme, respectivement, les voyelles "i" et "u", comme dans "juju" (distribuer), "tshij" (poivre), "we" (avoir), "aw" (tante). "j" est lu comme "y" après la voyelle ronde "u", comme pour "tuj" (fléau).

④ Quand "x" est mis avant des voyelles hautes, il se changera phonétiquement en un "ø", comme pour xie/øie (injurier).

⑤ "ŋ" est manifestement labialisé, comme dans "ŋuə" (lait de vache), "qəŋ" (cheveux). Mais "ŋ" dans les mots empruntés du chinois n'est pas labialisé, malgré quelques exceptions tels que "ten leŋ" (lanterne).

⑥ "r" n'apparaît pas comme shengmu comme une syllabe initiale; "y" peut être seulement mis au début de la consonne composée; "x" sous de nombreuses conditions, est pris comme une pré-consonne. "h" ne se fait entendre qu'au début d'une syllabe initiale.

⑦ Les syllabes commençant avec une voyelle ont toujours le coup de glotte "ʔ" avant la voyelle, comme pour "ʔas" (un jour). Parceque "ʔ" disparaît habituellement dans le courant des mots, il ne peut être utilisé comme un phonème.

Exemples:

| p | pə | acheter | ph | phə | ride |
| b | bə | abeille | m | mə | feu |
| Φ | Φa | vêtements | tsh | tshə | sel |
| dz | dzə | manger | ʁ | ʁu | pouvoir |
| h | har | regarder en arrière | x | xu | odorant |

(2) Consonne shengmu composée. Les consonnes composées sont toutes faites de deux parties, la plupart du temps une muette avec une muette, ou une voisée avec une voisée. Elles sont divisées en deux types: une avec des fricatives au début commest, st, sq；zd；ʂp, ʂk, ʂq l'autre avec des fricatives á la fin comme pour phʂ, khs, gz, qhs etc.

Exemples:

| st | stə | milan | sq | pie sqam | flocon |
| zd | zdə | pont d'une planche | zb | zbə | yack |

288

| ɤr | ɤrə | assez |  | gz | gzə | piquant |
| qhs | qhse | mouton sauvage |  | x ʧ | x ʧue | fermer (yeux) |

**2) Yunmu**

(1) Monophtongues yunmu (Figure 2). Il y a de nombreux monophtongues yunmu dans le langage Qiang. Dans le dialecte du nord, elles sont divisées en longues et courtes, rétroflexes et non-rétroflexes, nasalisé_s et non-nasalisé_s. Dans le dialecte du sud il existe aussi de telles caractéristiques linguistiques comme la rétroflexion et la nasalisation. Par exemple, le langage de Qugu a 8 voyelles médiolinguale yunmu, 8 longues voyelles yunmu, 5 voyelles rétroflexes yunmu, 3 longues voyelles rétroflexes yunmu, 2 voyelles nasalisées yunmu, 3 voyelles rétroflexes nasalisées yunmu, et 1 longue voyelle rétroflexe nasalisée yunmu; le langage de Yanmen a 8 monophtongues yunmu et 2 voyelles rétroflexes yunmu.

Figure 2   Yunmu monophtongue

| Ré troflexe | | | non-r é troflexe | | r é troflexe | |
|---|---|---|---|---|---|---|
| Longueur lèvres langue | | | court | long | court | long |
| haut | front | plat | i | i: | i ɻ | i: ɻ |
| | | rond | y | | | |
| | dos | rond | u | u: | u ɻ | u: ɻ |
| mi- | front | plat | e | e: | e ɻ | e: ɻ |
| | dos | rond | o | o: | | |
| bas | front | plat | a | a: | a ɻ | a: ɻ |
| | dos | rond | a | a: | a ɻ | a: ɻ |
| central | | | ə | | ə ɻ | ə: ɻ |

Notes:

① La langue montante pour les longues voyelles "i:" "u:" est un peu haute, comme les voyelles standard [i] [u]. La langue montante pour les courtes voyelles "i" "u" est plus basse, équivalent [I] [v]. Mais quand elles sont utilisées comme initiales yunmu, la langue montante est la même qu'avec [i] [u]. Quand "u" se trouve après l'uvulaire et l'apex central, l'ouverture des lèvres est approximativement comme pour le [o]; s'il est placé après le consonne médiolinguale, il sera prononcé comme [y]; si le shengmu "h" est devant, il sera nasalisé comme [Ǔ].

② La position de la langue pour "a" est comme le [æ] et est un petit peu plus en arrière que pour le [ʌ].

③ La position de la langue pour le "ɔ" est un petit peu plus basse et plus en arrière que la voyelle centrale [ə].

④ Sous l'influence de la rétroflexion, les voyelles rétroflexes sont produites avec la langue au milieu. "iɹ" n'apparaît que dans la voyelle composée "uiɹ", tandis que "i:ɹ, aɹ, a: ɹ" ne se produisent qu'en formation de mots.

Exemples:

| a: | ba: | vêtement | ə | p ə | acheter |
|---|---|---|---|---|---|
| o | oqu | famille | e | tshe | chèvre |
| a: ɹ | xa:ɹ | côte | aɹ | qhaɹ | rareté |

(2) Voyelle composée yunmu. La voyelle composée yunmu prend principalement la forme d'une post-sonorité excepté dans quelques dialectes de régions du sud où les voyelles prennent la forme d'une pré-sonoroité. La voyelle composée est divisée en diphtongue et triphtongue. Les diphtongues sont toutes post-sonorisées avec l'initiale yunmu "i" ou "u" au début. Les triphtongues ou "iau" et "uai" n'apparaîssent que dans les mots empruntés du chinois.

Exemples:

| ie | pie | cochon | ia | siaqa | choisir |
|---|---|---|---|---|---|
| ui | tuitue | harmonieux | iau | phiau | ticket (chinois) |

(3) Yunmu et coda consonnantal. 27 codas consonnantaux et 17 codas consonnantaux composés font en tout 189 combinaisons avec yunmu. Voici quelques exemples:

| p | kep | orphelin | n | tsun | puce |
|---|---|---|---|---|---|
| t | pet | bronze | d | sed | faucille |

Il y a de grandes différences entre les codas consonnantaux des dialectes du sud et du nord. La plupart des codas consonnantaux dans le dialecte du sud ont disparu, tandis que danns le dialecte du nord existe toujours un grand nombre de codas consonnantaux simples et composés. Plus de 30 consonnes dans le dialecte du nord peuvent se transformer en codas, ce qui crée plus de 250 combinaisons avec yunmu. Mais en général, le dialecte du sud a à peu près 20 consonnes, bien moins que celui du nord.

### 3) Ton léger

Le dialecte du nord n'a pas de tons pour distinguer le sens des mots. Néanmoins, presque chaque mot un ton fixe. La monosyllabe est principalement

élevée. Pour une disyllabe, sa première partie est habituellement de niveau moyen tandis que le reste est élevé. Les points concernant les mots empruntés au chinois sont flexibles. Certains sont ajustés en fonction de la prononciation habituelle du langage Qiang; certains suivent les tons du chinois local.

Il y a des mots dont les syllabes non initiales sont prononcées légèrement. Ces syllabes sont accompagnées d'un ton bas, d'une faible intensité et de voyelles dévoisées. Des syllabes comprenant des voyelles avec la marque dévoisée " ₒ " sont des syllabes légères.

Le dialecte du nord a une variété de changements phonétiques. Dans la formation des mots et la liaison apparaît souvent le phénomène suivant: réduction consonnantale, dévoisement, métathèse; harmonie de la voyelle, élision, et élision syllabique et fusion ensemble.

Le dialecte du nord n'a pas de ton. Certains mots utilisent des syllabes légères ou accentuées pour en distinguer le sens. Au contraire, le dialecte du sud a de deux à six sortes de tons. Cependant, ils contribuent peu à la différentiation des sens lexicaux et grammaticaux. Par exemple, le langage local de Qugu n'a pas de ton, tandis que celui de Yanmen en possède trois; leurs valeurs de ton sont respectivement de 55, 31 et de 35.

## 2. Caractéristiques grammaticales

Les principaux dispositifs grammaticaux du langage des Qiang sont les mots fonctionnels et l'ordre des mots. Comme il est impossible d'énumérer chaque langage local Qiang qui existe, le dialecte du nord, relativement représentatif, est pris en exemple pour montrer les caractéristiques grammaticales de base du langage des Qiang.

### 1) Formation des mots

(1) Monosémie. La plupart des monosémies sont des mots simples, tel mə (feu) et na (bon). Les monosémies disyllabiques, dans la plupart des cas, sont des verbes. De plus, beaucoup d'entre eux sont des mots avec des shengmu ou yunmu répétéz, comme tuətuə (plier), məma (barbouiller), tshutshuə (faire combattre les coqs) et khu(e)khu(e) (se mettre en colère). Il y a peu de monosémies avec plus de deux syllabes.

(2) Mots composés:

① Combinaison. La combinaison d'une racine plus une autre racine peut être divisée en deux types: l'un est la partie arrière portant le sens principal, comme dans dzuaʁl (moudre) tɕi (maison) →dzuaʁl tɕi (maison à moudre), l'autre place le

sens principal sur la partie première comme pour tɵui (poulet) pi (mâle) →tɵui pi (coq).

② affix (mots joints). Il y a deux sortes d'affix, le préfixe et le suffixe. Par exemple, "a-" (utilisé pour indiquer les titres des parents) et "ha-" (utilisé pour indiquer les nombres de onze à dix-neuf) sont tous deux des préfixes.

| | | | |
|---|---|---|---|
| apa | grand-père | akua | oncle (frère de la sœur) |
| opu | oncle (frère du père) | ow | grandmère |
| hekheɹ | dix-huit | hoŋ | quinze |

En raison de la présence de l'harmonie de la voyelle entre les préfixes "a-", "ha-" et l'etymons, "a-" et "ha-" prennent aussi d'autres formes, comme pour "e-", "o-", "he-" et "ho-".

Le suffixe "-m" est ajouté après un verbe morphème pour former un nom indiquant la personne agissant et un autre suffixe "-s" est mis après le verbe morphème pour former un nom se référant à l'objet en relation.

| | | | | |
|---|---|---|---|---|
| -m | qhuɹ | chasser | qhuɹm | chasseur |
| | təs pu | faire des affaires | təs pum | homme d'affaire |
| -s | dzə | manger | dzəs | nourriture |

(3) Mots empruntés. Il y a un grand nombre de mots empruntés au chinois, qui, parmi presque 4000 mots Qiang relevés, représentent approximativement 19%. Par exemple, χu (tigre), gantsə (selle), sen tshan tui (équipe de production) etc. Une fois que des verbes monosyllabiques et des adjectifs sont empruntés au chinois, le suffixe "-tha" est ajouté, comme dans khau tha (test) et pentha (idiot). Tandis que pour les verbes composés venant du chinois, le morphème pu est ajouté, comme dans ʁuakhu pu (faire la satire).

Il y quelques mots du tibétain. La plupart d'entres eux sont liés à la religion, comme piuru (corail).

**2) Classes des mots**

(1) Nom. "xsa" ajouté après un nom rend le nom à la forme plurielle; "tsi" ajouté après un nom signifie "petitesse". Les noms de localités, relativement abondants, peuvent être modifiés par l'adverbe "zui" (le plus). Et les noms de localité comme ceux indiquant les hauts et les bas, le cours supérieur et le cours inférieur, etc, peuvent être classifiés en quatre catégories, référence générique (A), référence de courte distance (B), référence de moyenne distance (C) et référence de longue distance (D).

|              | A       | B        | C        | D          |
|--------------|---------|----------|----------|------------|
| haut         | məq     | ʦuməp    | məχta    | mə:χta     |
| bas          | qəl     | ʦuqəl    | qəlla    | qə:lla     |
| cours supérieur | niz  | tsuniz   | nizta    | ni:zta     |
| cours inférieur | khsiz | tsukhisiz | khsizta | khisi:zta |

(2) pronoms personnels. Les pronoms personnels incluent la première personne, la deuxième personne et la troisième personne, chaque personne est divisée en nombre impair, nombre pair et nombre pluriel. La pronom de la troisième personne est a l'origine de la pronom demonstrative. Les formes redupliquées de tels pronoms sont employées a intensifier le ton pour les nombres impairs de la deuxième personne et la troisième personne, et pour les formes de monbre pair et de nombre pluriel des trois pronoms personnels.

La forme impaire de la première personne, la deuxième personne, la forme impaire et la forme paire de la troisième personne ont toutes leur pronom reflechi correspondant, tels que "gui" (moi-meme), "kui" toi-meme) et "nili" (eux-memes).

(3) nombres cardinauxles. Nombres cardinaux comptant d'un à neuf sont habituellement employés avec le mot de mesure "wu" (égale au "ge" dans le chinois); il y a deux autres expressions qui peuvent exprimer le concept de dix.

(4) spécificatifs. Il y a beaucoup de spécificatifs dans la langue des Qiang . Ceux-ci sont classés en quantifieurs verbaux et des quantifieurs nominaux, qui doivent généralement être employé en combinaison avec des numéraux et des pronoms démonstratifs. Les Quantifieurs doivent être placés après des numéraix. Beaucoup de quantifieurs se servent des racines nominales et verbales, comme le "quat" (un genre d'instrument de mesure) et "tsua" (une poignée de). Quand des quantifieurs sont employés avec des chiffres, leurs voyelles s'entendent harmonisées, comme dans le; du "o qhsu" (un saut) et "ra"(quatre morceaux).

(5) verbes. Les verbes changent selon la personne (première, deuxième et troisième), le nombre (singulier, pluriel), le temps (avant, présent, futur), mode (déclaratif, impératif, invocative, prohibitif, négatif), aspect (aspect perfectif auparavant, aspect perfectif actuel, aspect perfectif futur), ton (général, défini, indéfini), voix (active, passif), direction (à travers, en amont et en aval, vers l'intérieur et à l'extérieur, ici et là),  transitif et intransitif. Quand les adjectifs fonctionnent comme prédicat, ils partage également la plupart des catégories mentionnées ci-dessus.

Toutes ces catégories se réalisent au moyen de modification radicale et d'affixes.Le verbe "dzə"(manger) est donné ci-dessous comme exemple:

Généralement, l'utilisation de l'impératif est semblable au temps passée des deuxièmes personnes. Dans certains cas, préfixe est ajouté mais pour la forme singulière, on n'ajoute pas le préfixe "n". Par exemple, dans l'az (tu manges) et "aztɕin" (Vous mangez).

Les verbes de permission sont divisés en deux types:le premier indique que l'interlocuteur exige à l'auditeur de faire faire une chose par la troisième personne. Cette forme palatalise la consonne initiale du préfixe de l'impératif de la deuxième personne, (dans le cas d'une consonne initiale zéro, "j" est ajouté), comme dans le "jaz" (Vous lui demandez de manger), et "jaz e" (Vous leur demandez de manger). Le deuxième indique que l'intelocuteur demande à l'auditeur de permettre l'interlocuteur de faire quelque chose. Cette forme ajoute le "la" comme suffixe (quand l'interlocuteur est au singulier) ou "liə:ɹ" (quand l'interlocuteur est au pluriel). Par exemple, "azla" (Vous me demandez de manger) et "azliə:ɹ" (Vous nous demandez de manger).

Les verbes d'interdiction sont construits en ajoutant le préfixe "tɕa" avant des verbes du présent, comme le "tɕazən" (tu ne manges pas.), et "tɕaztɕin" (Vous (pl.) ne mangez pas). La voyelle "tɕa" devrait être harmonisé avec la voyelle de la racine du verbe, comme le "ta—tɕa" (prendre—ne prendre pas).

La négation est construite en ajoutant le "ma" dvant la racine du verbe. Si "ma" est ajouté devant le verbe qui indique le futur, le temps future devient négative; si "ma"est placé après le préfixe d'un verbe du passée, c'est le negation du passé. La voyelle dans le "ma"devrait être harmonisé avec la voyelle de la racine du verbe, comme le "za" (prendre avec une cuillère) — "maza"(ne pas prendre avec une cuillère) — "təmaza" (n'a pas pu prendre avec une cuillère).

Les expressions suivantes sont les formes employées pour exprimer les tons différents concernant les verbes:

Les tons précisés impliquent le lien entre l'interlocuteur et l'action exprimé par le verbe. Il y a plusieurs sortes d'affixes qui sont conformes à la personne. Quand la première personne est soulignée, le suffixe "k" est ajouté; quand la deuxième personne est soumise à l'importance, le suffixe "sa" est ajouté; quand la troisième personne est mise en accent, le suffixe "w" est ajouté. Par exemple:

sazək    (cette vache sûrement) a mangé (mes légumes)

sazsan   (cette vache sûrement) a mangé (vos légumes)

sazəw    (cette vache sûrement) a mangé (ses légumes)

Les tons imprécisés suggèrent que l'interlocuteur ait seulement entendu parler de ce qui a été fait et n'est pas sûr qu'il soit vrai ou pas. Il y a également plusieurs affixes qui sont conformes à la personne du sujet ou la personne du complément d'objet direct. Quand la première personne est soulignée, le suffixe "w" est ajouté; quand la deuxième personne est mise en accent, le suffixe "wan" est ajouté; quand la troisième personne est accentuée, le suffixe "wi" est ajouté. Par exemple:

səzwa    (cette vache probablement) a mangé (mes légumes)

səzwan    (cette vache probablement) a mangé (vos légumes)

səzwi    (cette vache probablement) a mangé (ses légumes)

(6) Les terminaison des adjectifs ressemblent à celles des verbes. De nombreau adjectifs emploient la forme de répétition. Le comparatif d'adjectif est exprimé en ajoutant un "s" final.

(7) Les adverbes de négation peuvent être insérés entre le préfixe et le verbe ou l'adjectif. Les adverbes contribuent également à la cohésion des phrases. En outre, les adverbs réitératifs travaillent ensemble pour former des phrases en rime vocalique.

(8) Les auxiliaires sont riches. Ils peuvent être divisés en auxiliaire de structure et auxiliaire de ton. Dans le premier groupe les auxiliaires incluent l'auxiliaire modifiant, auxiliaire agentive, auxiliaire passif, auxiliaire instrumental, auxiliaire comparatif, auxiliaire de lieu et auxiliaire de cause. Quand un auxiliaire de structure vient après un nom, un pronom ou un groupe nominal, il indique un rapport entre les mots ou entre les composants de phrase. Par exemple, "gu" (auxiliaire agentive ou instrumental), "ta" (auxiliaire de lieu), "ʁa" (indiquant le temps), "jgu de" (auxiliaire de cause).

qa χe gu Φa ja    (Je couds des vêtements avec une aiguille.)

Je aiguille (d'auxiliaire) vêtements coudre

the: ej ʁa doΦu    (Il s'est enfui une nuit.)

il une nuit (d'auxiliaire) s'enfuir

### 3) L'ordre des mots

l'ordre des mots dans une phrase est: sujet-complément-prédicat. Les noms et les pronoms déterminatifs viennent devant la partie principale de la phrase tandis que des adjectifs déterminatifs et les propositions quantitatives sont placés après la partie principale. Quand le pronom demonstrative, il est combiné avec un quantifieur ou un mot auxiliaire en tant que determinative. Il peut venir l'un ou l'autre avant ou après la partie principale. Généralement, l'ordre des mots est: nom (personne ou pronoun) —partie modifiée—ajectif—quantifieur.

Exemples:

(1) qa      stuaχa      dza:      [Je veux diner (manger).]
Je      repas      manger

(2) the: gu      qa      ma:      Φa      phʂiʂ      the: khsepe
haɭmaɭni      kantse aχlu

Il (auxiliaire) ma      mère      vêtement blanc      ces      trois
silencieusement propre laver

(Il a silencieusement lavé proprement ces trois vêtements blancs de ma mère.)

Dans une phrase compos é par deux propositions ou plus, il n'y a en general pas de conneteurs entre les propositions. Néanmoins, des connecteurs empruntés du Chinois sont parfois employés comme conjonction.

## III. Utilisation actuelle de la langue Qiang[①]

La langue des Qiang est principalement parlée par les Qiang de l'Autonomie Régionale Aba des Tibétains et des Qiang. Egalement elle est parlée par les Qiang dans le district Beichuan de la region Mianyang et dans le district Danba de l'Autonomie Régionale Ganzi. Il y a une population d'environ 160 000 qui parle cette langue dans la province du Sichuan. Il y a également plus de 40 000 Tibétains (principalement dans le distict de Heishui) qui parlent cette langue. La condition actuelle concernant l'utilisation de cette langue de Qiang est ainsi:

(1) Les régions principales où le Qiang est parlé sont les regions montagneuses (au sommet ou à mi-côte) des dstricts de Mao, Songpan，Wenchuan et Li. La majorité des habitants de ces régions utlitisent le Qiang dans leur vie quoditienne.

(2) Les régions où Qiang et Chinois sont employés l'un après l'autre restent dans les districts de Mao, de Wenchuan, et de Songpan. Dans les villages près des routes principaux et près des villes et bourgs du district Li, les deux langus s'emploient alternativement. Certains habitants des régions emploient le Qiang avec les gens de leurs villages ou de la famille. Les gens de certains ages: une quarantaine d'ans ou plus sont compétents en Qiang. Mais les au-dessus de quarante ans et les plus parlent Qiang de façon habiles. Pourtant parmi les au-dessous de quarante ans et les adolescents, ceux qui ont plus de contact avec le dehors parlent moins couramment le Qiang que ceux qui sortent rarement de leurs villages.

---

① Les chiffres d'ici sont cités du livre *Le Mistère de la Grande Nation Orientale* par Xu Ping et Xu Dan p96-98.

Certains d'entre eux ne comprennent que la parole du Qiang et n'arrivent pas à parler. En réalité, tout le monde peuvent parler chinois couramment.

(3) Les Tibétains s'appellant "Erma" dans le district de Heishui parlent aussi la langue Qiang. Selon une enquête faite dans les années 50 du siècle passé, peu de gens ont compris le chinois. Mais le nombre des gens qui peuvent parler le chinois a augmenté considérablement depuis les années 80. Cependant, la langue de Qiang a continué à être un de leurs moyens de communication. Selon la statistique d'après les faits, parmi les Qiang-parlants dans le comté de Heishui un peu de gens ont appris le Tibétain à travers les activités religieuses ou le commerce.

(4) La majorité des Qiang qui hatibent dans les districts Beichuan, Pingwu, Danba et dans le village de Baiyang du district Songpan, ceux qui restent dans les villes et bourgs des districte Wenchuan et Li et ceux qui vivent dispersés près des routes ne peuvent plus parler Qiang. Le Chinois est devenu la langue d'une utilité quotidienne.

Situations où la langue de Qiang est employée:

(1) Dans la famille. Dans la famille，les membres parlent Qiang, y compris la famille des Tibétains. Dans les districts Mao, Li et Wenchuan, les Qiang parlent chinois s'il y a des invités présents qui ne comprennent pas la langue de Qiang. Dans les villages Zhenping, Zhenjiang et Xiaoxing du district Songpan et dans la région Heishui; les indigènes parlent leur propre langue malgré la présence des invités qui ne comprennent pas le Qiang. Le mariage entre les Tibétains du nord et les Qiang conduit une communication en Qiang.

(2) Sur le marché. Les Qiang parlent leur langue sur le marché. Dans la majorité des cas, les gens de Songpan, de Mao, de Wenchuan et de Li parlent la langue de Qiang sur leurs marchés, mais le chinois est employé si les personnes d'autres nationalités sont présentes. Dans le district Heishui, la langue de Qiang est employée à tout moment.

(3) En public. Le Qiang est aussi utilisé dans les occasions publiques. Dans les districts Mao, Songpan, Wenchuan et Li, le Qiang est employé aux conférences administratives de villages. S'il y a la présence d'autres groupes éthniques, le chinois est employé à la place de Qiang. Cependant, dans le district Heishui, la langue de Qiang est employée non seulement aux conférences administratives de villages mais aussi à celles du district. Dans ce cas si les personnes d'autres groupes ethniques y assistent, des interprètes se servent. Dans les hôpitaux, les bureaux de poste, les salles de télécommunication, les magasins, et les arrêts de bus, le chinois

est souvent utilisé. Cependant, parmi de bonnnes connaissances, les indignènes se communiquent en leur propre langue.

(4) Dans le domaine de l'éducation. Jusqu'aux années 80 du siècle passé, les Qiang n'avaient pas eu leur langue écrite correspondante à leur langue orale, le chinois avait été enseigné dans les éceoles primaries et dans les collèges. Mais quelques écoles primaries dans les villages Chibusu et Shaba du district Mao ont essayé avec succès d'avoir une méthode bilangue. C'est à dire les professeurs chinois apprennent la langue Qiang d'abord et l'emploient ensuite dans leurs ensignements pour expliquer des difficultés du texte chinois. Actuellement, L'Ecole Normale Supérieur d'Aba et l'Ecole Normale supérieur Des Nationalités de Weizhou dans la province de Sichuan ont installé des départements de Qiang et ont commence des recherches sur cette langue. Plus de 100 écoles primaires et collèges dans les districts de Mao, Wenchuan, Li et Songpan ont adopté l'enseignement bilingue entre le Chinois et le Qiang. Maintenant il y a plus de 320 enseignant à temps plein et à temps partiel qui travaillent sur la langue de Qiang.

(5) Dans des activités religieuses. Les Qiang croient en religion primitive. Toutes les activités religieuses sont présidées par le "Shibi" (ʂpi ou ɕy, le "Duan Gong" en chinois, c.-à-d., prêtre de Qiang). Les activitée religieuse incluent la adoration de montagnes, vœu aux dieux, traitement des maladies, dispersion des fantômes, les marriage et les funérailles. Les prêtres de Qiang sont les utilisateurs les plus fidèles de la langue de Qiang. Ils ont préservé des chansons, des poésies et des légendes antiques de Qiang. Dans ce sens ils sont les vrais héritiers et convoyeurs de la culture de Qiang. La langue de Qiang est employée dans toutes les activités religieuses dans les régions de Qiang.

(6) Dans des activités culturelles. Quand les Troupes Artistiques de chaque district dans la région des Qiang donnent une représentation, le Qiang est employé pour présenter les programmes. Par exemple, le Troupes Artistiques du districte Mao donne environ une cinquantaine de représentations chaque année, parmi lesquelles un tiers des programmes sont présentés en Qiang. Ces programmes de chansons et de danses concernent habituellement des histoires des Qiang et leurs vies quotidiennes. En outre, les postes de radiodiffusion des villages préfèrent employer la langue des Qiang pour annoncer des affaires courantes de la région, des annonces et des programmes de la musique.

(7) Dans des cas légaux. Le tribunal dans la région de Qiang emploie souvent la langue des Qiang dans les investigations civiles ou criminelles. La conversation de

l'interrogation se fait en Qiang. Pendant les procès locaux, des interprètes sont prêts pour aider la partie en cause qui ne comprend pas le chinois s'il s'agit de la langue chinise. Le jugement final est prononcé dans les deux langues: le chinois et le Qiang.

## IV. Vernaculaire (La langue écrite des Qiang)

Avant les années 80 du siècle passé, les Qiang n'a pas eu une langue écrite et les caractères chinois ont été employés dans des régions des Qiang par l'administration locale et les écoles. Depuis la foundation de la République Populaire de Chine, beaucoup de fonctionnaires et de gens du pays de Qiang ont proposé de créer un système écrit pour les Qiang. Dès les années 50, l'Etat et le gouvernement chinois ont attaché une grande importance à la recherche de la langue des Qiang. À ce moment-là, l'Académie Chinoise des Sciences Sociales y a envoyé une équipe des linguistes appelée No. 7 Groupe pour les recherches de langue des Qiang. L'institut des Recherches des Langues Nationales a été également établi dans le préfecture Aba, essayant de créer un système écrit alphabétique pour les Qiang (basé sur le dialecte nordique du Qiang et la prononciation du Mawo vernaculaires est prise comme norme stantard). Des efforts ont été faits dans la recherche approfondie sur la langue des Qiang. Malheureusement ce travail a été arrêté pour des raisons diverses.

Avec le développement économique, la réforme du pays et l'ouverture au monde, surtout après la Troisième Session Plénière du 11ème Comité Central du Parti Communiste de la Chine, les Qiang ont exprimé de nouveau leur désir ardent pour créer une langue écrite. Selon les règles des affaires ethniques du pays, et dans la considération des besoins de Qiang, la Commission des Affaires Ethniques de la province de Sichuan a envoyée un groupe de recherche à Aba en 1984 dans le but d'examiner la langue. L'examen concerne la distribution de cette langue, la condition de l'emploi et le besoin si un système écrit soit nécessaire pour les Qiang. En juillet 1989, autorisé par le gouvernement provincial, un groupe de gestion pour créer un manuscrit alphabétique des Qiang a été formé. Pendant deux années succesives, le groupe a effectué les travaux suivants: formation des personnels enseignants de la langue écrite, proposition des plans, realization des experiences d'enseignement. Cela marquait le commencement de l'utilisation de l'écriture alphabétique des Qiang. En octobre 1991, le projet a été soumise à la Commission ethnique d'affaires d'état après avoir été approuvé par le gouvernement provincial de Sichuan. En mars 1993, Expertisés par des experts, la Commission Ethnique des Affaires de l'état a accordé la mise à l'essai du système écrit dans les régions de

Qiang. Maintenant, le système est avec succès en service pendant plus de 10 ans.

Mais certains chercheurs pensent que les Qiang antiques et les Huaxia (Han) co-formaient la culture chinoise, donc les caractères chinois actuels pourraient être considérés comme la langue des Qiang. Des autres pensent que la dynastie de Xi Xia a été fondée par les Qiang, les caractères de la dynastie de Xi Xia pourraient également être considérés comme des caractères des Qiang. Cependant, selon le trait des caractères que les "caractères ne sont que le symbole et le porteur de la langue (orale)", ni le chinois ni les caractères de Xi Xia devraient être vus comme caractères de Qiang. Les faits historiques nous indiquent que les Qiang actuels ne sont qu'une des nombreuses branches des Qiang antiques. Par consequent, leur origine culturelle est différente non seulement de celle des Qiang antiques qui ont co-vécu avec les Han de Huaxia mais également de celle qui ont fondé la dynastie de Xi Xia.

Le nouveau système écrit s'emploie la forme de l'alphabet du latin. La raison pour laquelle que l'alphabet est choisi, c'est que les lettres alphabétiques sont faciles à imprimer et à écrire. Elles simplifient un accès à la compréhendion et à l'apprendissage. Donc le système est facile à populariser. En janvier 1990, après une recherche complète et une discussion étendue, les cadres des Qiang, les intellectuels et les représentants de différents secteurs se sont réunis et ont unanimement adopté le système écrit. Le système se base sur le dialect nordique de Qugu, car le Qugu dialect est utilisé par la majorité des Qiang, donc il se comprend largement entre eux. De plus, il bien préserve les traits de la langue des Qiang et mieux représente la façon de prononcer des Qiang. Tout en prenant le Qugu dialect comme la base du système, les chercheurs ont profité de l'expérience de la formation des autres langues des minorités en Chine dans le but de faciliter la création.

En générale, l'ensemble du programme du système écrit alphabétique (première ébauche) inclut 8 sections et 4 annexes. Conformément aux principes phonétiques internationaux, le système lie la phonétique et les lettres écrites, c.-à-d., les lettres sont écrites selon la façon de se prononcer: la pornonciation détermine l'écriture. De plus, le système prend en compte les traits morphologiques de la langue des Qiang parce que la langue des Qiang y est très riche. Dans des cas en particulier, la pronunciation et l'écriture fonctionne de façon séparée.

La création et la popularisation du système écrit des Qiang jouent un rôle positif dans leur vie quotidienne. Elles prospéreront les régions des Qiang de manière politique, économique et culturelle. Elles leur aideront également à développer la culture des Qiang.

## CHAPITRE QUATRE   LITTÉRATURE QIANG

Pendant leur longue histoire, les Qiang ont créé une littérature splendide, s'étendant des récits oraux aux textes écrits. En plus d'être un trésor de la culture Qiang, ces patrimoines forment aussi une richesse spirituelle partagée par tous les Chinois.

### Ⅰ. Littérature populaire

Les histoires traditionnelles, passées de génération en génération sous la forme d'instruction orale, jouent un rôle le plus fondamental et le plus significatif dans la littérature Qiang. Elles trouvent leurs racines profondes dans l'histoire de la société où elles sont nées. En réalité, elles ont acquis une reconnaissance universelle. La littérature populaire des Qiang comprend des mythes, légendes, histoires, chansons traditionnelles (y compris chants épiques), fables et contes de fées, tous caractérisés par un contenu riche, des sujets vastes et des genres variés. De plus, beaucoup d'œuvres montrent un esprit idéal et un niveau artistique élevés.

La plupart des œuvres de la littérature populaire des Qiang, en dehors des mythes et des légendes, reflètent les réalités de la vie. Ils sont donc très sincères et simples. La plupart des travaux sont les éloges du cœur racontant les grands exploits des ancêtres. De surcroît, la mise en accent sur l'explication des faits et des narrations des histoires se trouvent également dans la littérature. Toutes les histoires emploient le dialecte local, paraissant ainsi naturelles, vivantes et très proches de la vie quotidienne.

### 1. Mythes

Le mythe est l'une des plus anciennes formes de la littérature populaire Qiang. En fonction de leur contenu, les mythes peuvent être divisés en huit catégories, à savoir les mythes sur la création du monde, sur l'origine des hommes, sur la nature et ses changements, sur les animaux et plantes, sur les totems et les ancêtres, sur les crues, sur la sécheresse et le feu, sur les origines de la culture, et sur les héros défiés. Les traits généraux de ces mythes sont: ① le lien avec la région locale; ② le rapport avec les pensées primitives survivantes et les croyances religieuses; ③ les

histoires en relation avec la lutte contre la nature; (4) l'imagination reflétant la réalité tout en se doublant d'un caractère esthétique.

De nombreux mythes Qiang concernent la création du monde, comme les célèbres *Création du Ciel et de la Terre, Chien—l'Oncle Maternel de la Terre, La Naissance de Pan Gu et Sa Création du Ciel et de la Terre*, etc. Ces mythes, reflétant les interrogations sur le mystère de la nature, expliquent l'imagination des Qiang vis-à-vis de la nature.

Les mythes sur l'origine de l'homme décrivent le commencement des êtres suivant une perspective différente, comme dans *L'Origine de la Fleur Yangjiao, Des Pithécanthropes aux Etres Humains, D' où venaient les Etres?* etc.

Dans *L'Origine de la Fleur Yangjiao*, l'histoire remonte à l'antiquité lointaine. L'Univers à ce moment n'était que l'air trouble dans les ténébres. Père Mubita, le dieu des Cieux, dit à Mubaxi de créer le ciel, et à la déesse Rubuxi de fonder la terre. Plus tard, le soleil, la lune, les étoiles et toutes les créations sur la terre furent façonnées. Comme il devint nécessaire d'organiser les créations, Mubita, imitant sa propre apparence, sculpta du tronc de yangjiao (azalée) neuf couples de petits personnages en bois. Il mit ensuite les couples dans un trou creusé dans le sol qu'il couvrit d'une dalle. Au jour du premier Wu (Wu signifie la cinquième des dix Tiges Célestes, qui sont combinées avec les douze Branches Terrestres, et qui désignent les années, les mois, les jours et les heures, dans l'astronomie traditionnelle Chinoise), les personnages furent capables de scintiller dès lors que la dalle fut découverte; au jour du deuxième Wu, les couples commencèrent à remuer la tête et les bras; quand le troisième Wu arriva, Père Mubita vint tout juste retirer la dalle, les personnages en bois s'échappèrent en un clin d'œil, grandirent, et devinrent adultes immédiatement. Depuis, il y a des hommes sur terre.

Les mythes des Qiang donnent aussi des observations sur les phénomènes de la nature et les explications simples de ses changements. A ce propos, deux ouvrages, *L'Origine de Vallée et de Terre Plat* et *Le Conte de Coqs Blancs*, racontent que le brûlis de la peau des crapauds et celle des coqs blancs entraînèrent certains changements à la surface de la terre. Dans l'histoire de *Le Soleil et La Lune*, le Soleil est dépeint en femme alors que la Lune est décrite en homme. Dans ce genre de mythes, les héros sont principalement les femmes. Cela indique probablement une période durante de la société matriarcale des Qiang, et également témoigne du caractère laborieux des femmes sous cette dynastie.

Dans les œuvres représentatives comme *L'Origine et la Perte des Graines* et

*L'Origine des Cinq Céréales*, les mythes sur les plantes mettent un accent particulier sur les origines des graines. D'après le conte *L'Origine et la Perte des Graines*, les céréales étaient en provenance des graines volées dans le ciel par un ancêtre Qiang appelé Danbaxiere. Depuis lors, les produits alimentaires et les légumes poussaient ensemble sur terre. Les mythes mentionnés ci-dessus démontrent l'épanouissement de la conscience collective des Qiang, ainsi que le développement de la société Qiang au cours de l'histoire.

Parmi les mythes liés aux totems, aux ancêtres Qiang, et aux héros déifiés, *Le conte de Dieu Jiaojiao, Femme Xiazhi Vole l'Eau* sont tous deux représentatifs. Le premier raconte le passé du Dieu Jiaojiao et son influence de génération en génération, et le deuxième dépeint l'histoire de Femme Xiaozhi, qui emmena l'eau du ciel à la terre, faute d'eau dans le monde originel.

Ayant des idées semblables, tout en conservant les caractéristiques distinctives de chacun, les mythes des Qiang partagent en général les thèmes suivants, inondation, sécheresse et feu. Ces histoires décrivent souvent l'extinction des êtres après un cataclysme, mais le mariage des frère et sœur survivants permet le recommencement d'un nouveau cycle de la reproduction des êtres humains. D'autres mythes concernant ce sujet sont *Inondation submerge le Ciel, Les Frère et Soeur s'installent sur Terre après être Descendu du Soleil*, et *Les Etres Humains Après le Feu*, etc.

Dans les mythes de la culture primitive sont souvent décrits l'esprit de découverte et l'imagination merveilleuse des Qiang. Ces points en particulier sont représentés dans les ouvrages *Garçon Ranbi Vole le Feu* et *Ababumo*, etc. La première histoire parle d'un garçon appelé Ranbi, qui vola le feu du ciel à la terre; la deuxième d'Ababumo, qui recueillit les herbes et les insectes pour guérir les malades faute de médicaments.

En conclusion, les mythes des Qiang reflètent leur esprit persévévant et leur volonté d'intrépidité. Ils font également ressortir le thème que les ancêtres Qiang commencent leur vie de façon laborieuse.

## 2. Epopées et longs poèmes

Durant la longue histoire des Qiang sont apparus un grand nombre d'épopées et de longs poèmes narratifs mythiques. Ces ouvrages représentent leur conscience collective et la sagesse des ancêtres des Qiang. En fait, ils ont exercé une grande influence sur la littérature Qiang et sur le côté artistique.

L'épopée *Guerres Entre les Qiang and les Ge* et les deux longs poèmes narratifs mythiques, *Mu Jiezhu et Dou Anzhu* et *Comment Dieux vivent A Part*, sont les exemples ayant la plus grande influence sur les œuvres littéraires traditionnelles des Qiang.

*Guerres Entre les Qiang et les Ge* (qui comporte les mêmes thèmes que deux autres oeuvres, *Gaerdu* et *Le Conte des Combats Entre le Peuple Qiang et le Peuple Geji*) décrit les batailles contre les indigènes, les Geji, habitant dans cette région depuis longtemps. Les Qiang s'y installèrent après leur migration vers l'amont du Fleuve Minjiang. L'épopée comprend sept parties, "*Overture*", "*L'Origine du Tambour en Peau de Mouton*", "*L'Origine de Grandes Montagnes Couvertes de Neige*", "*La Première Rencontre des Qiang et des Ge*", "*A la Recherche de la Bête Divine*", "*Guerres Entre les Qiang et les Ge*", et "*Rétablissement du Pays Natal*". L'ensemble de l'œuvre contient plus de 600 lignes. Décrivant les épreuves de la migration dans un style direct, les chants épiques glorifient le courage des ancêtres Qiang, leur sagesse et leurs luttes héroïques.

L'épopée, vivante et simple, démontre le style unique des Qiang. Ce genre de style dévoile un charme particulier de la littérature primitive. De plus, l'épopée apporte le culte des idoles divines, les émotions des êtres humains ainsi que la valeur de la vie quotidienne. Elle est le grand trésor pour la recherche de l'histoire et de la culture des Qiang. Elle nous fournit aussi les matériels pour étudier l'ethnologie et la religion.

Le long poème mythique narratif, nouveau style littéraire, basé sur les mythes et les chansons traditionnelles, vit le jour après les épopées. Il est représenté par l'œuvre célèbre *Mu Jiezhu et Dou Anzhu*. Avec son style poétique, il raconte de façon vivante un mythe. Il est caractérisé par le fait de mettre un mariage à l'épreuve. Un tel poème révèle la relation étroite entre les mythes et la religion primitive et explique la formation du mariage chez les Qiang.

Le long poème narratif mythique *Mu Jiezhu and Dou Anzhu* (ou *Mu Jiezhu et Garçon Ranbi*) décrit une histoire d'amour entre une fée et un jeune homme Qiang. L'idée générale du poème est: Mu Jiezhu, la troisième fille du dieu du ciel, était une fée à la fois très intelligente et jolie. Elle tomba amoureuse de Dou Anzhu, un berger gentil, honnête, travailleur, et chevaleresque, après qu'elle fut descendue sur terre sans la permission de son père. Ayant prit connaissance de cette liaison, son père tua le berger d'une colère noire. Cependant, avec l'aide de l'intelligente Mu Jiezhu, le brave Dou Anzhu déjoua avec succès trois pièges tendus par le dieu du ciel et obtint l'approbation pour marier la fée. Après avoir quitté le ciel, le couple s'installa dans un village Qiang. Ils bâtirent des maisons, dégagèrent des terres à l'abandon, cultivèrent les champs de leurs propres mains. Et finalement ils menèrent une vie heureuse. Le poème est divisé en dix chapitrs, "Une Princesse Bourrue", "Un Jeune Berger", "Rencontre au bord de l'Etang du Dragon", "Fiançailles par Offrir des Cheveux coupés", "Faire la Demande à la Princesse", "Surmonter les Trois Difficultés", "Survivre du Feu", "Refaire la Demande à la Princesse", "Echapper au Piège", et "Une Vie Heureuse". Le long poème crée un plaisir esthétique.

Les paragraphes suivants sont extraits du chapitre *Une Vie Heureuse*, de *Mu Jiezhu et Dou Anzhu:*

**Je changerai le monde de mes propres mains; je me consacrerai tout entier au labour de la terre. Laissez les montagnes et les eaux sous mon contrôle et je réduirai l'intervalle entre les hommes et les Génies.**

**Occupées à ramasser les herbes, les pies construisent des nids; occupées nuit et jour, les fourmis creusent des galeries. Transpirant énormément, Mu Jiezhu et Dou Anzhu aspirent à une vie meilleure.**

**Des maisons en pierre ont besoin d'une base solide, trois rochers blancs sont sur le toît. Les familles vivent à l'étage tandis que les animaux vivent au rez-de-chaussée.**

**L'orge du Tibet pousse sur la terre au sommet de la colline, tandis que le blé occupe la terre fertile d'en bas. L'herbe de montagne pousse si bien et c'est le bon moment pour élever chevaux, moutons et bovins.**

**De cette époque, les Qiang apprirent à cultiver, à élever des bovins et des moutons, partout sur les montagnes. La large plaine appartenait aux Qiang, leurs descendants se multiplièrent et se développèrent énormément.**

**L'automne doré apporte la joie des moissons, les vagues dorées roulent le long des montagnes et des champs. Des amoncellements d'orge du Tibet et de blé murs, volaille et bétail en grand nombre sont le signe de la prospérité.**

Le long poème mythique narratif "*Comment vivre A Part*", (*Mei Bu* et *Zhi Laduo*) a treize chapitres, qui sont "*Overture*", "*Zhi Laduo*", "*Mei Bu*", "*Chanson de Plats*", "*Demande la Main*", "*Shang Shu, Génie de Foyer*", "*Retour chez les Parents*", "*Forêt de Corbeaux*", "*Terre de Pies*", "*Peau des Araignées*", "*Baie des Fourmis*", "*Conversation*", et "*La Fin*". A travers l'histoire d'amour et le mariage entre la fille d'un dieu et un fils de chef de tribu Qiang, le poème reflète à la fois le

305

combat des hommes contre la nature ainsi que le rôle initiatif des hommes. Le poème chante aussi l'admiration pour se battre et la réalisation de s'ingénier.

Un autre long poème narratif mythique, *Zeqi Gebu*, appelle à un attachement aux valeurs de paix et de résistance face aux guerres injustes. Il exprime par là la solidarité des Qiang.

De longs poèmes sur des coutumes traditionnelles tels que *Paroles d'Entremetteuses*, *Chanson de Mariages*, *Chanson en Pleurs aux Mariages* et *Paroles à l'Enterrement* sont les reflets vivants des vœux des Qiang, de leurs rêves, de leurs coutumes traditionnelles ainsi que de leurs attitudes vis-à-vis de la religion et de la morale. Avec les procédés rhétoriques de personnification, de répétition et de comparaison, les poèmes transmettent des idées philosophiques dans leur langage simple.

## 3. Légendes

Les légendes traditionnelles des Qiang sont habituellement basées sur certains événements et sur des figures historiques, ainsi que sur des activités et des coutumes locales. Dans le même temps, les légendes font revivre les personnages et les événements afin que l'idéal idéologique ct style esthétique soient bien révélés.

La majorité des légendes Qiang sont ainsi: *Réincarnation de Shiniu, Pierre en Sang dans la Baignoire d'Enfants, Lit de Yu, Le Mont Wangchong, Montagnes des Herbes Médicinales, La Chaîne de Montagnes Comme le Dos de Yu, Le Conte de Yu le Grand, L'Empereur Yu de Xia Aménage un Cours d'Eau, La Légende de l'Empereur Yu de Xia, La Visite de LiBai à la Maison de Yu* etc.. Comme une perle éclatante dans la maison de la littérature traditionnelle Qiang, les légendes sur *Da Yu* décrivent de façon vivante comment *Da Yu* naquit dans l'Ouest Qiang, ses actes légendaires, et les traces remarquables qu'il a laissées aux générations futures. Beaucoup de legendes bien connues, expriment la richesse spirituelle des Qiang.

Des légendes locales rapportent les combats des ancêtres contre la nature, comme *l'Histoire de Le Xia*. Certaines parmi elles louent la grande vertu et la sagesse des mêmes ancêtres, telle l'œuvre *Fantôme Frappe la Pierre*; d'autres légendes locales décrivent la résistance du peuple face à l'oppression, raciale et sociale, comme dans *Tombe de Prince*.

Les légendes liées à la faune et à la flore couvrent principalement l'origine de certains animaux et plantes communs dans l'aire Qiang (y compris leurs habitues et leurs caractéristiques), telles *Femme Yu Hua, Legende d'un Oiseau avec Bec*

*Rouge*, *WaSha Rusé*, *Gui Gui Yang*, *Piennie*(né d'un taureau et d'un yak femelle), *Mouton and Léopard*, *L'Origine de Blé Noir*, etc. Par exemple, *Femme Yu Hua*, qui raconte un drame amoureux, chante la louange de ceux qui combattent les esprits; *WaSha Rusé* vante le travail et le zèle et critique la ruse. Les légendes sur les plantes parlent de la perception des gens et de la connaissance des plantes à différentes périodes de l'histoire, révélant la vérité sous des angles variés. Certaines critiquent ont pour habitude de comparer ses propres points forts avec les points faibles des autres; certains exposent les tragédies causées par l'éthique féodale.

Les légendes du dragon et du serpent se trouvèrent dans toute la région Qiang, enregistrant quelques variations d'un village à l'autre. Des légendes de dragons décrivent les luttes des hommes contre la nature, telles *Bataille avec des Armes Magiques dans une Mare de Dragon*, *Bataille entre Dragon Divin et Prêtre Taoïste*, et *Legende de Dragon dans la Mer Rouge*. Les légendes de dragons sur l'amour et le mariage sont classées en trois catégories. La première décrit le dragon tombant amoureux d'une fille Qiang, comme dans *Soeur Yasa*. La deuxième mélange des combats sociaux aux histoires d'amour des êtres humains et des dragons, telle *Lan Baji du Village Yinghong*. La troisième catégorie raconte comment le Roi Dragon contraint une fille Qiang à être sa femme, comme dans *Femme Huang San*. Le fil principal de ces légendes est le mariage entre les belles filles Qiang et les dragons. Les légendes qui reflètent les relations entre les êtres humains et les serpents sont représentées dans des oeuvres comme *Frères Serpent* et *l'Origine de Fête de Dragon* etc.

Les légendes sur les coutumes, à travers les histoires de fêtes, de foi, d'habillement et la façon dont ils se font beaux, racontent la longue histoire et les vies sociales colorées des Qiang sous de nombreux aspects. Elles sont perçues comme un moyen artistique important pour les Qiang de connaître leur société et leur histoire. Il y a quatre types de légendes sur les coutumes: ① les légendes sur les fêtes, comme *Fête de Chiens Suspendus*; ② les légendes sur les modes de vie, comme *L'Histoire de Marier les Filles*; ③ les légendes sur l'habillement et leur embellissement, comme dans *Mouchoir qui témoigne le Coeur* et *Legendes des Chaussures Yunyun*; ④ les légendes sur les divertissements traditionnels, telle *L'Origine de Flûte Qiang*, *L'Origine de Corde Orale*.

Les légendes qui ont le Shibi comme personnage central parlent de la sorcellerie du Shibi, et de la confrontation de ses pouvoirs magiques avec ceux du prêtre Taoiste et du Lama. Comme le Shibi l'emporte toujours dans de telles légendes, cela est donc la manifestation d'un profond sens religieux.

A côté de cela, il se trouve des légendes Qiang qui expliquent le phénomène des âmes et le concept du "chat poison" qui mélange matière et esprit.

Parmi ces légendes, un grand nombre traitent d'événements historiques et de figures des temps modernes, telles *Le Général Tigre Noir*, *Le Sang de Xiong Gui rougit le Village Xiawu*, *Liu Fan Exploite Puits Salant*, etc. Elles nous montrent ainsi, non seulement des caractéristiques locales, mais aussi des faits historiques de lieux locaux.

Ainsi, la victoire de l'Armée Rouge sur l'ennemi, grâce à l'alliance avec les Qiang, aboutit à de nombreuses et touchantes légendes, qui composent une importante part de la littérature moderne des Qiang, comme *La Tour de Guet de l'Armée Rouge* et *L'Attaque Chidou de Nuit*, etc.

## 4. Chansons traditionnelles

Les chansons traditionnelles Qiang sont emplies de caractéristiques locales, de couleur ethnique ainsi que de sentiments forts. Elles sont capables d'exprimer les désirs des gens et de déverser tristesse et bonheur. De plus, elles se rapportent à une large gamme de sujets, avec des mots simples, vivants, naturels et coulants, émettant un pur parfum de terroir. Comprenant quatre ou sept pieds dans chaque vers, les chansons sont parfois improvisées uniquement à la vue de certains objets, parfois créées librement suivant sa pensée. Certaines chansons sont mélodieuses, certaines sont sonores, certaines sont vivantes, certaines sont humoristiques, et certaines sont sentimentales, douces et touchantes. Quantitativement, les chansons dominent la littérature Qiang.

Les plus representatives des chansons traditionnelles sont les chansons sur le travail et les coutumes.

Les chansons de travail, telles *Ge Ximo*, *Chansons de Chasse*, *Chanson pour la Construction de Maisons*, *Chanson pour Recueillir le Thé*, etc, présentent de façon vivante des images de scènes de labeur. Les chansons de travail modernes, bien qu'ayant hérité des schémas mélodiques des chansons de travail traditionnelles, possèdent des contenus plus clairs et riches. Les chansons *L'Agent de la Reforme Agraire Travaille Tôt* et *Temps de Récoltes*, par exemple, affichent l'énergie déployée par les Qiang pour devenir leurs propres maîtres, et la grande ambition de se constituer des richesses matérielles par le biais de leur dur labeur.

Des chansons sur les coutumes, comme *Guo Guowei*, *Chanson de Toast au Moment d'Ouvrir la Jarre de Vin* à la *Cérémonie de Mariage*, *Chanson pour la*

*Construction de Maisons* sont encore plus riches et colorées. Il y a des chansons de mariage, comme *Paroles d'Entremetteuses*, *Chanson pour Presser le Mariage*. Certaines sont chantées par la mariée et ses sœurs avant la cérémonie, telle *Chanson pour Marier la Fille*, *Chanson de Mariée* et *Mélodie pour Quitter la Maison de Mariée*. Certaines sont chantées durant le banquet, après l'arrivée de l'épouse dans la maison de son époux, par exemple, *Chanson de Bienvenue*, *Eloges à Mariée*, *Eloges à Marié*, *Chanson pour Faire le Lit*, etc. Ces chansons sont mémorables en raison de leur langage vivant et fort. Les paroles qui suivent sont celles de *Mélodie pour Quitter la Maison de Mariée*:

**La remise colorée a été construite afin que le cochon puisse y être retenu. J'ai commencé à pleurer en entendant les cris larmoyants du cochon. Le cochon se désole d'être promis à la mort, mais rien n'est plus triste que de quitter ma mère à cause du mariage.**

Les chansons funèbres se chantent selon les processus de l'enterrement. *Chanson pour les Décédés* est chantée par les gens qui présentent leurs respects aux morts; *Chanson pour la Séparation Lamentable* est chantée par les enfants de la famille; *Elégies* est exécuté pour se rappeler le mort; *Chanson d'Obsèques* est chantée pendant la cérémonie funèbre; *Chanson de l'Enterrement* se réalise au moment de l'ensevelissement; *Discours de d'Obsèques* et *Chanson pour Appeler l'Ame de Mort* sont prononcés par le Shibi durant son travail occulte. Toutes ces chansons louent les bienfaits des défunts ou reposent les décédés en paix.

En fait, des chansons sont chantées respectivement à chaque cérémonie importante concernant la construction d'une maison, un mariage ou un enterrement. Toutes les chansons sont abondantes en quantité et en qualité.

Les anciennes chansons sur les affaires politiques témoignent des attitudes des Qiang avant 1949. Ces chansons s'attaquent violemment à la classe des propriétaires fonciers à cause de leur exploitation des travailleurs prolétariens. Certaines chansons reflètent l'idéal politique des Qiang, leurs idéaux de vie, ainsi que leur persévérance inébranlable; d'autres expriment leur résistance face aux pouvoirs ténébreux ainsi que leur aspiration à la liberté. Il y a des ouvrages influents comme *La Peine des Qiang*, *Feu brûle vers les Propriétaires Fonciers*, *Aller s'Engager dans l'Armée Rouge*, etc. Les nouvelles chansons politiques après 1949 sont principalement laudatives. Certaines admirent le Parti Communiste et le Président Mao, comme l'œuvre *Le Parti Communiste est la Libérateur des Qiang*; certaines apprécient la réforme de la république, telle la chanson *Ayant nos Champs*, etc.

Les chansons d'amour sont les plus importantes et nombreuses. Placées à un haut niveau d'idéal et de valeur artistique, les chansons d'amour expriment les tristesses et les joies des amoureux. Leurs rapports directs avec la vie sont évidents dans ces chansons telle que *J'ai 18 ans et Toi Aussi*.

**J'ai 18 ans, comme toi, nous jurons sous le ciel bleu.**

**Si tu tombes amoureux d'une deuxième fille, la foudre te frappe**

**Si je m'attache à un autre homme, je devienne aveugle.**

*Mon Amour n'est pas Rus*é est une autre chanson d'amour:

**Mon adorée demeure sur la crête de la Montagne, et je dois traverser neuf murs avant d'atteindre sa porte. Son chien est aussi fort qu'un tigre, alors comment puis-je la rejoindre ?**

**Sois malin, mon pauvre chéri, tu peux prendre avec toi un beignet cuit à la vapeur. Quand le chien te mords, lance loin le beignet, et ensuite tu peux venir à moi parce que le chien mangera le beignet.**

Les nouvelles chansons d'amour des Qiang sont non seulement le miroir de la nouvelle société, des nouvelles pensées et des nouvelles coutumes, mais aussi elles lient le sentiment d'amour personnel à la construction de la mère-patrie, comme dans *Un Cadeau Général* et *Adoration de mon amour travailleur* etc.

La ballade Qiang, comparativement de faible quantité parmi les chansons traditionnelles, célèbre principalement les activités concernant la situation de la ferme pendant les récoltes et la réalité sociale à des périodes historiques particulières. Voici un exemple qui décrit un vol par des bandits dans le district de Beichuan avant 1949: **vous devez surveiller votre porte-monnaie quand vous arrivez au Versant de Caoshan; après le Mont Jiuguan, vous serez rassuré quant à votre argent; après être passés par Liangfengya, vous êtes sain et sauf et il vous sera possible de rencontrer vos parents.**

## 5. Les Histoires Traditionnelles

Part importante de la littérature traditionnelle Qiang, les histoires traditionnelles comprennent des histoires fantastiques, d'animaux, de fantômes, de monstres, de vie, d'esprit, d'allégories, etc. A la fois dans le contenu et le contenant, elles tendent à refléter plus de réalité. D'un style Qiang unique, elles sont de bien meilleure qualité artistique.

Les histoires fantastiques couvrent plusieurs domaines telles l'histoire elfe de *Deux Soeurs*, l'histoire sur un enfant bizarre appelée *Enfant Apparu d'une Motte*

*de Viande* . De plus, il y a aussi des histoires de difformités, de trésors miraculeux, de frères, etc. A travers l'imagination et l'hyperbole, les histoires fantastiques présentent de nombreuses images symboliques par des descriptions esthétiques et impressionnantes.

Les histoires sur la vie quotidienne, en général, concernent la lutte des travailleurs engagée sur le long terme contre les propriétaires fonciers, comme dans *Propriétaires Fonciers et Valets de Ferme*. Il existe aussi des histoires d'amour et de mariage qui décrivent la résistance aux rites féodaux, telle que *Cheng Chengmen et Ala Zhaji*. Il y a également des histoires de beau-fils sots et des histoires pleines d'esprit. Avec des resources riches nombreuses, des styles divers et un choix juste de sujets, les histoires Qiang sont en relation étroite avec la réalité de la vie.

Les allégories Qiang, faisant aussi partie de la littérature populaire, suggèrent un certain sens de l'humour tout en montrant des styles de vigueur, de clarté et de sagesse. Elles se forment de façon brêve, avec la morale remontante et la significaiton actuelle. Les histoires drôles pourraient être considérées comme la dernière forme de la littérature populaire des Qiang. Les caractéristiques principales de ces histoires se doublent de ce qui se déroule dans la vie quotidienne et d'un caractère satirique. Il y a aussi la découverte des plaisanteries avec les sous-entendus.

## II. Littérature écrite

Dans une certaine mesure, la littérature Qiang, en dépit de sa longue histoire, s'est développée régionalement et sans discontinuité. Pendant ce temps, elle a été profondément influencée par la culture de la Chine du centre.

Avant de discuter en profondeur de la littérature écrite des Qiang, nous devons d'abord voir une notion que le mot 'Qiang' possède avec habituellement une connotation assez large et un peu vague. En fait, au niveau des régions, cette notion concerne de nombreuses branches qui sont très diverses. Considérant l'ensemble des régions des Qiang, la littérature écrite, ayant lieu en amont du fleuve Minjiang, est le produit principal de la culture de l'ensemble des régions et; elle a des rapports proches avec les coutumes locales et en a les traditions culturelles. Cependant, en dépit de leur littéraire apparue premièrement, ces anciens Qiang, au-delà de l'amont du fleuve Minjiang, n'étaient pas les indigènes de la partie en amont de Minjiang. Depuis la Dynastie Qing, les créations littéraires Qiang sont centralisées autour de la région en amont du fleuve Minjiang et elles attachaient donc beaucoup d'importance à la littérature traditionnelle de l'ensemble des régions. De ce fait il

est nécessaire de présenter l'historique ici. En résumé, n'ayant que peu de sources dans les amonts Minjiang, les ouvrages écrits avant la Dynastie Qing font aussi partie de la littérature écrite des Qiang.

## 1. Littérature d'avant la Dynastie des Jin de l'Ouest (572 av. J.C.— 264 ap. J.C.)

Les ouvrages de cette période semblent peu abondants, mais leur qualité est significative. D'après le matériel historique littéraire actuel, les écrits Qiang sont apparus au plus tard au milieu de la Période des Printemps et des Automnes. Le poème *Mouche Bleue*, écrit par le chef de la tribu Rong des Jiang Qiang à cette époque est le premier travail écrit Qiang que nous pouvons voir de nos jours. Caractérisé par son ancien style Qin, le poème exprime des mécontentements et des reproches. Il y a aussi la suite de chants appelée *Chanson d'un Loup Blanc*, un recueil d'émotions et de sentiments. Les œuvres de cette époque comprennent habituellement quatre mots par ligne, ce qui est le style caractéristique des compositions des anciennes chansons Qiang.

## 2. Les écrits de la période Hou Qin (384 ap. J.C.—417 ap. J.C.)

Avec la montée en puissance de la tribu Yao, Qiang, et l'établissement du régime de Hou Qin, les créations littéraires prospérèrent à cette époque. Deux œuvres représentatives, *Poème du Roi Langya* et *Poème de la Princesse Julu*, ont enrichi le style littéraire Qiang avec de nouvelles idées venant des poèmes Han. D'après les récits actuels, le *Poème du Roi Langya* serait le premier poème Qiang écrit avec cinq mots par ligne, tandis que *Poème de la Princesse Julu* serait le premier comportant sept mots. Ces poèmes qui s'expriment le style vigoureux avec les sentiments vrais ont contribué au développement des poèmes, surtout à l'art poétique. Les poèmes Qiang et ceux d'autres groupes éthniques vont de pair à cette époque. De plus, des prosateurs comme Yao Xing se sont distinguées à cette époque avec les écrits *Lettres à Seng Qian et Autres* et *A Travers les Trois Générations*. En définitive, la traduction des sūtras bouddhiques dans la période de Hou Qin a aussi influencé positivement la création littéraire Qing.

## 3. Les écrits de la période des Xia de l'Ouest (1038 ap. J.C.—1227 ap. J.C.)

Les travaux de cette époque consistent principalement en des proses, des poèmes et des inscriptions de stèle. Ces œuvres sont toutes de grande importance, non seulement parce qu'un grand nombre d'entre-elles ont été écrites par les Qiang, mais aussi parce qu'elles ont préparé une base solide pour le développement et la prospérité de la littérature Qiang, qui auraient eu lieu tout de suite après la Dynastie Yuan.

## 4. Les écrits des aïeux Qiang de la période des Xia de l'Ouest

En réalité, il n'est pas possible de passer cette période sans mentionner en particulier les travaux écrits par les ancêtres Qiang des Xia de l'Ouest. Ce sont des poètes et écrivains remarquables qui vécurent à cette époque. On peut citer des poètes tels que Yu Que, Zhang Xiongfei, Ang Ji, Wang Han, Woyuluntu, Wan Ze et Mai Zhu.

## 5. Les travaux écrits depuis la Dynastie Qing jusqu'aux jours de la République populaire de Chine

La littérature de cette période comporte principalement des poèmes et des proses, dont les sujets ne touchent que trois aspects: premièrement, la révélation et la critique de certaines réalités de la société; deuxièmement, la description de paysages, de montagnes et des étendues d'eau, ainsi que la vie des individus; troisièmement, la présentation des coutumes locales, des croyances des Qiang. En général, les caractéristiques des créations littéraires de cette époque se développèrent autour de trois points: tout d'abord, un certain nombre d'écrivains se font connaître, comme les "Cinq Gaos de Jiangqing", Gao Wanxuan, Gao Wankun, Gao Jian, Gao Huiguang et Gao Huidou, avec leurs œuvres représentatives *Le Col où le Sable s'envole*, *Visionner la Neige Ensoleillée en Passant le Col Yan Men*, *La Source Froide et Chaude*, *Ode aux huit paysages* à *Wen Yang* et *L'Ancien Chemin avec Sept Tournants*. Basés sur les spectacles locaux, ces travaux décrivent les montagnes et fleuves en chantant les paysages régionaux. Leur style est naturel et d'un trait vigoureux. Ils sont les premiers, dans la littérature Qiang, à décrire les montagnes et les rivières du pays natal sous la forme artistique de poème, comme dans les travaux poétiques *Le Village Suo Gu* et *Le Col Yan Men* de l'écrivain Zhao Chengjia. Enfin, la plupart des œuvres semblent très sophistiquées au sens propre de la littérature, certaines sont même de haute valeur artistique, en termes d'idéologie, de contenu et de style, tel que le poème *Sans Titre* par Gao Tiquan.

## 6. Les écrits modernes

La littérature d'aujourd'hui a beaucoup de genres, y compris la prose, le roman, la poésie, les pièces pour la télévision,etc. Les sujets sont variés et abordent différents aspects de la société. Ils sont le reflet de la nouvelle vie des Qiang et de

leur situations spirituelles dans cette nouvelle ère.

En fait, le roman est nouveau dans la littérature Qiang. Des romanciers représentatifs sont Gu Yunlong, Ye Xingguang, Xiang Shimao, Jiang Zonggui, Wu Gang, Yu Decheng, Zhang Xiangli, Que Yulan, et d'autres encore. Parmi eux, Gu Yunlong et Ye Xingguang ont réalisé des œuvres remarquables. Les romans de Gu Yunlong parlent des expériences des gens ordinaires. Modèles typiques de notre époque, ils reflètent les changements de la société et les esprits vifs des Qiang résultant des réformes du pays. Gu Yunlong a créé de nombreux ouvrages avec des perspectives nouvelles, des sentiments sincères et un style subtil. Son roman *Petals Perdus* a décroché le deuxième prix du Deuxième Concours Littéraire Nationale pour les Groupes Minoritaires en 1985. Il devint ainsi le premier écrivain Qiang à recevoir un prix national de création littéraire. Par ailleurs, son œuvre *Tant de Chaussures Usées chez Soi* a emporté le prix littéraire comme un excellent travail au Premier Concours Littéraire pour les Groupes Ethniques de la Province du Sichuan. L'écrivain Ye Xingguang a écrit des romans d'une manière polyvalente. D'un côté, il conserve de la littérature traditionnelle Qiang les caractéristiques naturelles et simples. D'un autre, il adopte audacieusement les styles et les structures des romans modernes. Ses ouvrages impressionnent les lecteurs avec son ouverture aux styles multiples et sa souplesse de caractère. En 1997, Ye Xingguang publia le premier scénario Qiang *L'Esprit d'Erma*. En 1998, il adapta la première pièce mythologique Qiang, *Mu Jie Zhu Coupe Papiers pour Sauver Cent Animaux*. Son roman *Le Dernier Amour* remporta le deuxième prix du Concours Lu Yao National en 1996. Plus tard, en 1998, il publia son recueil de ses romans intitulé *Montagne Divine, Arbre Immortel et Forêt Sacrée*. Le recueil est l'un des deux seuls recueils de romans dans l'histoire de la littérature Qiang.

La quantité de proses contemporaines Qiang s'accroît beaucoup. Un bon nombre d'écrivains ont composé des œuvres, qui traitent des sujets et des styles divers et variés. Ces écrivains Qiang sont à la hauteur de maîtriser l'écriture et de rédiger des textes avec habileté. Leurs écrits montrent leur capacité de refléter la vie des Qiang et leurs émotions. Des écrivains tels que Zhu Dalu, Gu Yunlong et Meng Fei s'efforcent à décrire la vie locale et les coutumes de leur patrie, ainsi que les changements historiques du pays et les pensées sur des réalités; Luo Zilan est excellent à peindre sans fioritures les esprits des gens qui vivent dans les régions montagneuses reculées; une série de présentations avec des informations de voyage sur Jiuzhaigou, par Zhang Shanyun, pourrait être considérée comme une ode aux hommes et à la nature. Parmi tous les écritains, Zhu Dalu et Zhang Shanyun sont les deux plus éminents. L'oeuvre de Zhu Dalu, *Un Bosquet de Clavalier dans le Village de Qiang*, qui fut récompensé du prix de création littéraire lors du Premier Concours Nationale de la Littérature Minoritaire, en 1980, est la première œuvre Qiang à remporter un prix national de création littéraire. Le caractère unique des écrits de Zhang Shanyun montre ses connaissances riches et approfondies. Il a déjà rédigé de somptueux essais à propos de Jiuzhaigou, comme *L'Esprit Reflété par les Feuilles Rouges de JiuZhai*, *Les Herbes à JiuZhai*, *Rosées sur les Feuilles*, *Un Spectacle Magnifique des Forêts*, et d'autres encore. Il y a aussi de beaux écrits par Luo Zilan, tels que *La Terre Tranquille* et *Crépuscule sur la Sable*.

Les poèmes Qiang contemporains sont généralement écrits d'un style différent de ce qui existait avant la fondation de la République Populaire de Chine. Les poètes contemporains, ayant l'esprit vivant, les conceptions nouvelles ainsi que des champs de vision plus larges, composaient des poèmes aux passions et sens de responsabilité. Leurs poèmes reflètent des vies sociales sous différents angles. Plus important, ils s'attachent davantage à l'historie, la culture et à la réflexion de la réalité de la vie de Qiang. A travers la description de l'expérience vécue par les anciens Qiang dans leur lutte pour leur survie et la démonstration de leur caractère typique et de leur mentalité unique, les poètes Qiang écrivent leurs désirs et pensées de nos jours et leurs espérances inspirées par le progrès culturel. Des poètes représentatifs sont Li Xiaojun, He Jian, Yu Yaoming. En juin 1994, Li Xiaojun mit tous ses poèmes dans un recueil nommé *Sous La Lumière des Etoiles*. Partagé dans cinq parties, le recueil accède à un passage de vie plein de difficultés traversé par le jeune poète toujours sincère. Dans un sens plus large, le recueil reflète aussi l'esprit véritable et la nature de la jeune génération Qiang, qui adore son histoire, aime sa patrie, fait des projets sur son avenir et aspire à un monde extérieur. La plupart des œuvres de He Jian sont composées par des groupes de vers, comme *Appels des Montagnes*, *Poèmes du Peuple Qiang*, etc. Du fait que les poèmes parlent de l'histoire culturelle et de la mentalité authentique du peuple Qiang, ils révèlent leur caractères récalcitrant. Les poèmes de Yu Yaoming sont réputés par style clair et simple, surtout celui qui montre la mentalité des Qiang, tels que dans *Tambour de Mouton, Une Paire de Chaussures Yun Yun Pour Vous*, *Pays Natal*, et plus encore.

La littérature Qiang prouve ses qualités et ses spécificités, avec des contenus riches, des styles variés et l'ancienne tradition littéraire, tout en constituant ensemble l'histoire colorée de la littérature chinoise.

# CHAPITRE CINQ   LES CROYANCES RELIGIEUSES DES QIANG①

Les Qiang ont une longue histoire et une culture très riche. Au cours d'une longue période de travail, les Qiang n'ont pas seulement créé des richesses matérielles et spirituelles, mais ils ont aussi développé des croyances religieuses qui leur sont propres.

## I. Polythéisme: Le Dieu du Ciel est le plus puissant

Comme les anciens Qiang ne pouvaient pas expliquer certains phénomènes naturels ainsi que la course des astres, et comme ils étaient effrayés par les calamités naturelles et désastres causés par l'homme, ils pensaient que chaque chose sur terre avait sa propre vie et son âme. C'est ainsi qu'ils développèrent des croyances religieuses primitives mêlant l'animisme et le culte de la nature. Existant encore aujourd'hui, elles sont une part importante de la culture Qiang.

Les croyances religieuses des Qiang restent au niveau du culte de la sorcellerie et des nimbes. Il n'y a ni institution ni organisation religieuse spécialement établies.

### 1. Divers Dieux

Généralement, les Qiang conservent plutôt des croyances religieuses primitives, incluant le culte de la nature, l'animisme, la vénération des ancêtres, le respect des sorciers, ainsi que la croyance aux fantômes.

Les Qiang croient et vénèrent des dizaines de dieux. En fonction de leur nature et de leur caractère, les dieux célébrés peuvent être divisés en groupes: le premier groupe est celui des dieux de la nature: dans les croyances Qiang, ces dieux sont les plus vénérés et les plus respectés, ils incluent les dieux du ciel, de la terre, du feu, de la montagne, des arbres et des chèvres. Comme le ciel, la terre, le feu, la montagne, les arbres et les chèvres ont la plus étroite relation avec la vie et le travail des Qiang, les dieux qui les représentent sont les dieux les plus célébrés et les plus respectés par les Qiang. D'après les croyances originelles des Qiang, le

---

① Dans les croyances religieuses des Qiang, le prêtre est appelé "Shibi" dans la langue Qiang. Dans d'autres livres, le prêtre est aussi appelé "Duangong", nom donné par les Chinois Han. Le livre adopte l'ancien nom.

dieu du ciel est le dieu suprême; c'est lui qui préside à la destinée de chaque chose sur terre et qui peut ruiner ou protéger les êtres humains et les troupeaux. Après le dieu du ciel viennent ceux de la montagne, du feu, des arbres, de l'eau, des chèvres, et d'autres encore.

En dehors des principaux dieux vénérés par les Qiang, il y a aussi différents dieux locaux célébrés dans chaque village Qiang. Ceux-ci forment le deuxième groupe de dieux vénérés par les Qiang. La plupart d'entre eux sont liés au culte de la nature. Parmi les dieux Qiang, les dieux locaux forment un large système, tels que les dieux et les propriétaires des villages, les dieux représentant les montagnes et les rivières autour des villages, etc. Dans ce système se trouvent aussi les dieux du Yin et du Yang. Les tours de guet possèdent également leur propre dieu: parce qu'elles protègent le village des invasions, elles sont aussi vénérées. Dans le concept primitif des croyances Qiang, chaque homme a une âme. Expliquant chaque chose sur terre par cette pensée, les Qiang croient que toutes les choses sont dominées par leur âme. Les concepts de fantôme et de dieu apparaissent en conséquence. Plus tard, on distingua le fantôme du dieu. Même les dieux sont classés en bien et en mal, en Ormazd et en Ahriman. Le bien se réfère à celui qui protège la vie et la propriété. Nous les appelons les Saints Patrons Locaux, tel le dieu du Pin des villages de Ruoda, Jiashan et Xishan (district de Li), le dieu de l'Aigle du rocher du village de Ganxi, etc. Le mal se réfère à celui qui blesse les gens et le troupeau, tel le dieu du Monstre de Vigne de Tianjiao, dans le village de Xingshangnawa (district de Li), le dieu de Citiaobazi dans le village de Muerda, le dieu du rocher dans le village de Jiuzi, etc. Il y a un conte de fées qui se rattache à chaque bon dieu, tandis que les mauvais dieux n'en ont pas. Chaque année, les Qiang demandent au Shibi de tenir une cérémonie pour faire des sacrifices pour les bons dieux et prier pour leurs bienfaits. Pour les mauvais dieux, les gens exécutent des rituels pour exorciser le mal et prier pour la paix, durant les quatre jours des trois premiers mois de l'année, à savoir le Jour du Cochon, le Jour de la Chèvre, le Jour du Dragon et le Jour du Cheval.

Les dieux du troisième groupe sont les ancêtres qui sont vénérés à la maison. Habituellement, nous appelons ces dieux "Pénates". Les ancêtres des Qiang, Mujiezhu et Douanzhu, anciens dieux mâle et femelle, dieux de protection, sont vénérés dans presque toutes les familles Qiang. Par exemple, certaines familles pratiquent le culte des trois différents dieux sur l'autel de la maison, situé au milieu de la pièce principale: les pénates sont placés au milieu de l'autel et suivent le

principe de "Ciel, Terre, Empire, Parents et Professeur" popularisés dans la culture chinoise Han; le dieu de la cuisine est placé sur le côté gauche, tandis que le Bodhisattva Kwan-Yin se trouve sur la droite. Tous les matins et soirs, les gens brûlent des bâtonnets d'encens pour montrer leur respect. Dans d'autres lieux, les dieux du grenier, de la porte et de la montagne sont aussi célébrés dans la maison. De même, les gens qui ont une activité spéciale font des offrandes au fondateur de leur profession.

Dans le culte des ancêtres des Qiang, Dayu est l'un des dieux les plus vénérés par les Qiang. Dans certains lieux Qiang, de nombreux vestiges et contes se rapportent à la naissance de Dayu, surtout dans le bourg de Yuli des Qiang (district de Bei Chuan). Les principales légendes sont "Dayu se réincarne dans le Shiniu", "l'origine de la pierre sanglante" et "l'origine de la caverne de Dayu" etc. Il y a aussi des vestiges et contes similaires dans d'autres lieux Qiang, par exemple, dans le district de Wen chuan, de Li et dans la région de Songpan. Dans les croyances des Qiang, les vestiges de Dayu (surtout Shiniu, le lieu où Dayu se réincarne) sont les lieux les plus sacrés et les plus purs. Si des Qiang partent au loin, ils emporteront des fragments de vestiges de Dayu pour bénéficier de la protection divine. Les Qiang croient que certaines ruines de Dayu (par exemple, la pierre sanglante et la caverne de Dayu) ont pour fonction de favoriser la procréation: une femme stérile peut rester un moment dans la caverne de Dayu ou prendre une pierre sanglante pour l'aider à procréer; aujourd'hui, cette coutume est encore très répandue. S'ils souffrent de la sécheresse ou des inondations, les Qiang peuvent tenir une cérémonie présidée par le Shibi pour supplier Dayu de dissiper le mal et pour prier pour la paix. Les ruines de Dayu sont considérées comme un lieu saint. Elles jouent ainsi un rôle très important dans les croyances religieuses des Qiang.

Avec les vicissitudes des Qiang, le contenu du culte des ancêtres devient de plus en plus compliqué: par exemple, tous les héros et tous les hommes qui apportent leur contribution à la vie locale sont considérés comme des dieux, tels que les dieux du bâtisseur, du tailleur de pierre, du forgeron, du chef de guerre, etc. Il y a un conte populaire qui se rattache à chaque héros des Qiang. Par exemple, le fils de l'Empereur de la Montagne du Dragon est respecté par les Qiang qui habitent dans le village de Keku (district de Wenchuan): il se dévoua pour mettre fin aux atrocités et protéger le peuple; mais finalement, il fut tué par des dominateurs cruels; son corps fut enterré au sommet de la Montagne du Dragon et vénéré de génération en génération par les Qiang. Le général du Tigre Noir est respecté par les Qiang du village de Heihu (district de Mao); il dirigea les Qiang pour lutter contre la domination de la Dynastie des Qing, mais il fut tué par ses ennemis.

Le culte du totem existe encore dans les croyances religieuses des Qiang; généralement, il s"agit du totem de la chèvre. On dit souvent que les Qiang s'appellent Ermie, dont la prononciation ressemble au bêlement des chèvres. Dans la guerre légendaire contre les Geji, tous les Qiang portaient un fil de laine à leur cou (ce qui se traduit par une imitation de la chèvre); encore aujourd'hui, le Shibi attache un fil de laine à chacun des Qiang qui participe à une cérémonie de sacrifices à la montagne, pour ainsi dire faire corps avec la chèvre. Dans la cérémonie funèbre, la chèvre est utilisée comme remplaçant du mort et elle guide son âme. A l'occasion des cérémonies de sacrifice, les Qiang saignent des chèvres et versent leur sang, avant de les brûler ou de les abandonner dans la nature. En tout cas, il est strictement interdit de manger de la chèvre. Toutes ces traditions devraient avoir certaines relations avec le culte du totémisme des anciens Qiang qui vivaient de l'élevage des animaux. Comme la chèvre avait une très étroite relation avec les Qiang, il est possible que les Qiang prenaient la chèvre comme un animal de consanguinité. La chèvre est donc considérée comme le totem des Qiang. Elle est ainsi protégée et vénérée par les Qiang.

Aux yeux des Qiang, l'âme de l'homme existe toujours, même après la mort du corps, et elle deviendrait fantôme. Les fantômes ne sont pas tous néfastes, sauf ceux des personnes qui étaient assassinées ou qui mouraient prématurément. Les Qiang pensaient que les fantômes provoquaient malheurs et maladies. On doit exorciser les fantômes sans les offenser. Par exemple, un fantôme appelé le Fantôme Toxique est considéré comme la source de toutes les maladies. N'importe quelle vieille femme à qui le fantôme toxique est attaché, est appelée femme de fantôme, (de même pour l'appellation fille de fantôme et homme de fantôme). Dans de telles circonstances, les gens cherchent l'aide du Shibi qui pratique ses rites magiques pour expulser le mauvais esprit et pour éviter le malheur.

Les Qiang n'ont pas de temple pour vénérer leurs dieux. Par contre, ils construisent une petite pagode en pierre au-dessus de laquelle se trouve une pierre blanche qui symbolise les dieux. Les dieux vénérés par les Qiang ont tous des relations étroites avec la vie et le travail des Qiang.

## 2. Le culte de la montagne

Les Qiang respectent et vénèrent les dieux justes qui les protègent. Le sacrifice au dieu du ciel est le plus commun tandis que le sacrifice au dieu de la montagne est le plus cérémonieux. Pendant des générations, les Qiang ont vécu dans les vallées profondes et les hautes montagnes, se répartissant essentiellement autour des Montagnes de Jiuding et de Zhegu (chaînons de la Montagne Min). Les vies des Qiang sont étroitement liées à ces montagnes, qui leur fournissent divers produits de nécessité tels que les graines, le bois de construction, les plantes médicinales, les animaux sauvages, et le bétail.

Comme les anciens Qiang ne pouvaient ni maîtriser les forces de la nature, ni connaître les relations entre l'être humain et la nature, et comme il n'y avait aucun approvisionnement fiable en produits de nécessité, les notions imaginatives au sujet des montagnes ont donné aux Qiang une croyance ferme dans l'existence du dieu de la montagne. Par conséquent, les Qiang célèbrent chaque année la cérémonie sacrificielle pour la montagne afin de rendre grâce à son dieu. C'est l'activité religieuse la plus importante des Qiang, comme le dit le proverbe: "L'empereur offre ses sacrifices aux ancêtres impériaux tandis que les gens du commun offrent leurs sacrifices à la montagne."

L'eau de pluie est un élément vital pour les Qiang qui vivent principalement de l'agriculture. Donc, en cas de sécheresse, des cérémonies sont tenues à grande échelle afin de prier pour la pluie. Si celles-ci sont sans effet, le Shibi conduit le peuple à la montagne sacrée (montagne la plus haute près de leur village) pour chercher un bois gravé. Ensuite, tous les participants offrent respectueusement du vin et des sacrifices, font des voeux et chantent leurs prières pour la pluie.

Dans certains endroits du comté de Wenchuan, pour prier pour la pluie, les gens pratiquent un genre de sorcellerie appelée "chasser Hanba" (le démon de la sécheresse); d'abord, une personne se déguise en Hanba et se cache dans la forêt; ensuite, le sorcier conduit le peuple, gongs battants, criant fort, pour chercher le démon de la sécheresse partout dans la montagne; quand il est trouvé, le démon de la sécheresse doit courir devant, avec le sorcier et les autres à sa poursuite, jusqu'à ce qu'il soit épuisé et rattrapé; ceci symbolise la dissipation du démon de la sécheresse et son prochain remplacement par la pluie.

## II. Le culte mystérieux de la pierre blanche (symboles des divers dieux)

Dans les croyances des Qiang, tous les dieux sont symbolisés par la pierre blanche, excepté le dieu du feu, qui est représenté par le foyer dans la maison, et le

maître suprême des Shibi, figuré par la tête de singe. Les Qiang, qui croient à l'animisme, mettent une (ou plusieurs) pierre blanche de quartz sur la pagode en pierre se trouvant sur leur toit. Celle-ci symbolise le dieu du ciel ou d'autres dieux. Cette pratique est un phénomène culturel distinctif du Qiang.

Le fait que les Qiang considèrent la pierre blanche comme symbole des dieux, tire son origine de la guerre légendaire entre le Qiang et la Geji. On dit que les ancêtres du Qiang ont été forcés de partir de leur terre natale. Plus tard, une des branches s'est installée dans la région de Qiang d'aujourd'hui, où ils ont été confrontés à un ennemi redoutable—les Geji. Avant que la guerre ne commence, le chef du Qiang a eu un rêve au cours duquel il a été instruit par un dieu lui indiquant qu'ils devaient employer des bâtons durs et des pierres blanches comme armes, et qu'ils devaient attacher un morceau de laine autour de leur cou, comme symbole. Les Qiang ont suivi ces instructions et ainsi, ils ont battu les Geji, ce qui leur a permis de vivre en paix; ils ont donc voulu remercier leur dieu pour sa bonté; mais comme le dieu n'avait pas d'image concrète, ils ont décidé de le symboliser par une pierre blanche, placée sur leur toit et destinée à recevoir des sacrifices quotidiens. Depuis, la vénération de la pierre blanche et l'offrande de sacrifices au Ciel sont devenues une coutume traditionnelle des Qiang.

Ce genre de culte a une longue histoire et la narration de cette histoire glorieuse est une partie incontournable dans toutes les cérémonies importantes du Qiang. Quand le Shibi fait des offrandes sacrificatoires et se voue aux dieux, il est requis de chanter cette histoire. Des pierres blanches sont présentes partout où les dieux sont adorés: dans les champs, les montagnes et les temples, sur les toits et le haut des pagodes, ainsi que dans la cuisine ou dans la forêt. Parmi elles, celle que l'on trouve sur un toit représente le dieu le plus puissant—le Dieu du Ciel. Il y a une ou plusieurs pierres blanches au milieu des toits dans toutes les maisons de Qiang. S'il y a cinq pierres sur le toit, une représente le dieu du ciel, une, le dieu qui distingue le jour et la nuit, une, le dieu de la terre, une, le dieu local et la dernière représente le dieu de la chasse. Ces cinq dieux sont les plus respectés et les plus vénérés.

Au début, le pierre blanche n'était considérée que comme symbole du dieu du ciel. Elle était placée non seulement sur le toit de chaque maison mais également dans la "forêt sacrée" de chaque village. Le toit de la maison servait de lieu de rites sacrificiels pour toutes les familles, tandis que la forêt sacrée (qui est une réserve verdoyante dans la montagne où tout déboisement est strictement interdit) était l'endroit où tous les habitants du village se réunissaient pour les cérémonies publiques. Plus tard, la pierre blanche est devenue le symbole de tous les dieux ainsi que le symbole des ancêtres du Qiang. En effet, le culte de la pierre blanche a un contenu substantiel; il n'est absolument pas le simple culte d'une pierre naturelle. C'est en fait une sorte d'idolâtrie. Les Qiang vénéraient non pas la pierre blanche elle-même mais les dieux et esprits dont l'existence était indépendante de la pierre blanche, et qui possédaient des pouvoirs magiques.

Dans la religion primitive, les images des dieux sont souvent créées sur la base des rêves ou en liaison avec des objets spéciaux. Même le bord des vêtements, de la saleté sur la peau, des insectes, des feuilles tombées, des animaux et des objets artificiels peuvent être pris comme symboles des dieux, incarnant la croyance animiste dans la religion primitive. Les Qiang vénèrent trois dieux abstraits, dieu-ancêtre des êtres humains et dieux régnants mâle et femelle; ceci fait partie du culte des ancêtres. Ces trois dieux sont représentés par les pierres blanches qui se trouvent dans la salle principale au premier étage de chaque maison.

En fait, le culte de la pierre des Qiang trouve son origine dans l'utilisation de la pierre comme outil et arme. Ceci, combiné avec l'estime des Qiang pour le blanc, s'est développé en phénomène unique du culte de la pierre blanche. La conception du Qiang "où il y a la pierre blanche, là est le feu" et le fait que la pierre blanche puisse produire le feu, démontrent que le culte de la pierre blanche porte une certaine empreinte du culte du feu. La pierre blanche, où réside le dieu du feu, est capable de produire le feu; elle devient ainsi le symbole du dieu du feu. D'ailleurs, une chose en produisant une autre, cela implique également l'idée de naissance ou de reproduction. Par conséquent, les Qiang croient à la fonction reproductrice de la pierre blanche, qui à leur avis peut expliquer l'origine du Qiang. Finalement, la pierre blanche devient le symbole des différents dieux. Elle est de ce fait vénérée au sommet de la pagode, sur les toits de toutes les maisons Qiang, ainsi que dans la forêt sacrée près des villages Qiang. Depuis des milliers d'années, la pierre blanche est toujours le trésor le plus important, dans le monde spirituel du Qiang.

## III. Le Shibi et sa position sociale élevée

L'animisme est le noyau de la croyance religieuse des Qiang. Les Qiang croient que tout est commandé dans ses changements et mouvements par l'esprit intrinsèque, et la puissance mystérieuse de l'esprit peut apporter aux gens la bonne fortune ou le désastre. Le Shibi, avec ses capacités surnaturelles, joue le rôle du

sorcier et du chef dans l'histoire de Qiang. Le Shibi est capable de transmettre des messages aux dieux et génies; il exerce de cette façon une grande influence sur la société et sur la vie des Qiang.

## 1. Le Shibi et les cérémonies religieuses

Dans les activités religieuses des Qiang, le Shibi est celui qui établit le contact avec les dieux et les fantômes. Dans la langue Qiang, il s'appelle également "Xu, Shigu et Bi", qui sont des variantes des translittérations du même mot dans les différents dialectes locaux. Bien que le Shibi ait un rôle religieux, il ne se détache pas du travail quotidien. Les Qiang comme leurs ancêtres croient que le Shibi est à l'origine venu du ciel, et possédait une puissance surnaturelle. Il est aussi considéré comme ayant la compétence de communiquer avec les dieux ainsi qu'avec les démons. C'est pourquoi le Shibi occupe une place très importante dans la société Qiang. Depuis longtemps, il est l'intellectuel le plus autoritaire et le plus érudit, et il jouit ainsi d'un grand prestige parmi les Qiang. Le Shibi apprend par coeur l'histoire et les légendes de Qiang; il peut aussi réciter toutes sortes de mythes, de contes et chanter des incantations non écrites. D'ailleurs, le Shibi possède un ensemble d'instruments rituels qui ont des puissances magiques. Par conséquent, les gens pensent qu'il est capable de maîtriser les forces de la nature, d'appeler le vent et la pluie, de faire prospérer les animaux et les plantes, d'influencer le destin des gens en changeant leur bonne ou mauvaise fortune. Le Shibi est également un médecin qui peut soigner toutes les maladies. Sous les pressions provenant des forces naturelles et sociales, les Qiang placent leur espoir dans le Shibi, espérant obtenir par son intermédiaire la bénédiction des dieux. Les événements tels que l'adoration des dieux, l'accomplissement des voeux, l'exorcisation des fantômes, la purification, le traitement des maladies, l'accompagnement de l'âme des morts, mais aussi les mariages et les enterrements, sont tous gérés par le Shibi. Il est donc une combinaison de prêtre, de sorcier et de docteur. Après avoir aidé les gens, le Shibi reçoit généralement du maïs, du blé, du porc, du mouton, du poulet, ou de l'argent comme récompense.

Le Shibi a une influence étendue sur les Qiang qui le considèrent comme chef spirituel. Les cérémonies religieuses qu'il effectue sont les moyens par lesquels sa valeur se concrétise. Selon la plupart des savants, il y a trois niveaux de cérémonies présidées par le Shibi. Selon leur objet, ces cérémonies peuvent être classifiées comme suit: le haut (au sujet des dieux), le milieu (au sujet des affaires humaines),

et le bas (au sujet des fantômes). Elles peuvent également être divisées en quatre types de cérémonie selon la nature de leur but: divination, rites sacrificatoires, rappel du bien et exorcisation du mal.

Dans la tradition des Qiang, la divination est une sorcellerie très habituelle. Elle pourrait être effectuée soit comme activité indépendante, soit comme prélude ou partie composante d'autres cérémonies religieuses. Les activités de divination des Qiang sont clairement enregistrées sur les inscriptions antiques de carapaces et d'os.

Ses formes diverses sont énumérées ci-dessous.

(1) Divination avec le fémur de mouton. C'est une méthode antique de divination du Qiang. Pour accomplir la divination, le Shibi doit utiliser le fémur prélevé sur un mouton sacrifié, après que ce dernier soit abattu et avant qu'il ne soit brûlé. La personne qui veut demander des signes tient de l'orge du Tibet dans sa main et explique ses demandes au Shibi. En chantant des prières, le Shibi tord une feuille d'armoise en petite boule puis la brûle sur le fémur du mouton. Une fois que des dessins apparaissent sur le fémur, le Shibi annonce si la personne en question aura une bonne ou mauvaise fortune selon la longueur et l'orientation des lignes. Il évalue également quelles mesures nécessaires devraient être prises pour répondre à la situation. Cette méthode est souvent employée pour prévoir la chance ou deviner la cause d'une maladie ou la fortune des personnes qui sont loin de la maison.

(2) Divination avec l'orge du Tibet, appelée également la "divination de blé" Elle est principalement répandue dans le comté de Wenchuan. Ce genre de divination est employé pour prévoir la volonté des dieux et la future chance de tout le village.

(3) Divination en utilisant des branches de cyprès. Elle est fréquemment employée et a trois fonctions: deviner et comprendre le dessein des dieux; deviner la volonté de l'ancêtre du Shibi et obtenir un enseignement clair de la façon dont la danse sacrée du Shibi doit être exécutée; voir si les activités du Shibi sont bénies par le dieu à la tête de singe.

(4) Divination en suspendant un chien blanc. Cette méthode est employée pour savoir si la moisson sera bonne; les Qiang de la région de Tumen (comté de Mao) suspendent un chien vivant; si le chien est encore en vie au bout de sept jours, ils pensent qu'ils auront de bonnes récoltes, en revanche, s'il est mort, ils croient qu'ils auront une mauvaise année.

Les Qiang ont de nombreuses autres méthodes de divination, telles que les

divinations utilisant des nerfs de mouton, de la laine de mouton, une colonne d'eau, des becs de poulet, des oeufs, des mains de personnes, de l'eau, etc.

Les divinations populaires des Qiang se caractérisent par les trois points suivants: d'abord, la divination est une pratique fréquente liée à pratiquement chaque aspect de la vie quotidienne; ensuite, les différentes méthodes de divination ont différents buts; enfin, la divination traditionnelle du Qiang est étroitement liée aux moutons. L'existence continue de la divination est liée à sa fonction instructive, guidant le comportement des gens et, dans une certaine mesure, les influençant psychologiquement.

Les rites religieux présidés par le Shibi concernent des cérémonies de virilité, des cérémonies de mariage, des cérémonies funèbres, et des vœux aux dieux: par exemple, ils consistent à prier pour la sécurité de la famille et pour le rétablissement des patients.

Exorciser le mal est une pratique par laquelle le Shibi est invité à éloigner les maladies, le malheur, les démons et les monstres des personnes ou de leurs maisons.

Généralement la pratique prend deux formes: l'une est d'employer divers arts magiques pour traiter les maladies; l'autre est une cérémonie où un animal est employé comme substitution pour sauver la vie d'une personne.

Le rappel du bien vise principalement à faire revenir de bons génies ou quelque chose qui apporte de la bonne fortune, par exemple, le rappel du dieu de la terre, du dieu de la vache et l'évocation des âmes.

## 2. Comment le savoir du Shibi est transmis entre générations

Le Shibi est choisi par un système de maître et d'apprenti. Puisqu'il n'y a aucun texte écrit, toutes les formules magiques sont enseignées par l'instruction orale. Il n'y a aucune limite au niveau du nombre d'apprentis suivis par un même Shibi. L'enseignement a lieu généralement en soirée, parce que cela le rend encore plus mystérieux, mais aussi parce que c'est le moment où les gens ont fini le travail. L'apprentissage dure habituellement trois à cinq années. Lorsque l'apprenti connaît par coeur toutes les formules magiques et qu'il sait les appliquer correctement, et quand il est connaît tous les rituels, il tient une cérémonie appelée "Gaigua" pour remercier son maître et pour annoncer formellement la sortie de l'apprentissage. Pendant le rituel, l'apprenti offre à son maître un baquet, ainsi que des chaussures et des vêtements comme cadeaux de remerciement. En retour, le maître donne à son apprenti un ensemble d'instruments rituels, signifiant que l'apprenti est qualifié pour exécuter indépendamment la sorcellerie. Les autres Shibi du village et des autres villages sont également invités à assister à cette cérémonie.

Les instruments du Shibi, y compris tous les outils utilisés à chaque cérémonie, sont les matériaux religieux avec lesquels le Shibi entre en contact avec les fantômes et les dieux. Ils sont considérés par le Shibi comme sacrés et réservés uniquement à cet usage. Personne d'autre n'est autorisé à les toucher.

Pendant les rituels le Shibi porte généralement un gilet de basane et une jupe blanche. Certains Shibi portent également un chapeau en fourrure de singe et une pièce de fourrure de léopard sur leurs épaules. L'instrument principal employé par le Shibi quand il chante les textes sacrés est un tambour de basane d'environ 45 cm de diamètre. On dit que le premier Shibi acquit et maîtrisa les textes sacrés sous la direction d'un singe divin. A ce moment-là, les textes sacrés étaient écrits sur l'écorce de bouleau blanc. Malheureusement, cette écorce a été mangée par un mouton blanc alors que le Shibi dormait. Dès lors, les Qiang n'ont plus eu de textes écrits. Mais au même moment, un autre singe d'or est venu indiquer au Shibi que s'il tuait le mouton, mangeait sa viande et fabriquait un tambour à partir de sa peau, alors à chaque battement du tambour, il se rappellerait un morceau des textes sacrés. C'est pour cette raison que le Shibi doit battre le tambour en chantant des textes scripturaires.

Il y a également d'autres instruments. Un bâton sacré en bois, avec une tête gravée au-dessus et une pièce de fer couvrant la partie inférieure, est utilisé dans les rituels pour chasser les fantômes. Le couteau du Shibi, habituellement long de plus de 30 cm, est également utilisé pour chasser les fantômes. Une cloche de cuivre est employée en chantant des textes sacrés et des incantations. Quand le Shibi exécute ses arts magiques, il porte autour du cou un chapelet blanc constitué d'os d'animaux. La tête de singe dorée est vénérée comme objet sacré. Un sac en cuir est également l'un des instruments du Shibi. Les divers instruments sont décorés de poils d'animaux , de corne de mouton et de lames de fer ou de cuivre, etc. Ils peuvent produire des sons spéciaux lorsqu'ils sont frappés; ils accompagnent ainsi le chant du Shibi et créent une atmosphère mystérieuse.

## 3. Les textes oraux du Shibi

Le Shibi chante ces textes quand il effectue ses rituels lors des diverses cérémonies religieuses. Ces chants, issus de la sagesse collective du peuple Qiang , sont une mémoire de la longue histoire de leur civilisation. Dans l'histoire des

Qiang, la philosophie, la littérature, l'art et la religion ne se sont pas développés de façon indépendante, mais sont intégrés dans une sorte de conscience sociale. Les textes oraux du Shibi, résumé de cette conscience sociale, généralisent la vie sociale et décrivent une série de personnages vivants. Au niveau de l'organisation structurale, ils montrent une très bonne qualité artistique et un très haut niveau littéraire. Les textes du Shibi peuvent être divisés en trois parties. La première partie, l'autel supérieur, traite des Dieux; elle contient une préface et un texte principal. La deuxième partie, appelée l'autel moyen, traite des affaires humaines. La dernière partie, appelée l'autel inférieur, traite des fantômes. Le Shibi chante différentes parties des textes oraux selon la nature des cérémonies. Les mythes, les légendes et les textes oraux du Shibi sont basés sur les principaux faits historiques du peuple Qiang. Les textes oraux du Shibi sont une représentation vivante et encyclopédique de la société et de l'histoire des Qiang et ils contribuent de façon importante à la recherche historique et ethnographique de ce peuple. Ils sont en effet une encyclopédie vivante du peuple Qiang.

Les textes oraux du Shibi sont passés de génération en génération par l'instruction orale. Ils décrivent souvent le procédé de divers rites religieux et la nature et l'origine des coutumes locales. Ils jouent un rôle important dans la transmission des informations sur les coutumes et la croyance des Qiang. Ils sont également chargés d'expliquer les origines de diverses traditions des Qiang. Tous les textes oraux du Shibi sont riches en contenu, différents selon les personnages et étroitement liés à la vie des Qiang. Ils montrent également l'idée philosophique de Yin et de Yang, attribuant à tout élément de la nature une identité masculine ou féminine. Le mâle et la femelle se joignent, comme s'unissent le Yin et le Yang, pour produire tout dans le monde.

## IV. Divers tabous avec une longue histoire

Dans la croyance religieuse des Qiang, les fantômes et les dieux existent partout et peuvent dominer le destin humain. Pour éviter le malheur et encourager la chance, les Qiang ont établi divers tabous qui peuvent être généralement divisés de la façon suivante:

### 1) Tabous de la vie

(1) Tabous de la maison. Dans la maison, on interdit ce qui suit: entrer en portant un chapeau de paille ou en tenant un parapluie ouvert; orienter les pieds vers

l'autel de la maison ou y accrocher des vêtements; cracher; tuer des êtres vivants; percer un trou. Pendant les dix derniers jours du premier mois lunaire, le Shibi est invité à effectuer des rituels afin que les dieux pardonnent les péchés des personnes qui ont violé des tabous l'année passée.

(2) Tabous de mariage. Dans certains villages Qiang, on ne permet pas le mariage entre les hommes et les femmes qui portent le même nom de famille ou qui viennent du même village. Quand la mariée quitte sa maison, elle ne doit pas regarder en arrière.

(3) Tabous de naissance. Quand un bébé naît, les étrangers ne doivent pas entrer dans la maison. Dans certaines familles, on accroche un drapeau rouge à la porte pour avertir les étrangers de ne pas entrer. Un miroir de cuivre est habituellement accroché autour du cou du bébé et le bébé porte un chapeau décoré de conques. Les étrangers ne doivent pas toucher le bébé. Après qu'une femme ait donné naissance à un bébé, on ne lui permet pas d'entrer dans la cuisine ou d'aller à l'extérieur jusqu'à la fin d'un mois complet suivant l'accouchement. La présence d'étrangers est également néfaste quand les animaux domestiques tels que les moutons et les vaches mettent bas. Les Qiang pensent que la présence d'un étranger tarira le lait des animaux, donc ils attachent un paquet de bâtons correspondant au nombre d'animaux nouveau-nés au seuil de leur maison pour montrer que les étrangers ne doivent pas s'approcher.

(4) Tabous funèbres. Pour les enterrements, les gens habillent les morts avec six articles d'habillement et mettent de l'or, de l'argent, du porc et des légumes dans leur bouche. Ils mettent également "un billet de voyage" publié par le Shibi dans la poche du défunt de sorte que l'âme puisse arriver sans risque jusqu'au monde souterrain. Tous ceux qui meurent de mort violente doivent être incinérés. Et la date choisie pour l'incinération ne doit coïncider avec l'anniversaire d'aucun des membres de la famille. Si par hasard, la date de l'incinération coïncide avec l'anniversaire d'un membre de la famille, cette personne doit se cacher dans un endroit élevé, transformant de ce fait la malchance en chance. Quand une personne âgée meurt, sa famille abat une chèvre pour guider son âme. La famille dissèque alors la chèvre pour y trouver l'organe responsable de la mort de la personne. Ensuite les étrangers sont invités à manger la viande de cette chèvre; par contre, il est interdit aux membres de la famille d'en manger. Si une personne tombe d'un précipice et meurt, le Shibi sera invité pour rappeler son âme. Une chèvre, considérée comme bouc émissaire, est jetée de l'endroit où le mort a fait la chute. Si

la chèvre survit et revient à la maison, on considère ceci comme l'indication sinistre qu'une deuxième personne tombera du même précipice et mourra. Si une personne meurt de maladie, sa famille ne doit pas avoir de contact avec d'autres personnes jusqu'au sixième jour après l'enterrement.

(5) Tabous de festivités. Chacun dans le village doit arrêter le travail pendant les fêtes de la nouvelle année Qiang. Il y a également certains tabous qui doivent être observés en mangeant, en voyageant ou en étant malade.

### 2) Tabous de production

Aucun travail des champs ne doit être effectué le jour du Réveil des insectes (une des 24 quinzaines de l'année solaire qui tombe vers le 5 mars) ou les jours de Wu (le cinquième des 10 Troncs Célestes servant à désigner les ans, mois, jours et heures dans la tradition chinoise). Comme le Wu représente aussi la terre, travailler aux champs ces jours-là porte malheur. En outre, l'abattage d'arbres pour le bâtiment est interdit dans la forêt sacrée et les chasseurs ne doivent pas utiliser de feuilles jaunes pour couvrir leur tête quand ils chassent, etc.

### 3) Tabous sacrificiels

Quand le Shibi est invité à exorciser les fantômes d'une personne malade, l'entrée dans la salle est interdite aux étrangers. Le 12 mars, une chèvre est abattue dans le village et le peuple demande au dieu de la terre de bénir ses récoltes. Les routes et les chemins sont fermés et personne n'est autorisé à entrer dans le village. Ce jour-là s'appelle le "jour du plant vert".

### 4) Tabous observés par le Shibi en communiquant avec les dieux et les fantômes

Pendant le mois précédent toute cérémonie sacrificielle à grande échelle, le Shibi ne doit manger ni ail ni oignon. Avant d'effectuer ses rituels, le Shibi doit se baigner et se laver les mains. Personne d'autre que lui ne peut toucher ses instruments rituels. En outre quand les sacrifices sont offerts au dieu le plus puissant, il ne doit pas utiliser la tige sacrée.

La naissance et la continuité des tabous folkloriques des Qiang reposent sur des éléments qui se transmettent oralement. Selon cette particularité, les tabous des Qiang se divisent en deux catégories: premièrement, les expressions brèves et abstraites, qui servent à expliquer et illustrer certains tabous d'une manière abstraite et concise. La plupart d'entre eux esquissent simplement les raisons des tabous et les dangers de les casser, sans fournir de détails; deuxièmement, la littérature

folklorique vivante qui sert à expliquer et illustrer des tabous par des histoires folkloriques, des légendes ou des extraits des textes sacrés du Shibi.

En tant que phénomène culturel spécial, les tabous Qiang ont les caractéristiques suivantes:

Premièrement, bon nombre d'entre eux sont influencés par la croyance religieuse. Selon la pensée reflétée par les tabous des Qiang, nous constatons que ces tabous prennent principalement leur origine dans les pensées religieuses ainsi que dans les évènements principaux de la vie. Deuxièmement, ils sont étroitement liés à la religion primitive avec beaucoup de tabous concernant le culte de la nature et le polythéisme primitif. Troisièmement, un grand nombre de tabous a une signification symbolique. Comme genre de loi folklorique antique, les tabous sociaux servent à influencer et contenir le comportement des gens, et, de ce fait, à protéger l'ordre social, tandis que les tabous religieux sont le principal moyen pour les Qiang d'exprimer leur dévotion et leur révérence aux Dieux.

Le Taoïsme constitue un autre pan important de la croyance religieuse des Qiang. Bien que le bouddhisme, le bouddhisme tibétain, le catholicisme et le christianisme se soient étendus jusque dans le pays des Qiang, ceci n'a pas influencé l'adhérence des Qiang à leur propre croyance religieuse.

La civilisation des Qiang, qui dure depuis des milliers d'années et qui contient la croyance religieuse typique des Qiang, fait partie intégrante de la culture chinoise.

# CHAPITRE SIX   MUSIQUE QIANG

Les Qiangs, courageux et travailleurs, sont d'excellents chanteurs et danseurs. Comme une forme de sagesse historique et collective, la musique traditionnelle Qiang devient non seulement un de leurs patrimoines culturels les plus importants, mais aussi un excellent chapitre de l'histoire de l'art chinois. D'une manière générale, la musique Qiang peut être classée dans la catégorie de la musique folklorique.

## I. Chansons folkloriques Qiang

Puisque la langue Qiang n'a aucune forme écrite, les chansons folkloriques Qiang se transmettent de génération en génération par l'instruction orale. Cependant, en raison de la diversité des dialectes locaux, certaines chansons sont devenues très difficiles à comprendre. Les chansons aujourd'hui survivantes se rapportent principalement à l'histoire et à l'étiquette Qiang. Elles ont préservé la simplicité de leur modèle original. Depuis des centaines d'années, de nombreux chanteurs et de Shibi ne cessent de créer et de corriger ces chansons dont les mélodies ont été considérablement enrichies et améliorées.

### 1. Chansons de travail

Les chansons de travail sont chantées pour diriger le travail, encourager les travailleurs, et coordonner leurs mouvements. Elles peuvent également inspirer les ouvriers et leur donnent de l'enthousiasme. Le travail effectué par les Qiang, tel que le battage des grains, le calage des pierres et le portage des bois, est souvent accompagné de ces genres de chansons, chantées à l'unisson par les hommes et les femmes alternativement, et créant une atmosphère animée. Le "Ah, La Shan Jue" de village de Heihu, comté de Mao, est une chanson typique de ce groupe.

**Ah, La Shan Jue (andante, un peu plus vite, vif, puissant)**

(齐唱) 啊   啊拉山觉，啊米收基 牧 勒(哦)，  山觉呃，拉一呃(索   呃)。

L'idée principale de la chanson est: Allons, travaillons ensemble !

Quand les fermiers Qiang moissonnent l'orge ou le blé de montagne, ou sarclent des champs, ils préfèrent chanter des chansons dans un tempo modérément lent, telle que la chanson "Yue Yue".

**Yue Yue (andante, temps fort et temps faible distinctifs)**

Les chansons de travail mentionnées ci-dessus sont populaires et faciles à apprendre par cœur. Elles sont semblables aux "Haozi", chansons de travail dans la culture Han, la différence est que la tonalité et la mélodie de l'appel "à travailler" ne sont pas aussi claires que dans les chansons Han. De plus, elles sont principalement chantées à l'unisson ou en alternance, plutôt qu'avec un premier chanteur dirigeant.

Un examen de la teneur des paroles des chansons, de la forme structurale et du modèle de la musique, indique rapidement que ces chansons folkloriques sont le résultat des changements du style de vie des Qiang, du nomadisme à l'affermage. Les paroles des chansons de travail se composent des interjections telles que "hai", "le", "yo", "he", "yi", et "oh" etc. Jusqu'à présent, ces chansons de travail des Qiang ont préservé leurs dispositifs distinctifs: mélodies simples, rythmes distincts, brièveté de structure, et rapport étroit avec le travail collectif.

## 2. Chansons de montagne

Quand les Han chantent, ils aiment chanter au sujet de la création de l'univers par Pan Gu; quand les Tibétains chantent, ils aiment chanter au sujet du Na Li Xi Qi; quand les Qiang chantent, ils aiment chanter au sujet de "Na Ji Na Na". "Na Ji Na Na" est une expression dans le dialecte Qiang du Nord, qui signifie "la chanson de nos ancêtres". Ce genre de chanson est souvent placé dans un environnement

naturel particulier, et à l'aide de la métaphore, il exprime l'aspiration et la quête des Qiang pour une vie heureuse. Quand les Qiang font paître le bétail ou travaillent aux champs, ils commencent souvent à chanter "Na Ji Na Na, Na Ma You Xi, You Xi Re Na, Re Na Zha Sha", un quatrain dont chaque ligne est composée de quatre mots, et qui peut précéder une série entière de textes substantiels. Ces quatre lignes sont riches en connotation. Elles peuvent être traduites comme "chanson de nos ancêtres, la chanson que nous devons toujours chanter! La chanter à haute voix, et ne jamais oublier nos ancêtres". En conséquence, "Na Ji Na Na" est devenu synonyme de chanson de montagne dans la musique folklorique Qiang. La musique provient de la mentalité et de la culture commune des Qiang, un produit de langue, de localité, d'économie et de style de vie partagés, et elle est devenue un genre spécial de musique rapportant les traditions Qiang. Les pensées et les sentiments exprimés en chantant ces chansons sont simples et pourtant profonds, les chanteurs traduisant un esprit aisé et insouciant, ainsi qu'un sens profond d'amour-propre ethnique.

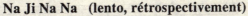

**Na Ji Na Na   (lento, rétrospectivement)**

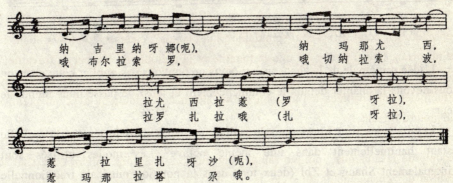

## 3. Ballades

Les ballades Qiang sont habituellement chantées à côté du foyer où le dîner est préparé ou lors d'activités particulières de groupe. Lorsqu'elles sont chantées, les gens s'assoient souvent en cercle sur le sol, avec au milieu, leur "vin à sucer" favori; pendant qu'ils boivent le vin, un des aînés chante, et de cette manière enseigne leur culture aux plus jeunes. Ces ballades, chantées à l'unisson, racontent les histoires glorieuses des héros Qiang, évoquent le passé, louent les mérites et les vertus de leurs ancêtres, et décrivent la beauté des montagnes et des fleuves.

"Chuan A Wang Te", par exemple, est une ballade racontant les exploits accomplis par Wang Te, un héros légendaire des tribus Qiang. Les textes de la

chanson sont divisés en dizaines de sections. On dit que Wang Te est né dans un endroit appelé Mahuangzhai dans le village de Sanlong (comté de Mao). Au début de la dynastie des Qing, il a mené les Qiang dans la résistance contre l'oppression et l'exploitation des Tusi, leurs gouverneurs locaux, et contre le système féodal, à la poursuite de la liberté et de l'égalité. Malheureusement, la rébellion a été réprimée et Wang Te a été tué. Depuis, les Qiang le considère comme un héros, et exalte ses exploits dans leurs chansons.

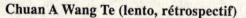

**Chuan A Wang Te (lento, rétrospectif)**

纳　　吉 纳娜 （哟）　　　哦）.　　也日阿　姆 尤西　　（哟）,
日阿　冷 扎沙 （哟）　　　哦）.　　也米　 出尔米色　（哟）.

尤　　 西日阿拉（哟）　　　也）,　 日阿　冷　扎沙　（哟）,
斯　　出尔惹 色（哟）　　　也）,　 各　 古　回巴　（哟）,

（哟）　 尤　 西 （哟）　也　　尤　 西 日阿拉（哟）。
（哟）　 尤　 西 （哟）　也　　尤　 西 日阿拉（哟）。

L'idée principale de la chanson est: Nous ne pouvons pas oublier cette chanson. Nous devons la chanter depuis le commencement et ainsi, le passé nous inonde le cœur.

Les ballades sont libres dans le rythme et lentes dans le tempo, la mélodie restant habituellement dans une même octave. Les modes utilisés sont principalement Shang et Zhi (deux tons dans la notation musicale traditionnelle chinoise), et parfois une combinaison des deux. Généralement, on préfère un mélange des genres, et chaque phrase coule librement sans être divisée en plusieurs mesures. On trouve la plupart des ballades chez les Qiang qui habitent la région de Shaba (comté de Mao).

## 4. Chansons se rapportant aux coutumes

### 1) Chansons d'amour

Il n'y a pas de terme conventionnel pour l'ensemble des chansons qui traitent de l'amour et du mariage dans la culture Qiang. Autrefois, le mariage était arrangé par les parents et les jeunes n'avaient aucun droit de choisir leur conjoint. Dans leur désir de choisir leur propre compagnon à vie et dans leur rejet du système de

mariage arrangé, les jeunes avaient l'habitude de chanter pour déverser leur tristesse et pour épancher leur cœur à leurs aimés. C'est ainsi que les chansons d'amour ont été produites.

Selon les légendes folkloriques des Qiang, ceux-ci sont des descendants de Na Ji et de Na Na, leurs premiers ancêtres. Par conséquent, toutes les chansons folkloriques Qiang commencent par chanter "Na Ji Na Na".

D'autres folklores racontent l'histoire d'amour entre un premier immortel et un homme mortel, qui sont les premiers ancêtres d'une certaine branche des Qiang. Les textes classiques chantés par le Shibi, par exemple, nous indiquent que Mu Jie Zhu et Dou An Zhu étaient amoureux l'un de l'autre et se sont mariés. Chanter "Na Ji Na Na" est devenu une pratique courante pour déclarer l'amour entre un homme et une femme dans la région nord du Qiang, en amont du fleuve Min Jiang.

Les textes de la chanson "Na Ji Na Na" sont divisés en dix sections décrivant l'amour entre Na Ji et Na Na. Puisqu'ils ont éprouvé la douleur et la souffrance dans leur rapport, la chanson traduit la tristesse. Aujourd'hui, il n'y a que très peu de personnes âgées qui peuvent chanter cette chanson dans sa totalité.

### Na Ji Na Na  (andante, avec sentiment)

纳 吉(啊)　　　纳　　娜(欧)，　　　纳　姆(啊)　　咿)
日阿姆(啊)　　拉)　扎　沙(嘞)，　　玛 穿(啊)　　咿)

尤　西(啊)，　　　(啊)　　　　尤　西(啊)
钦　匹(啊)，　　　(啊)　　　　穿阿斯(啊)

尤　惹姆拉，　　哈　尤(啊)　　呀)　哈　尤(啊)。
尤　尤玛内，　　哈　尤(啊)　　呀)　哈　尤(啊)。

L'idée principale de la chanson est:

**Chanter Na Ji Na Na me rappelle leur histoire, qui est bien triste!**

**Quand je commence à chanter Na Ji Na Na, je pense à eux et je les plains !**

D'autres chansons d'amour expriment les émotions joyeuses des jeunes hommes et femmes travaillant dans les montagnes ou aux champs, après qu'ils soient tombés amoureux les uns des autres. "Ga Si Zhi La Wu Er Ba" est une chanson typique de ce style, qui décrit deux amoureux, inspirés par leur amour et vivant heureux ensemble malgré les difficultés de la vie. Une mélodie fluide s'élève et s'abaisse naturellement avec une joyeuse vitalité.

### Ga Si Zhi La Wu Er Ba (andante)

L'idée principale de la chanson est:

**Je commence à chanter Na Ji Na Na; nous sommes jeunes et c'est le meilleur moment de la vie. Puisque nous nous aimons, escalader les montagnes escarpées et dangereuses semble facile pour nous.**

Les chansons d'amour répandues le long du fleuve de ZaGuNao (comté de Li et comté de Wenchuan), sont habituellement exécutées sur un mode de questions-réponses, qui s'appelle "Pan Ge", dans des dialectes locaux. Comparée aux chansons d'amour communes dans la partie Nord de la région du Qiang, la "Pan Ge" a son propre modèle. Cependant, en termes de paroles et de forme musicale, elle n'est pas aussi représentative que celles de la région Nord du Qiang.

#### 2) Chansons de vin

"Xi Ren Mu" signifie la chanson de vin dans le dialecte du Qiang du Nord. C'est une forme de musique très répandue dans les comtés de Mao et de Heishui, ainsi que dans quelques parties du comté de Songpan.

Boire du "vin à sucer" et chanter les chansons de vin sont des activités indispensables dans les traditions Qiang. A l'occasion d'un mariage, d'un enterrement, d'une fête, de la construction d'un bâtiment, d'un banquet, et en particulier d'activités religieuses, des cruches de vin scellées sont placées près de l'autel ou de la cheminée. Selon des règles cérémonieuses solennelles, un aîné de grande vertu et de prestige élevé est appelé à effectuer le rituel de "l'ouverture de la cruche", invitant avec respect les dieux du ciel et de la terre à apprécier les premiers le goût du vin, avant que les gens du commun puissent y participer à leur tour. Les Qiang croient qu'ils sont ainsi bénis et protégés par les dieux et qu'ils auront la bonne fortune. Après un

336

discours de l'aîné, toutes les personnes assises autour de la cheminée boivent du vin l'une après l'autre, selon leurs positions dans la hiérarchie familiale. Après plusieurs tours de vin, elles commencent à chanter, l'une d'entre elles dirigeant le chant.

Les Qiang s'appellent souvent "les Qiang altérés" car ils ont depuis longtemps la réputation de boire jusqu'à la plus grande limite, accompagnés du chant enthousiaste. Aujourd'hui, les Qiang sont bien connus pour leur méthode de fabrication de l'alcool, dans laquelle l'orge du Tibet, le blé ou le maïs, a fermenté puis a été scellé pendant des jours dans des cruches de terre avant qu'il soit prêt à servir. Ce genre de vin s'appelle "vin à sucer".

"Ren Mu La • Song Wa" signifie "la chanson destinée aux invités" dans le dialecte du Qiang du Nord. Selon la coutume Qiang, quand les invités ou les amis intimes viennent à la maison, on les invite à goûter "du vin à sucer", tandis que les hôtes âgés chantent cette chanson pour leur souhaiter la bienvenue.

Pendant cette manifestation, les hommes et les femmes s'alignent en demi-cercles séparés, chacun tenant avec ses petits doigts les ceintures des deux personnes qui l'entourent. La cérémonie exprime le grand respect pour les invités. Dans cette atmosphère cérémonieuse, les chanteurs se balancent de gauche à droite d'une façon élégante, suivant le rythme insouciant de la musique.

Quand une section de la chanson est finie, les hommes se tiennent toujours avec respect, alors que les femmes tapent les pieds avec élégance sur un rythme particulier, leurs hanches se déplaçant dans les deux sens, de plus en plus rapidement jusqu'à ce qu'elles s'arrêtent brusquement devant les invités, chacun reprenant alors la chanson de vin.

## Kui La Oh Ren

行板

也 拉 罗 索 梅 罗 劳 嗬
央, 嗬 呀 纳 哈 克 呀 嘞
噜 若, 索 奎 拉 哦 嗬
哦 嗬 央, 呃 哈 嗬 罗 鲁
呃, 莫 嗯 索 嗬 莫 索 呃 哦 日 阿 纳。

L'idée principale de cette chanson est:

**Pourquoi ne pas prendre du repos et boire du vin ? Détendez-vous, et la main dans la main, chantons et dansons.**

Les chansons de vin sont souvent chantées avec un meneur, habituellement une personne âgée. Les chansons font principalement l'éloge des héros passés et du beau paysage de montagne et de rivière, racontant les contes de leurs migrations historiques, invitant les gens à boire et chauffant l'ambiance. Bien que les paroles de chanson soient la plupart du temps improvisées, les chansons de vin commencent habituellement par quatre mots monosyllabiques: "Pao", "Hai", "le" et "Re", qui signifient respectivement "reposez-vous, invités de loin", "nous te donnons le bon vin en signe de bienvenue", "détendez-vous et buvez tout votre content" et "merci de nous rendre visite". Une telle sincérité et amitié reflètent vraiment les qualités d'amabilité, de naturel, et d'honnêteté des Qiang.

## 5. Chansons à partitions multiples

Des chansons folkloriques Qiang à partitions multiples sont produites principalement dans les régions du dialecte du Nord qui se trouve en amont du fleuve Minjiang, tels que les villages de Zhimulin et de Xiaoxing du comté de Hei Shui, dans le comté de Sonpan, le Songpinggou et le village de Taiping dans le comté de Mao. Cette forme d'art n'a été découverte que ces dernières années.

Dans le secteur de Zhimulin, il y a presque mille habitants indigènes qui parlent la langue Qiang et portent les costumes et les ornements tibétains. Ils s'appellent "A Er Mai" ce qui signifie "des personnes Qiang" et ce qui est une prononciation alternative pour "Erma" ou "Ri Mai" dans la langue Qiang, indiquant qu'ils sont également Qiang. Les gens de ce secteur excellent dans l'exécution d'une chanson folklorique antique avec double partition, que l'on peut entendre lors de mariages ou en tant qu'accompagnement de danse ou de travail quotidien. C'est une forme unique d'exécution et un style typique de chant. La chanson "Guo Ta Na Ma", par exemple, est un duo folklorique au sujet de la migration des Qiang et de leur origine historique.

### Guo Ta Na Ma (duo de voix masculines)

L'idée principale de la chanson est:

**Chantant la chanson des immigrés, nous venons de loin. Nous quittons "Ba Shi Gu", jour après jour.**

**Dans la chanson crée par nos ancêtres, nous trouvons les notes hautes ainsi que les notes basses. C'est Atai qui a chanté la première fois la chanson.**

Quand deux chanteurs exécutent des chansons folkloriques semblables à "Guo Ta Na Ma", ils doivent retenir par cœur cette phrase: "l'un des deux chanteurs devrait chanter la partie mince tandis que l'autre devrait chanter la grosse, et il devrait y avoir un pied au fond". En plus, les deux pièces vocales devraient également être plates aux deux extrémités avec une bosse au milieu. Ici, "la partie mince" signifie la partie haute, "la partie grosse" la partie basse, et "un pied au fond" indique que la partie basse sera entendue clairement. En ce qui concerne "les extrémités platés avec une bosse au milieu", il s'agit de commencer et terminer la chanson sur la même note. Quant au reste de la chanson, les deux chanteurs chantent en deux différentes parties. Prenons la chanson "Guo Ta Na Ma" comme exemple, dans la première phrase de la chanson, les deux chanteurs commencent par l'homophonie, qui se transforme ensuite en deux parties, celles de supérieur et d'inférieur. Ces deux parties reviennent de nouveau en homophonie.

Pendant que la chanson se développe, une harmonie fougueuse en deux parties apparaît avec des intervalles principalement de seconde et de tierce. Les deux exécutants effectuent ensuite un vibrato de tierce mineure sur la note longue de même degré. En conclusion, les deux pièces vocales finissent sur la note principale. Ceci démontre merveilleusement la condition artistique "des extrémités plates avec une bosse au milieu".

## 6. Chansons de sacrifice et de célébration

"Ji Nong Ji Sha" est le nom général des chansons exécutées en offrant des sacrifices aux dieux ou en célébrant une moisson abondante. A ces occasions, les Qiangs construisent devant leur village une tonnelle en couleurs vives, au dessus de laquelle sont décorés des couteaux, des pistolets et des balles pour exorciser les démons. Tous les jeunes hommes qui se réunissent en dehors du village s'habillent de couleurs variées, mettent à leur ceinture colorée une perche en bambou de plus de 70 centimètres et au milieu de laquelle sont insérées trois plumes de faisan. Quant aux personnes âgées, portant de nouveaux vêtements, ils rendent visite à chaque famille pour leur souhaiter le bonheur. Dans chaque famille, des bœufs et des moutons sont abattus. Les gens boivent du "vin à sucer", célèbrent la fête en chantant et dansant. Toutes ces activités de célébration durent plusieurs jours. Pendant cette période, deux séries de "Ji Nong Ji Sha" sont souvent exécutés. La première série inclut douze chansons avec une mélodie régulière et douce, exécutée par un groupe de personnes assises, et âgées de plus de cinquante ans. Un des chanteurs dirige le chant tandis que les autres chantent en chœur. La deuxième série comprend environ treize ou quatorze chansons vives d'une mélodie simple, qui sont exécutées joyeusement et accompagnées de danse.

## 7. Chansons d'appel des dieux

A l'occasion d'une fête importante, d'un banquet de mariage, de la célébration d'un anniversaire, de la mise en place de la poutre principale d'une maison, ou de l'achèvement de la construction d'une maison, les Qiang célèbrent toujours la cérémonie d'appel des dieux. Les cérémonies commencent en appelant les dieux: "OH, suo, ya! Er, er, er..." C'est une scène spectaculaire avec une couleur religieuse très forte.

Ensuite, tout le monde commence à chanter la chanson "Ji Oh Suo"

### Ji Oh Suo (andante)

L'idée principale de la chanson est:

**Ah, dieu du ciel, le suprême, veuillez me bénir, Dieu!**

Cette chanson est chantée accompagnée de la danse et de temps en temps, des cris des personnes. Après la cérémonie religieuse, l'ambiance change tout de suite. Les sujets des chansons se tournent vers de plus joyeux, tels que la célébration de la fête, le banquet de mariage ou la félicitation d'anniversaire. Les chansons portent principalement sur la louange des qualités morales, des talents et des apparences des jeunes mariés. Il s'agit également de souhaiter aux hôtes une famille riche et nombreuse, ainsi qu'une vie tranquille. Ce genre de chanson est riche en contenu, simple et pure dans la forme et unique dans le modèle. De plus, elles sont étroitement liées à la vie quotidienne des Qiang. Aujourd'hui, ce genre de culture traditionnelle, rencontré dans les rituels, les chants et les danses, joue un rôle important dans la vie du Qiang. Ces chansons qui ont un registre très étendu, de belles mélodies et leur propre originalité, et qui sont chantées d'une voix énergique avec beaucoup d'émotion, constituent une partie indispensable de la musique du Qiang.

## II. Danses folkloriques du Qiang

A l'occasion d'une moisson abondante, de la fête, du mariage, de l'enterrement

ou de la cérémonie sacrificatoire, les Qiang aiment toujours exprimer leurs pensées et sentiments en chantant et en dansant. Les mouvements des membres inférieurs sont les plus importants dans la danse traditionnelle du Qiang. De plus, ces mouvements sont simples, libres et faciles à suivre. La chorégraphie de danse est souvent tirée directement des observations de la vie quotidienne.

## 1. Sa Lang

Le mot "Sa Lang" dans le dialecte du Qiang du nord signifie chanter et danser en même temps. Il s'appelle également "Guo zhuang". Le Sa Lang est la danse de divertissement préférée des Qiang et la plus fréquente pour exprimer leur joie ou leur tristesse.

Le "Sa Lang" est exécuté principalement à l'occasion des célébrations des fêtes, des bonnes récoltes, des mariages ou des enterrements. Il est dansé avec un cercle ou un arc d'hommes sur l'avant et de femmes à l'arrière, dans un espace ouvert ou autour d'un foyer. Après avoir bu et chanté joyeusement, les gens dansent autour du feu en se tenant les mains. Pendant qu'ils dansent, les hommes et les femmes forment respectivement une ligne ou se rassemblent en cercle. En secouant une grappe de cloches, le meilleur chanteur dirige le chant. Les hommes chantent d'abord une section à l'unisson, puis les femmes répètent avant que tout le monde se mette à danser. La danse est accompagnée du chant a capella avec un ou un demi-tempo ajouté avant la première phrase de la chanson. Le chant allant de plus en plus vite, le meneur de la danse accélère soudainement son rythme et passe à une autre série de pas de danse. Après un cri qui finalise toute la chanson, tout le monde se remet à boire du vin. Quelques minutes plus tard, quand une autre chanson commence, les gens reprennent la danse joyeusement. Ces activités durent normalement toute la nuit.

La plupart des "Sa Lang" sont liés aux coutumes locales ou à la croyance du Qiang. Il y a généralement deux genres de "Sa Lang", l'un pour des occasions heureuses et l'autre pour des occasions tristes. Par contre, tous les deux partagent presque les mêmes chansons et mouvements de danse. Prenons comme exemple la danse des "angles des vêtements": les danseurs dansent en tenant les deux angles du pan avant de leur robe, et les danseuses tiennent également les deux angles de leur tablier tout au long de la danse. Accompagnés d'un chant doux, ils dansent en différentes formations: en cercle, en ligne ou en deux lignes opposées.

## 2. Xi Bu Cu

"Xi Bu Cu" signifie "danse de banquet" dans le dialecte du Qiang du sud. Il s'appelle également "Yue Bu Bu" ou "Suo Da Xi". Ce genre de danse se rencontre dans la région de Longxi du comté de Wenchuan et dans Tonghua et Xuecheng dans le comté de Li.

Comme la danse de "Sa lang", le "Xi Bu Cu" est également exécuté pendant les célébrations des fêtes, des mariages, des enterrements, et quand les travaux des champs sont finis. En tant que forme d'art, le "Xi Bu Cu" et le "Sa lang" se sont développés dans les mêmes environnements culturels, ils sont ainsi semblables au niveau du modèle de représentation. Cependant, il y a des nuances entre les deux danses. C'est que le "Xi Bu Cu" est une danse en salle, dont les pas sont plus lourds que ceux du "Sa lang"

### 3. Danse de sorcellerie

La danse de sorcellerie, danse des rites sacrificatoires, est également connue comme danse de Shibi. Quand le Shibi pratique ses arts rituels, il porte un chapeau en fourrure de singe décoré des plumes de faisan et de papier de diverses couleurs. Il chante en dansant et profère des incantations. Il secoue parfois son couteau rituel, se déplaçant sans à-coup avec lenteur et légèreté. De temps en temps, il brandit vigoureusement sa canne magique. Quand il bat son tambour de basane, ses mouvements sont agiles. Quand il secoue sa tessère de commandement, il crée une ambiance mystérieuse. Généralement, il accélère ou ralentit sa danse en fonction du rythme des incantations et du battement du tambour. Il y ajoute de temps en temps des volte-face ou des sauts.

Les rituels des ShiBi sont suivis d'une danse de tambour de basane. Le danseur principal porte "une tige sacrée" sur son épaule gauche, tout en battant la mesure avec une cloche dans sa main droite. Il est suivi d'un groupe de danseurs de tambour de basane qui dansent en courbe qui se transforme ensuite en cercle. Les étapes de danse sont simples et énergiques, et les battements de tambour sont audacieux et sans contrainte. Au final, ce genre de danse a une connotation ethnique qui lui est propre.

### 4. La danse de tambour

La danse de tambour est également connue comme danse de tambour de basane ou de tambour de cloche. Les Qiang ont une croyance religieuse primitive et exécutent souvent une danse sacrificatoire en tant qu'élément de leurs rites sacrificiels. Ce genre d'activité religieuse s'appelle "Ce Bai Ju • Su De Sa" dans le dialecte du Qiang du Nord, et "Mo En Na Sa" au sud.

Lors d'événements heureux, tout le monde porte des vêtements de fête colorés et donne un bal de danse de tambour où l'on peut trouver des danses en solo, des danses de couple et des danses en groupe. Les danseurs portent les gilets de basane, les coiffes "Yunyun" et les chaussures "Yunyun". Ils portent les tambours à simple

face dans leurs mains gauches et les battent avec de petits bâtons en bois. Ils commencent à danser d'une manière élégante, accompagnés de la musique du "Suona" (un instrument à vent semblable au hautbois) et de cloches.

Un Shibi, habillé presque comme dans la danse de sorcellerie, dirige la danse du groupe. Trois joueurs de cloche, portant un chapeau confectionné à partir d'une mâchoire d'animal et décoré de rubans rouges, tiennent les cloches de cuivre et portent sur leurs épaules des balais de paille qui sont décorées de drapeaux de papier colorés et de petits bâtons de papier. Il y a également plusieurs batteurs de tambour qui portent des vêtements de chanvre descendant sous le genou, des gilets de basane sans doublure, des chaussures de tissu ou des sandales de paille, des bandes molletières de feutre de laine et des ceintures brodées de pêches en fleurs. Avec les tambours dans leurs mains gauches et le pilon dans leurs mains droites, ils forment deux lignes et dansent au rythme du danseur principal et des joueurs de cloche.

Tout en dansant, le danseur principal soulève lentement "le bâton magique" et le brandit vers le ciel. Alors les joueurs de cloche élèvent les cloches et les sonnent trois fois pendant que les batteurs poussent un cri fort. Soudain, le danseur principal retire le bâton et se retourne. Les joueurs et les batteurs de cloche poussent un long cri qui remplit l'air, le bruit des tambours et des cloches s'intensifie dans un crescendo, puis, la chanson prenant fin, les interprètes ralentissent et arrivent graduellement à une halte.

## 5. La danse d'armure

Elle s'appelle aussi "Ke XI Ti • Hu Su De (Ren) " dans la langue du Qiang. La danse d'armure est une ancienne danse sacrificatoire. Les danseurs portent l'armure de cuir de bœuf, des casques ou des chapeaux décorés de plumes de faisan et de tiges de blé, ainsi que des ceintures rouges. Ils tiennent dans leur main des lances, de longues épées, des couteaux ou des poignards. Tous portent des arcs et des flèches sur leur dos et un ou deux ont un pistolet de chasse. Les danseurs se tiennent en ligne en formation de combat et, suivant le chef, ils battent leurs tambours, poussant en rythme des "Ho ha !" Commençant la danse en cercle, ils se déplacent ensuite en deux lignes de bataille, en agitant leurs arcs. Les sons créés par les cloches sur leurs épaules, sont mélangés de cris rythmiques et des bruits des armes. Les chansons accompagnant la danse d'armure racontent habituellement les grands exploits des ancêtres des Qiang ou l'histoire des guerres entre les Qiang et d'autres tribus.

## 6. Ba Rong

Le "Ba Rong", une transcription phonétique de la langue du Qiang, signifie

l'antiquité. Cette danse sert à ouvrir le chant et la danse. Elle est répandue surtout dans la région de Chibusu du Comté de Mao. Avant que la danse ne commence, une femme plus âgée fait un discours et propose du vin. Toutes les femmes dansent et elles s'alignent selon leur âge, avec la danseuse principale à leur tête. Quand elle commence à chanter, les autres s'associent et commencent à danser. Le chant et la danse évoluent de plus en plus vite, et la formation continue à chanter, toujours sous la direction de la danseuse principale.

### 7. La danse de Ha Ri

Le Ha Ri s'appelle également "Heu Ri", indiquant des manœuvres de troupe dans la langue du Qiang. C'est une danse militaire pour haranguer les troupes avant le combat. Des Qiang de différents villages se réunissent avec leurs propres armes sous le drapeau triangulaire de la tribu. Ils chantent avant de danser. Quand la danse commence, les étapes de danse sont simples, avec les danseurs qui changent constamment de formation. En même temps, ils poussent des cris en répondant à ceux des autres. Ils brandissent leurs armes en accompagnant ces cris. Ils se ruent face en face vers le milieu et combattent par paires, comme contre des ennemis imaginaires. La danse est entremêlée de chants et finalement portée à son apogée avec des cris joyeux et les armes brandies vers le ciel. Le grand élan et le spectacle magnifique du Ha Ri en ont fait une danse puissante, renforçant le moral et la prouesse militaire des Qiang alors qu'ils s'engageaient et demandaient la victoire avant d'aller faire la guerre.

Quelques danses folkloriques du Qiang sont semblables à ceux du Han, tel que la danse de dragon et la danse de bateau. En outre, beaucoup d'artistes du Qiang de nos jours ont créé de nombreuses danses modernes avec des caractéristiques ethniques, continuant et développant les traditions des danses locales.

### III. Opéra antique du Qiang

L'opéra du Qiang s'appelle "Ci La" ou "Yu Ou" dans la langue du Qiang. Il provient d'une danse antique de "Nuo" qui était une étape transitoire dans l'évolution de l'opéra du Qiang. Le contenu et les intrigues sont habituellement simples mais étroitement liés aux activités religieuses des Qiang.

Fondamentalement il y a quatre genres d'opéras de Qiang: l'opéra de Shibi concernant les activités religieuses, l'opéra solennel inspiré de la guerre, l'opéra de village qui est simple et franc, et l'opéra de lanterne pour la fête. Ils sont généralement exécutés dans les dialectes du nord ou du sud des Qiang.

L'opéra de Shibi a une plus longue histoire que les trois autres et dérive de la danse de "Nuo". Il concerne principalement la vénération des dieux et l'accomplissement de ses vœux aux dieux, tels que prier pour la bénédiction, demander que l'âme du défunt monte rapidement au ciel, et demander l'affranchissement du mal, des difficultés et des désastres. Il comprend des textes parlés, des textes chantés, de la mélodie et de la danse. L'accompagnement est fourni par les instruments musicaux tels que la flûte Qiang, harpe de bouche, suona, tambour de basane, et gong. Les interprètes ont des costumes et des accessoires spéciaux. L'opéra de Shibi consiste essentiellement en rituels sacrificatoires du Shibi, y compris les offres sacrificatoires, les prières, et le rachat des vœux. Les livrets et les dialogues riches de l'opéra de Shibi sont principalement des versions simplifiées de l'histoire, des mythes, et des légendes du Qiang, telles que "Mu Jie Zhu et Dou An Zhu" et "la bataille du Qiang et de la Ge". La teneur principale de l'opéra de Shibi change peu et est largement connue de chaque famille du Qiang. Puisqu'il est exécuté par les Qiang et que les Qiang n'ont pas leur propre langue écrite, l'opéra de Shibi n'est transmis sous aucune forme écrite.

L'opéra de guerrier raconte la guerre et les migrations dans l'histoire antique du Qiang. Les intrigues sont relativement plates; il s'agit par exemple des représentations de la vengeance audacieuse du Qiang sur les tribus envahissantes. Les acteurs ont toute liberté pour improviser selon leur désir et leur connaissance des légendes. Ils sont tous volontaires, ils se réunissent spontanément et exécutent l'opéra principalement pour leur propre divertissement.

L'opéra de village est organisé dans différents villages comme forme d'individu-divertissement. Il y a quelques manuscrits simples d'opéra écrits en caractères chinois dans Wenchuan, par exemple, "le papier de coupes de Mu Jie Zhu pour sauver cent animaux" et "combattre le démon de sécheresse". C'est le Shibi qui écrit le manuscrit, organise l'opéra, et agit en tant qu'acteur principal. L'opéra de village est toujours à un niveau assez fondamental en termes de développement de caractère et conception de l'intrigue.

L'opéra de lanterne exprime principalement le désir du Qiang du bonheur et de la paix. Il est populaire dans la région du fleuve de Tumen, à côté de Beichuan et du comté de Mao. L'opéra de lanterne le plus célèbre s'appelle "la lanterne du village de Xu" qui provient du village de Xu dans le comté de Beichuan. On dit qu'il emprunte beaucoup de caractéristiques de l'opéra de Sichuan et que s'est graduellement développé l'opéra de lanterne sous la forme d'art unique du Qiang. Il

a lieu souvent entre le premier jour de l'année lunaire et le début du deuxième mois, et il est exécuté par neuf à douze acteurs.

L'intrigue est souvent basée sur des histoires traditionnelles du Qiang telles que "Mu Jie Zhu descend pour mettre à la terre" et "la montagne des fleurs blanches". Une combinaison des rythmes émotifs d'expression, de récit et de danse est employée pour exprimer les personnalités de caractères et les conflits entre eux. Les mélodies dans l'opéra de lanterne incluent "appeler les fleurs", "ouvrant la porte avec Dix bouts du doigt", "la floraison des branches", et d'autres. Selon l'intrigue de l'opéra, différentes lignes sont combinées avec différentes mélodies accompagnées des gongs, des tambours, des suonas, et des flûtes. Avant chaque chanson, on exécute un prélude instrumental qui est un morceau relativement indépendant avec un battement régulier et une mélodie attrayante.

## IV. Instruments musicaux du Qiang

### 1. La flûte de Qiang

La flûte de Qiang s'appelle également la "la flûte verticale de deux-pipes"; c'est un instrument tubulaire fait en bambou. À l'origine, la flûte de Qiang était seulement une simple pipe. Ce n'est qu'à la dynastie de Han occidentale (ou légèrement plus tôt) qu'elle a été changée en deux pipes et que c'est devenu un instrument musical ethnique célèbre en Chine. La flûte moderne de Qiang, appelée "Qie le" dans la langue du Qiang et appelée également "Xu Xu", se compose de deux pipes verticales adjacentes, chacune avec une anche et six trous de doigt, capables de produire six notes musicales. La flûte est longue de quinze à vingt centimètres, elle ressemble à de longues baguettes, le diamètre de chaque pipe étant de la taille du petit doigt. La flûte est faite à partir de matériau soigneusement choisi, en utilisant seulement une spécialité locale appelée le bambou éternel de flèche (également appelé le bambou d'huile). Celui-ci doit être droit et rond avec de longues sections; la peau ne doit être ni trop épaisse, ni trop mince. La texture doit être dense, mais pas craquante. Le bambou est ramassé tous les ans avant l'hiver et, une fois qu'il est complètement sec, l'enveloppe externe est retirée et le bambou est poli à plusieurs reprises avant d'être coupé en tubes courts. Deux tubes sont placés côte à côte et fermement attachés ensemble, aux deux extrémités et au milieu. Les six trous équidistants sont forés dans chaque tube et une anche en bambou est insérée dans le dessus de chaque tube. La flûte de Qiang est alors terminée. Quelques flûtes sont frottées avec de l'huile ou de la cire pour les faire durer plus longtemps et sont ornées avec deux rubans rouges ou

découpés selon des modèles attrayants, pour rendre la flûte plus belle. Les embouchures tubulaires font environ 3 à 4 cm de long avec un diamètre intérieur de 0,5 cm. La gamme musicale de la flûte est limitée. Les notes des six trous de doigt, dans la clef de G (sol), sont A (La), B (Si), C (Do), D (Ré), E (Mi) et F (Fa). Pourtant les notes "bB" et "#F" ne peuvent pas être produites. Les deux pipes produisent les même notes qui sont douces, claires, mélodieuses et agréables, mais elles n'ont pas un diapason très large. La flûte de Qiang a été fréquemment mentionnée dans les poésies célèbres dès les dynasties de Tang et de Song il y a environ mille ans.

## 2. La harpe de bouche

La harpe de bouche, qui s'appelle "E Luo" dans la langue du Qiang, est également un instrument musical très populaire chez les Qiang. Pour faire une harpe de bouche, le bambou fort, à peau épaisse, flexible, est découpé en tranches, en morceaux plats d'environ 10 centimètres de long. Ensuite, une lame mince de sept centimètres de long est découpée à l'intérieur (parfois deux lames). Une corde solide est alors attachée à chaque extrémité de l'instrument. La harpe de bouche est placée entre les lèvres, tenue dans la main gauche par une petite poignée et secouée, alors que la main droite tire la corde. Des airs attrayants peuvent être produits en ajustant la position de la langue et la forme de la bouche pour commander le flux d'air. La harpe de bouche est la plupart du temps jouée par les jeunes et les personnes entre deux âges ainsi que par les femmes plus âgées.

Une autre particularité de la harpe de bouche est qu'elle apporte de la couleur aux relations amoureuses des jeunes. Quand ils ont un rendez-vous, ils s'amusent non seulement en chantant et en jouant la harpe de bouche mais également en créant une variété de mélodies riches et colorées de harpe de bouche. La chanson "musique de mariage", par exemple, exprime le sentiment mélangé du bonheur et de la tristesse de la fille de Qiang avant qu'elle se marie. "La musique funèbre" exprime des condoléances et le deuil pour les morts. "La musique amère" exprime la douleur et le mécontentement des femmes concernant le vieux système des mariages arrangés. La "musique de berger" et la "chasse avec des chiens dans les montagnes" expriment l'humeur joyeuse des Qiang quand ils travaillent ou qu'ils chassent.

## 3. Le tambour de basane

Le tambour de basane, appelé "Ri Wu" ou "Ce Bai Ju" dans la langue du Qiang, est un instrument rituel indispensable du Shibi. Il est fait en basane étroitement étirée avec un diamètre d'environ 45cm. Le tambour a une tonalité haute variable et

il est joué avec la cloche peu profonde. Le bruit profond et mûr du tambour et la tonalité métallique de la cloche se mélangent pour créer un genre de musique de percussion rythmé. Le battement de tambour est principalement un battement itéré simple, fait en battant le visage du tambour, ou le côté, ou les deux ensemble.

## 4. Cloche peu profonde

La cloche peu profonde, formée comme une petite capsule peu profonde inversée, est un genre d'instrument musical utilisé lors de rituels religieux. Les personnes de Qiang l'appellent "Kulu". Fait de cuivre, son côté de dessous est semblable à la base d'un instrument à vent avec un diamètre d'environ 10cm. Une courte corde filetée par un trou dans le dessus de la cloche relie un marteau minuscule à l'intérieur de la cloche à une poignée sur le dessus. Quand la cloche est secouée par la poignée, le marteau minuscule heurte la surface intérieure, produisant un bruit clair sonnant de lumière. Il est souvent exécuté avec le tambour de basane pendant les danses aux occasions religieuses. Parfois il est joué par une personne avec une cloche dans chaque main, et parfois par le batteur avec sa main gauche tenant le tambour et la cloche, ce qui a pour résultat des rythmes identiques de cloche et de tambour.

## 5. Tambour de bassin de pied

Le tambour de bassin de pied a une armature en bois avec la basane étirée étroitement à travers le dessus. Le diamètre du visage de tambour est d'environ 40 cm tandis que la base est d'environ 35cm. Il ressemble à un bassin de pied employé par les personnes de Qiang et est habituellement joué avec un pilon en bois.

Outre les instruments mentionnés ci-dessus, beaucoup d'autres instruments à vent et à percussion, tels que le suona, le gong, les cymbales, et les petites cymbales, sont utilisés pour les mariages, les enterrements, les festivals d'un dieu de montagne et d'autres rituels religieux.

La musique du Qiang a accompagné la survie et la lutte des personnes de Qiang pendant des siècles de changement et de développement, constituant progressivement une forme complète et systématique d'expression artistique avec son propre modèle distinctif. En même temps, elle a été considérablement enrichie par le contact avec d'autres formes d'art folklorique en Chine. Aujourd'hui, les chansons folkloriques mélodieuses, danses colorées des Qiang, opéras de divertissement et art d'instrument musical antique, sont devenues les symboles immortels de l'histoire et de la civilisation du Qiang.

# CHAPITRE SEPT    FÊTES DU PEUPLE QIANG

En plus des fêtes qui sont identiques à celles de Han, telles que la fête du printemps, la fête de Qingming, la fête de Duanwu et la fête de la Mi-Automne, le peuple Qiang a aussi ses propres fêtes, comme son nouvel an, la fête de sacrifice aux montagnes, la fête du roi taureau et la fête de chanson.

## I. Le Nouvel An

Dans la langue du Qiang, le nouvel an est appelé "Rimeiji", qui signifie une journée de fête ou de la célébration du nouvel an. Le nouvel an est la fête la plus importante pour le peuple Qiang, à l'occasion de laquelle on offre des sacrifices aux ancêtres et aux dieux, après la récolte de céréales, pour accomplir d'anciens vœux et faire de nouveaux vœux. Dans "L'histoire de la Dynastie Sui", on a écrit: "Le peuple du Qiang de Supi offre des hommes et des singes comme sacrifices aux dieux au commencement de l'année, puis entre dans la montagne pour les observer." On peut voir que cette fête a une très longue histoire et qu'elle est plutôt religieuse. Les anciens peuples de la tribu Di de Qiang se servaient d'un calendrier spécial selon lequel un an est divisé en 10 mois et le premier jour du dixième mois est considéré comme le commencement d'une année. Ce jour-là est donc le moment pour dire adieu aux vieux et accueillir des nouveautés. A cause des conditions climatiques et géographiques variées des différentes régions, les dates exactes des fêtes et leur façon de les célébrer ne sont pas forcément identiques. Après la réforme et l'ouverture de Chine, les représentants venus des comtés de Qiang, Mao, Wenchuan, Li, Songpan, et Beichuan ont demandé leur opinion aux Qiang de toutes les régions et se sont mis d'accord pour rendre le premier jour du premier mois lunaire, le nouvel an officiel du Qiang. Et cette fête dure normalement 3 à 5 jours.

Lors du nouvel an, tous les membres de la famille portent de nouveaux vêtements et se rejoignent chez eux, sans partir loin, sans travailler (comme chasser ou ramasser des morceaux de bois dans les montagnes). Chaque famille offre des os de taureau et de mouton comme sacrifice sur les pierres blanches, symbole de dieu. D'après l'ordre de Dieu Mubita, on colore les sacrifices et on les met sur le feu ou on les apporte aux forêts sacrées pour les partager après une danse collective.

Chaque village tue des taureaux et des moutons devant les forêts sacrées et place leurs têtes et sang sur la pagode en pierre blanche. Quand les activités de sacrifice sont terminées, quatre hommes enlèvent la pierre blanche, symbole de dieu, et font un tour dans le village. Puis chacun a un morceau de viande et rentre chez lui pour continuer la célébration. Pendant la fête, les jeunes hommes de Qiang mettent de nouveaux vêtements et une ceinture colorée, décorée de trois plumes de faisan. Ils visitent toutes les familles et souhaitent une bonne année en chantant et en dansant.

Le banquet de la fête est appelé aussi "Alcool de Récolte". Au premier jour du dixième mois lunaire, tout le monde brûle des branches de cyprès devant le Lekexi (une petite tour sur laquelle il y a une pierre blanche) qui est sur le toit de la maison, afin d'offrir aux dieux et aux ancêtres des sacrifices comme des galettes à la viande et des petits pains en forme de taureau, mouton, poulet et cheval. Puis toute la famille prend du vin, mange du porc, danse Sa Lang. Le lendemain, on invite ses proches et ses voisins à manger, à boire et tout le monde chante et danse.

Dans la région de Mao, Wenchuan et Yadu, les Qiang ont une tradition spéciale selon laquelle lors du nouvel an, on dessine un signe spécial "卐" sur le mur s'il n'y a pas eu de mort d'adulte au cours de l'année écoulée dans le village.

## II. Fête de sacrifice aux montagnes

Cette fête est appelée aussi la fête de sacrifice au ciel, la fête du dieu de montagne, la fête de la tour, la fête du roi de montagne. C'est une grande cérémonie Qiang pour offrir des sacrifices au dieu du ciel et à celui de la montagne et pour demander une bonne santé et une bonne récolte. Dans "L'histoire de Dynastie Nord: l'histoire de Dangchang", on a écrit: "Le peuple du Qiang de Dangchang organise une réunion tous les trois ans, lors de laquelle des taureaux et des moutons sont tués comme sacrifice au ciel." On peut voir ainsi que cette fête a une longue histoire.

A cause des différentes saisons agricoles ou des origines différentes des tribus, cette fête n'a pas de date déterminée. En général, un ou plusieurs villages célèbrent la fête ensemble dans la forêt sacrée près de leurs villages. Dans la montagne près du village, il y a une pagode en pierre de deux mètres de haut, sur le toit de laquelle on met quelques pierres blanches qui représentent le dieu du ciel, le dieu de montagne et celui d'arbre. Autour de la pagode, il y a une forêt formée par des cyprès et des sapins que l'on appelle la forêt sacrée. La place vide devant la pagode s'appelle la Place d'arbre sacré. C'est l'endroit où la fête est organisée.

Les cérémonies de cette fête sont très compliquées. En général, les participants doivent être les hommes adultes de la famille. Les familles qui sont en deuil ou qui ont des femmes en couche ne sont pas autorisées à participer à la cérémonie. Chaque famille peut présider la cérémonie à tour de rôle. La famille de présidence est chargée d'organiser et de préparer la cérémonie. La cérémonie est présidée par un Shibi local. La famille de présidence prépare tous les sacrifices, y compris un bouc noir, un coq rouge, de l'alcool, de la viande, des céréales, des petits pains, des encens, des bougies et des monnaies en papier. Le Shibi porte un chapeau en cuir de singe, avec un couteau rituel à la ceinture, un collier de perle d'os. Il tient dans les mains une cloche peu profonde, un tambour Balang et un tambour de basane. Lors de la cérémonie, ses élèves le suivent en apportant d'autres appareils rituels. Un autre homme apporte une branche de cyprès (symbole de dieu d'ancêtre) décorée des drapeaux en papier et des bandes. Ces personnes sont suivies par les autres participants à la cérémonie de sacrifice. Le Shibi frappe le tambour de basane, tient une canne dont la tête ressemble à une tête d'homme. Avec le bruit des instruments, ils entrent dans le lieu de cérémonie—la Place d'arbre sacré. La cérémonie commence ainsi: le Shibi allume les encens et les bougies devant la pagode, met en place les sacrifices et offre du vin aux dieux. Il chante "la chanson d'ouverture de temple et de purification" et brûle des branches de cyprès. Les participants et le bouc noir franchissent les branches brûlées. Tous les sacrifices et les équipements de cérémonie doivent être fumés par les branches, qui signifie la pureté, afin d'accueillir les dieux. C'est l'étape de préparation de la cérémonie. Quand elle commence, le Shibi lit la parole d'accomplissement des vœux anciens, informe les dieux de la bonne volonté du peuple. Il demande aux dieux, Taiyizhi et Re A hong, une année de bonnes récoltes et la bonne santé du peuple et de son bétail. Ensuite le Shibi chante "la parole de la création du monde" et "l'Ode du dieu de montagne", puis, "la parole de bouc émissaire" pour inviter les dieux à prendre les sacrifices. En chantant, le Shibi essuie le bouc de la tête jusqu'à la queue avec une branche de l'orge du Tibet. Il fourre quelques grains de l'orge du Tibet dans ses oreilles et l'arrose trois fois ainsi que le coq. Stimulés par l'eau froide, les deux animaux tremblent trois fois, ce qui signifie que les dieux les acceptent. C'est alors que tout le monde pousse des cris de joie. Puis on tue le bouc, on relâche le coq dans la montagne, et on met les cornes du bouc sur le sommet de la pagode. La peau de l'animal est offerte au Shibi. Sa viande est cuite sur place et partagée entre les familles. Après "la parole de bouc émissaire", le Shibi chante quelques chansons anciennes, comme "Eviter le malheur", "Immortalité" et "Bonne récolte". Ensuite, le Shibi demande aux dieux des semences de l'orge du Tibet, avec un chant compliqué qui est accompagné par le tambour. Comme il chante de plus en plus vite, le son du tambour s'accélère. Soudain, le Shibi tourne le

tambour et saute. On écoute les bruits des semences de l'orge du Tibet entrant dans le tambour. Tout le monde acclame, admirant la puissance magique du Shibi. C'est l'apogée de la cérémonie. Le Shibi chante la parole "Inviter des animaux à manger les sacrifices", l'ode de la famille de présidence et du peuple. On s'asseoit par terre, on porte un toast au Shibi, et tout le monde boit et chante ensemble.

A la fin, le Shibi chante "la parole de la fin de cérémonie". On suit le Shibi, qui fait trois fois le tour de la pagode en chantant et dansant. Quand la prochaine famille de présidence est choisie, tout le monde rentre au village.

Dans les autres régions, il y a des coutumes différentes, par exemple, tuer un chien, un coq , un taureau comme sacrifice de montagne. Les sacrifices sont différents, tandis que les cérémonies demeurent presque identiques à celles que l'on vient de voir ci-dessus.

## III. Fête du roi taureau

Cette fête, appelée aussi fête de taureau est normalement célébrée au premier jour du dixième mois lunaire, le même jour que le nouvel an des Qiang. On dit que ce jour est l'anniversaire du dieu taureau (le roi taureau). Le dieu taureau ou le bodhisattva taureau, est appelé Ba Zha Se dans la langue des Qiang.

L'origine de cette fête est la vénération du taureau, une coutume très ancienne des Qiang. Dans les régions des Qiang, on appelle le taureau "parent qui nous donne la nourriture et l'habit". Dans une chanson du Qiang, on chante: "La vie du taureau est dure, on n'a rien à manger ni à se mettre sans le taureau". Dans la "chanson de la fête de taureau", on chante: "Le dixième mois vient...Tous les travaux sont finis. Tu dois être très fatigué. Après une année de dur labeur, l'hiver est le moment de te reposer". Les chansons montrent la sollicitude des Qiang au taureau. Quand le bétail est malade, au sud des régions des Qiang, on a une coutume qui s'appelle "Zhao Niu Cai"; c'est un rituel du Shibi pour demander au dieu taureau de rendre la santé au bétail car le dieu taureau est protecteur du bétail. En général, toutes les familles offrent des sacrifices au dieu taureau. Au vingtième jour du premier mois lunaire, ils vont chercher un papier dessiné chez le Shibi et le collent sur un pilier de l'étable. Auparavant, le peuple du Qiang ne mangeait pas de taureau. En revanche, quand le taureau est mort, on l'enterre où on appelle la tombe de taureau. Avant de l'enterrer, on enlève sa peau et on l'accroche à l'arbre, ce qui signifie que le taureau se détache de la dure vie et qu'il se réincarnera en être humain. De plus, on dépose la corne du taureau sur la pagode qui se trouve sur le toit de la maison ou bien à l'emplacement de l'arbre sacré.

En général, on célèbre cette fête avec le nouvel an. On allume des encens, des bougies, et des monnaies en papier dans le temple du dieu taureau. Les sacrifices sont un coq et une chèvre, pour que le dieu taureau protège le bétail. Ce jour-là, tous les taureaux restent au repos et on leur offre des petits pains de blé et de maïs. Dans certaines régions, on met plusieurs pains en forme de soleil et de lune sur les cornes des taureaux et on les lâche hors des étables.

## IV. Fête de chanson

C'est la fête pour les femmes Qiang. Elle est appelée Wa Er Wo Zu dans la langue du Qiang, ce qui signifie aussi le cinquième jour du cinquième mois lunaire. Elle est populaire dans les régions de Mao et de Bei Chuan. En fait, elle commence à partir du troisième jour de ce mois et dure trois jours. La fête provient de cette histoire: dans le village de Xihu de Qugu, une fille belle et intelligente qui s'appelait Sa Lang, s'était installée à côté du lac, dans la montagne près du village. Chaque année, elle chantait et dansait autour du lac le cinquième jour du cinquième mois lunaire. Sa belle voix et sa danse attirèrent le peuple Qiang qui ne pût s'empêcher de l'imiter. Mais le méchant chef du village voulut s'emparer de Sa Lang. Elle ne lui a pas obéi et elle fut tuée par le chef. Le peuple était triste; il a déposé Sa Lang sur un lit d'azalées et l'a incinérée. Ensuite, une pagode de pierre fut construite en sa mémoire. Depuis, cet endroit est nommé Sa Lang Liangzi. Quand les azalées s'épanouissent, les femmes chantent et dansent à cet endroit. La fête de chanson continue à se développer.

Au troisième jour du cinquième mois de chaque année, plusieurs femmes du village se rendent à la forêt sacrée pour offrir des sacrifices à Sa Lang (ou Mizhu ou Rumizhu) et lui demandent ce qu'elles doivent chanter pour la célébration de la fête. Le lendemain, toutes les femmes du village suivent une femme âgée qui sait bien chanter et danser. Elles mettent de jolis vêtements traditionnels et se maquillent, et puis se rejoignent pour rendre visiteàtoutes les familles du village en chantant et en dansant pour célébrer la fête. Des hôtes les accueillent avec de bons plats et du bon vin. Après cette visite, les femmes se réunissent sur une place pour chanter et danser. La célébration dure normalement trois jours.

Les femmes du Qiang travaillent pendant toute l'année, tant à la maison qu'aux champs, sauf à l'occasion de la fête de chanson, durant laquelle tout travail est accompli par leurs maris et leurs fils. C'est pourquoi la fête de chanson est une vraie fête pour les femmes du Qiang.

# CHAPITRE HUIT    *LES NÉCESSITÉS DE LA VIE DES QIANG*

## I. Habillement

L'habillement des Qiang se distingue éthniquement et régionalement.

Dans *"L'histoire de Qiang du nord: l'histoire de Dangchang"*, il est érit: "le peuple du Qiang de Dangchang porte des vêtements en cuir d'animaux." Dans *"Les annales de Mao: coutume"*, il est écrit: "Les hommes portent un chapeau de feutre alors que les femmes tressent leurs cheveux et mettent un turban. On s'habille en lainage à chaque saison. Les femmes tricotent des vêtements elles-même." Dans *"Les annales de Wenchuan"*, il est écrit: "Les femmes ont toujours la coutume de tisser du lin". Dans *"Les annales de Shiquan* (Beichuan, maintenant):*coutume"*, il est écrit: "les femmes du Qiang de Beichuan ont des tresses fines. Comme il n'y a pas de coton dans cette région, on porte des vêtements en lainage, on tisse un genre d'étoffe très épaisse à partir du lin... Les femmes tricotent des tapis."

Après 1950, dans les régions des Qiang, il n'y a presque plus d'atelier familial de textile. Les Qiang ont ainsi beaucoup changé leur habillement. Actuellement, les hommes Qiang portent un turban blanc, noir ou bleu, une robe longue, une bande molletière en lainage ou en lin, avec des chaussures en toile, de caoutchouc, ou de paille. Ils portent également une ceinture, à laquelle ils attachent un couteau, un sac en cuir et un Huolian (un équipement pour allumer le feu) . Pendant les fêtes, ils mettent les chaussures Yunyun. En ce qui concerne les femmes, elles aiment porter des bracelets et des boucles d'oreille en argent. Elles mettent normalement à la tête une écharpe dont le style et la couleur varient selon les régions et les différentes saisons. A Muka du comté de Li et à Qugu du comté de Mao, les femmes Qiang aiment porter des écharpes en tissu bleu en forme de tuile. Quelques-unes unes d'entre elles sont décorées de parures en argent ou brodées de fleurs ou de dessins. Dans les comtés de Mao, Huilong, Sanlong, Baixi et Wadi, les femmes portent en hiver des écharpes carrées brodées de dessins, au printemps et en automne des écharpes brodées de fleurs. Les femmes du comté de Heihu mettent des écharpes blanches, dont une partie est en surplomb derrière la tête. On l'appelle "Wan Nian Xiao". Les jeunes filles mettent des écharpes colorées à l'occasion des fêtes. En fait, les femmes Qiang ont des coiffes très variées. En plus d'une écharpe, les femmes portent une robe longue jusqu'aux pieds, un tablier brodé de fleurs, une ceinture de ruban et une veste de basane.

La veste de basane et les chaussures Yunyun méritent une attention particulière. Les hommes et les femmes aiment tous la veste de basane qui les protègent du froid et de la pluie. En plus, on peut s'en servir comme coussin au moment de la pause du travail. Les chaussures Yunyun ressemblent à des bateaux car les bouts des chaussures se redressent légèrement. L'empeigne de chaussure est brodée de dessins de nuages ou décorée de tissu coloré en forme de nuage. Selon la légende, quand les ancêtres des Qiang se sont installés près de l'amont du fleuve Min, ils rencontrèrent la résistance du Peuple de Geji, habitants locaux de cette région. Au début, les Qiang étaient surpassés par les Geji, mais un jour, après avoir reçu l'ordre des dieux, les Qiang s'enfuirent sur des nuages à l'aide des chaussures Yunyun. Ils attaquèrent ensuite leurs ennemis avec des pierres blanches et des bâtons et finirent par vaincre les Geji qui se servaient de perches et de boules de neige comme armes. (Certains experts disent que c'est incorrect). En tous cas, dans l'esprit traditionnel des Qiang, les chaussures Yunyun sont des chaussures de bonne fortune, qui sont également le témoignage d'amour entre les jeunes. Dans une chanson Qiang, on chante: "Mon cher, je te donne cette paire de chaussures Yunyun, est-ce que tu les aimes ? C'est moi qui les ai fabriquées, elles sont plus précieuses que l'or et l'argent..."

## II. Alimentation

Le peuple Qiang habite dans des secteurs accidentés près de l'amont du fleuve Min, où la terre est pauvre, les conditions agricoles sont mauvaises, ce qui leur rend la vie dure. Cependant, les Qiang ont une alimentation variée et typique.

La nourriture de base traditionnelle des Qiang est le maïs, la pomme de terre, le blé noir, le blé, l'orge du Tibet et le riz. Les Qiang prennent normalement trois repas par jour, mais pendant la saison des grands travaux agricoles, ils prennent quatre ou même cinq repas par jour. Par contre, pendant la morte saison d'hiver, ils prennent parfois deux repas par jour. Ils ont différentes méthodes pour cuisiner les céréales. Prenons le maïs comme exemple: ils en font la bouillie, le "Jiaotuan", le pain grillé et le pain à la vapeur. Ils font également du pain à la vapeur avec du maïs et du riz moulus mélangés. Si la quantité de maïs moulu est plus importante que celle de riz, on l'appelle "l'argent enveloppé d'or"; à l'inverse, on l'appelle "l'or enveloppé d'argent". Les nouilles sont normalement fabriquées à partir d'un

mélange de farine de blé et de farine de blé noir. Pour les gens qui chassent, qui font paître un troupeau, ou qui partent loin pour le travail, on prépare de la farine sautée à partir de l'orge du Tibet, du blé et du blé noir. La pomme de terre est non seulement une nourriture de base, mais aussi un légume que l'on cuisine de multiples façons.

L'alimentation secondaire des Qiang est constituée des produits de la viande, tels que porc, mouton, bœuf, yak, poulet et autres animaux domestiques et volailles. Parmi eux, le lard est le plus typique. Pour les fêtes, les Qiang tuent le cochon et coupent sa viande en quartiers. Après avoir mariné, ces morceaux de viande sont suspendus et fumés au-dessus de la cheminée (jusqu'au moment où la viande est demi-sèche) puis ils seront placés dans un endroit bien ventilé. Ce genre de viande ressemble beaucoup à "La rou" (viande salée et fumée) du Sichuan. Dans les régions Qiang, on l'appelle "Zhubiao" (le lard). Quand on veut la manger, on la coupe en morceaux et on la fait cuire dans l'eau bouillante. L'alimentation secondaire inclut aussi les légumes suivants: le navet, le chou chinois, le pois, la fève et les produits du soja (notamment le pâté de soja et la gelée de soja), ainsi que différentes herbes sauvages comestibles. Le chou chinois picklé est un des plats principaux des Qiang. Le chou picklé se différencie de deux façons: le grillé et l'ordinaire. Le chou picklé est normalement légèrement sauté, préparé dans la soupe ou simplement accompagné de sauce pour être servi froid. Les assaisonnements Qiang sont le poivre du Sichuan, le piment, le gingembre, la ciboulette, l'ail, le sel, la sauce de soja et le glutamate de monosodium. Avec la soupe de chou picklé, on peut faire des pâtes, des "Jiaotuan"et des boulettes de riz glutineux au chou picklé.

Les boissons traditionnelles des Qiang sont l'alcool et le thé. Le vin à sucer est une spécialité nationale du Qiang. C'est le favori des hommes et des femmes de tout âge. Dans la région des Qiang, il y a un proverbe qui dit: " Un jour sans alcool est pire que trois jours sans plat." On produit l'alcool avec l'orge du Tibet, le blé ou le maïs qui sont cuits à la vapeur, puis fermentent avec la levure pendant quelques jours. Ensuite, c'est prêt à servir. Pour le prendre, il faut ajouter de l'eau bouillante et le sucer avec une paille en bambou. Puis on ajoute de l'eau froide et on continue à boire, jusqu'à ce qu'il n'ait plus de goût. Il y a des étiquettes spéciales pour boire du vin à sucer. A l'occasion des fêtes, des noces, des célébrations pour les nouveaux-nés ou simplement pour boire au quotidien, il faut toujours qu'il y ait une personne plus âgée qui prononce "la parole de l'ouverture de la cruche". Le contenu de cette parole diffère selon la réunion, mais en général, il comporte des éloges aux dieux, aux héros du Qiang, aux ancêtres, aux hôtes et aux invités. Pendant que la parole est prononcée, la personne la plus âgée trempe trois fois la paille dans la cruche, sort une goutte de vin à chaque fois et la jette vers le ciel, ce qui signifie respect aux dieux et aux ancêtres. Ensuite, on partage le vin selon l'âge et on se porte un toast. On chante des chansons de vin, et on danse le "Guo zhuang" jusqu'à la fin de la réunion. Les chansons de vin ont beaucoup de style, comme le chant en couple, le chant tour à tour et le chant à plusieurs parties. Le chant tour à tour est très riche en contenu et raconte des histoires avec des intrigues subtiles. C'est pourquoi on appelle ce genre de chant "théâtre de vin". En outre, il y a encore les chants de vin pour le mariage, l'anniversaire et le rituel sacrificatoire. Le thé est indispensable dans la vie quotidienne des Qiang. Ils préfèrent le thé sauté et le thé séché au soleil. Les Qiang mettent du thé dans le cercueil du mort, au moment de l'enterrement.

Le peuple Qiang habite dans les montagnes; ils ont donc beaucoup de légumes et d'animaux sauvages à manger. Il y a notamment le sanglier, le muntjac, le faisan, le faisan de bambou et le porc-épic. Les légumes sauvages ordinaires sont la pousse de cédrel, la fougère, la vesce, le portulaca, l'igname de Chine, l'herba houttuyniae, la ciboulette savage et les champignons variés. Tous ces produits de la montagne contribuent à la richesse de l'alimentation du peuple Qiang.

## III. Habitation

Le Diaolou (la tour de fortification) et la maison "Zhuang" où habite le peuple Qiang se distinguent ethniquement et régionalement.

Depuis 2000 ans, le peuple Qiang est réputé pour son excellente technique de construction. Dans *"L'histoire de Dynastie Han dernier: la minorité nationale du Sud-ouest"*, il est écrit: "le peuple Qiang habite près des montagnes et construit des maisons en pierre, qui font dix Zhang de haut (3,33 mètres par Zhang)." Ces maisons sont appelées "Qilong", ce qui signifie tours de fortification dans la langue ancienne des Qiang. Dans *"The strengths and weakness of the various regions of the Realm"*, écrit par GuYanwu dans la dynastie de Ming, on peut lire: "à Wei et Mao, l'ancienne région de Ranmang, le peuple habite dans des tours de fortification construites en pierre, comme la pagode boudhhiste. Comme elles ont plusieurs étages, les habitants utilisent des escaliers pour monter et descendre. Normalement, on met les stocks de provisions en haut, on habite au milieu et le bas est réservé au bétail. Celle qui fait deux ou trois Zhang de haut est appelée Ji long; par contre celle qui fait dix Zhang de haut, ou plus, est appelée Diao lou."

Les tours de fortification servent à se défendre contre les ennemis. On ne s'en sert pas quotidiennement, mais lorsqu'il y a des ennemis, les Qiang portent leur armes et montent dans la tour pour se défendre. Généralement, les tours de fortification sont construites dans les endroits stratégiques ou au centre du village. Elle ont une forme d'hexagone ou d'octaèdre, et mesurent au moins dix Zhang de haut. Elles comportent généralement treize ou quatorze étages.

La maison "Zhuang" où habite le peuple Qiang, est appelé aussi la maison "Diao". En général, entre trente et cinquante familles Qiang habitent ensemble dans un village qui se trouve au sommet ou au millieu de la montagne, ou près du fleuve c'est à dire là où il y a de l'eau et où il est facile de travailler et de se défendre. La maison "Zhuang" comporte généralement deux ou trois étages. Le rez-de-chaussée est l'étable. Les gens habitent au premier étage. En plus d'une chambre à coucher, il y a une autre chambre au milieu de l'étage où se trouvent une cheminée et un autel adossé au mur; c'est l'endroit où l'on accueille les invités et où ont lieu les rituels, par exemple, les mariages ou les cérémonies funèbres. Au deuxième étage, on stocke les provisions importantes comme les céréales. Sur le toit, on bat les céréales et on les fait sècher. Aux quatres coins du toit et au milieu du coté qui fait face à la montagne, on construit des petites pagodes d'environ un mètre de haut, au sommet desquelles on dépose quelques pierres blanches. Ce genre de pagode s'appelle "Wo Lu Pi" ou "Na Ke Xi" dans la langue Qiang; c'est l'endroit où la famille offre des sacrifices aux dieux du ciel et de la montagne.

La construction des maisons est très importante dans la vie du peuple Qiang. Elle comporte solennité et contenus riches en folklore. Avant la construction, il faut demander au Shibi de vérifier l'endroit où la maison sera édifiée et de déterminer l'emplacement des portes et de l'autel. Quand le travail est terminé, il faut aussi demander au Shibi de choisir une belle journée pour organiser une cérémonie. Ce jour-là, l'hôte de la maison doit inviter ses proches et ses amis. La cérémonie doit être présidée par son oncle maternel. Pendant cette cérémonie, de la poutre de la maison, le charpentier chante plusieurs ballades et éparpille des petits pains, des noix et des monnaies en papier. Trois petits pains doivent être récupérés par l'hôte de la maison dans les pans de son vêtement, ce qui signifie que la richesse est apportée à l'hôte. Ce qui reste est distribué aux invités. Cette activité est appelé "Diu Qian Bao Zi" (Eparpiller des pains d'argent). En outre, au cours de la cérémonie, on écrase la crête d'un coq rouge avec l'ongle et on offre son sang

comme sacrifice aux dieux. Les paroles des chansons que chante le charpentier signifient que l'emplacement de cette maison offre des conditions favorables, que les gens qui habitent ici auront une famille nombreuse, du bonheur et une très longue vie, et que l'on remercie les dieux. Après la construction de la maison, on doit placer un bâton de cèdre (symbole de dieu) sur le toit pour vénérer les dieux. Puis il faut demander au Shibi d'organiser une autre cérémonie rituelle.

## IV. Déplacement

Les régions du Qiang comportent de hautes montagnes et des vallées profondes. Le chant du coq et l'aboiement d'un chien du village peuvent être facilement entendus par les gens du village d'à côté. Quand les gens de deux villages chantent en alternance, il semble qu'ils chantent face à face. Néanmoins, les déplacements entre les différents villages sont vraiment difficiles. Comme l'indique une ballade du Qiang: "Gravir la montagne est aussi difficile que d'aller au ciel. Quand on descend de la montagne, on a les jambes qui flageolent. Même si l'on peut communiquer en face d'un côté à l'autre de la vallée, il faut une demi-journée pour se rejoindre à pied." Autrefois, les seules routes principales des régions du Qiang n'étaient que des sentiers en zigzag aux bords des vallées et des falaises.

Quand des passants regardent en l'air dans la montagne, ils ne peuvent voir qu'un fil de ciel, comme une fissure entre deux falaises. Quand on regarde d'en haut, le fleuve en bas ressembleàun ruban blanc. Afin d'éviter les chutes, on dispose des marques au bord des routes pour indiquer aux passants où monter sur son cheval, où il faut en descendre et où monter dans le palanquin. Pour traverser les montagnes et les vallées, le peuple Qiang, intelligent et courageux, a créé plusieurs équipements de transport comme "Zhan Dao" (la passerelle de bois fixée le long d'une falaise), "Liu Suo" (la corde à glisser) et "Suo Qiao" (le pont suspendu).

"Zhan Dao", appelé également "Ge Dao" ou "Fu Dao", est utilisé dans les régions de Qiang et du Sichuan depuis des milliers d'années. Dans *"l'histoire de Sichuan"*, il est écrit: "la route en planche a été inventée dans les dynasties de Qin et de Han. On a creusé des trous dans les falaises et on y a inséré des bâtons. Puis on a posé des planches sur les bâtons pour faire le sol, et des rampes au bord de la route." En fait, la construction de la route de planches peut dater des dynasties de Yin et de Shang. L'ancien peuple Qiang a inventé un excellent procédé de construction des routes: d'abord, les roches ont été chauffées avec du feu puis elles ont été arrosées à l'eau froide; elles ont alors éclaté à cause des brusques changements de température; ce procédé a accéléré la construction des routes.

"Liu Suo", appelé également "Liu Tong" ou "Sheng Du", est une façon très ancienne de traverser les fleuves. Il y a deux façons de glisser: horizontalement et en pente. La corde horizontale est un fil qui est attaché à deux roches de même niveau; la corde en pente comporte deux fils en pente qui communiquent avec les deux rives du fleuve; elle est appelée aussi "la corde de canards mandarins". Dans *L'histoire du voyage de Kangyou*, il est écrit: "A Songpan et Mao, le courant du fleuve est très rapide. Il est imposible d'utiliser le bâteau et difficile de construire des ponts. Le peuple a ainsi construit la corde à glisser. Ils ont buriné les roches des deux rives, puis ils y ont attaché une très grosse corde. Pour la corde qui va vers le sud, son extrémité nord est plus haute que celle du sud. Pour la corde qui va vers le nord, c'est le contraire, son extrémité sud est plus haute que celle du nord. Il y a toujours quelques tubes en bois aux deux extrémités de la corde; les passants peuvent ainsi les saisir pour mieux arriver de l'autre côté." La corde à glisser est non seulement utilisée pour le simple déplacement des gens, mais aussi pour les gens portant des bagages, voire du bétail ou autre chose d'encombrant. Les tube en bois que l'on vient de mentionner ci-dessus sont fabriqués à partir de bois d'environ trente centimètres de long et en forme de colonne. Ces bois sont fendus en deux parties, qui sont creusées séparément avant d'être fermement rattachés à la corde. Ce genre de tube s'appelle "Liu Ke". La personne qui veut traverser le fleuve attache une ceinture ou une corde à sa taille et s'accroche elle-même à la corde à glisser. Puis elle glisse de l'autre côté du fleuve. Ce procédé de déplacement est dangereux, mais le peuple Qiang qui l'utilise depuis des milliers d'années, s'y est habitué.

"Suo Qiao" (le pont suspendu) est appelé aussi "Sheng Qiao". Dans la langue ancienne du Qiang, il s'appelle "Zuo". Selon les légendes, la tribu "Zuo" des Qiang inventa le pont suspendu, qui a pu être développé sur la base de la corde à glisser. Pour construire un pont suspendu, deux piliers sont d'abord placés dans l'eau, sur lesquels on place une poutre en travers. Ensuite, on ajoute sur la poutre des cordes de bambou, dont les extrémités sont attachées aux deux rives du fleuve. A la fin, on met des planches sur les cordes de bambou et on installe les rampes qui sont faites à partir du bambou ou du rotin.

Il est vraiment difficile de construire des ponts dans les régions des Qiang. C'est pourquoi on utilise généralement la corde à glisser et le pont suspendu. Mais tous les deux sont dangereux. Alors le peuple Qiang, intelligent et créatif, a inventé le pont "Gong Gong". Il est aussi appelé le pont de bois en arc. Pour construire ce

pont, il faut construire des piliers fermes en pierre sur les deux rives du fleuve. Les travaux se déroulent séparément, simultanément sur les deux rivres. On place des rondins sur les piliers sur lesquels on pose des pierres plates. On répète ces opérations, mais chaque fois, on allonge la couche d'environ deux mètres de plus vers le milieu du fleuve, jusqu'à ce que les rondins venant des deux rives se rejoignent au milieu du fleuve. En fin, on ajoute une dernière couche des rondins enjambant les rondins qui se rejoignent. Pour terminer la surface du pont, on ajoute des branches et de la terre sur les rondins; on dame pour que la surface soit plane et régulière. Après la mise en place des rampes, un pont "Gong Gong" est construit et prêt à servir. Le pont "Gong Gong" est stable et confortable. Il est une bonne solution pour la construction des ponts sur les fleuves torrentueux. C'est une grande innovation dans l'histoire de la construction de pont en région montagneuse.

Les chemins dans la montagne sont escarpés, étroits et dangereux. Traverser un fleuve est extrêmement difficile. Vu que les véhicules et les chevaux ne sont pas utilisables dans ces conditions, et qu'il est même impossible de porter des objets sur l'épaule avec une palanche, les Qiang se sont habitués depuis des milliers d'années, à porter des objets sur le dos.

# CHAPITRE NEUF   L'AGRICULTURE ET LA VIE DU PEUPLE QIANG

## I. Culture et protection agricole

Les Qiang habitent des régions montagneuses où les mauvaises conditions naturelles déterminent la façon de cultiver, les caractéristiques et les coutumes de l'agriculture Qiang.

Les Qiang cultivent principalement le maïs, l'orge du Tibet, le blé, le blé noir et la pomme de terre, ainsi que des cultures industrielles comme le sésame et le tabac. Les Qiang plantent également le zanthoxylum, la noix, la pomme et les herbes médicinales. Le maïs et la pomme de terre, cultures à rendement élevé, ont été importés dans les régions Qiang pendant la Dynastie de Qing. Les outils agricoles, qui s'adaptent au sol maigre et pierreux, comprennent principalement la houe, la houe en forme de graine de tournesol (avec le bout pointu), la bêche en forme de bec de canard (avec le bout rond et large), et la bêche en forme de bec de poulet (avec le bout pointu et étroit). Habituellement, on laboure le sol à l'aide d'un couple de boeufs. Depuis 1950, la technique et les outils agricoles se sont progressivement développés. Les Qiang commencent à utiliser des engrais chimiques et des insecticides, ce qui leur permet d'augmenter l'efficacité productive et la quantité de céréales.

Dans les régions Qiang, il y a beaucoup de proverbes d'agriculture. Par exemple: "Ramasser des pierres au cinquième jour du premier mois lunaire", "Un printemps sans cultiver, une décennie sans produire", "cultiver sans peine, récolter sans gain", "On ne pêche pas dans les fleuves peu profonds, on ne cultive pas dans les hautes montagnes", "Un début d'automne sec entraîne une réduction du rendement", "une sècheresse au printemps n'est pas aussi sévère que celle en automne, qui a normalement un effet catastrophique sur le rendement". Ces proverbes résument des expériences et des savoirs d'agriculteurs dans les régions montagneuses.

Avant 1949, à cause des épreuves de la culture et de la vie, le peuple Qiang organisait de grandes cérémonies en avril, pour offrir des sacrifices aux dieux de la terre et des céréales afin d'avoir une bonne récolte.

Dans les régions Qiang, la terre cultivée, dont la majeure partie est en pente, est

souvent séparée par des forêts où il y a beaucoup de fauves, surtout des ours et des sangliers qui sont très nuisibles. Dès que germent les céréales, il faut les protéger jusqu'à leur maturité. Le peuple Qiang construit des cabanes en paille; il y habite avec des fusils de chasse pour protéger les cultures et expulser les animaux tels que sangliers et ours, hérissons, rats, corbeaux et faisans. Quand la nuit tombe, ils allument le feu pour intimider les fauves. Avant 1950, le peuple Qiang protégeait les cultures également par la sorcellerie, en espérant que les dieux éloignent les fauves. Cette activité est appelée "Re che" dans la langue Qiang, qui signifie "expulser les fauves". Pendant la cérémonie qui a lieu chaque année après la récolte d'automne, on demande au Shibi de présider les affaires religieuses pour expulser les insectes nuisibles. Cette activité comporte une cérémonie solennelle et des coutumes compliquées. La cérémonie commence avant l'aube. Le Shibi chante des chansons anciennes pour expulser les fauves. Quand il a terminé, un jeune homme tenant un coq, suit d'autres jeunes hommes qui tiennent des flambeaux. Le Shibi les suit, en chantant la chanson ancienne *"Reche"*. Ils visitent tous les villages ainsi que les champs. Le Shibi marche en clamant le nom des endroits, et les autres membres du groupe l'imitent... Cela signifie que tous les fauves sont expulsés. A la fin, on tue le coq et on offre son sang aux dieux en faisant couler le sang sur de petits drapeaux blancs qui seront déposés dans les champs au lever du soleil. Ensuite, on cuit le coq et on le partage avant de le manger. Cela signifie que tous les fauves sont mangés. Tout cela montre le désir de bonne récolte du peuple Qiang et son respect pour les dieux. Cela reflète en même temps la pauvre force productive des régions montagneuses dans l'antiquité.

## II. L'élevage et la chasse

Xu Shen a écrit dans *"ShuoWen JieZi"*: "Qiang, le berger de Xirong." Fan Ye a écrit dans *"L'histoire de la Dynastie de Han: l'histoire de Qiang"*: "La région ancienne du Qiang se trouve dans le bassin du fleuve de Ci Zhi, s'étend jusqu'à la source de ce dernier, et couvre une distance de milliers de kilomètres." "Les Qiang vivent en nomades le long des fleuves et cherchent des pâtures. Ils vivent principalement de l'élevage, et complètent par la culture de céréales." Cet extrait nous montre que les Qiang sont un peuple nomade dont l'élevage des moutons constitue la production principale. Elle est complétée par l'agriculture primaire. Une tribu Qiang s'est installée plus tard en amont du fleuve de Min, et s'est intégrée aux habitants locaux du peuple Ran Mang. Ils sont ainsi devenus sédentaires. L'agriculture devient progressivement leur activité principale, et l'élevage

traditionnel demeure une activité auxiliaire très importante.

Dans les régions Qiang modernes, on élève principalement moutons, boeufs et cochons. Dans les régions proches de celles de Han, on élève des cochons. Dans les régions proches du Tibet, on élève des boeufs ou des yacks. Normalement, on fait paître les moutons en troupeaux. La nuit, on enferme les moutons dans l'étable qui se trouve au rez-de-chaussée de la tour de fortification. Il y a aussi des étables dans les montagnes. Les bergers habitent dans les cabanes en paille, avec des fusils de chasse pour protéger leurs moutons. L'élevage des moutons était le secteur d'activité principal de l'ancien peuple Qiang. Les moutons occupent une place très importante dans la vie des Qiang qui leur sont très attachés. C'est pourquoi pendant les fêtes, les Qiang offrent des sacrifices au dieu du roi taureau et au dieu du mouton. Il y a une chanson de berger très populaire: "Pour mener paître des moutons dans le premier mois de l'année, au début du printemps, nous nous levons très tôt. Les moutons marchent devant nous. La rosée mouille nos talons. Nous menons paître les moutons dans le deuxième mois de l'année, au printemps. Il y a partout des herbes vertes. Les moutons préfèrent les herbes vertes aux feuilles vertes des arbres." La parole décrit la vie des bergers pendant tous les mois de l'année, nous décrit leurs joies et leurs difficultés, ainsi que leur affection pour les moutons.

Le peuple Qiang élève des boeufs principalement pour labourer les champs secs. Cette activité semble commencer après leur installation en amont du fleuve du Min et dès que l'agriculture est devenue leur production principale. Avant 1949, les Qiang ne mangeaient pas de boeuf car ils pensaient que les boeufs travaillaient toute leur vie comme l'être humain et qu'ils méritaient le respect. Quand les boeufs mourraient, on les enterraient dans les tombes de boeufs. Il était strictement interdit de les fouler. Le premier jour du dixième mois de chaque année, il y a des cérémonies solennelles pour célébrer la fête du roi taureau, comme nous l'avons indiqué dans les parties précédentes.

On élève les cochons pour manger la viande et pour les vendre. Ces dernières années, beaucoup de familles élèvent des cochons. Dans les régions Qiang, il y a un proverbe qui dit: "les pauvres doivent élever des cochons, tandis que les riches doivent étudier les livres."

La chasse est une autre occupation secondaire importante pour le peuple Qiang. Dans *"la chanson de chasse"*, on chante: "je suis né pour chasser. J'ai grandi en mangeant du lait de chienne. Je riais comme un chien quand j'avais un mois. Je m'asseyais comme un chien quand j'avais trois mois. Je faisais deux canines quand j'avais sept mois. Je rêvais de chasser quand j'avais douze ans." Cette chanson est à la fois romantique et humoristique; elle montre l'enthousiasme du chasseur qui vit avec son chien de chasse depuis son enfance.

Dans les différentes régions Qiang, il y a des coutumes et des histoires de chasse fantastiques. Dans les régions du nord, le dix-septième jour du premier mois lunaire est la fête de la chasse. On dit que la quantité de gibier de ce jour-là montre la chance de chasse que l'on aura dans l'année. Ce jour-là, les personnes qui ont au moins 30 ans vont chasser dans les montagnes avec des fusils de chasse et avec des petits pains en forme d'animal. Quand la chasse est finie, les chasseurs placent des petits pains en ligne et les tirent en chantant des incantations... A midi, Les femmes "tuent" leurs petits pains en forme d'animal avec des pierres ou des couteaux. Puis on les mange. Les enfants "tuent" aussi des petits pains avec des armes et donnent les têtes des "animaux" aux parents.

Dans certains villages Qiang, on a une activité "Su Yue" le jour de la fête de la chasse. C'est en fait un concours de tir des petits pains en forme d'animal. Ceux qui atteignent la cible auront de la chance pour la chasse de cette année. Ce sont des coutumes de chasse laissées par les anciens Qiang. Ces activités montrent que le peuple Qiang prête une grande attention à la chasse et que tout le monde participe à la chasse.

Dans les régions Qiang, il y a beaucoup d'histoires de chasse. Dans le comté de Li, le peuple Qiang vénère le dieu de la chasse Hun Mou. On dit qu'il était le maître des chasseurs. Il a inventé des piéges pour capturer des animaux. Mais un jour il a capturé le dieu de la montagne. Le dieu s'est alors transformé en tigre et l'a mangé. Dans les comtés de Beichuan et de Mao, le peuple Qiang vénère le dieu Mei Shan. On dit qu'elle était une excellente chasseresse. Chaque fois qu'elle chassait, elle était sûre de rapporter du gibier. Elle est ainsi considérée comme dieu de la chasse. Malheureusement, elle a été tuée par un tigre; pendant la lutte, le tigre a déchiré ses vêtements; c'est pourquoi ses statues sont toujours nues. Le dieu Mei Shan est souvent vénéré dans les endroits couverts. Quand un chasseur n'arrive pas à trouver de gibier, il s'asseoit et chante *"la chanson du dieu de la foudre"*, *"la chanson de Meishan"*. Restant nu, il fait des rites de sorcellerie en priant le dieu Meishan de diriger les animaux vers les piéges.

Le peuple Qiang appelle le chasseur "Diao Lu Zi" ou "Da Lu Zi". Les chasseurs Qiang appellent le sang "Ran Zi", le chien "Léopard". Les chasseurs chantent beaucoup de chansons, comme *"la chanson de chevrotain"*: "Chasseur, que fais-tu? Installer des pièges, capturer des chevrotains. Pour décider où installer

les pièges, il faut connaître les points suivants: premièrement, trouver les empreintes des chevrotains, en forme de fleurs; deuxièmement, trouver sur les troncs d'arbre les traces faites par le frottement des chevrotains; finalement, trouver leurs excréments, qui sont en forme de poids." Cette chanson nous décrit les expériences de la chasse au chevrotain.

Les hommes Qiang adultes sont non seulement d'excellents paysans, mais aussi des experts de la chasse. Ils sont bons tireurs et connaissent différentes techniques de chasse; ils savent comment bien installer le piège de corde, l'arbalète, la vanne lourde, et le piège d'étable (on construit des étables dans les endroits fréquentés par les fauves et on y met des petits animaux comme un mouton ou un lapin, pour attirer les fauves. Dès que les fauves touchent les dispositifs de déclenchement des pièges, ils sont capturés.) Ce sont des connaissances précieuses laissées par les ancêtres des Qiang. Cependant, comme l'arbalète est dangereuse pour l'être humain, elle est maintenant interdite.

## III. Autres occupations secondaires

Le peuple Qiang a d'autres occupations secondaires comme l'industrie textile de famille, la cueillette des plantes médicinales, des noix et des zanthoxylums. Avant 1949, le tissage famillial était la seule source des vêtements de tous les membre d'une famille. Quant aux plantes médicinales et aux noix, elles sont des ressources économiques importantes pour les Qiang.

En plus des travaux de culture et d'élevage, les femmes Qiang tissent et filent le lin et la laine. Dans *"la chanson de la peine de femme"*, on chante: "Au huitième jour du quatrième mois lunaire, je dois faire paître les moutons pendant la journée et filer le lin pendant la nuit. Il y a beaucoup de moutons à faire paître et beaucoup de lin à filer jusqu'à l'aube. Du lin dans la main, je pleure. Mes beaux-parents disent qu'ils vont peser le lin que je file. Ayant entendu cette conversation, la voisine me passe discrètement une liasse de lin." Dans *"la chanson de berger"*, on chante: "Je dois faire paître les moutons en avril et je commence à filer le lin de bon matin. Si le textile que je file est gros, les beaux-parents m'accuseront, mais pour filer du textile fin, j'ai très mal aux yeux. Je suis en colère mais que puis-je faire?" Ces chansons reflètent la dureté de la vie des femmes Qiang. La filature est très fatiguante. Par exemple, quand une femme file du lin, elle coupe le lin avec ses dents, la main droite tirant des filaments et la main gauche tournant le fuseau. Pour fabriquer des fils de lin à tricoter une veste, elle doit filer plusieurs mois.

Grâce au rôle important que les femmes jouent dans la vie de famille et dans la société Qiang, elles sont respectées par tout le monde. Parmi les dieux Qiang, il y a le dieu de l'ancêtre maternel, le dieu domestique maternel et le dieu des bellefilles. C'est un phénomène particulier dans la culture Qiang.

La cueillette des plantes médicinales est une autre occupation secondaire traditionnelle des Qiang. Les forêts des régions Qiang sont riches en plantes médicinales rares, comme le cordyceps, la fritillaire, le "Qiang Huo" et la racine de codonopsitis, etc. La personne qui recueille les plantes médicinales est appelée "maître de médicament". Les cabanes en paille qu'ils construisent dans la montagne s'appellent "cabanes de médicaments". Avant d'aller dans les montagnes, ils préparent la nourriture et les objets indipensables. Après une divination pratiquée par le Shibi pour décider le jour du départ, un groupe de "maîtres de médicament" monte dans la montagne. Selon la coutume, on ne sort pas aux dates en "sept" et on ne rentre pas aux dates en "huit". Quand on choisit un emplacement pour construire une cabane, on doit allumer de l'encens, des bougies et tuer un coq comme sacrifice au dieu de la montagne. En général, mai et juin sont les périodes pour recueillir le cordyceps et la fritillaire, juillet et août le "Qiang Huo". Dans "la chanson de la cueillette des plantes médicinales", on chante: "Au mois de mai, la montagne est couverte de fraises rouges, alors que le cordyceps commence à germer. Tout le monde les recherche attentivement. On n'a que sept ou huit jours pour les cueillir. Au mois de juin, la saison chaude, la fritillaire s'épanouit comme une lanterne. Prenez les petites houes et sortez-les de terre." Cela nous indique les saisons et l'expérience de la cueillette des plantes médicinales.

Normalement, on cherche des plantes médicinales seul ou en couple. Le peuple Qiang a comme idée que chaque chose a son âme. En outre, il pense qu'il y a des montagnes masculines et d'autres féminines; il faut donc faire attention de ne pas enfreindre les dieux. On a différentes façons pour offrir des sacrifices aux montagnes de genre différent.

Dans les régions Qiang, il y a beaucoup de spécialités, notamment les plantes médicinales, les noix et le zanthoxylum, qui sont beaucoup vendus à l'extérieur. Dans une chanson populaire Qiang, on chante: "il y a des bambous dans la montagne, que l'on coupe pour fabriquer des paniers. Le panier est si grand que je peux y mettre huit Dou (équivalent à 10 litres) de céréales. Le panier est assez ferme pour que j'y ajoute mes noix et mes zanthoxylums." Dans les régions Qiang, les montagnes sont hautes et les routes sont très difficiles. Le transport est réalisé

par l'homme et par le bétail. On transporte nos produits sur le dos pour les vendre à l'extérieur et on ramène du thé et des articles d'usage courant de l'extérieur. Ce mode de transport est appelé "porter à dos", et celui qui le prend comme travail est appelé "dos-porteur". Les "dos-porteurs" grimpent les montagnes en portant des articles très lourds. Un instant d'imprudence pourrait leur coûter la vie. Donc, avant de partir, ils se préparent minutieusement et vérifient leurs équipements de transport: le panier, l'étagère à porter, le bâton en forme de "T" pour aider à la marche et faire balancier. Ce qui est important est de demander au Shibi d'organiser des cérémonies religieuses pour que les dieux de la montagne les protègent. Le peuple Qiang pense qu'à chaque endroit (village, montagne, fleuve ou place), il y a un dieu particulier, de même que nous avons un chef dans chaque village. Quand le Shibi préside la cérémonie, il clame le nom des dieux des endroits où les porteurs vont passer et fait des voeux. Quand les "dos-porteurs" rentrent au village sains et saufs, ils offrent des sacrifices aux dieux et accomplissent leurs voeux. Les "dos-porteurs" risquent de perdre la vie à chaque trajet, ce qui crée une crainte profonde dans leur esprit. Il y a un proverbe Qiang qui dit: "On préfère être un boeuf pendant trois ans que livrer des articles à l'extérieur une seule fois."

# CHAPITRE DIX   FAMILLE ET SOCIÉTÉ QIANG

## I. Famille et nom

La famille est l'unité essentielle de la société Qiang. Les familles sont souvent composées des parents en ligne directe. Trois générations habitent souvent ensemble dans une même maison, mais beaucoup de familles ne sont constituées que de deux générations: les parents et leurs enfants. Dans une famille nombreuse, les fils se séparent de leurs parents et vivent indépendamment après le mariage, sauf le dernier-né qui reste toujours avec les parents et qui s'occupe d'eux quand ils sont âgés. Dans chaque famille Qiang, il y a un autel où les ancêtres et les dieux sont vénérés. Quand un enfant quitte la maison pour vivre séparément de ses parents, il doit respecter les même dieux dans sa nouvelle maison. Cependant, ces dieux sont plus "jeunes" que ceux qui se trouvent dans l'ancienne maison. Selon la tradition Qiang, "l'âge" des dieux de différentes maisons décident l'ordre de présentation des vœux du nouvel an. Comme les dieux dans l'ancienne maison sont plus vieux que les autres, les frères aînés rendent toujours visite au frère cadet pour lui souhaiter une bonne année. En effet, la présentation des vœux du nouvel an est par sa nature, la vénération des ancêtres. Quand les enfants déménagent, l'allume-feu est aussi emporté de l'ancienne maison à la nouvelle.

Les familles Qiang adoptent un système patriarcal. Quand le père meurt, le fils assume sa position. Si la famille n'a pas de fils, le gendre entrera dans la famille comme fils adoptif et héritera de la fortune de son beau-père. Les femmes occupent essentiellement une position dominée, mais elles jouent un rôle important dans la production et le travail quotidiens. De ce fait, elles sont souvent sollicitées pour donner leurs conseils lorsque de grandes décisions sont prises pour toute la famille.

Aujourd'hui, les mariages Qiang sont en général monogames. Le mariage doit être assorti au niveau économique et au statut social. Il existe encore des phénomènes comme le mariage arrangé par les parents, le mariage précoce, le mariage entre cousins, voire le mariage entre la veuve et son beau-frère.

En ce qui concerne les noms des Qiang, comme il est écrit dans *"l'histoire de la dynastie Han Orientaux: l'histoire du Qiang occidental"*, "Les Qiang étaient

370

d'une même tribu. Ils se sont divisés ensuite en plusieurs clans, utilisant le prénom de leurs pères ou le nom de leurs mères comme celui du clan." A partir de là, les anciens Qiang ont développé un système de nomination qui a été pratiqué pendant longtemps, à savoir se nommer en empruntant un ou deux caractères du nom du père.

Tous les Qiang habitant en amont des fleuves Min et Fu ont leurs propres noms ancestraux, qui deviennent progressivement leurs noms actuels. Par exemple, les noms ancestraux comme Mao Er Zhi, He Bi Zhi, He Wo Shao et Luo Zhi, dont les initiales deviennent respectivement leur noms Han, soit Mao, He et Luo. Ce phénomène date de la dynastie Han. Depuis, les Qiang préfèrent prendre le premier caractère de leurs noms ancestraux comme leurs noms Han. Dans l'histoire, certains Qiang ayant été auteurs d'exploits militaires significatifs ont été nommés par les souverains impériaux. Les Qiang ont beaucoup de branches, et il est pratiquement impossible de savoir quand exactement ont eu lieu ces changements de noms. Donc, contrairement aux Han, les Qiang n'ont pas de registre généalogique.

A l'époque contemporaine, les enfants Qiang sont souvent nommés comme les parents le désirent. Ils ont normalement deux prénoms, l'un donné par le Shibi, et l'autre par un des membres âgés de la famille. Un gendre adopté par les parents de sa femme, doit changer son nom de famille en celui de sa femme. Pour avoir un nom complet, il place son nom de famille original après celui de sa femme, et ajoute un autre caractère entre les deux. Son enfant prend normalement le nom de sa femme. Néanmoins, s'ils ont beaucoup d'enfants, certains d'entre eux peuvent être nommés après le nom du père.

## II. Le Statut spécial des oncles maternels

Comme le dit un proverbe Qiang: "au paradis, il y a le dieu du tonnerre, et sur terre, il y a l'oncle maternel. Le plus jeune frère de ma mère est le plus proche, tandis que son frère le plus âgé est le plus respecté." Cela manifeste les caractéristiques Qiang en matière de contrôle social. Bien que la structure sociale du peuple Qiang soit établie sur la base de la consanguinité patriarcale, le contrôle social dépend principalement de la consanguinité matriarcale. Représentant de la ligne maternelle, les oncles maternels prennent une position spéciale dans la société Qiang. Parmi les "quatre parents importants", à savoir, oncle maternel, oncle paternel, mari de la tante maternelle et mari de la tante paternelle, l'oncle maternel est le plus influent.

Dans la vie quotidienne des Qiang, l'oncle maternel joue un rôle particulier et important. Il a le droit de décision définitive dans beaucoup d'évènements importants, par exemple, le mariage des enfants ainsi que le choix des positions de la porte, de l'autel et du fond conseillé par le Shibi pour la construction d'une nouvelle maison. Pendant le banquet de mariage, les oncles maternels et les frères de la nouvelle mariée continuent à jouir d'un deuxième tour des mets et boissons, après la desserte du premier tour. Cette pratique est appelée "Ya xi jiu".

A l'occasion des cérémonies funèbres, les fils du défunt doivent envoyer quelqu'un chez ses oncles maternels pour leur annoncer le décès. Quand les oncles maternels viennent présenter leurs condoléances, les fis du défunt doivent les accueillir en dehors de la maison, en se mettant à genoux des deux côtés de la rue qui donne accès à la maison. Puis une personne offre aux oncles maternels un plateau en bois rempli de vin et de viande. La personne portant le titre de "Zhi ke si", qui est responsable de la réception, chante avec les fils du défunt la chanson "Bienvenue aux oncles maternels", accompagnée du chœur des autres présents. Ensuite, les fils en deuil racontent aux oncles maternels comment le décédé est tombé malade, comment le Shibi a exorcisé les démons et soigné le malade, et comment ils ont préparé les funérailles. Avec l'approbation des oncles maternels, les fils en deuil peuvent finalement enterrer le défunt.

Dans *"l'histoire de la dynastie Han Orientaux: l'histoire du Qiang occidental"*, il est écrit "Les Qiang respectent les femmes et favorisent le clan maternel." Le statut social spécial des oncles maternels devrait être issu de cette ancienne coutume.

## Ⅲ. "Yi hua ping", la Réflexion de la démocratie primitive

"Yi hua ping" signifie littéralement un terrain plat qui sert de place publique où les affaires importantes sont discutées. Il est appelé "Er mu zi ba" dans la langue Qiang. Avant la révolution de 1911, chaque village avait son propre "Yi hua ping". Dans certains villages reculés , ce système de discussion a duré jusqu'à 1949. Bien que ce système n'existe plus dans sa forme ancienne, les Qiang gardent l'habitude de rassembler tout le monde pour discuter des événements importants et pour résoudre ensemble les problèmes. Les documents enregistrent le système de prise de décision du Qiang de Dangxiang. Le système de discussion du Qiang moderne est en effet une réflexion de la démocratie primitive de l'ancien peuple Qiang. Ce système de discussion est une partie indispensable de l'éthique sociale et des lois du peuple Qiang. Les décisions prises de cette manière réglementent la conduite du peuple, jugent qui a raison ou qui a tort, et gèrent la vie sociale des Qiang.

"Yi hua ping" était autrefois l'endroit public où l'on passait en revue l'armée Qiang, élisait le chef du village, s'entraînait au combat, et prenait les décisions importantes comme celle de la guerre. Dans les temps modernes, il sert principalement à régler les affaires publiques, comme l'élaboration et la promulgation des règlements, la résolution des différends, l'interdiction de l'accès à la montagne pour la reforestation naturelle, ainsi que l'élection du chef du village. Cette conférence publique a lieu généralement tous les ans ou tous les deux ans. Le chef de la conférence a un mandat de sept ou huit ans. En cas d'évènement important qui nécessite une discussion urgente, le chef de la conférence délivre une convocation au dernier moment. Les participants de la conférence sont tous des hommes adultes. Chacun a son droit de parole. Une fois la décision prise, elle a effet de loi du village et doit être respectée par tous les gens du village. Avant 1949, dans le village Zengtou du comté Li, le chef du village présidait chaque année au 5 juillet la conférence de "Yi hua ping" qui réunissait tous les chefs de famille. Habituellement, ils tuaient un coq et arrosaient des drapeaux en papier du sang du coq. Les drapeaux étaient ensuite enfoncés dans les champs et dans la forêt, tandis que le coq était suspendu à l'arbre, pour avertir tous les villageois que ceux qui violeraient les règles mourraient comme le coq. Si quelqu'un viole ce règlement après la conférence, il sera puni ou recevra une amende, selon les circonstances. Les décisions prises dans les autres villages Qiang par ce système de discussion publique ont également effet de loi.

## IV. Les traditions de respect des personnes âgées et d'amour des enfants, l'appréciation de l'assistance mutuelle et de la solidarité du peuple

Respecter les personnes âgées et prendre soin des enfants sont des vertus traditionnelles du peuple Qiang. Les Qiang servent les parents avec une grande piété filiale, respectent les personnes âgées, aiment les enfants, prennent soin des jeunes membres de la famille, montrent leur sympathie et offrent leur aide aux personnes handicapées, faibles ou solitaires. Toutes ces pratiques sont des vertus communes dans la société Qiang. Les grandes cérémonies sont souvent présidées par des personnes âgées. Un jeune homme doit respecter les personnes âgées même si ces dernières sont inférieures à lui dans la hiérarchie familiale. Avant 1949, même les officiers locaux, comme "Bao jia zhang" et "Tuan zong", devaient également respecter les vieillards.

La solidarité, la fraternité et l'aide mutuelle sont une autre réflexion du sens moral des Qiang. La sauvegarde des intérêts communs du village et du peuple Qiang est la norme de parole et de conduite partagée par tous les Qiang, comme dit un proverbe répandu dans la région Qiang: "Quand vous construisez une maison, tout le monde vous aide; quand vous vous mariez, tous vos proches vous aident; quand vous avez de grands travaux dans les champs, tous les villageois vous aident." Au moment des grands travaux des champs, les voisins ont l'habitude de former une équipe pour s'aider mutuellement. Ils peuvent également échanger la main d'œuvre ou demander à une personne libre de les aider gracieusement. A l'occasion de la construction d'une maison, du mariage ou des funérailles, les Qiang sont prêts à offrir leur aide. L'hôte ne s'occupe que d'offrir la nourriture. Les gens venant aider ne prêtent jamais attention à la qualité des repas. S'il manque des tables, des bancs ou des couverts, les voisins sont prêts à les leur prêter.

Dans certains villages près de la région tibétaine, des Qiang, des Han et des Tibétains habitent ensemble. Ils vivent en harmonie et n'hésitent pas à s'aider mutuellement, comme chante une chanson Qiang *"Construire la maison Diao"*: "Des frères Qiang, Han et Tibétains se réunissent dans la montagne afin de construire une maison pour des Qiang. Les Han transportent des pierres, les Tibétains malaxent le mortier, tandis que les Qiang maçonnent le mur. En transpirant et riant, tout le monde concerte ses efforts... Quand la maison est construite, l'hôte Qiang offre un banquet. Mes frères Han et Qiang, veuillez prendre les sièges d'honneur. Merci, mes frères, pour votre aide."

# CHAPITRE ONZE COUTUMES QIANG ET CÉRÉMONIES DE MARIAGE ET FUNÈBRES

## I. Coutume de la réception des proches

Les Qiang sont réputés pour leur hospitalité et leur convivialité. Ils attachent de l'importance au principe de "répondre à la courtoisie par la courtoisie".

Quand quelqu'un rend visite un ami ou à un parent, il doit le signaler en arrivant à la porte de sa maison. Ayant entendu la voix de cet ami ou de ce parent, l'hôte doit sortir et accueillir chaleureusement le visiteur. Si l'hôte ne répond pas, le visiteur ne peut pas entrer dans la maison, sinon sa démarche sera considérée comme impolie. S'il y a une femme qui accouche ou un patient dans la maison de l'hôte, le visiteur ne doit surtout pas entrer; au contraire, il doit s'en aller immédiatement et poliment. Une fois que le visiteur est bienvenu à la maison, on lui offre un siège, du thé, et on lui allume une cigarette. Si le visiteur est plus âgé que l'hôte, ou supérieur à ce dernier dans la hiérarchie de la famille, il sera invité à s'installer le plus près possible de l'autel de la maison. Le visiteur ne doit pas flâner en toute liberté dans la maison de son hôte. Il n'a pas le droit d'entrer dans une chambre, surtout celle de la fille de l'hôte. Si jamais cela se produit, il sera considéré offensif, et tout le monde se moquera de lui. En ce qui concerne le cadeau offert par le visiteur, l'hôte le décline généralement d'abord pour montrer sa modestie, puis l'accepte et le garde dans la pièce réservée aux articles importants. De cette façon, l'hôte montre son respect au visiteur.

Les Qiang reçoivent généralement les visiteurs avec les spécialités locales, composées de plats de viande et de légumes. Au moment du dîner, il est de tradition que l'hôte persuade le visiteur de boire de l'alcool, normalement du vin à sucer ou de l'eau-de-vie. Quand l'hôte porte un toast au visiteur, ce dernier, qu'il aime ou pas, doit boire trois verres de vin. Tout refus de boire pourrait être interprété comme une détestation de la nourriture et de la boisson préparées pour l'hôte. Avant de boire, on chante d'abord "l'ouverture de la cruche" ou la "chanson de toast". Plus le visiteur boit, plus l'hôte est satisfait. Le boire est souvent accompagné du jeu de la mourre, de la chanson de vin, ou de la danse autour du foyer. Il y a des coutumes spéciales dans

certains régions: par exemple, les Qiang qui habitent dans les comtés de Hei shui et de Mao, tirent un coup de feu vers le ciel pour accueillir le visiteur, puis l'invitent à s'installer dans le siège d'honneur à côté du foyer et lui offrent du vin à sucer.

Avant de partir, le visiteur doit dire au revoir à l'hôte. Il est impoli de partir sans rien dire. Si le visiteur est pauvre, l'hôte lui offrira des cadeaux. Ensuite, ils se donnent rendez-vous pour la prochaine visite avant de se séparer.

## II. Coutumes de la vie

Les Qiang ont des rituels variés et des coutumes concernant toute la vie. Toutes ces coutumes reflètent les caractéristiques distinctives des croyances de la société du peuple Qiang. Elles constituent ainsi une partie importante de la civilisation Qiang.

### 1. coutumes de la naissance

#### 1) Prier pour avoir un enfant

Les Qiang croient en une déesse qui s'appelle "Bodhisattva" ou "Trois étoiles". On dit qu'elle se charge de la procréation. Elle peut ainsi protéger les femmes enceintes et leurs bébés. Le trois ou le vingt du troisième mois de chaque année, toutes les femmes mariées se réunissent au temple de la déesse pour offrir des sacrifices. Celles qui n'ont pas encore eu d'enfant prient pour en avoir un; celles qui sont enceintes prient pour avoir un accouchement facile; quant à celles qui ont déjà des enfants, elles prient pour que les enfants soient protégés par la déesse et grandissent sans encombre. Depuis l'antiquité, les Qiang croient en la "caverne de procréation" qui se trouve dans une falaise près de leur village. On dit qu'elle a un pouvoir magique pour la procréation. Ceux qui désirent un enfant disent d'abord la prière devant l'entrée de la caverne, et puis jettent une pierre dedans. Si la pierre atteint la cible, cela signifie que le dieu accorde un enfant à cette personne. Les comtés de Song Pan, de Bei Chuan et d'autres régions ont tous des cavernes de ce genre, parmi lesquelles "Yu Xue Gou" de Beichuan est particulièrement mystérieuse et impressionnante. Selon les légendes Qiang, "Yu Xue Gou" était le lieu de naissance de Da Yu. On y trouve encore des vestiges comme la caverne Yu, le bassin où Da Yu était lavé, et la pierre sanglante. Les habitants locaux croient fermement que toutes les femmes stériles, qui s'assoient ou se couchent une nuit dans la caverne Yu, ou y ramassent une pierre et la tiennent dans la main, peuvent concevoir un enfant et avoir ultérieurement un accouchement facile. A Mian Si dans le comté de Wen Chuan, il y a

une autre façon de demander un enfant. Après le mariage, au premier mois de l'année qui vient, les nouveaux mariés font venir à leur maison une équipe de danseurs qui y exécutent la danse du lion ou la danse du dragon illuminé. Durant la danse, le lion ou le dragon vomit un "Trésor rouge" qui est préparé antérieurement et qui est une noix enveloppée d'un papier ou d'un tissu rouge. L'hôte de la maison adresse ses remerciements en s'agenouillant, puis il place le "trésor rouge" dans l'autel de la maison, en espérant avoir un bébé le plus tôt possible.

### 2) Grossesse

Quand une femme enceinte a des réactions de grossesse comme des vomissements, le Shibi est invité à effectuer des rituels. En plus, on place un parapluie ouvert sur le toit. On dit que cela protège le fœtus contre les fantômes, et évite les incidents majeurs comme l'avortement, l'accouchement prématuré ou le fœtus mort-né. Dès qu'elle est enceinte, la femme a un statut plus élevé qu'auparavant. Les membres de la famille prennent soin d'elle attentivement. Puisque la femme enceinte est considérée comme corps impur, elle doit veiller à certains tabous pour ne pas offenser les dieux. Quelques jours avant l'accouchement, les parents de la femme enceinte apportent des petits vêtements, des chapeaux, des chaussures, des chaussettes, des oeufs, du riz glutineux et du sucre brun. Ces cadeaux sont appelés "la hâte de l'accouchement". Certaines familles suivent même les anciennes traditions consistant à frapper le fond du bassin en bois jusqu'à ce qu'il cède, ou à déplacer la chaudière en fer du foyer. Ils pensent que la femme aura ainsi un accouchement facile.

### 3) Accouchement

Avant 1949, les femmes Qiang accouchaient normalement dans l'étable du bétail, sans l'aide de l'accoucheuse. Elles coupaient le cordon ombilical avec une pierre ou avec leurs dents. Si le placenta ne descendait pas, la femme devait s'asseoir sur un banc et son postérieur devait être chauffé avec de l'eau chaude. Après 1949, ces anciennes coutumes ont été abandonnées. Néanmoins, les femmes ne sont pas autorisées à accoucher dans les chambres où les sacrifices sont offerts aux dieux. Après la naissance du bébé, un miroir en bronze ou en verre est suspendu dans la chambre, et le chapeau du bébé est décoré de la coquille pour exorciser les fantômes. Le premier visiteur visitant la maison du nouveau bébé est accueilli chaleureusement par le maître. La famille lui offre des oeufs cuits au vin fermenté. Le visiteur est attendu pour présenter ses vœux au bébé. Les Qiang préfèrent un

visiteur mâle pour une fille nouveau-née, un visiteur femelle pour un fils nouveau-né. Ils pensent également que le caractère et les futures dispositions du bébé ont une relation étroite avec ceux du premier visiteur, et avec son humeur lorsqu'il entre dans la maison du bébé.

### 4) Coutume et Tabous de l'enfance

Après la naissance du bébé, les proches et les voisins lui offrent des "cadeaux de félicitation", comme des oeufs, des poulets, ou des lards fumés. Les parents de la mère apportent également des cadeaux pour leur petit-enfant. Au troisième jour après la naissance, on prépare la décoction aux plantes médicinales avec laquelle on baigne le bébé. Après le bain, la décoction ne doit pas être jetée n'importe où, car cela peut être considéré comme une action offensive aux dieux qui engendrerait des catastrophes. Avant 1949, quand un bébé anormal venait au monde, le Shibi était invité à exercer des rituels pour exorciser "Ye Xian", qui, dans l'esprit des Qiang, était le responsable de cette anomalie. Les Qiang croient que les rituels effectués par le Shibi peuvent empêcher le démon de causer la naissance d'un autre bébé anormal. Un mois après la naissance, la mère fait sortir le bébé de sorte que les proches et les voisins puissent le voir et le caresser. Chacun présente au bébé ses compliments et ses meilleurs veux. La nomination du bébé a lieu le même jour. On invite à la maison tous les enfants de cinq à huit ans des proches et des voisins. On prépare un pot de vin à sucer ou d'eau-de-vie, et trois petits pains en forme d'homme. Une fois que le bébé est nommé par son père ou un membre d'une génération précédente ou le membre le plus âgé de la famille, tous les enfants sont invités à partager les petits pains et le vin. Le nom donné de cette façon est un nom non officiel. Autrefois, certaines familles demandaient au Shibi de nommer le bébé selon la date et l'heure de la naissance du bébé. Le nom donné par le Shibi est le nom formel du bébé. Désormais, le 12 et le 24 du premier mois de chaque année, les parents accompagnent l'enfant pour offrir des sacrifices aux dieux, et prier pour la bonne santé durant toute la vie du bébé. Si la date et l'heure de naissance du bébé présagent qu'il sera difficile pour les parents biologiques de bien élever cet enfant, le bébé sera adopté et élevé par quelqu'un d'autre. Il appellera ses parents biologiques "oncle" et "tante". Autrefois, il y avait même une coutume consistant à faire adopter un bébé par un arbre ou une pierre. Dans ce cas, une lettre d'adoption était écrite sur une pièce de papier rouge et collée sur l'arbre ou la pierre. Les encens et les papiers étaient ensuite brûlés. L'enfant se prosternait et un nouveau nom était choisi pour lui. Si un enfant attrape la variole ou une autre maladie suscitée par une frayeur survenue, le Shibi sera invité à effectuer des rituels.

Les coutumes Qiang concernant la naissance reflètent leur désir très fort de se multiplier malgré le niveau très bas de la production et les mauvaises conditions hygiéniques. Elles montrent également la lutte des Qiang pour la survie de leur groupe ethnique.

## 2. La cérémonie de la majorité

La cérémonie de la majorité marque un nouveau point de départ dans la vie d'un homme Qiang. Cette cérémonie a lieu à l'âge de douze ans ( il y a d'autres versions comme 18 ans ou 16 ans). Le Shibi préside la cérémonie, mais avant la cérémonie, il nettoie la maison pour exorciser l'infortune. Ensuite, il offre au dieu du ciel des sacrifices ( coq ou mouton). Tous les membres du même clan s'installent autour du foyer. Et le garçon qui recevra la cérémonie s'habille de nouveaux vêtements et chapeau. Quand toutes les préparations sont faites, le Shibi s'agenouille devant le dieu, prenant une perche de cyprès en haut de laquelle figure une image de l'ancêtre de l'être humain. Il offre ensuite des sacrifices aux dieux du ciel et de la montagne, etc. Le garçon s'agenouille devant le dieu de l'ancêtre de l'être humain, pendant qu'un autre Shibi lui apporte des cadeaux de l'ancêtre, à savoir de la laine de mouton blanc et un tissu de cinq couleurs qui seront attachés au cou du garçon afin de montrer la sollicitude des ancêtres et la relation étroite entre les ancêtres et le garçon. Pour terminer la cérémonie, le Shibi chante des textes concernant la cérémonie de la majorité, puis le chef du clan ou une personne âgée récite des poèmes sur l'histoire Qiang et offre des sacrifices aux ancêtres du clan.

Dans certaines régions, il y a d'autres manières d'exécuter la cérémonie de la majorité. Par exemple, dans des villages Qiang des comtés de Mao et de Beichuan, on n'exécute pas la cérémonie séparément à la maison; elle sera effectuée comme une partie de la cérémonie annuelle de l'offre des sacrifices à la montagne, à laquelle participe tout le village ou plusieurs villages. Après que la cérémonie de l'offre des sacrifices soit terminée, en tournant autour de la pagode à côté de l'arbre sacré, le Shibi chante les épopées Qiang comme "Mu Jie Zhu et Dou An Zhu" et "la guerre entre les Qiang et les Geji". Il attache un fil de laine et met un peu de saindoux sur le front des garçons. Cela signifie que les garçons seront protégés par les dieux. Le même jour au soir, la mère du garçon préside sur le toit de la maison une cérémonie sacrificielle pour les dieux comme le dieu de grenier.

379

Dans certains villages du comté de Beichuan, en tant que partie de la cérémonie de la majorité, un tonneau d'eau est placé sur une dalle de pierre couverte de boue. Il est demandé au garçon de lever le tonneau. Si la dalle de pierre adhère au tonneau et ne se sépare pas, le garçon sera considéré comme chanceux avec un avenir prometteur. Cette activité est appelée "inviter le dieu de majorité".

Une fois qu'un jeune homme a expérimenté la cérémonie de la majorité, il est formellement considéré comme un adulte et a le droit d'agir indépendamment. Il peut participer aux activités publiques et sociales. Il a en même temps les droits et les obligations de l'adulte. Il est désormais considéré comme un membre formel de la société.

## 3. Système du Mariage

Les mariages Qiang sont généralement monogames. Beaucoup de ballades et de légendes sur les coutumes du mariage se répandent dans les régions Qiang. *"La chanson de la cérémonie du mariage"*, par exemple, chante "le système du mariage a été établi par Mu Jie. Elle a établi toutes les règles auxquelles les générations futures ne peuvent ni ajouter ni réduire. Ces règles se transmettent de génération en génération. Nous devons obéir aux règles que notre ancêtre nous a laissées". Dans les croyances Qiang, la déesse Ebabase est responsable des affaires du mariage. Selon la légende, après avoir créé l'être humain, le dieu Mu Bi Ta était très en colère en constatant que les hommes et les femmes se mariaient au hasard. Il demanda donc à la déesse Ebabase de se charger des affaires du mariage dans le monde humain. A l'aide de son frère qui était le dieu chargé de la réincarnation, Ebabase appariait les hommes et les femmes en couple avant leur réincarnation. Ebabase habitait au jardin d'azalée dans la montagne frontière entre le monde humain et celui des dieux. Elle apportait beaucoup de cornes de mouton du monde des dieux. Avant qu'un couple se réincarne, Ebabase leur donnait une paire de cornes de mouton; l'homme prenait la corne gauche, la femme celle de droite. Après avoir cueilli une botte d'azalée, le couple allait se réincarner. Tout le monde était désormais apparié en couple. Quelque soit l'endroit où un couple se trouvait après la réincarnation, ils arrivaient à se retrouver et à se marier. C'est pourquoi les Qiang appellent l'azalée "E Si La Ba", et les fiançailles "l'insertion des fleurs".

Dan la littérature folklorique Qiang, il y a beaucoup d'histoires sur le mariage entre les frères et les sœurs qui avaient ensuite beaucoup de descendants. Cela reflète les faits du mariage collectif et du mariage consanguin qui existaient dans

l'histoire de la haute antiquité. Dans *"l'histoire des Han postérieurs: l'histoire du Qiang occidental"*, il est écrit: "Les Qiang étaient un seul clan, et ils se sont ensuite séparés, se nommant en empruntant le prénom du père et le nom de la mère. Après douze générations, les gens venant de différents clans se sont mariés entre eux."

Cela montre que les Qiang ont établit le système du mariage monogame entre des clans il y a plus de deux mille ans; désormais, ce système de mariage déterminé par les dieux du ciel est considéré comme inviolable.

Néanmoins, d'anciens Qiang étaient répartis en groupes variés dans différentes régions. Ils avaient différents niveaux économiques. Leurs formes de mariage n'étaient pas forcément identiques. En ce qui concerne les Qiang habitant en amont des rivières de Min et de Fu, le matriarcat a duré longtemps. Jusqu'aux temps modernes la principale forme de mariage était toujours "Ru Zhui Hun", à savoir le mari entre dans la famille de ses beaux-parents et y vit comme un fils adoptif. Dans *"Les annales de Wen Chuan"* de 1912 à 1949, il est écrit "Le mariage du style Ru Zhui est très répandu". Les textes du Shibi disent aussi "Par rapport à l'ancien temps, le mariage a aujourd'hui beaucoup changé." Auparavant, les hommes Qiang entraient dans la famille de leurs beaux-parents. Le couple a le droit de décider s'il veut ce genre de mariage. Si la femme est vierge, tous les rituels de mariage seront entrepris, sauf que la famille du mari ne donnera pas de cadeau de mariage; par contre, la famille de la femme doit offrir des cadeaux à la famille du mari. Le mari doit prendre le nom de famille de sa femme et signer un contrat avec la famille de sa femme, dans lequel sont stipulés les engagements et les responsabilités qu'il doit accomplir après le mariage.

Avant 1949, les mariages Qiang étaient principalement arrangés par les parents. Quand les enfants étaient encore jeunes, leurs parents invitaient quelqu'un à prédire la bonne aventure des enfants en analysant les caractères de leurs noms. Si un garçon et une fille étaient considérés assortis, les parents concluaient des fiançailles pour eux. Le mariage était choisi selon de strictes restrictions hiérarchiques, par exemple, les familles du futur couple devraient être égales au niveau du statut social et économique. On préférait le mariage entre cousins et cousines. En plus, le mariage précoce était un phénomène universel. Les garçons se mariaient normalement à l'âge de sept à dix ans, les filles à l'âge de douze à dix-huit ans. Une chanson folklorique Qiang très caustique et satirique dit: "Nous sommes une femme de 18 ans et un mari de 3 ans. Chaque soir, je te porte au lit dans mes bras. A minuit, tu veux sucer le sein, mais je suis ta femme, pas ta mère. Si tes parents n'étaient pas là, nous serions comme mère et fils." A cette époque-là, quand deux personnes se mariaient, la famille du mari demandait beaucoup d'argent à la famille de la femme, comme le dit un proverbe populaire: "Si vous ne demandez pas aux beaux-parents de votre fille de vous donner assez d'argent, une pauvre vie vous attend."

Après 1949, au fur et à mesure du développement économique et du progrès social, beaucoup de mauvaises coutumes ont été supprimées. Les jeunes sont libres de choisir leurs épouses.

## 4. Noces

Dans la vie des Qiang, le mariage est considéré comme un des évènements les plus importants, par conséquent, les coutumes du mariage sont assez compliquées. En effet, un mariage est composé traditionnellement des étapes suivantes: "banquet de la demande en mariage", "banquet de fiançailles", "banquet de l'annonce de date des noces", "banquet de l'ouverture du pot", "banquet de la construction de la cabane", "la veille du mariage", "banquet formel du mariage" et "retour à la maison des parents de la nouvelle-mariée".

Généralement, la famille de l'homme prend l'initiative de demander une femme en mariage. Un marieur rend une visite chez la femme avec le cadeau appelé "cadeau de l'eau" et préparé par la famille de l'homme. Si les parents de la femme acceptent le cadeau, cela signifie qu'ils sont d'accord sur le mariage entre les deux enfants. Ils écrivent ensuite l'heure et la date de naissance de leur fille sur une lettre que le marieur emmènera à la famille de l'homme. Puis la famille de l'homme invite le Shibi à calculer si les dates de naissance de ce couple sont bien assorties. Si elles sont bien assorties, le marieur va choisir un jour pour ramener cette "lettre de naissance" à la famille de la femme, ce qui signifie que l'agrément sur le mariage est bien établi entre les deux familles. La famille de l'homme doit donc offrir des cadeaux à l'autre famille, et aller chez la femme pour boire le "vin de la demande en mariage". A ce moment-là, les deux familles précisent explicitement leur relation et se mettent d'accord sur la date du banquet des fiançailles.

Le banquet des fiançailles a lieu respectivement dans les deux familles. La famille de l'homme organise un banquet familial auquel tous leurs parents sont invités. A cette occasion, ils sont informés de cet engagement. Le Shibi est également invité à effectuer des rituels pour implorer la protection des dieux pour ce futur couple. La famille de la femme invite de son côté leurs parents pour leur annoncer ce mariage. Le banquet des fiançailles signifie que le mariage est

formellement confirmé par les deux parties. Désormais, à l'occasion des fêtes ou des anniversaires des beaux-parents, le fiancé doit visiter la famille de sa fiancée et offrir des cadeaux.

La prochaine étape est de décider la date de la cérémonie du mariage. La famille de l'homme invite le Shibi à sélectionner une date propice en fonction des dates de naissances du futur couple. Cette date est ensuite communiquée à la famille de la femme par le marieur et des parents de la famille de l'homme, qui amènent avec eux des cadeaux comme du riz, des nouilles, du vin, des vêtements, des ceintures, des chaussures et des chaussettes, etc. En même temps, la famille de la femme prépare un banquet et invite ses proches pour leur confirmer la date du mariage. Ils discutent tous les détails du mariage, par exemple, ceux qui accompagneront la nouvelle mariée à la maison du mari, combien d'argent et quel genre de cadeaux demander à la famille du mari. Tout cela déterminé, ils doivent informer le marieur de leurs décisions. Ce banquet est normalement appelé "banquet de l'annonce de date des noces". Après ce banquet, les deux parties commencent à se préparer pour le mariage.

La cérémonie d'ouverture du pot a lieu normalement quelques jours avant le mariage. A cette occasion, les deux familles invitent séparément leurs propres parents de haut prestige à discuter les arrangements du mariage et à désigner les responsables des différentes tâches. Toutes les affaires sont sous la direction d'un organisateur principal. Les autres membres sont chargés des tâches variées.

Deux jours avant le mariage, la famille du mari construit devant leur maison une baraque qui servira de salle de cadeaux où on recevra les cadeaux offerts par les proches. A ce moment-là, on doit inviter tous les aides du mariage et les quatre proches les plus importants, à savoir le mari de la tante paternelle, l'oncle maternel, le mari de la tante maternelle et l'oncle paternel.

"La veille du mariage" marque le début de la célébration à la famille de la nouvelle mariée. Tous les proches viennent offrir leurs cadeaux. La famille de la nouvelle mariée les reçoit avec une chaleureuse hospitalité. Au moment du banquet, les invités dansent le "Sha Lang d'évènement joyeux". La célébration en dansant et chantant dure normalement toute la nuit.

La nouvelle mariée est la personne clé de la veille du mariage. Cette nuit-là elle se prosterne devant l'autel des dieux de la famille, puis exprime ses remerciements à tous les proches et à tous ceux qui aident à la préparation du mariage. Après cela, elle demande au maître de cérémonie de distribuer les chaussures "Yunyun" qu'elle a confectionnées depuis des années, aux proches et aux membres âgés de la famille. En plus de cela, elle doit leur chanter une chanson de remerciements. Enfin, le maître de cérémonie fait sortir les parents de la nouvelle mariée devant lesquels la fille s'agenouille.

Le lendemain matin est le moment pour la nouvelle mariée d'aller chez son mari. Après le banquet du matin, la famille de la nouvelle mariée prépare un banquet devant l'autel comme sacrifice aux dieux. Un membre âgé du clan récite l'éloge du départ de la nouvelle mariée, demandant au dieu de la bénir, de la protéger et de lui donner une vie heureuse. Ensuite, le père de la nouvelle mariée se prosterne devant les dieux. Avant de sortir de la maison, la nouvelle mariée doit pleurer pour montrer sa tristesse de quitter la famille. Les aides portent dehors toutes les dots. En même temps, l'oncle maternel de la nouvelle mariée exprime à haute voix ses vœux pour elle, en disséminant vers elle de l'orge du Tibet, du blé et du riz qui sont utilisés pour montrer leur respect aux dieux. Enfin, accompagnée des proches, la nouvelle mariée est portée sur le dos de son jeune frère et amenée à la maison de son mari.

Le banquet formel est le rituel le plus cérémonieux de la famille du mari. La vielle du banquet formel, la famille du mari envoie à la maison de la femme une équipe d'une vingtaine de personnes, qui est composée du marieur, de la demoiselle d'honneur et d'autres aides du mariage, afin de ramener la nouvelle mariée et d'offrir de généreux cadeaux, comme des vêtements pour la nouvelle mariée, ainsi que des cigarettes, du vin, du riz et de la viande dont la famille de la nouvelle mariée aurait besoin pour préparer le banquet dans sa maison. Quand l'équipe arrive chez la nouvelle mariée, elle doit payer pour l'ouverture de la porte, la descente de cheval, l'entrée dans la maison. Selon les coutumes, les parents de la nouvelle-mariée et les quatre proches les plus importants doivent les accueillir devant la porte. Dès que les visiteurs entrent dans la maison, ils mettent leurs cadeaux sur la table devant l'autel de la famille. Le marieur adresse un discours de réception de la nouvelle mariée de la part du nouveau marié, et quelqu'un de la famille de la nouvelle mariée fait une allocution pour exprimer leur remerciement. En même temps on allume des pétards ou on tire au fusil de chasse comme signe de bienvenue.

Quand la nouvelle mariée sort de la maison, on tire une salve de trois coups de canon, on allume des pétards, et on joue ensemble au "suo na", en harmonie. Les frères de la nouvelle mariée la portent alternativement sur le dos et la placent dans le palanquin ou sur un cheval. Quand la nouvelle mariée et tous les accompagnateurs arrivent à la maison du mari, tous les proches du mari, y compris

les quatre proches les plus importants, les accueillent devant la porte et rendent hommage aux accompagnateurs de la famille de la femme en allumant des pétards et en tirant une salve de trois coups de canon. La nouvelle mariée s'arrête devant la porte où l'oncle maternel du mari ou un autre membre âgé de la famille du mari lui couvre la tête avec un foulard rouge. A ce moment-là, le Shibi effectue un rituel de l'exorcisation des démons. En disséminant des pois ou de l'orge du Tibet en dessus de la tête de la nouvelle mariée, il récite les incantations suivantes: "En ce jour faste et à ce moment propice, comme le témoignent le ciel et la terre, la nouvelle mariée arrive à sa nouvelle famille. Quel moment de bonheur! ... Un nuage blanc se lève de l'Est, un nuage violet de l'Ouest. Les deux nuages se rencontrent, tandis que les nouveaux mariés se rejoignent. Le ciel et la terre, veuillez ne pas être jaloux de ce couple... Tous les démons s'abstiennent." Après le rituel, le Shibi se tourne vers les parents du nouveau marié et les principaux proches des deux familles, les félicite et leur souhaite la bonne fortune et la prospérité.

Ensuite, les nouveaux mariés sont conduits dans la salle principale de la maison. Maintenant, les encens et les chandelles sont allumés et les sacrifices sont offerts aux dieux. Les nouveaux mariés se tiennent debout devant l'autel puis se prosternent trois fois, suite aux instructions du maître de la cérémonie. La première fois est pour le ciel et la terre, la deuxième pour tous les ancêtres et la dernière fois pour les parents et les personnes âgées. Enfin le nouveau marié dévoile sa femme, puis ils se prosternent face à face. Quand les nouveaux mariés se prosternent devant les parents et les membres âgés, les oncles maternels des deux familles leur donnent des conseils sur leur vie de mariage. Après ce rituel, le maître de la cérémonie leur présente ses félicitations puis le couple entre dans la chambre nuptiale.

Après être restés un petit moment dans la chambre, les nouveaux mariés sortent pour offrir des sacrifices aux dieux, pour honorer les visiteurs et pour tenir une cérémonie afin d'exprimer leurs remerciements au marieur. A ce moment-là, les aides du mariage distribuent les chaussures "Yunyun" apportées par la famille de la nouvelle mariée aux proches du nouveau marié, selon leur rang dans la famille. Le nouveau marié porte un toast et allume des cigarettes aux oncles maternels et aux frères et sœurs de la nouvelle mariée, afin de les remercier d'accompagner cette dernière à la maison du mari. Ensuite le maître de la cérémonie chante au nom de la famille du mari la "chanson de remerciements au marieur" et lui offre des cadeaux. Ayant accepté les cadeaux, le marieur chante une chanson pour exprimer sa gratitude pour l'hospitalité et la gentillesse de la famille du mari.

Après tous ces rituels, on organise un grand banquet à midi pour régaler tous les proches, les amis et les voisins. Le soir, la famille du nouveau marié organise une grande soirée et tous les visiteurs dansent et chantent autour du foyer.

Le lendemain du mariage est le jour pour remercier les visiteurs. Les accompagnateurs de la nouvelle mariée rentrent chez eux. Les nouveaux mariés préparent des cadeaux et rendent visite aux parents de la femme. Quand les nouveaux mariés arrivent chez les parents de la femme, on effectue les rituels pour offrir des sacrifices aux dieux et se prosterner devant les proches et les membres âgés de la famille de la femme. Ensuite la famille de la femme offre un banquet aux nouveaux mariés et aux visiteurs. A ce moment-là, les cérémonies du mariage chez les deux familles sont complètement terminées.

## 5. Mort

Les Qiang sont généralement conscients de la loi naturelle qui veut que "Où il y a la vie, il y a aussi la mort". Selon les Qiang, si une personne est morte à l'âge de soixante ans ou plus, elle est considérée comme ayant eu une mort naturelle; par contre, si quelqu'un est mort à moins de soixante ans, sa mort est considérée comme une infortune. Nous allons raconter ci-après les principales coutumes funéraires du peuple Qiang.

### 1) Mise en bière

Quand quelqu'un est mourant, il est déplacé de la chambre au lit dans la salle de séjour. On l'appelle "changement du lit". Cela aide l'âme du défunt à se mettre en route vers l'ouest où se trouve le lieu d'origine du peuple Qiang. Quand il est mort, les membres de sa famille mettent du thé, du riz, de l'argent et de l'or, emballés d'une pièce de papier rouge, dans la bouche du défunt pour ses frais de voyage. Le mort est ensuite placé à côté du foyer pour qu'on lui nettoie le corps et qu'on lui change ses vêtements. Dès que le corps est complètement froid, il est placé dans le cercueil. D'abord, on disperse dans le cercueil de la cendre du foyer, sur laquelle on réalise quelques empreintes avec une tasse. Puis on étale une couche de papier avant de poser le corps dessus. Certains objets favoris du défunt, par exemple, sa béquille et sa pipe, sont placés près de lui comme objet funéraire. En plus de cela, on doit encore mettre dedans un couteau de 16.5 centimètres de long et une petite cruche de vin. D'ailleurs, sur l'épaule du défunt est placé un sac dans lequel on met cinq genres de céréales, de la cendre de papiers (qui est considérée comme l'argent des morts) et un papier d'incantation qui sert de laisser-passer pour le voyage.

**2) Annonce de la mort**

Quand quelqu'un décède, on tire trois coups de fusil vers le ciel pour dire adieu au défunt et pour annoncer sa mort aux membres du village. En même temps, les fils du défunt doivent informer immédiatement les proches de cette mauvaise nouvelle. L'oncle maternel est le premier à être informé. Recevant cette nouvelle, l'oncle maternel prépare tout de suite des cadeaux de condoléances et se hâte vers la maison du défunt avec d'autres proches, criant sur la route pour montrer leur tristesse. Quand l'oncle maternel arrive, les enfants du défunt lui racontent les détails de la mort du défunt, y compris la maladie, la mort et la mise au cercueil. En plus de répondre aux questions de l'oncle maternel, les enfants doivent apprécier son arrivée et lui exprimer leurs remerciements

**3) Recherche de la cause de la mort**

La famille en deuil invite quelques Shibi à effectuer des rituels. D'abord, avant de mettre le corps dans le cercueil, les Shibi récitent les incantations, purifient le corps du mort, et l'habillent. Puis un membre âgé de la famille tue un mouton afin qu'il montre le chemin au défunt. Ce mouton est appelé "le mouton de guide" ou "le bouc émissaire". Avant de tuer le mouton, le Shibi chante des incantations et vaporise de l'eau froide dans l'oreille du mouton. Si le mouton tremble d'effroi, on le considère comme substitut du défunt, qui souffrira à sa place. Puis le mouton est tué et disséqué pour trouver la cause de la mort du défunt. Tous les organes internes sont examinés et si quelque organe est anormal, on considère que le même organe du corps du défunt était la source de sa maladie et de sa mort. Ensuite, un rituel funéraire compliqué est effectué pour offrir des sacrifices au défunt et pour présenter ses condoléances à sa famille. Quand les Shibi effectuent le rituel, ils se déguisent en dieu de l'armure, en portant une armure de cuir de bœuf et un chapeau de cuir. Selon la légende, le dieu de l'armure est un des huit dieux protecteurs, qui sont appelés ensemble "les huit généraux". Lorsque les enfants du défunt s'agenouillent, les Shibi commencent le rituel: certains d'entre eux secouent leurs cloches et le tambour, certains battent le tambour de basane, certains chantent, d'autres dansent pour rendre un hommage attristé au défunt. En tout état de cause, la cérémonie dont les détails sont extrêmement compliqués est un spectacle vraiment impressionnant.

**4) Soir d'adieux**

La veille des funérailles est appelé "Soir d'adieux". Ce soir-là, toutes les

lumières sont éteintes sauf un flambeau de paille. Le cercueil est ouvert de sorte que l'oncle maternel et d'autres proches adressent un dernier regard au défunt. Ensuite, le cercueil est refermé et toutes les lampes et bougies sont allumées. Une cérémonie mortuaire a lieu, à l'occasion de laquelle le Shibi effectue des rituels pour guider l' âme du défunt au cimetière.

### 5) Crémation

La crémation est la plus ancienne forme de funérailles de l'histoire Qiang. Les enregistrements de l'emploi de la crémation des Qiang peuvent être trouvés dans les anciens documents datant des temps pré-impériaux. Dans *"l'ancienne histoire de la dynastie Tang: l'histoire du Qiang de Dangxiang"*, il est écrit que les Qiang de Dangxiang dans la dynastie Tang "brûlent le défunt; cela s'appelle crémation". Tous ceux qui ont le même nom partagent le même cimetière, qui comporte une fosse de crémation, au-dessus de laquelle se trouve une petite cabane en bois où sont présentées toutes les tablettes des ancêtres du clan. A l'occasion de la crémation, la cabane est déplacée, puis le cercueil est mis dans la fosse. Le fils du défunt allume le feu en personne. Ensuite, le Shibi effectue des rituels, quelqu'un tire un coup de fusil vers le ciel, les membres de la famille et les proches s'assoient en cercle, crient et chantent la chanson funéraire, dansent la danse funéraire et boivent du vin funéraire. Dès que le feu s'éteint, les os du défunt sont collectés et enterrés.

### 6) Enterrement

Selon certaines études, sous l'influence de la culture Han et avec l'encouragement des autorités, les Qiang ont adopté progressivement l'enterrement, à partir du milieu de la dynastie Qing. Selon les croyances Qiang, l'être humain a trois âmes et sept esprits. Après la mort d'une personne, ses esprits disparaissent, mais ses âmes restent toujours: l'une garde son tombeau; la deuxième reste à la maison pour recevoir des sacrifices et pour protéger ses descendants, et la troisième rentre au bercail pour rejoindre ses ancêtres. Par conséquent, les Qiang préfèrent parler de "saluer le départ" plutôt qu'employer le mot "enterrer" dans leurs coutumes funéraires. Guidées par un flambeau, le chemin frayé par un sabre tenu par l'oncle maternel, les âmes du défunt sont orientées vers les endroits propices grâce au pouvoir surnaturel du Shibi.

La famille en deuil invite le géomancien à choisir un bon site funéraire, puis y creuse une fosse. A la veille des funérailles, on organise des activités pour rendre hommage au mort. Par exemple, on chante la chanson funéraire, on danse la danse

funéraire. Le Shibi effectue des rituels pour demander au défunt de protéger sa famille et tout le village. Le lendemain, de bon matin, les fils en deuil et les proches transportent le cercueil au cimetière, suivant le Shibi et le "dieu de l'armure" qui sont en tête de la procession funéraire. Sur le toit de la maison du défunt, l'oncle maternel fraye le chemin pour son âme. Le Shibi effectue des rituels, chante ou récite la prière, accompagné du son lourd du tambour et des sons enroués des autres instruments musicaux. Tout cet ensemble crée une atmosphère triste. Sur la route, au bout d'une certaine distance, on tire au fusil vers le ciel, ce que l'on répète plusieurs fois jusqu'au cimetière. Un coq ou un mouton est attaché au cercueil pour éviter tout malheur éventuel. Avant que le cercueil soit mis dans la fosse, le coq ou le mouton est tué et son sang est versé autour du tombeau pour montrer que cet endroit est réservé au défunt. Après, le cercueil est mis dans la fosse; on le couvre d'abord d'un petit peu terre, puis tous les membres de la procession funéraire, sauf les fils du décédé, entourent le tombeau, chantent la chanson funéraire et dansent le "Guo Zhuang funéraire". Ensuite, le Shibi exécute des rituels pour offrir des sacrifices aux dieux et pour appeler les âmes du défunt, ce qui est suivi par la cérémonie d'adieux et d'hommage au défunt. Enfin, la famille en deuil offre le petit-déjeuner au Shibi, au dieux de l'armure et à tous les invités. Après cela, les invités rentrent chez eux, alors que le Shibi, le dieu de l'armure et les proches parents restent pour construire le tombeau. Les funérailles prennent ainsi fin.

# 参考文献

[ 1 ] 冉光荣，李绍明，周锡银. 羌族史. 成都：四川民族出版社，1984.

[ 2 ] 王康，李鉴踪，汪青玉. 神秘的白石崇拜. 成都：四川民族出版社，1992.

[ 3 ] 李明，林忠亮，王康. 羌族文学史. 成都：四川民族出版社，1994.

[ 4 ] 徐平，徐丹. 东方大族之谜. 北京：知识出版社，2001.

[ 5 ] 中央民族大学少数民族语言研究所. 中国少数民族语言. 成都：四川民族出版社，1987.

[ 6 ] 徐其超等. 族群记忆与多元创造. 成都：四川民族出版社，2001.

[ 7 ] 毛星主编. 中国少数民族文学. 长沙：湖南人民出版社，1983.

[ 8 ] 黄银善，董方权. 中国少数民族传统音乐（上）. 北京：中央民族大学出版社，2001.

[ 9 ] 杨羽健. 羌族音乐. 中国大百科全书·音乐舞蹈卷. 北京：中国大百科全书出版社，1989.

[10] 乐声编著. 中国少数民族乐器. 北京：民族出版社，1999.

[11] 覃光广，李民胜等. 中国少数民族宗教概览. 北京：中央民族大学出版社，1988.

[12] 宋恩常. 中国少数民族宗教（初编）. 昆明：云南人民出版社，1985.

[13] 四川省文联. 四川民俗大典. 成都：四川人民出版社，1999.

[14] 卢丁等. 羌族历史文化研究. 成都：四川人民出版社，2000.